D1715366

To the Tashkent Station

To the Tashkent Station

*Evacuation and Survival in
the Soviet Union at War*

Rebecca Manley

Cornell University Press
Ithaca and London

First published 2009 by Cornell University Press

Printed in the United States of America

Library of Congress Cataloging-in-Publication Data

Manley, Rebecca, 1973–
    To the Tashkent station : evacuation and survival in the Soviet Union at war / Rebecca Manley.
        p. cm.
    Includes bibliographical references and index.
    ISBN 978-0-8014-4739-6 (cloth : alk. paper)
    1. World War, 1939–1945—Evacuation of civilians—Soviet Union.   2. Refugees—Uzbekistan—Tashkent—History.
3. Soviet Union—History—1939–1945.   4. Tashkent (Uzbekistan)—History.   I. Title.

    D809.S65M36 2009
    940.53086'91409587—dc22

2009010905

Cornell University Press strives to use environmentally responsible suppliers and materials to the fullest extent possible in the publishing of its books. Such materials include vegetable-based, low-VOC inks and acid-free papers that are recycled, totally chlorine-free, or partly composed of nonwood fibers. For further information, visit our website at www.cornellpress.cornell.edu.

Cloth printing   10 9 8 7 6 5 4 3 2 1

To Andrew and Anna

CONTENTS

ACKNOWLEDGMENTS

The idea for this book first took shape in Moscow, as I was poring through archival files on housing in the 1930s. Quite by chance, I stumbled on some letters penned in the final years of World War II. The letters were petitions written by Muscovites who had spent much of the war years elsewhere, in evacuation, and had returned to find their apartments occupied by other people. The letters were standard Soviet fare: in an economy of shortage, Soviet citizens were perpetually petitioning for something. At the same time, the letters described a much larger drama, a drama of wartime displacement, of separation from family and friends, and of a struggle to survive hundreds and often thousands of miles from home. I returned to the University of California at Berkeley with a new project and a lot to learn.

I owe my first thanks to Yuri Slezkine who, more than anyone else, helped me conceptualize this project and find the right way to tell the story. Reginald Zelnik was an enthusiastic supporter from the outset, and his attention to detail and breadth of knowledge added immeasurably to my first few chapters. Like so many others, I still feel his loss. I am grateful to Margaret Anderson, whose careful reading of the manuscript and astute comments helped guide my revisions. A special thanks to Irina Paperno for her penetrating reflections on my work, her personal support, and her active engagement with all aspects of this project.

A number of others contributed to this book along the way as mentors and interlocutors. I thank Lynne Viola for first stimulating my interest in Russian history; Nathalie Moine and Catherine Gousseff for their informative joint seminar on the war at the Centre d'études des mondes russe, caucasien et centre-européen (CERCES) in Paris; Peter Gatrell and Amir Weiner for their encouragement, comments, and criticism.

Parts of this book were presented at the *Travaux en Cours* at CERCES, the speaker series of the Institut für osteuropäische Geschichte in Tübingen, the American Association for the Advancement of Slavic Studies Conference in Toronto; the International Council for Central and East European Studies Conference in Berlin; and the University of Chicago Russian and East European Studies Workshop. I thank the audiences and organizers for their helpful feedback.

I am happy to acknowledge the intellectual companionship provided by numerous people in the research and writing stages of this book, including Charly Coleman, Arianne Chernock, Victoria Frede, Olivia Gomolinski, Malte Griesse, Ben Kafka, Tracy McDonald, Marline Otte, Olga Pichon, Emmanuel Saadia, Dana Simmons, Paul Stronski, to whom I owe a special debt for his invaluable help in Tashkent, Anoush Terjanian, and Mikhail Zaitsev. Thanks also to the many friends whom I have leaned on for support, most notably Giulio Federico, Berta Figueras, Fong Ku, Jessica Manley, Shaloub Razak, and Rachel Simeon. I am particularly grateful to Priya Satia, for her intelligence, humor, and constant support and for pushing me on the big questions.

At Cornell University Press I benefitted from John Ackerman's enthusiastic support and incisive comments, and from the careful work of Carolyn Pouncy and Susan Specter. I am particularly grateful to the anonymous readers for the Press, whose reviews helped shape the final product.

Research for this project was generously funded by the Social Sciences and Humanities Research Council of Canada; the Andrew W. Mellon Foundation; the Chancellor's Office, Institute of International Studies, Graduate Division, and History Department of the University of California at Berkeley; and the Advisory Research Council of Queen's University. I am grateful to the archivists and reading room staff, too numerous to name, at archives and libraries in Moscow, St. Petersburg, Tashkent, Odessa, and Volgograd. For their help acquiring materials I thank Polina Aksenova, Durdona Pirmukhamedova, and Lyudmila Shutova. I am further indebted to my colleagues in the history department at Queen's, who have been a source of encouragement and support.

Parts of this book have been published before, and I am grateful for permission to republish them here. A section of chapter 8 appeared in "'Where Should We Resettle the Comrades Next?': The Adjudication of Housing Claims and the Construction of the Post-War Order," in *Late Stalinist Russia: Society between Reconstruction and Reinvention*, ed. Juliane Fürst (London: Routledge, 2006), 233–46. A section of chapter 6 appeared in "The Perils of Displacement: The Evacuee between Refugee and Deportee," *Contemporary European History* 16, no. 4 (2007): 495–509. Finally, a very early version of parts of chapters 2 and 3 appeared in "L'URSS en guerre: la question de l'évacuation de la population civile," trans. Olivia Gomolinski, *Communisme: Revue d'études pluridisciplinaires* 70–71 (2002): 159–79.

I thank my parents, Katherine and Paul Manley, for their unflagging love and support and their keen interest in my work. I am indebted to both for their helpful comments on the manuscript and to my father, who has always loved maps, for his help preparing mine.

Finally, this book could not have been written without Andrew Jainchill, who made the journey with me—from Berkeley all the way to Tashkent, and to various places in between. His spirit of adventure, intellectual rigor, incisive comments, and cooking helped make this book what it is. I dedicate this book to Andrew and to Anna, who made the completion of this book so much more fun.

Note on Translation and Transliteration

All translations are the author's, unless otherwise indicated. Common Russian names such as Maria and Alexander have been rendered in the standard English spelling in the text, as have the names of familiar Russian figures. Otherwise, I have followed the Library of Congress transliteration system, except that diacritical marks have been used in the citations only.

ABBREVIATIONS

GAGT	Gosudarstvennyi arkhiv goroda Tashkenta/Toshkent shahar davlat arkhivi
GAOO	Gosudarstvennyi arkhiv Odesskoi oblasti
GARF	Gosudarstvennyi arkhiv Rossiiskoi Federatsii
GAVO	Gosudarstvennyi arkhiv Volgogradskoi oblasti
OR OIKM	Otdel rukopisei Odesskogo istoriko-kraevedcheskogo muzeia
OR RGB	Otdel rukopisei Rossiiskoi gosudarstvennoi biblioteki
OR RNB	Otdel rukopisei Rossiiskoi natsional'noi biblioteki
RGAE	Rossiiskii gosudarstvennyi arkhiv ekonomiki
RGALI	Rossiiskii gosudarstvennyi arkhiv literatury i iskusstv
RGASPI	Rossiiskii gosudarstvennyi arkhiv sotsial'no-politicheskoi istorii
RGVA	Rossiiskii gosudarstvennyi voennyi arkhiv
TsAGM	Tsentral'nyi arkhiv goroda Moskvy
TsAOPIM	Tsentral'nyi arkhiv obshchestvenno-politicheskoi istorii Moskvy
TsDNA	Tsentr dokumentatsii "Narodnyi arkhiv"
TsDNIVO	Tsentr dokumentatsii noveishei istorii Volgogradskoi oblasti
TsGAIPD SPb	Tsentral'nyi gosudarstvennyi arkhiv istoriko-politicheskikh dokumentov Sankt-Peterburga
TsGAKFFD RU	Tsentral'nyi gosudarstvennyi arkhiv kinofotofonodokumentov Respubliki Uzbekistan/Ozbekistan respublikasi kinofotofonohujjatlar markaziy davlat arkhivi
TsGAKFFD SPb	Tsentral'nyi gosudarstvennyi arkhiv kinofotofonodokumentov Sankt-Peterburga

TsGARUz   Tsentral'nyi gosudarstvennyi arkhiv Respubliki Uzbeki-
              stan/Ozbekistan respublikasi markaziy davlat arkhivi
TsGASPb   Tsentral'nyi gosudarstvennyi arkhiv Sankt-Peterburga

TO THE TASHKENT STATION

INTRODUCTION

In the fall of 1941, the Polish writer Aleksander Wat, recently released from confinement in a Soviet prison, made his way east across the vast expanses of the Soviet Union. In his memoirs, he depicts a railway station en route: "I saw a striking image of suffering there. . . . All of Russia was on the move . . . peasant men and women, whole families, middle-class people, workers, intellectuals, all on the miserable floor of the train station."[1] Wat described the scene as an expression of "Russian nomadism."[2] Those en route, however, were not traditional Russian migrants. Nor, properly speaking, were they refugees. Unlike the archetypal European refugee, they were displaced but not stateless. In official Soviet parlance, moreover, they were "evacuees," not refugees. The term highlights the specificity of their experience. They were compelled to depart not only by a devastating war but by a government, their own government, which sought to protect the lives of its citizenry, to keep valuable "human resources" from falling into enemy hands, and to assure the security of the state by clearing frontline regions.

Between the German invasion in June 1941 and the autumn of the next year, approximately 16.5 million Soviet citizens were evacuated to the country's interior. The scale of the operation was unprecedented. Evacuations were carried out in eight different Soviet republics and from territory that was home to approximately 40 percent of the Soviet population on the eve of the war.[3] As Wat's description of the train station suggests, moreover, the evacuation touched Soviet citizens from all walks of life.

---

[1] Aleksander Wat, *My Century: The Odyssey of a Polish Intellectual*, trans. Richard Lourie (New York: New York Review of Books, 2003), 307, 309.

[2] Ibid., 307, my translation.

[3] The eight republics were the Russian, Ukrainian, Belorussian, Estonian, Latvian, Lithuanian, Moldovan, and Karelo-Finnish Soviet Socialist Republics.

What follows is a story of this displacement, told from the vantage point of both those who experienced it and those who conceived, organized, and implemented the operation. It is at once a history of World War II, on its most brutal front, and a history of Soviet society and the Soviet state as revealed in a moment of crisis. Although the tale begins and ends in Moscow, home of the council that oversaw the operation and the site of a substantial evacuation in its own right, the intervening pages take the reader on a journey across the ever-expanding front lines and then eastward to the Central Asian city of Tashkent. In Tashkent, over one hundred thousand Soviet citizens found a temporary refuge. Their number included some of the country's greatest writers, figures such as Anna Akhmatova, Alexei Tolstoi, and Kornei Chukovskii, as well as many more ordinary people, tailors and teachers, engineers, workers, and children. They came from Moscow and Leningrad, from Odessa and Kiev, and from a host of smaller cities and towns. Many were Russian or Jewish, but there were also Ukrainians, some Belorussians, even the odd Lithuanian and Latvian.

Their displacement constitutes a quintessentially twentieth-century story. Over the course of the century, in Europe alone, tens of millions of people were uprooted from their homes. At no time, moreover, was the upheaval more substantial or dramatic than in the decade spanning World War II.[4] As Anna Akhmatova, in evacuation in Tashkent, wrote in her *Poem without a Hero*:

> And that happy phrase—at home—
> Is known to no one now,
> Everyone gazes from some foreign window.
> Some from New York, some from Tashkent,
> And bitter is the air of banishment—
> Like poisoned wine.[5]

In Akhmatova's telling, evacuees had been forced to drink from the same bitter cup as Europe's many refugees. She universalizes their plight: it is shared by "everyone." Although Akhmatova and her compatriots were caught up in a continent-wide upheaval, theirs is at the same time a distinctly Soviet story. It is a story about a war that touched each and every Soviet citizen and shook the Soviet state to its foundations. It is a story about the nature and limits of the Soviet state and about the perils of displacement in a society where the state had made residence a keystone of rights.

[4] One estimate puts the number of people in Europe displaced during the war alone at sixty million. See Malcolm J. Proudfoot, *European Refugees: 1939–1952* (London: Faber and Faber, 1957), 20.

[5] Anna Akhmatova, *The Complete Poems of Anna Akhmatova*, expanded ed., ed. Roberta Reeder, trans. Judith Hemschemeyer (Boston: Zephyr, 1989), 575.

• • •

World War II was a seminal event in the lives of several generations of Soviet citizens. As one woman put it in the opening pages of her unpublished memoirs of the evacuation, the war "divided the history of Soviet people in two parts: 'before the war' [*dovoennyi*] and 'after the war' [*poslevoennyi*]."[6] For many Soviet citizens, the war became *the* defining experience of their lives. Although a handful of recent studies have begun to probe the nature of "Ivan's war," few have delved into the war beyond the front lines, where millions of evacuees experienced their own wartime upheaval.[7] For many women in particular, the evacuation, rather than the front, shaped their understanding and experience of the war. It is surely telling that in the burgeoning memoir literature emerging from the former Soviet Union, "in evacuation" has emerged as a common organizing rubric.

For the Soviet state, the war was a test, the greatest it had yet encountered. The evacuation has particular significance in this regard, for it stands as one of the state's most notable wartime achievements. No less a person than Red Army Chief of Staff General Georgii Zhukov later affirmed that "the heroic feat of evacuation and restoration of industrial capacities during the war . . . meant as much for the country's destiny as the greatest battles of the war."[8] To be sure, there were, in the words of authorities, "deficiencies" or "negative moments." The process was chaotic. Factories were left behind; trains took people in the wrong direction; machinery and parts were abandoned on the sides of railway tracks. All too frequently, moreover, authorities fled, abandoning factories and the population to the proverbial "mercy of fate." Nonetheless, amid the disorder and the disarray, millions of people and a substantial number of factories were successfully transferred to the safety of the rear. The evacuation was in many respects a triumph of the Soviet system of mass mobilization, the modus operandi of the Soviet state. At the same time, the operation underscored the system's limits. It points to the vast zone of human action that fell beyond the reach of state control and to the detrimental effects of a highly centralized and secretive regime.

The war not only tested the regime; it transformed it. Over the course of the war, the boundaries of the body politic shifted. Wartime experience quickly emerged as a benchmark of one's place in the polity, while ethnic markers came

---

[6] A. V. Sorokina, "Tri goda na vsiu zhizn'," TsDNA, f. 18, op. 1, d. 18, l. 4.

[7] The phrase "Ivan's war" comes from Amir Weiner, "Saving Private Ivan: From What, Why, and How?" *Kritika: Explorations in Russian and Eurasian History* 1, no. 2 (2000): 305–36 and, more recently, from Catherine Merridale, *Ivan's War: Life and Death in the Red Army, 1939–1945* (New York: Metropolitan Books, 2006).

[8] Quoted in John Barber and Mark Harrison, *The Soviet Home Front, 1941–1945: A Social and Economic History of the USSR in World War II* (London: Longman, 1991), 131.

to play an increasingly important role as criteria for inclusion and exclusion.[9] The evacuation was intimately bound up with these processes. Those who were designated for evacuation and refused to depart were viewed with suspicion by state security organs. By contrast, those who departed too hastily were roundly condemned: state and party authorities charged them with cowardice and panic while the population at large branded them as traitors. When authorities fled, a gulf was created between population and leadership that threatened to undermine the very legitimacy of Soviet power. A popular perception that Jews fled first, moreover, gave rise to a new wave of popular antisemitism. After the war, derisive references to the "Tashkent front," where Jews were widely said to have "served" in the war, helped place Jews outside the boundaries of the polity.

The war also constituted an important juncture in the evolving relationship between citizen and state. For many Soviet citizens, the war was more than an ordeal to be survived. Like the revolution more broadly, it demanded sacrifice and service. The evacuation in particular thrust questions of allegiance onto center stage. As one woman from a town near Leningrad noted in her diary: "The boundary between 'defeatists' and 'patriots' has taken shape with unusual precision. The patriots strive to evacuate themselves as quickly as possible, whereas the others, like us, attempt by all means possible to hide from the evacuation."[10] In reality, the boundary was substantially more complex: individuals had to balance the dictates of multiple loyalties, and the question "to stay or to go" was by no means easily resolved. Few, however, failed to identify with the war effort on some level. Indeed, the invasion of the country drew many Soviet citizens closer to the state. It created a common ground of shared outrage, shared enemies, and shared hopes. A war that initially threatened to undermine Soviet power thus emerged as a powerful source of legitimation.

The story of the evacuation is not only an important chapter in the history of the war but a window onto the workings of the Soviet system. Conceived not to purge but to protect, the evacuation constitutes a unique moment in the history of Soviet population displacement. The operation was shaped both by the advent of total war and by the increasingly important role played by the modern state in generating, organizing, and categorizing migration. The Soviet state was particularly active in this regard. Over the course of the two decades preceding the war, the state had come to deploy population transfer, both forced and unforced, as an important tool of economic development, ethnic cleansing, and social purification. As a humanitarian initiative, the evacuation differed substantially from both deportations and the more

---

[9] Amir Weiner, *Making Sense of War: The Second World War and the Fate of the Bolshevik Revolution* (Princeton, N.J.: Princeton University Press, 2001), 8.

[10] Diary of L. Osipova, in N. A. Lomagin, ed., *Neizvestnaia blokada (Dokumenty, prilozheniia)*, vol. 2 (St. Petersburg: Neva, 2002), 443.

routine practice of agricultural resettlement. Like both these practices, how-ever, evacuation was conceived as a form of managed migration. Through evacuation policy, Soviet authorities sought to change the face of contemporary warfare. Instead of an uncontrolled exodus of people, they envisaged a policy whereby the state would designate selected sectors of the population for an organized transfer to the rear. When the evacuation did not turn out as planned, and they were confronted with a mass and largely uncontrolled movement of people, the authorities attempted to confine evacuees to their regions of resettlement, blurring the distinction between evacuees and deportees. The evacuation thus casts light on the vast gray zone dividing forced from unforced migration in Soviet society under Stalin. It further sets some of the distinguishing features of Soviet population politics into sharp relief: the attempt to channel all social phenomena into the strictures of state planning and control; the deep suspicion, and stigmatization, of anything "disorganized"; and the attempt to sculpt the polity through population transfer.

The evacuation is also a tale of privileged people and privileged places. In designating people for evacuation and return, the state defined their place in Soviet society. It is not incidental that diary entries and memoir passages on evacuation frequently contain reflections on the place of privilege in Soviet society: as one Muscovite, reflecting on the evacuation, mused, "our society is, of course, not a class-based one, but it is nonetheless stratified."[11] Privileges were defined occupationally as well as geographically. The evacuation of the population transpired in discrete places defined not only by the enemy's advance but also by the spatial hierarchies that informed the way Soviet authorities dealt with the country's territory and its inhabitants.

At the most basic level, the evacuation is a story about the struggle to survive. Although wartime conditions imposed a burden on all Soviet citizens, evacuees were at a particular disadvantage. The process of displacement both deprived them of a place to live and broke up their communities: husbands were separated from wives, parents from children, individuals from the organizations that employed them, and friends from one another. "In evacuation," Soviet citizens struggled to reconstitute the networks they depended on for personal sustenance, and for survival—access to food, housing, and work. The ways that Soviet citizens coped with displacement demonstrate the importance of both formal and informal networks in everyday life under Stalin.[12]

---

[11] L. I. Timofeev, "Dnevnik voennykh let," *Znamia*, no. 6 (2002): 157, entry of October 13, 1941.

[12] On the role of personal networks in the constitution of social and political life in the Soviet Union, see Sheila Fitzpatrick, "Blat in Stalin's Time," in *Bribery and Blat in Russia: Negotiating Reciprocity from the Middle Ages to the 1990s*, ed. Stephen Lovell, Alena Ledeneva, and Andrei Rogachevskii (New York: St. Martin's, in association with the School of Slavonic and East European Studies, University of London, 2000), 166–82; Alena V. Ledeneva, *Russia's Economy of Favours: Blat, Networking, and Informal Exchange* (Cambridge: Cambridge

• • •

This book aims to reintegrate the war into the social, cultural, and political history of the Soviet Union. It reflects the perspectives of institutions and people involved at all levels and in all stages of the evacuation, from Stalin and the members of the Evacuation Council selected to organize the operation to the millions of Soviet citizens whom it affected. While Moscow occupies a central position in the story, the geographic sweep of the book is broad, ranging from Leningrad to Odessa, from Stalingrad to Tashkent. By and large, it is an urban tale. Although some evacuees hailed from villages, and many more lived in villages "in evacuation," the overwhelming majority of evacuees were urban residents, many of whom sought out cities in the rear.

Among the dozens of cities that served as shelters in the war, this story focuses on one: Tashkent, the capital of the Soviet Socialist Republic of Uzbekistan. In Tashkent, which in many ways came to symbolize the evacuation, evacuees found a city that was at once both foreign and familiar: differences in climate, culture, and architecture were offset by an institutional landscape that replicated that of the cities they had left behind. Among the multitudes who sought refuge in the city were some of the most illustrious members of Soviet society as well as some of the most destitute. Shared literature, as much as shared experiences, has produced a particular set of reminiscences of the Tashkent evacuation. Anna Akhmatova drafted and recited her *Poem without a Hero* while in Tashkent, Elena Bulgakova circulated clandestine copies of her late husband's magnum opus, *The Master and Margarita*, and Alexei Tolstoi worked on and read from his play *Ivan the Terrible*. Though the voices of the intelligentsia loom large in this story, they are set alongside a range of other voices, reflecting the full diversity of the evacuated population.

The story begins in Moscow, in the halls of power where evacuation policy was first formulated. From there, our gaze spans out across the front lines to the local authorities who had to implement the operation and finally to the individual Soviet citizens who sought to make sense of it. The book then follows evacuees on their arduous journey east, terminating at the station in Tashkent. Life in evacuation was far from easy. On the "Tashkent Front," evacuees struggled to survive and found their own ways of contributing to the war. The story ends with the return of evacuees to the war-torn landscapes they had left behind. At the end of their journey, evacuees confronted a new set of challenges as they sought to reassemble the pieces of their prewar lives and to find their place in the world "after the war."

University Press, 1998); and Barbara Walker, "(Still) Searching for a Soviet Society: Personalized Political and Economic Ties in Recent Soviet Historiography. A Review Article," *Comparative Studies in Society and History* 43, no. 3 (2001): 631–42.

1

CONCEIVING EVACUATION
From Refugee to Evacuee

Population displacement has been a perennial feature of war. In the lands of the former Russian Empire, as elsewhere, successive wars have wrought successive waves of people on the move. One need think only of the flight from Moscow in 1812, immortalized by Tolstoy in his epic *War and Peace*, to appreciate that wartime population displacement is not a purely twentieth-century phenomenon. Tolstoy's depiction of Muscovites quitting their homes during the Napoleonic Wars resonates with the contemporary reader in part because the scene is so familiar. For Russians living through World War II, it was eerily so. Almost a century and a half after the events Tolstoy described, history seemed to be repeating itself: in the fall of 1941, Moscow was subject to evacuation, and the city's inhabitants again took to the roads heading east as enemy forces approached the capital. Although the evacuation of 1941 harked back both to the flight of 1812 and the veritable deluge of refugees during World War I, it was conceptually distinct from the displacements that preceded it. Indeed, as a concept the evacuation was of relatively recent vintage. It was forged in the crucibles of total war and Stalinism and was indelibly marked by the priorities and practices of the Soviet state.

The very term "evacuation" (*evakuatsiia*) appeared as something of a novelty in 1941. It was, as one memoirist put it, a "terrible and unaccustomed word." To this writer, a young boy at the time of the German invasion, the word seemed to have "suddenly tumbled down from somewhere."[1] Another memoirist similarly recalled that "until the war we didn't know the word [evacuation]; in historical novels and films only the word 'refugee' was used."[2] "Refugee" (*bezhenets*) was indeed a familiar term in the Soviet Union of the interwar years. The "refugee" populated not only "historical novels and films,"

---

[1] Mikhail German, *Slozhnoe proshedshee* (St. Petersburg: Iskusstvo SPb, 2000), 83.
[2] V. Peterson, "Iz blokady—na bol'shuiu zemliu," *Neva*, no. 9 (2002): 151–52.

but living memory. World War I in the Russian Empire had been accompanied by large-scale population displacement, and what contemporaries referred to as the "refugee" had become a common figure. With the outbreak of World War II, however, the term was largely eclipsed. The change in terminology is neatly summed up in the memoirs of Anastasia Sorokina, who, reflecting on her experiences in both wars, noted: "then they called us 'refugees,' and now we are 'evacuees.' "[3]

The passage from refugee to evacuee reflected an important transformation in the state's approach to wartime population displacement. Early Soviet refugee policy was formulated against the backdrop of World War I and was predicated on a tacit acceptance of wartime displacement: its primary concern was organizing and providing for the inevitable mass of people who would *choose* to leave their homes in a future war. In the 1930s, however, it was effectively subsumed by another, and heretofore distinct policy: evacuation. Since World War I, evacuation had been conceived first and foremost as an economic measure, designed to effect the transfer of selected material and human resources to the safety of the rear. The focus on the evacuee as the central figure of wartime population politics reflected a radical rethinking of the premise underpinning state policy. In effect, it constituted a rejection of the very principle of choice. Instead of planning for an already displaced population, evacuation aimed to manage and control displacement itself. The elaboration of a unified approach to population displacement under the rubric of evacuation was a corollary of Stalin's revolution from above, which thrust the Soviet Union onto a path of rapid industrialization and forced collectivization. It reflected the militarization of Soviet society, the development of new practices of population transfer, and changing practices of war. At issue were not only conceptions about a future war, but basic suppositions about Soviet society and the Soviet state.

THE CRUCIBLE OF TOTAL WAR: REFUGEEDOM AND EVACUATION IN WORLD WAR I

The wartime population policies of the Soviet state were crucially shaped by the experience of World War I. In the lands of the Russian Empire, as elsewhere, the war was a transformative experience that inaugurated an era of increased government involvement in all spheres of life. Faced with the prospect of seemingly indefinite warfare in an industrial era of mass conscription armies, war was reconceived as a struggle not only between opposing armies but also between nations and entire economies. In many respects, the war was a watershed: it gave birth to the concept of total war and to a range of new practices including surveillance, grain requisitions, and rationing. From

[3] A. V. Sorokina, "Tri goda na vsiu zhizn'," TsDNA, f. 18, op. 1, d. 21, l. 13.

this crucible, two further phenomena emerged that would lay the ground-work for subsequent Soviet policy on wartime population displacement.[4]

World War I had confronted the imperial Russian government with a refugee crisis of unprecedented proportions. Within a couple of years, over three million imperial subjects had become refugees as Russian forces re-treated and substantial tracts of territory were ceded to the enemy.[5] The scale of population displacement was unanticipated. Tsarist authorities, more-over, were completely unprepared. There was no policy in place to deal with refugees; and as the Soviet General Staff later noted of the experience, "the tsarist government conducted no preparatory work" until 1915, when the mass of refugees could no longer be ignored.[6] The absence of an imperial refugee policy reflected not only the government's mismanagement of the war but also the novelty of the phenomenon. Until World War I, refugees were simply not part of military planning. On the eve of the war in Russia, more-over, they were barely part of public consciousness.

Refugeedom had emerged as a distinct and identifiable concept in imperial Russia only in the late nineteenth century. Although Tolstoy's *War and Peace*, penned in the latter half of the 1860s, was peopled with numerous refugees, the term itself is nowhere to be found in his oeuvre. Indeed, it was only in 1891 that "refugee" first appeared in a Russian dictionary. In this entry, the refu-gee was defined as a "fugitive" who had been "compelled" to leave his "home-land, place of service, or of dwelling . . . by some kind of calamity."[7] Accord-ing to the dictionary, the Russian term was first used to designate Bosnian civilians who fled the Ottoman Empire in the wake of a brutal repression of tax revolts in 1875. Until the outbreak of World War I, however, the term was used only rarely and appeared neither in the third edition of Dal's mag-isterial dictionary of the Russian language, published in the early twentieth century, nor in the multivolume *Russian Military Encyclopedia*, published

---

[4] On World War I and the concept of total war, see Roger Chickering, "Total War: The Use and Abuse of a Concept," in *Anticipating Total War: The German and American Experiences, 1871–1914*, ed. Manfred F. Boemeke, Roger Chickering, and Stig Forster (Cambridge: Cam-bridge University Press, 1999), 13–28; and Stig Forster, "Introduction," in *Great War, Total War: Combat and Mobilization on the Western Front, 1914–1918*, ed. Roger Chickering and Stig Forster (Cambridge: Cambridge University Press, 2000), 6. On the transformations wrought by the war in the Russian Empire, see Peter Holquist, *Making War, Forging Revolution: Rus-sia's Continuum of Crisis, 1914–1921* (Cambridge, Mass.: Harvard University Press, 2002); and Holquist, "'Information Is the Alpha and Omega of Our Work': Bolshevik Surveillance in Its Pan-European Context," *Journal of Modern History* 69, no. 3 (1997): 427–32.

[5] On the refugee crisis, see Peter Gatrell, *A Whole Empire Walking: Refugees in Russia dur-ing World War I* (Bloomington: Indiana University Press, 1999).

[6] GARF, f. 8418, op. 2, d. 99, l. 23.

[7] Vtoroe otdelenie Imperatorskoi Akademii nauk, *Slovar' russkogo iazyka* (St. Petersburg, 1891). In Russian, both "refugee" (*bezhenets*) and "fugitive" (*beglets*) are derived from the verb "to run" (*begat'*). The German term for refugee, "Fluchtling," has a similar etymology. See Michael Marrus, *The Unwanted: European Refugees in the Twentieth Century* (Oxford: Oxford University Press, 1985), 9.

only a few years before the war.[8] Moreover, when Russia was confronted with a refugee crisis of its own in the mid-1890s, as Armenians streamed across the border from the Ottoman Empire in the wake of a series of massacres, the term applied was not "refugee" but "migrant." The use of this more general term suggests that at this point there was little consciousness that refugees suffered from any specific plight. Indeed, individuals attempting to raise funds for the displaced Armenians bemoaned the fact that the Russian public failed to distinguish the plight of the Armenian "migrants" from that of Russia's own peasant "migrants."[9]

Not until World War I, in the wake of the displacement of millions of Imperial subjects, did the term "refugee" acquire common currency in Russia. Although today we tend to think of refugees as those who are forced to leave their countries of origin, refugeedom entered onto the Russian stage as a phenomenon denoting not statelessness but homelessness. Indeed, refugees were sometimes referred to as "refugees—homeless people" and were described in a proclamation of a committee convened to care for them as "our civilian inhabitants" dispersed by the war.[10] The widespread adoption of a new term signaled both an emergent consciousness of the distinct plight of those displaced by war and a new set of administrative practices designed to deal with the particular problems they posed: refugees frequently clogged essential transit routes—they had to be moved; they were homeless—they had to be resettled; they lacked even the most basic provisions—they had to be clothed and fed.

World War I thus transformed refugeedom into an object of public concern and administrative regulation. In a sense, the war gave birth not simply to a new consciousness of refugeedom, but to the phenomenon itself. Though population displacement was by no means a novel feature of war, its unprecedented scale in World War I stemmed from a new approach to warfare. The refugee crisis was the product not only of flight but of forcible expulsions, a situation reflected in the juridical definition of refugees as people "who have abandoned localities threatened or already occupied by the enemy, or who have been expelled by order of the military or civil authority from the zone of military operations."[11] Although World War I witnessed the expulsion of

[8] See, for its absence, K. I. Velichko et al., *Voennaia entsiklopediia*, vol. 5 (St. Petersburg: I. D. Sytyn, 1911–15).

[9] The term in Russian was *pereselenets*. G. A. Dzhanshiev, ed., *Bratskaia pomoshch' postradavshim v turtsii armianam. Literaturno-nauchnyi sbornik*, 2d ed. (Moscow: I. N. Kushnerev i ko., 1898), F.

[10] The term in Russian was *bezhentsy-bezdomnie. Komitet Ee Imperatorskogo Vysochestva Velikoi Kniazhny Tat'iany Nikolaevny po okazaniiu vremennoi pomoshchi postradavshim ot voennykh deistvii, 14 sentiabria 1914 g. po ianvariu 1916 g.* (Petrograd, 1916).

[11] Quoted in Gatrell, *Whole Empire Walking*, 12. Initially, the categories of expellee and refugee were regarded as distinct, but the former were increasingly assimilated to the latter, masking, in Gatrell's view, the actions of the Russian Army (ibid., 31–32).

civilians across Europe, in the Russian case the targets were not only foreign subjects but subjects of the Russian Empire itself.[12]

The forcible expulsions of World War I were rooted in a new approach to population management elaborated within the military establishment. They were driven in part by concerns about the loyalty of the domestic population, which military authorities separated, in conformity with ethnic markers, into "reliable" and "unreliable" elements. During the war, those deemed "unreliable" were expelled from particularly sensitive regions to preclude the possibility of collaboration with the enemy.[13] Russia's ethnic Germans and Jews, as well as foreign passport holders, were subject to expulsions on these grounds. Expellees were either simply evicted from their homes or, less frequently, deported farther east.[14] The forcible removals also stemmed from concerns about the size and strength of the enemy's labor force. During World War I, German occupying forces on both the Western and the Eastern fronts routinely conscripted civilians for forced labor in defense work. In response, the Russian Army began to remove civilians from territory under threat of occupation, thus depriving the enemy of crucial resources. While pursued only sporadically, these expulsions further swelled the ranks of refugees.[15]

The recourse to expulsions to win the war of resources underscores the way in which economic concerns were transforming the conduct of war. The principle of removing resources to protect them found its fullest expression in another novel phenomenon born of the war—evacuation. The evacuation of factories, valuables, and specialized workers from the frontline regions to the rear had not been foreseen in any prewar plans. As the chairman of the Evacuation Commission of the Northern Front later recalled, the country was "completely unprepared" for evacuations.[16] Only in the summer of 1915 did evacuations begin in earnest, and only in the fall of that year was the "Evacuation Commission" finally established under the auspices of the Special Conference of Defense to oversee the operation.[17]

[12] This was also the case in the Ottoman Empire. For a general overview of population expulsions in Europe, see John Horne and Alan Kramer, "War between Soldiers and Enemy Civilians, 1914–1915," in *Great War, Total War*, ed. Chickering and Forster, 153–68.

[13] On the evolution of this policy and its prewar antecedents, see Peter Holquist, "To Count, to Extract, to Exterminate: Population Statistics and Population Politics in Late Imperial and Soviet Russia," in *A State of Nations: Empire and Nation-Making in the Soviet Union, 1917–1953*, ed. Terry Martin and Ronald Suny (New York: Oxford University Press, 2001), 111–44.

[14] Deportations generally targeted ethnic Germans, whereas expulsions tended to target Jews. Both operations were referred to in Russian as *vyselenie*. See Eric Lohr, *Nationalizing the Russian Empire: The Campaign against Enemy Aliens during World War I* (Cambridge, Mass.: Harvard University Press, 2003), chap. 5.

[15] Gatrell, *Whole Empire Walking*, 15, 27.

[16] Quoted in A. L. Sidorov, *Ekonomicheskoe polozhenie Rossii v gody pervoi mirovoi voiny* (Moscow: Nauka, 1973), 215.

[17] Ibid., 216–17.

Like the term "refugee," the term "evacuation" entered the Russian language only in the latter half of the nineteenth century.[18] Derived from the French *évacuation*, it initially denoted "the planned dispatch of the wounded and the sick from field hospitals to hospitals in their home country."[19] The term had come into usage in Russia during the Russo-Turkish War of the 1870s, which had witnessed the first large-scale efforts at transporting wounded soldiers far from the theater of war.[20] With World War I, "evacuation," heretofore reserved for soldiers, came to denote the organized transfer of resources to the rear.

The transposition of "evacuation" from an exclusively military domain onto the domestic economy reflected a new consciousness of and systematized approach to the economic problems posed by contemporary warfare. Both the theory and the practice of war had changed. Mass displacement, population expulsions, and the evacuation of resources were all a measure of these changes. Although the tsarist regime did not survive the war, the transformations it inaugurated shaped the way the subsequent rulers of the land conceived of warfare.

PREPARING FOR WAR IN THE EARLY SOVIET ERA

When the Bolsheviks seized power in 1917, they sought to enact a clean break with the imperial past, to create both state and society anew. Ultimately, however, they could not entirely escape the past. World War I, in particular, left an indelible imprint on the nascent Soviet regime. Denounced by the new authorities as an "imperialist war," World War I nonetheless bequeathed to the Soviet state a way of thinking about and managing war. When Soviet officials set about preparing for a future war, they did so with the concepts and practices of both the Russian Civil War and World War I firmly in mind. An experience to be alternately emulated and improved on, World War I was an inescapable point of reference.[21]

Serious preparations for a future war began only in the late 1920s, in the wake of a war scare. Caused by a series of setbacks in international relations, the war scare of 1927 convinced the Soviet leadership that war was imminent and set into motion a flurry of activity geared toward "strengthening the de-

---

[18] The term entered Dal's dictionary of the Russian language only in its third edition, published in the early twentieth century. See Vladimir Ivanovich Dal', *Tolkovyi slovar' zhivogo velikorusskogo iazyka*, 2d ed., 4 vols. (St. Petersburg: M. O. Vol'f, 1880–82); Vladimir Ivanovich Dal', *Tolkovyi slovar' zhivogo velikorusskogo iazyka*, 3d ed., vol. 4, ed. Jan Niecisław Baudouin de Courtenay (St. Petersburg: M. O. Vol'f, 1909).

[19] S. N. Iuzhakov, *Bol'shaia entsiklopediia* (St. Petersburg, 1905), 448.

[20] Ivan Efimovich Andreevskii et al., *Entsiklopedicheskii slovar'*, vol. 40 (St. Petersburg: F. A. Brokgauz and I. A. Efron, 1890–1904), 118.

[21] For literature on this topic, see Holquist, "'Information Is the Alpha and Omega of Our Work'," 432 n. 46.

fense" of the country.[22] Policies and plans proliferated, all under the umbrella of the Council of Labor and Defense. Given the experience of World War I, it was perhaps inevitable that refugeedom and evacuation would both be part of the equation. Nor was it surprising that the two issues, although handled by overlapping administrations, were nonetheless conceived of as separate.

Soviet refugee policy was predicated on the "assumption that the quantity of refugees in a future revolutionary class war could be as great as in the World War."[23] From the vantage point of the 1920s, it seemed safe to conclude that in the future warfare would only be more brutal. Chemical weapons and other technical innovations "directed at the merciless destruction of the civilian population," as well as mistreatment at the hands of enemy armies, would "create such horrors of war from which wide circles of the population cannot help but seek salvation in displacement to the rear." Whereas peasants might be reluctant to flee due to the hardships they endured during World War I and their assumed attachment to the land, the "class character" of a future war would assure a "whole [new] category" of refugees: those subject to repression on class or ideological grounds. This category, which included workers as well as government and party officials, would substantially swell the mass of refugees. For "economic as well as political reasons," then, refugeedom would be unavoidable.[24]

Refugee policy was not formulated by Soviet authorities as a humanitarian response to suffering so much as a pragmatic attempt to "help prepare the country for defense."[25] In 1928, Soviet authorities prepared the country's first refugee statute under the direction of the Council of Labor and Defense. Drafted by the Red Army General Staff with input from a handful of other administrations, it was formulated, in the words of the preamble, "on the basis of the experience of the war of 1914–18."[26] Refugees in World War I had posed a significant problem for which neither the army nor the government had been adequately prepared. As one official put it, they had "blocked military roads and interrupted the free movement of troops, spread various diseases, and frequently served to demoralize the rear."[27] Moreover, they had proved to be an "exceptionally heavy burden on the state budget." The result was a crisis of "political, economic, and strategic" dimensions.[28]

Soviet refugee policy was designed to avoid the mistakes of the previous war by organizing refugee movement and providing aid to those in need. In

[22] N. S. Simonov, "'Strengthen the Defense of the Land of the Soviets': The 1927 'War Alarm' and Its Consequences," *Europe-Asia Studies* 48, no. 8 (1996): 1355–64.

[23] This was the position of the General Staff, shared by the Soviet Red Cross. See GARF, f. 8418, op. 2, d. 99, ll. 23–24; 68.

[24] Ibid, ll. 68–69.

[25] GARF, f. 8418, op. 2, d. 99, l. 23.

[26] Ibid.

[27] Ibid., l. 41.

[28] Ibid., l. 23.

the first place, it aimed to "organize the movement of refugees" to minimize disturbances to military supply and communication. "Refugees" were defined as Soviet citizens who had "voluntarily left their permanent residences for the rear during an enemy attack" or had been "expelled from the zone of military activity on the order of military authorities," as well as "subjects of countries at war with the USSR" who had chosen to come to the Soviet Union to escape repression at home or "out of sympathy with the Red Army."[29] The concept of "voluntary" displacement strikes a discordant note for today's readers, accustomed to thinking of wartime population displacement in terms of "forced migration" or "involuntary displacement." The term was intended, however, to distinguish between different modalities of displacement, the first of which stemmed from an individual decision (and was thus "voluntary") and the second of which issued from an order from above. The notion of "voluntary refugeedom" reflected the prevailing view that departure was ultimately a matter of personal choice, a phenomenon that could be discouraged but not prevented. Although the General Staff proposed a program of vigorous propaganda designed to dissuade the population from departing, policy ultimately aimed to channel flight rather than forestall it.[30]

The policy's second objective was to ensure that refugees received adequate provisions. In World War I, the needs of refugees had been met by a series of organizations, all of them charitable. Soviet authorities, however, viewed this solution as inadequate and even inappropriate. The charitable organizations had arisen, in the words of the General Staff, "by chance." Soviet policy sought to replace the "chance" and decentralized organizations of the tsarist regime with the centralized organs of the socialist state. The "rational" and "maximal" use of refugee labor would accomplish what charity could not.[31] To this end, the General Staff proposed limiting government aid to refugees "who have not found work and are not settled on the land" and prohibiting refugees from refusing work "if it corresponds to their physical capabilities and profession." This would resolve not only the financial but also the psychological problems associated with the care of refugees, for charity, in the eyes of the General Staff, "engendered a dependent sentiment among refugees."[32] In keeping with the dominant Soviet ethos, labor rather than charity would provide the key to well-being.

For the most part, the statute on refugees seemed to meet the expectations of the various officials who reviewed it. A discordant note, however, was struck by officials in the Commissariat of Transportation, who challenged the very premise of refugee policy. "[T]he People's Commissariat of Transportation categorically rejects the idea whereby voluntary refugeedom is permitted,

---

[29] GARF, f. 8418, op. 2, d. 99, ll. 23, 25.
[30] Ibid., l. 29.
[31] Ibid., ll. 23; 24.
[32] Ibid., ll. 26; 24.

that is, the idea that those citizens who would like to leave their permanent residences for the rear during an enemy invasion can do so without impediment." The commissariat's rejection of "voluntary refugeedom" was based on the position that, if tolerated, it would result in the "spontaneous and disorganized flight of the population" and would undermine attempts to maintain order. In place of the unregulated departure of masses of people that had characterized World War I, officials in the commissariat proposed the "evacuation" of a limited number of people, "people who, if left in [such] zones . . . , could be in danger of repression at the hands of the [enemy]." To enforce the new and more restrictive regime, moreover, they advocated not only the standard methods of persuasion, but also "measures of a repressive nature, directed against people who willfully leave their region of residence." To this end, their proposal called for the organization of special police detachments, which would be stationed along major roads during a retreat and would stop all those "who have not received permission to depart."[33]

The commissariat's proposal contested the very concept of refugeedom, as the Council of Labor and Defense was well aware. The council representative who reviewed the proposal was clearly skeptical. Scrawled in the margins beside the Commissariat of Transportation's rejection of "voluntary refugeedom" is the question: "and can refugeedom really be anything but voluntary?" The representative further underlined the commissariat's proposed repressive measures, scribbling the following question over the text: "and what will we do with those who flee anyway?" Officials in the Commissariat of Defense raised similar questions. The proposal, in their eyes, neglected the needs of the population ("what about people whose homes have been destroyed?" one official queried) and was hardly feasible (the proposed police detachments were rejected as the "kind of measure that could spark a riot").[34] In 1928, the proposals of the Commissariat of Transportation seemed outlandish and impractical. Ten years later, they would be commonplace. Both the principle of restricting and controlling displacement and that of selectively removing certain sectors of the population to protect them would be incorporated into Soviet policy on wartime population displacement. This would happen, however, under the rubric not of refugeedom, the very notion of which had been challenged, but of evacuation.

Like planning for population displacement, Soviet evacuation planning was informed by the experiences of World War I and by contemporary reflections on the determinant role of the economy in warfare. The preeminent Red Army General and military theorist M. V. Frunze wrote in 1925:

the fundamental and most important conclusion to be drawn from the experience of the imperialist war of 1914–18 is the reappraisal of the question of the

---

[33] GARF, f. 8418, op. 2, d. 99, ll. 31; 33.
[34] RGVA, f. 7, op. 10, d. 730, l. 17.

role and significance of the rear in the general progress of military operations. The position that holds that "the outcome of the war will be decided not only directly on the battle front, but also on the lines where the civilian forces of the country stand" has now become a popular axiom.[35]

Like many others in the Soviet Union and abroad, Frunze maintained that the ability to wage war in the future would depend in large measure on the successful mobilization of the economy. It was in precisely this context that Soviet administrators broached the question of evacuation. A 1926 tract titled "Contemporary War and the Role of Economic Preparation" pointed to the central role of evacuation on the economic front, arguing that the "evacuation plan is one of the most serious aspects of the mobilization work of the Supreme Soviet of the National Economy [Vesenkha]."[36]

Not surprisingly, then, economic concerns were preeminent in defining whom and what to evacuate. A statute on the preparation of evacuation plans issued in 1928, in the midst of the more general preparations for war, clearly identified the objects of evacuation as the "human and material resources" needed to assure the "stability of the economy and defense capacity of the country" as well as anything that would "strengthen the enemy."[37] Conceived in military-industrial terms, evacuation policy targeted not the "population" at large (a category that is notably absent from evacuation planning in this period) but only select "human contingents." A meeting on evacuation held by the General Staff warned of the danger of evacuation being used as a "cover" for "mass refugeedom," and insisted on the necessity of limiting the categories of people subject to evacuation.[38] Much of the debate between the administrations involved in drafting the statute concerned exactly which categories to include.

At the top of everybody's list, in keeping with the stated objectives of the operation, were skilled workers and employees, who were to be evacuated only when "their use in the interior of the country . . . is not in doubt." Next were political and administrative cadres, who would be needed to reinforce Soviet power in the rear and to aid in the "restoration of Soviet power" once abandoned territories had been reclaimed.[39] Who else would be subject to evacuation, and on what conditions, was a source of controversy. Many felt that rural authorities, the infirm, invalids, and the families of evacuated work-

[35] M. V. Frunze, *Izbrannye proizvedeniia* (Moscow: Voennoe izdatel'stvo, 1984), 182.

[36] Quoted in A. A. Meliia, "Stanovleniia evakuatsionnogo planirovaniia kak elementa mobilizatsionnoi podgotovki ekonomiki (1921–1928 gg.)," *Ekonomika i finansy*, no. 2 (2002): 46.

[37] GARF, f. 8418, op. 1, d. 123, l. 86. Preparation of the statute began in 1927 and involved the Council of Labor and Defense, the General Staff, the All Union State Political Administration (OGPU), the Commissariats of Transportation and Labor, Vesenkha, and the Revolutionary Military Soviet of the USSR. It was intended to replace a statute issued in 1923.

[38] RGVA, f. 7, op. 10, d. 444, l. 85.

[39] Ibid., l. 261.

ers and employees should be evacuated only if they were "in danger of possible repression at the hands of the enemy."[40] The Commissariat of Internal Affairs (NKVD), for one, considered the evacuation of rural authorities "inexpedient" on the grounds that "it might elicit dissatisfaction."[41] Ultimately, while rural authorities were indeed excluded from the operation, the families of qualified workers were not.[42] Their evacuation might not serve the "defense capacity of the country," but officials in both Vesenkha and the Commissariat of Labor maintained that it was inexpedient *not* to include them. "Tearing workers and employees from their families" was "unrealistic" and would undermine, in the words of both administrations, the "voluntary" character of the operation.[43] Their position, set out in separate communications, was rooted in a politics of accommodation based on assumptions about the behavior of the population. In effect, they advocated evacuating families in the interest of placating workers, who, it was assumed, would otherwise resist evacuation. Their concern with convincing workers to cooperate suggests that at this point planners still drew distinctions between mobilization on the economic front and mobilization on the battlefront. The mobilization of civilians was subject to fundamentally different modalities from that of combatants, and was conceived as voluntary. A decade later, this would no longer be the case.

STALIN'S REVOLUTION: FROM REFUGEE TO EVACUEE

The relationship between refugeedom and evacuation was fundamentally reordered in the 1930s. The policy debates of the late 1930s were separated from those of 1928 by Stalin's revolution from above, heralded by the collectivization of agriculture and the adoption of dizzying plans for rapid industrialization. The "great turn," as Stalin referred to it, was also accompanied by a more heavy-handed approach to population circulation. Passportization, introduced in 1932, made internal migration and travel dependent on official authorization.[44] In addition, the period saw the widespread application of new forms of population transfer. Collectivization was followed by the large-scale deportation of wealthy peasants, or kulaks, to newly estab-

---

[40] GARF, f. 8418, op. 1, d. 123, ll. 88–89. A similar position is set forth in an earlier draft of the statute in RGVA, f. 7, op. 10, d. 444, l. 262.

[41] GARF, f. 8418, op. 1, d. 123, l. 148.

[42] Ibid., l. 2.

[43] Ibid., ll. 82, 174.

[44] On passportization and the passport system, see Gijs Kessler, "The Passport System and State Control over Population Flows in the Soviet Union, 1932–1940," *Cahiers du monde russe* 42, no. 2–3–4 (2001): 477–503; Nathalie Moine, "Passportisation, statistique des migrations et controle de l'identité sociale," *Cahiers du monde russe* 38, no. 4 (1997): 587–600; V. P. Popov, "Pasportnaia sistema v SSSR," *Sotsiologicheskie issledovaniia*, no. 9 (1995): 3–13; and David R. Shearer, "Elements Near and Alien: Passportization, Policing, and Identity in the Stalinist State, 1932–1952," *Journal of Modern History* 76, no. 4 (2004): 835–81.

lished "special settlements," to which deportees were legally confined. The deported kulaks were only the first of a long list of people subject to deportation over the course of the decade. Deportations targeted people across the country, but special measures were reserved for the border zones, from which so-called unreliable elements were routinely expelled. Though these were not, technically speaking, wartime measures, they nonetheless served a military function and harked back to the forced expulsions of World War I. Over the course of the 1930s, the expulsion of "unreliable" elements from border and other sensitive regions developed into a systematized practice of the state under the charge of the NKVD.[45] This was only one of several ways in which military concepts and practices came to organize civilian life under Stalin.

The 1930s also saw important changes in the theory and practice of war. Aerial bombardment, only in its infancy during World War I, emerged as a signature feature of war in the interwar period. In the latter half of the 1930s, the Japanese invasion of China and the Spanish Civil War put the new technology and its destructive capabilities on prominent display. The fate of cities such as Guernica, destroyed by German aircraft in a deliberate attack on a defenseless population, cast the realities of modern warfare into sharp relief. Henceforth, it was no longer possible to draw neat distinctions between civilian and military, homefront and battlefront.

Taken together, these developments set the stage for a substantive change in Soviet policy. The transformation was heralded by an administrative reorganization of policy on population displacement at the end of the 1930s. In 1937, a decree "on procedures for removing and resettling refugees" transferred responsibility for refugee policy from the Red Cross and the party, to whom it had previously been entrusted, to the Soviet political police, the NKVD. The next year, the General Staff informed the NKVD that they were drawing up a new "statute on evacuation," which contained important directives on the "removal of the population."[46] Henceforth, refugees appeared only rarely in policy statements, and all planning for war-related population displacement was carried out under the rubric of evacuation. This had certain immediate implications: whereas the objects of refugee policy were, in the words of many of the proposals, the "human masses" who "had left their places of permanent residence," evacuation policy targeted specific "human

---

[45] For an overview of Soviet deportations in this period, see Pavel Polian, *Against Their Will: The History and Geography of Forced Migrations in the USSR*, trans. Anna Yastrzhembska (Budapest: Central European University Press, 2004). On the deportation of kulaks, see Lynne Viola, *The Unknown Gulag: The Lost World of Stalin's Special Settlements* (Oxford: Oxford University Press, 2007). On deportations from the border zones, see Terry Martin, "The Origins of Soviet Ethnic Cleansing," *Journal of Modern History* 70 (December 1998): 813–61. On specifically urban expulsions see Paul M. Hagenloh, "'Socially Harmful Elements' and the Terror," in *Stalinism: New Directions*, ed. Sheila Fitzpatrick (New York: Routledge, 2000), 286–308.

[46] GARF, f. 8418, op. 12, d. 470, ll. 1; 7.

contingents." Whereas "masses" took shape spontaneously and on their own, "contingents" were selected, the product of an organized procedure. In evacuation policy, the state was the sole agent of displacement. The replacement of the "voluntary" refugee by the designated evacuee was accompanied by several substantive changes in policy, involving both an enlargement of the scope of evacuation and a simultaneous restriction of the overall scope of displacement.

The most obvious changes to Soviet evacuation policy stemmed from the advent of aerial bombardment. In a memo describing a new draft statute on evacuation prepared in the late 1930s, the General Staff noted that the 1928 statute "did not single out with sufficient sharpness the question of the evacuation of children and the nonworking population from points where enemy aviation is active."[47] In fact, the 1928 statute contained not a word on either children or the nonworking population, nor, for that matter, on enemy aviation. Despite the long-standing conviction that a future war would radically erode the boundary between front and rear, preparations for the defense of the "rear" had been confined to what contemporaries referred to as "civil defense," essentially the construction of bomb shelters and the distribution of gas masks.[48] It was not until 1937, as Soviet papers reported on the devastation wreaked by aerial attacks on Republican bastions in Spain, that those concerned with wartime population displacement began to take aerial bombardment into account. As a Soviet manual on civil defense put it, the "action of Fascist aviation in Spain and of Japanese aviation in China demonstrate that the targets of aerial bombardment consist not only of military factories, warehouses, and government institutions but also the population itself."[49] In the spring of 1937, the head of the Leningrad Soviet, "basing himself on the example of Madrid," put the question of the "removal of children and the inactive population" on the table.[50] The evacuation of children and the nonworking population subsequently became an important component of prewar evacuation policy.

---

[47] GARF, f. 8418, op. 22, d. 55, l. 35.

[48] For a brief survey of Soviet civil defense initiatives, see John Erickson, *The Soviet High Command: A Military-Political History, 1918–1941* (London: St. Martin's, 1962), 306–8. Soviet planners were not alone in their failure to grasp the danger posed by aerial bombardment. French officials also minimized the threat of bombardment, persuaded by the experience of World War I that French aircraft would successfully defend the country from aerial attack. Among British officials, by contrast, the threat of aerial bombardment was the driving force behind the elaboration of evacuation policy from the early 1920s. See Jean Vidalenc, *L'Exode de mai–juin 1940* (Paris: Presses universitaires de France, 1957), 15; Nicole Dombrowski, "Beyond the Battlefield: The French Civilian Exodus of May–June 1940" (Ph.D. diss., New York University, 1995), 18; Michael Fethney, *The Absurd and the Brave: CORB—The True Account of the British Government's World War II Evacuation of Children Overseas* (Sussex, UK: Book Guild, 1990), 22.

[49] N. F. Mainin and Osoaviakhim SSSR, *Kolletivnaia zashchita ot vozdushno-khimicheskogo napadeniia* (Moscow: Glavnaia redaktsiia khimicheskoi literatury, 1938), 5.

[50] GARF, f. 8418, op. 12, d. 426, l. 17.

Heightened attention to the new technologies of war was accompanied by an increasing concern with the psychological dimensions of warfare. Since World War I, theorists of modern war, the champions of aerial bombardment in particular, had seen morale as a decisive element of warfare. "Morale" accordingly became a target of enemy attack, and its maintenance a key component in any plan of defense. It was only in the 1930s, however, that the term was introduced into evacuation policy debates. Cities were now reconceived as "moral bastions" for the country. Thus the first principle animating the statute drafted by the Chief of the General Staff, B. M. Shaposhnikov, stipulated that the "major political and industrial centers and points of operational significance located in the frontline regions or the regions of military action should not be evacuated in the sense that everything is removed. They must be unassailable fortresses against the enemy and serve as moral buttresses for our troops." Such was the concern with morale that the Committee of Defense actually opposed the evacuation of the non-able-bodied population on the grounds, among other things, that it would "elicit a decline in the moral-political state of the unevacuated population." At issue was not the satisfaction of particular groups within Soviet society, but rather the collective will to fight. From the perspective of both the Committee of Defense and the General Staff, the maintenance of morale was simply incompatible with a large-scale evacuation.[51]

Morale was one of a range of considerations that helped seal the fate of "voluntary refugeedom." The very premises of policy had changed. In contrast to the late 1920s, when administrators insisted that families be included in the evacuation of specialized workers to preserve the "voluntary" character of the operation, the policy debates of the 1930s took almost no account of the population's own desires or inclinations. Although the Committee of Defense expressed concern that the evacuation of children would "split up the family," its comments seem to have fallen on deaf ears. Policy in the 1930s was based on the dictum that the primary allegiance of Soviet citizens was owed not to their families but to the state. More important, it was premised not on assumptions about the behavior of the population but on regulations that prescribed this behavior. Increasingly, civilian labor was recast as a military obligation, and the politics of accommodation that had underwritten policy in the previous decade were accordingly rejected. This was expressed nowhere more explicitly than in an NKVD memo to the General Staff, which proposed that "all able-bodied adults living on the front lines" be excluded from the evacuation and "recruited for specific work of a defensive character. Those who refuse to fulfill their appointed work, or depart for the rear, will be regarded as labor deserters." This was a critical moment in the shift from refugee to evacuee as the organizing principle of policy, for the notion of

[51] GARF, f. 8418, op. 12, d. 470, ll. 7; 38.

civilian mobilization transformed the refugeedom of World War I into nothing short of desertion. The NKVD further stipulated that local party committees and city soviets, or councils, would be responsible for "preventing the spontaneous and disorganized departure of the population." The Commissariat of Transportation proposal that had seemed so outlandish in 1928 thus became an accepted dictum: there would be no "voluntary refugeedom" in a future war.[52]

$$\bullet \quad \bullet \quad \bullet$$

The draft statute on evacuation of 1938 remained just that—a draft. Despite repeated interventions by the General Staff requesting that the Committee of Defense "hasten the presentation to the government of the draft statute on evacuation," the draft appears to have been neither accepted nor rejected.[53] It was not until early June 1941, less than three weeks before the German armies invaded, that a new draft statute was presented for approval. The draft statute of 1941 was based on the earlier one but was altered to accommodate the geopolitical changes of the past two years, namely the annexations of eastern Poland, the Baltics, Bessarabia, and northern Bukovina in keeping with the secret clauses of the Molotov-Ribbentrop pact. Titled "On Procedures for Developing Evacuation Plans," the statute defined evacuation as the "carrying out in wartime of fundamental measures to remove valuable property, institutions, factories, and human contingents from regions under military threat."[54]

The statute of 1941 reflected the transformations of the previous decade. It laid out a unified approach to wartime population displacement in which the key term was not "flight" but "removal." Only those sectors of the population designated by the state would be subject to displacement. Although the statute contained no statement as strong as that initially proposed by the NKVD in 1938, whereby those who departed without authorization were to be branded "labor deserters," such language may no longer have been necessary. A series of labor laws passed in 1940 placed significant strata of the civilian workforce under a state of military mobilization. Moreover, the statute charged the NKVD with "ensuring that no evacuations take place outside the general plan" and with "liquidating" any unauthorized departures.[55]

---

[52] Herein lay one of the distinguishing features of Soviet evacuation policy. Although the French were also faced with the prospect of a land-based invasion and, like the Soviets, feared the destabilizing effect on morale of a mass evacuation, French planners tended to accept that many civilians would "depart of their own accord." Vidalenc, *Exode*, 16. For the NKVD memo, see GARF, f. 8418, op. 22, d. 55, l. 1.

[53] GARF, f. 8418, op. 22, d. 55, ll. 34, 40.

[54] GARF, f. A-259, op. 40, d. 3028, ll. 82–83.

[55] Ibid., l. 79.

Another significant feature of the statute of 1941 was the enlargement of the territorial scope of projected evacuations. Whereas evacuation policy of the 1920s conceived of evacuation as an operation designed to remove people and things only from regions threatened by invasion, the 1941 statute reflected a more contemporary awareness of the danger posed by aerial bombardment. The 1938 manual on civil defense cited above aptly expressed the new premise of policy: the "entire zone accessible to enemy aviation will become part of the theater of war. The depth of the 'active' rear of the army, considering the average flight capacities of contemporary aviation, will extend to 1,000 kilometers from the front lines."[56] The new evacuation statute laid out what may be termed a topography of evacuation, defining three zones of evacuation, each with its own priorities. Evacuation from zones of army deployment (the border regions, in which the army was supposed to take up its positions) targeted children and the elderly as well as industry, educational institutes, state valuables, and natural and industrial resources. The second zone, "regions threatened by the enemy," would see the evacuation of the most important state organizations and factories, resources that "could be used by the enemy," "the entire male population eligible for military service," and children and the elderly, depending on the military situation. The final zone consisted of the "most important centers of the country" and included preschool children with their mothers; school children up to fifteen years of age, organized by school and accompanied by their teachers; the elderly over sixty years of age; machinery and other industrial equipment, as well as the workforce required to service it; principal scientific and educational institutions; and the "most important" museum valuables.[57]

The guidelines were predicated on the assumption that in a future war the urban population would be systematically targeted by the enemy. Indeed, the most extensive evacuations were planned for the cities. The guidelines were likewise informed by the belief that the population represented a potential resource in the eyes of the enemy, and that victory would depend on the mobilization and retention of all possible sources of labor. In this vein, men fit for military service would be targeted for evacuation from regions threatened by enemy occupation, and industrial resources and manpower would be evacuated from each of the three evacuation zones.

The statute of June 1941 placed responsibility for the evacuations in the hands of the NKVD. The operation would be initiated by different authorities depending on the zone—in the border regions by the Council of People's Commissars (Sovnarkom), in threatened regions by the army, and in urban centers by Sovnarkom, with the sanction of the NKVD. Most immediately, the NKVD was charged with the preparation of concrete evacuation plans,

[56] Mainin and Osoaviakhim SSSR, *Kollektivnaia zashchita*, 5.
[57] GARF, f. A-259, op. 40, d. 3028, l. 81.

which were to be drawn up before the onset of military action.[58] By 1941, evacuation was thus firmly established as a full-blown part of Soviet planning for war. The role of planning, and the extent of preparation, would be put to the test within weeks of the preparation of the statute. For on June 22, 1941, Nazi Germany launched a surprise attack on the Soviet Union, setting into motion the largest military operation in history.

[58] Ibid., l. 76.

2

THE OFFICIAL MIND OF EVACUATION
Policy in the Wake of the Invasion

In late June 1941, as German forces penetrated deep into Soviet territory, Nikolai Dubrovin, a top-ranking official in the Commissariat of Transportation, was dispatched on a research expedition. He had been appointed to a newly established council responsible for "directing the evacuation of the population, institutions, military and other transports, factory equipment and other valuables."[1] As Dubrovin recalled many years later, however, "we didn't have concrete, well-developed evacuation plans in case of an unfavorable course of events. . . . On orders from higher up we searched the archives and the libraries of Moscow, including the Lenin State Library, to find even a scrap of information on evacuations during World War I, but we found almost nothing."[2]

Dubrovin's account is at first glance perplexing. After all, the Soviet Union had been drafting evacuation statutes since the 1920s. Despite a succession of evacuation statutes, however, preparations remained incomplete on the eve of the invasion. Not only was the latest evacuation statute still in draft form but few concrete plans had been established. Moreover, one of the few known initiatives to establish such plans, a draft decree prepared by the Moscow Soviet on the "partial evacuation of the city's population in the event of war," had been stymied.[3] Stalin himself had intervened, sending the following brief note to Pronin, the head of the Moscow Soviet, only weeks before the German invasion: "Comrade Pronin. I consider your proposal for the 'partial' evacuation of the population of Moscow during war untimely. I request that you disband the commission for evacuation, and cease

---

[1] "Iz istorii Velikoi Otechestvennoi voiny," *Izvestiia TsK KPSS*, no. 8 (1990): 208.

[2] N. F. Dubrovin, "Eshelon za eshelonom," in *Eshelony idut na Vostok: iz istorii perebazirovaniia proizvoditel'nykh sil SSSR v 1941–1942 gg. Sbornik statei i vospominanii*, ed. Iu. A. Poliakov (Moscow: Nauka, 1966), 208–9.

[3] The draft decree is in GARF, f. A-259, op. 40, d. 3073, l. 32.

all talk of evacuation. If and when it is necessary to prepare for evacuation, the Central Committee and the Council of People's Commissars will inform you."[4]

Stalin's refusal to countenance any "talk of evacuation" stemmed in part from his insistence that a future war would be fought on foreign soil and would be almost exclusively offensive. The principle of an offensive war was a veritable dogma of Soviet planning. Such was the commitment to offensive goals that when the Soviet military held war games in the winter of 1941, a defensive reaction to a projected German invasion was not even included in the action.[5] Stalin's suggestion that plans for evacuating Moscow were "untimely" also reflected his steadfast, almost desperate conviction that there would be no war in the summer of 1941. Despite ample intelligence that the Germans were preparing to invade, Stalin was convinced that Hitler would not dare to risk a second front.[6] He feared, moreover, that preparations for war were liable to provoke the enemy. Thus a proposal on the eve of the invasion by the commander of the Kiev Military District to prepare defenses and evacuate some three hundred thousand people from the border zone was rejected as a potential "provocation."[7]

Stalin's position resulted in a failure to anticipate the June 22 attack and to prepare for what the attack would entail. When the Germans did invade, the country was taken by surprise: aircraft were lined up on Soviet bases in plain sight like sitting ducks; border fortifications were in the process of being replaced; many of the troops closest to the border lacked ammunition. Soviet authorities, moreover, were utterly unprepared. Hence the dispatch of a top-ranking official in the Commissariat of Transportation to the archives at a moment when the demands placed on the commissariat had never been greater.

Dubrovin's brief and unsuccessful foray into the archives underscores the irrelevance of prewar plans to wartime evacuation policy. Indeed, the precepts and objectives of evacuation policy were formulated anew in the wake of the invasion. To be sure, the wartime architects of Soviet evacuation policy had much in common with the officials who had elaborated the new approach to policy in the preceding decade. In particular, they shared a basic set of suppositions regarding the priorities of the operation and the need to

---

[4] Quoted in G. A. Kumanev, *Podvig i podlog: stranitsy Velikoi Otechestvennoi voiny, 1941–1945* (Moscow: Russkoe slovo, 2000), 245.

[5] P. N. Bobylev, "For What Kind of War Was the Red Army General Staff Preparing in 1941?" *Russian Studies in History* 36, no. 3 (1997–98): 56.

[6] On the information available to Stalin regarding German intentions and military build-up and his assessment of German intentions, see Gabriel Gorodetsky, *Grand Delusion: Stalin and the German Invasion of Russia* (New Haven: Yale University Press, 1999).

[7] The case was related by Nikita Khrushchev in his secret speech to the Party's Central Committee and was meant to demonstrate Stalin's mishandling of the war. See John Erickson, *The Soviet High Command: A Military-Political History, 1918–1941* (London: St. Martin's Press, 1962), 581–82.

control population displacement. Neither the administrative apparatus established to oversee the evacuation nor the designated objects of evacuation, however, fully conformed to the provisions of the prewar statutes. In the face of the inadequacy of prewar plans, the urgency of the problem, and the prevailing chaos in the Kremlin, Soviet authorities were forced to improvise. As a result, evacuation policy was modeled on existing forms of population transfer and informed by existing visions of the Soviet polity.

Evacuation was conceived by the Soviet state, in keeping with prewar developments, both as a form of economic mobilization and as an attempt to manage migration from the front lines. Although not punitive in nature, the operation was heavily indebted to the practices of population transfer developed over the previous decade. Furthermore, the operation was structured around a hierarchy of people and places that reflected both an existing system of privilege and an ideologically informed vision of the Soviet polity. Finally, evacuation was conceived to protect not merely certain sectors of the population but the entire socialist state. At its core, the operation aimed to retain control over Soviet space, threatened, in the eyes of the state, not only by German forces, but by "enemy elements" and internal dissolution.

THE ADMINISTRATIVE APPARATUS

On June 24, 1941, two days after the German invasion had begun, an Evacuation Council was hastily created by joint decree of the Central Committee and the Council of People's Commissars. Evacuation was in many ways thrust on the Kremlin. German forces had already wreaked havoc along almost the entire length of the Soviet Union's western border: taking advantage of the state of surprise, they had destroyed communication lines, dispersed defending forces, and broken through the system of frontier defenses. By the time the decision to establish the Evacuation Council was made, officially sanctioned evacuations had already begun in both Latvia and Belorussia. Panteleimon Ponomarenko, then first secretary of the Communist Party of Belorussia, recalls having called Stalin on June 23 to request permission to commence evacuations in the Belorussian Republic. Stalin was allegedly surprised by the request and wondered whether it was really necessary. Still captive to the principle of an offensive war and slow to grasp the scale of the disaster unfolding on the front lines, Stalin had, only the day before, ordered the General Staff to launch a counteroffensive and to invade enemy territory. Ponomarenko's report, however, left little doubt as to the gravity of the situation: such was the rapidity of the German advance that a large-scale evacuation from some of the western regions of the republic was, in his estimation, no longer possible, and any delay in the evacuation of Minsk and the eastern regions would be "irreparable."[8] The next day, following countless hours of impromptu meetings in Stalin's office, the Evacuation Council was established.

The establishment of an Evacuation Council had not been foreseen in the prewar statute, which entrusted the NKVD with overseeing the operation. It was, in part, a measure of the irrelevance of prewar planning to the actual administration of evacuation that this provision was largely ignored. The creation of an ad hoc council invested with authority over government organs from the local to the republican levels signaled a new approach to the problem of wartime administration. Like the State Defense Committee, created less than a week later, the council was conceived as a central command structure capable of quick and effective action. Composed of top-ranking individuals drawn from a range of different ministries, the Evacuation Council would, it was hoped, be able to bypass standard bureaucratic procedure and coordinate the activities of various branches of government.[9]

Decisions regarding the evacuation of people and things were made by a handful of Soviet leaders who were deeply engaged in almost all aspects of the war effort. The council's members were drawn from among the most powerful figures in the Soviet Union. At its head stood Lazar Kaganovich, people's commissar of transportation and long-standing member of the Politburo. His deputies were Aleksei Kosygin, deputy chairman of the Council of People's Commissars, and Nikolai Shvernik, chairman of the All-Union Council of Trade Unions. Among the council's five other members were S. N. Kruglov, first deputy to the NKVD; P. I. Kirpichnikov, of the State Planning Committee (Gosplan); and B. M. Shaposhnikov, a marshal of the Soviet Union who was soon to be appointed head of the General Staff and had already played a critical role in the elaboration of civilian evacuation policy in the late 1930s. In subsequent days their ranks would be expanded to include Anastas Mikoian, the people's commissar of internal trade, and Lavrenti

[8] G. A. Kumanev, *Riadom so Stalinym: otkrovennye svidetel'stva (vstrechi, besedy, interv'iu, dokumenty)* (Moscow: Bylina, 1999), 125.

[9] On the administration of the operation, see Sanford R. Lieberman, "Evacuation of Industry in the Soviet Union during World War II," *Soviet Studies* 35, no. 1 (1983): 90–102. The establishment of the Evacuation Council and even more so the Defense Committee signaled a continuation of a prewar trend to concentrate power in ever fewer, and state rather than party, hands. On this, see Oleg Khlevniuk, *Politbiuro: mekhanizmy politicheskoi vlasti v 1930-e gody* (Moscow: Rosspen, 1996), 249–56. On the reliance on ad hoc committees throughout the war, see Sanford R. Lieberman, "Crisis Management in the USSR: The Wartime System of Administration and Control," in *The Impact of World War II on the Soviet Union*, ed. Susan J. Linz (Totowa, NJ: Rowman and Allanheld, 1985), 59–76. On the Defense Committee, see Iu. A. Gor'kov, "K istorii sozdaniia goskomiteta oborony i stavki verkhovnogo glavnokomandovaniia po novym arkhivnym materialam," *Novaia i noveishaia istoriia*, no. 4 (1999): 17–34; A. A. Pechenkin, "Gosudarstvennyi Komitet Oborony v 1941 godu," *Otechestvennaia istoriia*, no. 4 (1994): 126–42.

Beria, the head of the NKVD and a member of the Defense Committee.[10] Evacuation Council members were thus involved in several key spheres of the wartime administration. Moreover, Stalin himself played an active part in the operation, formulating evacuation policy and issuing evacuation orders as head of the Defense Committee.

The evacuation was an operation of gargantuan proportions. As Mikoian later reflected, "circumstances did not turn out as intended, and after two days, it was already clear that evacuation would take place on a massive scale."[11] From the outset, activity on the Evacuation Council was feverish. According to Dubrovin, "in the first months of the war, the council met almost every day."[12] Mikoian, who served on both the council and the Defense Committee, later recalled of this period that he and his colleagues "usually worked until five or six in the morning . . . and returned to work at ten."[13] While presumably not all council members kept such hours, work on the council was demanding. According to L. I. Pogrebnoi, who served as a council plenipotentiary, "we literally lost count of the days." Pogrebnoi could not recall this period of the evacuation "without emotion." These were, in his words, "bitter and difficult days." Like other Soviet citizens, members of the Evacuation Council "took the news of Red Army retreats and enemy occupation of Soviet cities and villages hard."[14] Each day brought news of fresh losses. Within weeks of the invasion, vast tracts of territory had been ceded to the enemy, including all of Latvia and Lithuania, most of Belorussia, and much of western Ukraine. By the end of September, the invading forces had cut Leningrad off from the rest of the country, captured Kiev, surrounded Odessa, and initiated an all-out assault on Moscow. The council was thus faced with what Dubrovin aptly described as an "extremely difficult task."[15]

Responsibility for the evacuation was divided between the Evacuation Council and local military commands, which were charged with overseeing evacuations on the front lines. Both were expected to cooperate with regional state authorities, who were instructed to designate the objects of evacuation in accordance with central state directives and with the help of local "organs of Soviet power," responsible for organizing the evacuation of the population on the ground.[16] By far the greatest burden of organizing the

---

[10] The other members of the Evacuation Council, in order of their appointment, were P. S. Popkov, chair of the Executive Committee of the Leningrad Soviet, and N. F. Dubrovin, from the People's Commissariat of Transportation; M. G. Pervukhin and K. D. Pamfilov, both deputy chairmen of the Council of People's Commissars; and M. V. Zakharov, the deputy to the Chief of the Main Administration of the Red Army Rear.

[11] A. I. Mikoian, "V sovete po evakuatsii," *Voenno-istoricheskii zhurnal*, no. 3 (1989): 31.

[12] Dubrovin, "Eshelon za eshelonom," 209.

[13] Mikoian, "V sovete po evakuastii," 33.

[14] L. I. Pogrebnoi, "O deiatel'nosti soveta po evakuatsii," in *Eshelony idut na Vostok*, ed. Poliakov, 205.

[15] Dubrovin, "Eshelon za eshelonom," 208.

[16] GARF, f. A-259, op. 40, d. 3022, l. 34.

transfer of people and things, however, fell on the Evacuation Council. The responsibilities of the council, as laid out a few weeks after its creation, included the "realization" of the evacuation; the establishment of plans, timelines, and priorities; the provision of the required means of transport; the resettlement of evacuated people and enterprises; control over the implementation of the operation; and the "resolution of all other questions related to the evacuation."[17] The council was thus invested with authority over all aspects of the process, and its decisions were binding.

As the scope of the operation became evident, the ranks of the initially eight-member body were expanded; and Kaganovich, unable to fulfill his responsibilities as both head of the council and as commissar of transportation, was replaced by Shvernik.[18] Successive modifications to the structure of the Council saw the development of distinct administrative divisions, each with its own personnel and responsibilities.[19] Responsibility for the evacuation of the population, initially entrusted to a single member on the council, was quickly shifted to an entire subgroup, which was instructed to "prepare all questions on the resettlement of the evacuated population, the timing and order of evacuation, and the provision of evacuees with food and medical care during evacuation, as well as financing all measures connected to the evacuation of the population."[20] In late September 1941, this group was replaced by an "administration for the evacuation of the population" to which Pamfilov, deputy chairman of the Sovnarkom of the Russian Republic, was appointed head.

Within months, the Evacuation Council had developed a sizable bureaucracy. According to one of the council's personnel, the apparatus "was composed of personnel from Sovnarkom, Gosplan, the trade unions, and the people's commissariats of both the SSSR and the RSFSR. Altogether there were eighty to eighty-five employees."[21] The council worked closely with the people's commissariats, each of which was required to establish an apparatus of three to five people under the direction of a council plenipotentiary, appointed in early July.[22] In organizing the evacuation of civilians, the council likewise drew on existing infrastructure, relying on the cooperation of municipal and district soviets. While the council thus worked with the party and state apparatus, it made extensive use of council plenipotentiaries, the first of whom were sent out in early July 1941, and whose activity permitted

---

[17] GARF, f. 6822, op. 1, d. 420, l. 3.

[18] Kaganovich nonetheless remained a member and continued to play a key role in the organization of evacuee transport. See Mikoian, "V sovete po evakuatsii," 32. Kosygin and Pervukhin were appointed as Shvernik's deputies.

[19] GARF, f. 6822, op. 1, d. 420, ll. 4–5.

[20] Ibid., l. 3.

[21] Pogrebnoi, "O deiatel'nosti soveta po evakuatsii," 202.

[22] GARF, f. 6822, op. 1, d. 420, l. 24; and Pogrebnoi, "O deiatel'nosti soveta po evakuatsii," 203.

the council to bypass regular channels of government. By the early fall, the council had hundreds of plenipotentiaries posted across the country.[23] Typically dispatched to a particular area for the duration of two weeks, council plenipotentiaries were invested with authority over local Soviet and party officials in all matters relating to the evacuation.

The Evacuation Council retained responsibility for the evacuations through January 31, 1942, when it was disbanded following the first successful Soviet counteroffensive outside Moscow. On June 22, 1942, however, in the wake of renewed German offensives in the Caucasus and the lower Volga, an Evacuation Commission was created within the Defense Committee. Although administratively distinct from the defunct Evacuation Council, the commission's membership was drawn from previous council members.[24] At its head was Shvernik, former chair of the Evacuation Council, and among its additional six members were both Kosygin and Mikoian. The decision to create a commission within the Defense Committee rather than to reestablish the Evacuation Council merely formalized the Defense Committee's direct involvement in the process of evacuation, which was already marked in the initial operation.

Given the lack of advance preparation, officials on the Evacuation Council were required to improvise. Dubrovin described how he and his colleagues lacked the "required experience" for such an operation. "We acquired experience," he later reflected, "during the course of the war."[25] The Soviet government, it is true, had little experience in the evacuation of factories. It had extensive experience, however, in the transfer of populations. By 1941 there were several existing templates for population resettlement in the Soviet Union. They ranged from the rational redistribution of agricultural labor organized by a specially designated Resettlement Administration to deportation, the domain of the NKVD. Not surprisingly, both organizations were assigned important roles in initial proposals on evacuation. The first evacuation order, on the evacuation of civilians from a handful of cities in the Republic of Latvia, called on the Latvian NKVD to draw up the plan.[26] In the initial drafts on the structure of the Evacuation Council, moreover, it was none other than a member of the NKVD, Abakumov, who was put in charge of the evacuation of the population.[27] In a similar vein, the Resettlement Administration was entrusted with establishing a network of evacuation centers in an early draft of a directive on evacuation.[28]

---

[23] GARF, f. 6822, op. 1, d. 420, l. 39.

[24] RGASPI, f. 644, op. 1, d. 40, l. 54.

[25] Dubrovin, "Eshelon za eshelonom," 209.

[26] This decree was issued by the Council of People's Commissars and the Central Committee of the Republic of Latvia on June 22, 1941. GARF, f. 6822, op. 1, d. 43, l. 21.

[27] Ibid.

[28] Ibid., d. 221, ll. 103, 104.

While neither the NKVD nor the Resettlement Administration ultimately played a leading role in the evacuation of civilians, the Evacuation Council made use of the expertise and personnel of both administrations. Three of the council's handful of members were drawn from the NKVD, including Beria himself. Moreover, NKVD units organized the evacuation of specific sectors of the population and assisted in the evacuation of particular regions, including Leningrad.[29] The Resettlement Administration, for its part, was subordinated with its entire apparatus to the Administration for the Evacuation of the Population, to which E. N. Kobzin, the former head of the Resettlement Administration, was appointed deputy director.[30]

Like both the Resettlement Administration and the NKVD, the Evacuation Council aimed to effect an organized redistribution of the population. "Distribution" (*razmeshchenie*) and "employment" (*trudoustroistvo*) were key terms in the elaboration of evacuation policy. Authorities attempted to organize the distribution of evacuees in accordance with the needs of wartime economic production. To this end, the Evacuation Council drew up elaborate graphs charting the distribution of factories and institutions. In addition, authorities on the ground were instructed to record the job qualifications and experience of each evacuee, so that on arrival in a particular region, regional authorities could direct them to the specific settlements where their skills were required. Whereas skilled workers were sent to industrial settlements, the unskilled workforce was directed to the countryside, where the labor force had been substantially depleted by conscription. The redistribution of the population was also prompted by a desire to ease the pressure on the state-run distribution networks responsible for feeding the urban population. Mikoian recalled that the evacuation of children from Moscow was undertaken "both with the aim of securing their safety and with the aim of relieving pressure in the provision of goods to the capital's several million inhabitants."[31] Like the authorities who organized the peacetime transfer of peasants to less populated areas in the Soviet east, evacuation authorities were engaged in a complex attempt to manage state resources through population transfer.

Conceived as a form of managed migration, the evacuation of Soviet civilians was modeled on the practices of population transfer elaborated over the previous decade. The decrees of the Evacuation Council bear a striking resemblance to the deportation orders of the NKVD, which were themselves informed by military models. Both frequently operated on the principle of quotas, a preferred tool of Soviet administrative practice. The conditions of departure, moreover, were laid out in strikingly similar terms. Like deportation

---

[29] V. P. Sal'nikov, S. V. Stepashin, and N. G. Iangol, *Organy vnutrennikh del Severo-Zapada Rossii v gody Velikoi Otechestvennoi voiny* (St. Petersburg: LAN, 1999), 145–70.

[30] RGASPI, f. 644, op. 1, d. 10, l. 94.

[31] Mikoian, "V sovete po evakuatsii," 32.

orders, decrees on the evacuation of specific categories of people established both the weight and range of items they could bring with them.[32] Moreover, the operation relied not on regular passenger trains but on "echelons," a term and model of transportation drawn from military practice. The echelon, a key element in Soviet population transfers, was essentially an organized convoy. Order within the echelon was maintained by elders or directors, appointed from among the echelon's members. Travel by echelon differed significantly from individual travel as disembarking en route was, at least in theory, forbidden. In the elaboration of evacuation policy, the echelon figured as an important means of regulating population movement and controlling access to the Soviet interior. It was the tool of a state that conceived of itself as the ultimate arbiter of who and what would be subject to evacuation.

THE OBJECTS OF EVACUATION: PRIVILEGED PEOPLE AND PRIVILEGED PLACES

Reflecting on his experience on the Evacuation Council, Mikoian observed: "it was not possible to evacuate everything. We had neither the time nor the means. We had to decide as we went what was in the interests of the state to evacuate first."[33] Decisions about whom and what to evacuate were among the most significant of the policy issues facing the Soviet state in the aftermath of the German invasion. Scholarship on the priorities of the civilian evacuation, however, is limited. Soviet scholars have tended to repeat the claim, initially made in the six-volume history of the Great Patriotic War put out in 1961, that priority in the civilian evacuation was given to "children's organizations, women with children, and the elderly."[34] Non-Soviet scholarship has focused primarily on the question of whether or not Soviet evacuation policy specifically aided the Jewish population.[35] Refuting early

---

[32] In many cases, the terms were identical, although the allocations for deportees tended to exceed those accorded to evacuees. A decree of July 2, 1941, stipulated a maximum of 100 kilograms of baggage for evacuated workers, with an additional 40 kilograms per family member. A deportation order issued a few months later, in October 1941, stipulated a maximum of 200 kilograms per family member. GARF, f. 6822, op. 1, d. 423, l. 1; ibid., d. 417, l. 145.

[33] Mikoian, "V sovete po evakuatsii," 31.

[34] The same phrase is found in I. I. Belonosov, "Evakuatsiia naseleniia iz prifrontovoi polosy v 1941–1942 gg.," in *Eshelony idut na Vostok*, ed. Poliakov, 18; and M. I. Likhomanov, L. T. Pozina, and E. I. Finogenov, *Partiinoe rukovodstvo evakuatsiei v pervyi period Velikoi Otechestvennoi voiny* (Leningrad: Izdatel'stvo Leningradskogo universiteta, 1985), 12.

[35] See Mordechai Altshuler, "Escape and Evacuation of Soviet Jews at the Time of the Nazi Invasion: Policies and Realities," in *The Holocaust in the Soviet Union: Studies and Sources on the Destruction of the Jews in the Nazi-Occupied Territories of the USSR, 1941–1945*, ed. Lucjan Dobroszycki and Jeffrey S. Gurock (Armonk, N.Y.: M. E. Sharpe, 1993), 77–104; Vadim Dubson, "On the Problem of the Evacuation of Soviet Jews in 1941 (New Archival Sources)," *Jews in Eastern Europe* 3, no. 40 (1999): 37–56; and Dov Levin, "The Attitude of

claims that Soviet authorities gave priority to Jews, some scholars have gone so far as to claim that there was no effective policy of saving civilians during the war.[36]

In fact, Soviet evacuation policy was conceived with multiple objectives in mind, reflecting its position at the nexus of several key spheres of Soviet wartime policy: industrial production, food distribution, population transfer, and the maintenance of social order. In the most general terms, the priorities of the operation were, as Mikoian stated quite plainly above, the "interests of the state." As Stalin allegedly remarked to Ponomarenko, the first secretary of the Communist Party of Belorussia, "everyone must understand that evacuation is also an element of war."[37] Evacuation was thus conceived first and foremost as a component of the war effort, and the priorities of the operation were determined accordingly. This is not to say that saving lives was not an objective of evacuation policy—it certainly was. Human life was not, however, an operative category of the evacuation. Instead, priorities were structured around the military and industrial needs of the state as well as a prewar hierarchy of people and places that shaped exactly which human lives authorities were most concerned with protecting.

The fundamental priorities of the operation were first articulated in a June 27 government decree on the "removal and distribution of human contingents and valuable property." The decree established the categories of people and things that were to be evacuated "on first priority." As the only coherent articulation of evacuation policy and the fundamental reference point for the civilian evacuation, the June 27 decree provides valuable insight into the priorities of the operation. It reflects the perception held by Stalin and his inner circle that the war would be won or lost not only on the battlefield but also in the factories and in the fields.[38]

Evacuation policy, as set forth 'in the decree, was predicated on the twin objectives of protection and deprivation. It involved the transfer of people and things to safety as well as a policy of systematic destruction to deprive the enemy of crucial resources. Point 3 of the decree stipulated that "all valuable property, raw materials, food reserves, and standing crop that cannot be removed . . . and could be used by the enemy should, to avert such

the Soviet Union to the Rescue of the Jews," in *Baltic Jews under the Soviets, 1940–1946* (Jerusalem, 1994), 159–70.

[36] This argument is made in S. Shweibish, "Evakuatsiia i sovetskie evrei v gody katastrofy," *Vestnik Evreiskogo universiteta v Moskve* 9, no. 2 (1995): 36.

[37] Interview with P. K. Ponomarenko in Kumanev, *Riadom so Stalinym*, 125.

[38] It is unclear who prepared the initial draft of the decree, but the final version appears to have been largely the work of Kaganovich, whose modifications to his own copy of the draft were for the most part retained. See RGASPI, f. 81, op. 3, d. 351, l. 30. The final version of the decree is in "Iz istorii Velikoi Otechestvennoi voiny: nachalo voiny," *Izvestiia TsK KPSS*, no. 6 (1990): 208. Its status as the basis of the civilian evacuation was reaffirmed in a July 5 decree "on the procedure for evacuating the population during war." GARF, f. A-259, op. 40, d. 3022, l. 34.

use, . . . be demolished, destroyed, and burnt." This was, in effect, the first articulation of the scorched earth policy that would be made public only a few days later in *Pravda*.[39] Its initial formulation as an integral component of evacuation policy points to an important affinity between the logic of the two operations. Like scorched earth tactics, evacuation was conceived by the Soviet leadership as a crucial component of the war effort, a tactic to win the war of resources even as the Red Army retreated and Soviet territory fell into enemy hands.

In this vision, civilians figured into the evacuation only insofar as they were necessary to the Soviet war effort. The categories of people to be evacuated "on first priority," set out in point 2 of the decree, consisted of "qualified workers, engineers, and employees with enterprises evacuated from the front; the population, in the first place youth fit for military service; Soviet and party leadership cadres."[40] Evacuation would thus secure industrial output, ensure a steady supply of army recruits, and provide the country with continued leadership and administration.

The consideration given to the civilian populace as a whole is encapsulated by the fate of the term "population" in the evolution of the decree. In an earlier draft, the category "population" had stood, unqualified, at the head of the list of "human contingents" slated for evacuation. Kaganovich, who made a few critical revisions to the text, crossed it out, reinserted the term toward the end of the list, and significantly restricted its scope. Instead of "population," the statement now read, the "population, in the first place youth fit for military service." While Kaganovich inserted a clause on children up to age fifteen, this alone among his amendments did not make it into the final draft. More striking still was the change he effected to the scorched earth policy. After instructing those responsible to destroy resources remaining in enemy territory, the draft statement had stipulated that the population be evacuated. Once again, Kaganovich struck this out, drawing a line through "population." His deletion symbolized the priorities of the regime. The decisive issue was the industrial and military capacity of the Soviet Union and its enemy on the battlefield, not the fate of the civilian population.

In keeping with the June 27 decree, subsequent formulations of the scorched earth policy contained no reference to civilians. In Stalin's famous speech of July 3 authorities and citizens alike were instructed, in the event of a retreat, to "drive away the railway rolling stock, leaving the enemy not a single

[39] Most scholars of the war trace the inception of the scorched-earth policy to the Sovnarkom and Central Committee directive of June 29, 1941, which was, however, issued only after the evacuation decree. See, for example, John Erickson, *The Road to Stalingrad: Stalin's War with Germany* (Boulder, Colo.: Westview, 1984), 138; and Mark Harrison, *Soviet Planning in Peace and War, 1938–1945* (Cambridge: Cambridge University Press, 1985), 64.

[40] On the list of material objects, priority was assigned to industrial equipment, raw materials and foodstuffs, and "other valuables of state significance." "Iz istorii Velikoi Otechestvennoi voiny," 208.

locomotive, not a single wagon, not a kilogram of bread, not a liter of fuel. The collective-farm workers should drive away their livestock and turn their crops over to state organs for their transportation to the rear. All valuable property, including nonferrous metals, grain, and fuel, that cannot be transported must without fail be destroyed."[41]

Not once did Stalin refer to any imperative to evacuate the population. In conditions of forced withdrawal, when, in Mikoian's words, there was neither the "time nor the means to evacuate everything," the non-able-bodied population was low on the list of priorities. In a subsequent clarification of what to do in the event of withdrawal, Stalin instructed Khrushchev, then secretary of the Ukrainian Communist Party, "to take the entire adult male population, draught animals, grain, tractors, combines from the zone extending seventy versts [just under 50 miles] from the front, and to direct them to the east." The evacuation of the population as a whole was neither projected nor anticipated, for in a subsequent clause Khrushchev was instructed to "leave poultry, small livestock, and other foodstuffs for the remaining population."[42]

While the scope of the civilian evacuation was thus deliberately restricted, there was considerable indecision at the highest level of authority regarding whom, exactly, to include. Consider the drafting of the June 27 decree: children were absent from the initial draft, were added to a subsequent version, and eliminated from the final one. In a similar vein, the families of command personnel and NKVD cadres were initially included, only to be struck off at a later stage.[43] In the end, however, the operation was significantly more expansive than the final, more restrictive version of the decree would suggest. Over the summer and fall of 1941, select categories of the population not mentioned in the final June 27 decree came to occupy a central place in evacuation policy, albeit on terms that would significantly restrict their scope.

Just one week after the June 27 decree was passed, an additional decree was approved by Sovnarkom authorizing the evacuation of the "families of leading party and Soviet cadres and the families of the command personnel of the Red Army, the Navy, and troops of the NKVD from the frontline zones."[44] Like the June 27 decree, this decree was directed to authorities across the front lines. The inclusion of these groups in general evacuation policy points to an additional calculus in the determination of evacuation priorities: privilege. Over the course of the 1930s, privilege had become a defining feature of Soviet society. Even as the Stalin constitution of 1936 boldly proclaimed that

[41] K. I. Bukov, M. M. Gorinov, and A. N. Ponomarev, eds., *Moskva voennaia, 1941–1945. Memuary i arkhivnye dokumenty* (Moscow: Mosgorarkhiv, 1995), 63.
[42] "Iz istorii Velikoi Otechestvennoi voiny: nachalo voiny," *Izvestiia TsK KPSS*, no. 7 (1990): 207.
[43] Kaganovich crossed these groups out. RGASPI, f. 81, op. 3, d. 351, l. 30.
[44] GARF, f. A-259, op. 40, d. 3022, l. 40.

class divisions had finally been overcome, Soviet society had never been so stratified. Those identified in this decree were among the most privileged sectors of Soviet society. Before the war, they had enjoyed access to the highest rations and to the best-supplied stores.[45] As the decree suggests, moreover, family had become a crucial site for the state's assignation of privilege. The object of vigorous attacks for over a decade, the family had emerged in the 1930s as a central administrative category. It was an operative element of criminal law and a key factor in determining access to a wide range of state-controlled goods.[46] The evacuation of the families of the administrative and military elite was predicated on the new role of the family in the Soviet administrative system as well as a reconfiguration of elite gender roles. The 1930s witnessed the emergence of a new model of elite womanhood in which wives were cast as helpers to their husbands.[47] In evacuation policy, as in Soviet society more broadly, the privileged position of the wives of elites was a function of their husbands' status.

Yet another group targeted for evacuation, at least in part because of their privileged position, was the intelligentsia. Cultural figures, scientists, and scholars, like the groups cited above, enjoyed privileges in the prewar period. The evacuation of the intelligentsia reflected both its privileged status in the Soviet hierarchy and the exalted role it was expected to play in the struggle for the fatherland. As the film director Sergei Eisenstein wrote of his evacuation to Alma-Ata, "we are soldiers of art, going to assume our assigned positions."[48] Among the organizations slated for evacuation were the Academy of Sciences, the Bolshoi Theatre, Moscow State University, and a slew of other pedagogical institutes, research centers, and theaters. In addition, lists were drawn up of the country's leading writers, artists, and architects, who received first priority in the evacuation.

Soviet scholarship on evacuation long repeated the dictum that priority in the civilian evacuation was given to women, children, and the elderly. Yet neither women nor the elderly appeared in even a draft of the June 27 decree; and children, although added by Kaganovich, were ultimately struck off the list of priorities. From the very beginning of the war, however, "family members of workers and employees" as well as "children" and "women and children" were the objects of a series of evacuation orders issued in in-

[45] See Elena Osokina, *Our Daily Bread: Socialist Distribution and the Art of Survival in Stalin's Russia, 1927–1941*, trans. Kate Transchel (Armonk, N.Y.: M. E. Sharpe, 2001), 70–77.

[46] Individuals were regularly deported as the family members of deportees. This was the case in the deportation of kulaks, for example, and in the removal of nationalist and other elements from the annexed territories in 1940–41. Furthermore, during the war the families of traitors were subject to repression.

[47] This was particularly marked in the *Obshchestvennitsa* movement (a movement of "public-spirited women"), which began in the mid-1930s. See Mary Buckley, "The Untold Story of Obshchestvennitsa in the 1930s," *Europe-Asia Studies* 48, no. 4 (1996): 569–86.

[48] Sergei Eisenshtein in Bukov, Gorinov, and Ponomarev, *Moskva voennaia*, 156.

dividual locales. In fact, children were the object of the first evacuation order of the war, issued by the Council of People's Commissars of Latvia on
the day of the German invasion, a full two days before the formation of the
Evacuation Council. The goal of this operation, as outlined in the plan, was
"to protect the non-able-bodied [*netrudosposobnoe*] population (women,
children, the elderly, etc.) from the consequences of aerial bombardment by
the enemy."[49] In keeping with this objective, evacuees from the cities of
Riga, Liepaia, Dugavpils and Elgava were to be resettled in the surrounding
countryside.

The Latvian evacuation order was the first of dozens of specific decrees
to treat the civilian population. Never again, however, would a category as
inclusive as the "non-able-bodied population" appear in an evacuation order. In the future, evacuees would be defined in terms that were at once nar-
rower and more consonant with existing social categories. In Belorussia,
where evacuations likewise began before the formation of the council, authorities ordered the "evacuation of children from cities subject to enemy
bombardment in the zone of military activity and from Minsk." This was
followed, one day later, by an order on the "evacuation of children and their
mothers from Minsk," issued "in connection with the intensive bombardment" of the city.[50] Even after the June 27 decree, children remained at the
center of localized evacuation efforts. On July 1, the Moscow Soviet issued
a decree "on the procedures for evacuating children." This was followed, one
week later, by a resolution on the "evacuation of the family members of workers and employees." In September, the Defense Committee ordered a further
evacuation of children from the city.[51] In October, with German forces rapidly
advancing on the capital, a series of further decrees were passed "on the additional evacuation of women and children," "on the evacuation of preschool children," and "on the evacuation of children's homes." Similar orders were issued in Leningrad, Kiev, and Odessa and in a host of other
cities that grew in number as the war progressed. Frequently issued by municipal authorities, these orders nonetheless had the clear sanction of the
Evacuation Council, which, for its part, issued similar orders on several
occasions.[52]

The operative categories in specific decrees on the evacuation of the
"population" thus became, variously, "children," "family members" (of either army, state, and party personnel or of "workers and employees"), and
"women and children." Although a significant number of decrees mentioned
women, "women" did not itself constitute a category of evacuation. This is
clearly demonstrated by an Evacuation Council resolution of August 1941,

[49] GARF, f. 6822, op. 1, d. 43, l. 21.
[50] RGASPI, f. 17, op. 22, d. 216, ll. 3, 8.
[51] GARF, f. 259, op. 40, d. 3035, ll. 19, 74; RGASPI, f. 644, op. 1, d. 9, l. 23.
[52] See, for example, for Odessa, GARF f. A-259, op. 40, d. 3053, l. 15.

which condemned the evacuation of "childless women" and instructed regional authorities to ensure that in the future evacuation efforts were concentrated on "women and children."[53] In a country in which women were integrated into the workforce well before the onset of war, women counted among the "able-bodied," and would be called on to serve the fatherland as members of civilian defense units, factory workers, partisans, and combatants.[54] As civilians, women were thus subject to evacuation only in their capacity as mothers, and, in the case of party, soviet, and army officials, as wives.

The categories of the civilian evacuation clearly reflected not only the priorities of the regime but also a particular vision of Soviet society—one that was urban, composed of youth, workers and employees, the party and the state, the army, the NKVD, and leading teachers, scientists, and cultural figures. Most notably absent from the evacuation categories were the elderly. Singled out in the Latvian evacuation order of June 22, they all but disappeared from subsequent directives and decrees. The category of "family members," potentially broad enough to include the elderly, was frequently followed by the brief notation "women and children." While people aged sixty and over were evacuated in practice, there was an official silence on such people on the Evacuation Council. In a polity so focused on youth, the older generations, absent from official discourse, constituted an invisible sector of Soviet society.

The evacuation of "women and children" reflected a model of evacuation in which the perceived danger was bombardment rather than occupation, and the "evacuation zone" consisted of urban centers, not frontline regions. This was essentially evacuation on the English model, based on the transfer of children from circumscribed "target zones" to the surrounding countryside, no further from enemy reach but less likely to be bombed. Evacuation, in this context, was conceived not to prevent resources from falling into enemy hands but, in the words of the decree issued by the Council of People's Commissars of Latvia, "to protect the non-able-bodied population from the consequences of aerial bombardment by the enemy."[55] In the eyes of Soviet authorities, however, the evacuation of nonproductive sectors of the population also served economic needs. As Mikoian later noted, the evacuation of children from Moscow was undertaken "both with the aim of securing

[53] GARF, f. 6822, op. 1, d. 422, l. 70.

[54] On the changing conception of women's roles in the 1930s see Anna Krylova, "Stalinist Identity from the Viewpoint of Gender: Rearing a Generation of Professionally Violent Women-Fighters in 1930s Stalinist Russia," *Gender and History* 16, no. 3 (2004): 626–53. On the role of women on the front lines, see John Erickson, "Soviet Women at War," in *World War 2 and the Soviet People*, ed. John Garrard, Carol Garrard, and Stephen White (New York: St. Martin's, 1993), 50–76.

[55] GARF, f. 6822, op. 1, d. 43, l. 21.

their safety and with the aim of relieving pressure on the provision of goods to the capital's several million inhabitants."[56]

The war on Europe's Eastern front, however, was not the Battle of Britain. With German armies rapidly occupying the country, the populations of smaller towns and villages, who made up over half of the prewar Soviet population, were often in greater danger than their urban counterparts. Although the heavy bombardment of Soviet cities did necessitate special measures for urban centers, Soviet authorities focused on cities to the neglect of the surrounding countryside. Moreover, a select group of cities received considerably more attention than others. In effect, the evacuation of the "population" transpired in discrete spaces defined as much by existing hierarchies of people and places as by enemy attacks, which targeted Soviet territory as a whole.

The general decrees laying out the contours of the operation, in their application to the entire territory of the USSR, thus masked the existence of what turned out to be a specific topography of evacuation. Operations involving people of "state significance," on one hand, and those encompassing the more general population, on the other, were to take place in distinct spaces: the first in the frontline regions, an ever-changing yet broad swath of territory that included all regions officially subject to evacuation; the second within highly circumscribed regions, defined in specific decrees, and, for the most part, limited to urban centers. In a real sense, the story of the evacuations is a story of privileged people and privileged places, categories that often overlapped.

The division of Soviet territory into distinct zones of evacuation, each with its own priorities, was first articulated in the prewar statute on evacuation. The statute had identified three areas from which evacuations would take place. The first was the zone of army deployment, which before the onset of fighting extended 75 and 100 kilometers into Soviet territory from the border, and the second consisted of regions that were in danger of enemy occupation. The first two regions of evacuation were thus indeterminate zones, to be defined over the course of military operations. The third, however, was composed of a set of identifiable, unchanging places. These were the "most important centers of the country: Moscow, Leningrad, Minsk, Kiev, and Odessa."[57] The most extensive evacuation of civilians was projected not for the operational or threatened zones but for these five urban centers.

The decrees on evacuation issued in the wake of the German invasion did not explicitly distinguish between different zones of evacuation. Rather, policy statements were oriented to the "frontline regions," the boundaries of which changed in accordance with the movement of the German armies.

---

[56] Mikoian, "V sovete po evakuatsii," 32.
[57] GARF, f. A-259, op. 40, d. 3028, l. 82.

Nonetheless, evacuation policy effectively differentiated between major cities and the Soviet countryside. Evacuation orders aimed at the "population" were, for the most part, restricted to urban centers. Among these, Moscow was the clear priority. As the political, industrial, and cultural capital of the country, Moscow was at the pinnacle of the prewar urban hierarchy.[58] Following closely on the list of priorities was Leningrad, the second most important industrial center and the second capital of the country.

The geographical priorities of the operation were set into sharp relief by two evacuation plans prepared by the council in early July 1941. The first, a plan for the evacuation of the population for the first ten days of the month, initially projected the evacuation of 1,665,000 people from across the front lines. Within days, however, in the face of formidable logistical challenges, the number was reduced to 395,000, a mere quarter of the initial projections.[59] At the same time, the Evacuation Council authorized the additional evacuation of up to five hundred thousand women and children from Moscow and Leningrad.[60] The statistics for railway use are telling: of a total of over one hundred thousand train wagons deployed in evacuations in the first two months of the war, a full 44 percent of them served the population of the capital, a city which did not come under threat of actual occupation until mid-October. Seventeen percent served Leningrad; and the vast swath of territory known as the "frontline regions," effectively the rest of the country from which evacuations had or were taking place, was serviced by only 39 percent.[61]

In sharp contrast to the concentrated efforts on behalf of the country's major cities, the inhabitants of villages and smaller settlements were largely left to their own devices. Access to trains, the principal mode of transport, was restricted to the inhabitants of urban centers. Thus, while a significant portion of the country's railway reserve was devoted to Moscow from the first days of the war, peasants in Moscow oblast, in the words of the NKVD chief of the region, "do not have the means to move and do not know the regions where they should evacuate themselves."[62] Even the inhabitants of the capital's suburbs, because they did not fall under the jurisdiction of the Moscow Soviet, were unable to purchase train tickets to depart.[63] The topography of the operation was laid bare in a letter penned by an executive member of the regional Leningrad Soviet in early August 1941: "thus far, from the frontline regions we have mainly evacuated the families of party

[58] Residents of Moscow, for instance, enjoyed the highest rations in the country. Osokina, *Our Daily Bread*, 70–77.

[59] GARF, f. A-259, op. 40, d. 3028, ll. 36, 60.

[60] GARF, f. 6822, op. 1, d. 415, l. 12.

[61] GARF, f. A-259, op. 40, d. 3032, l. 28.

[62] O. B. Mozokhin and V. P. Iampol'skii, eds., "Vlast', kotoraia grabit naselenie," *Istoricheskii arkhiv*, no. 2 (2000): 142.

[63] GARF, f. A-259, op. 40, d. 3055, l. 32.

and Soviet activists, children and their mothers from the cities, but the collective-farm population has been left until the last minute and has departed on its own. A significant proportion of the population has remained behind enemy lines."[64]

EVACUATION AND DEPORTATION

Evacuation policy was only one branch of Soviet wartime population policies, emerging as part of a broader Soviet approach to the populations of regions adjacent to the front. The other principal branch consisted of deportations. Over the course of the war, some 1.5 million Soviet citizens were expelled from their homelands and deported further east in a series of ethnic operations. The deportations targeted entire peoples—Germans and Finns in the first year of the war, and later, as the Red Army regained previously occupied territory, a range of peoples from the Caucasus and the Crimea who were accused of collective collaboration with the enemy.[65] Although the war thus marked, in the words of Amir Weiner, "a stark shift in the purge paradigm from cleansing certain areas to cleansing entire groups of people," deportations were nonetheless initially concentrated in regions threatened by the enemy.[66] Soviet authorities, much like the imperial army in World War I, displayed a heightened concern with the populations of these areas. It is thus not coincidental that evacuations and deportations were frequently carried out simultaneously from within the same spaces.

The policies of evacuation and deportation stemmed from a unified Soviet approach to population displacement. In contrast to the practices of the Imperial Russian Army during World War I, the operations launched by the Soviet regime in the summer and fall of 1941 aimed to manage migration from the front. Although authorities in both wars aimed to "cleanse" the border regions of "unreliable elements," Soviet authorities confined the victims to specially designated regions, usually remote, whereas their tsarist predecessors let a large portion resettle at will.[67] Increasingly, the operative term in the Soviet operations was not "expulsion" (*vyselenie*) but "resettle-

[64] GARF, f. 6822, op. 1, d. 355, l. 90.

[65] For a general treatment of wartime deportations, see J. Otto Pohl, *Ethnic Cleansing in the USSR, 1937–1949* (Westport, Conn.: Greenwood, 1999); Pavel Polian, *Against Their Will: The History and Geography of Forced Migrations in the USSR*, trans. Anna Yastrzhembska (Budapest: Central European University Press, 2004).

[66] In the Crimea, Leningrad, and Moscow, deportations of ethnic Germans and Finns closely followed the movement of the front lines. The only exception to this general pattern in the first two years of war was the deportation of ethnic Germans from the Volga region in late August 1941. Amir Weiner, *Making Sense of War: The Second World War and the Fate of the Bolshevik Revolution* (Princeton, N.J.: Princeton University Press, 2001), 14.

[67] Among the "unreliable elements" expelled from frontline regions in 1915, only the German colonists were transferred to a specific region to which they were confined. See Eric Lohr,

ment" (*pereselenie*). As far as the civilian population at large was concerned, Soviet authorities attempted to achieve an organized transfer of people in place of the unregulated flow of refugees that had plagued the Russian Empire in its final years. The similarities in the organization of the evacuation and deportation further underscore the existence of a unified model of population displacement based on state regulation and planned distribution.

Carried out within overlapping spaces and modeled on a similar operational procedure, evacuation and deportation became imbricated in the official mind. Indeed, the first wartime deportation of ethnic Germans was carried out by the NKVD on the orders of the Evacuation Council, which issued a decree ordering the "evacuation" of some sixty thousand Soviet citizens of German ethnicity from the Crimea in mid-August 1941.[68] This operation is one of only two known occasions in which evacuation policy, which was generally constructed around occupation and family rather than ethnicity, targeted a specific ethnic group. The order was issued less than two weeks after Stalin instructed Beria, in an order scrawled on a report about the behavior of the German population in the frontline regions, to "kick them all out." A response to fears about "untrustworthy elements" in regions threatened by the enemy, the evacuation of Crimean Germans was conceived as a "preventative" measure to preclude the possibility of collaboration.[69] In mid-August, when the order was issued, the Crimea was considered part of the "frontline regions" and was subjected to a more general evacuation only a few days after the evacuation of Germans had begun.[70] It was a measure of the operation's ambiguity that the evacuated Germans were initially resettled in neighboring regions and were included in statistics on the evacuated population. Only in early September, when a more general deportation of the entire German population west of the Urals was initiated, did the state transfer them to "remote regions of the union" to which they were confined as "special settlers".[71] A similar ambiguity surrounded the deportation of Finns and Germans from the Leningrad region in late August 1941. Although the operation was put under the charge of the NKVD, it was carried out under the rubric of "evacuation." The evacuees were all issued "evacuation certificates" and their final destination was determined

Nationalizing the Russian Empire: The Campaign against Enemy Aliens during World War I (Cambridge, Mass.: Harvard University Press, 2003), 135.

[68] The decree is mentioned in a report by the director of the NKVD's special settlement division. See Nikolai F. Bugai, *"Mobilizovat' nemtsev v rabochie kolonny—I. Stalin": sbornik dokumentov (1940-e gody)* (Moscow: Gotika, 1998), 30.

[69] The report itself requests that local authorities be ordered to expel *neblagonadezhnye elementy*. Bukov, Gorinov, and Ponomarev, *Moskva voennaia*, 77.

[70] See GARF, f. 6822, op. 1, d. 43, l. 8.

[71] Bugai, *"Mobilizovat' nemtsev v rabochie kolonny"*, 18, 30–31. On the status of special settlers, see Nicolas Werth, "'Déplacés spéciaux' et 'colons de travail' dans la société stalinienne," *Vingtième siècle* 54 (April–June 1997): 34–50.

by the Evacuation Council.[72] Although subsequent transfers of ethnic Germans did not involve the Evacuation Council, ethnic German deportees were routinely included in counts of the "evacuated" population.[73]

A similar conflation of evacuation and deportation occurred a few months later in an operation carried out in Moscow. On this occasion, the Evacuation Council, in a decision signed by Kosygin, ordered the "evacuation" of "people with no fixed occupation or place of residence, the criminal element, people who have been arrested and tried, unregistered residents, and the population that has accumulated at the city's evacuation centers." In this instance, a standard NKVD operation undertaken, in the words of the NKVD agent involved, "to cleanse the city," was carried out under the auspices of the Evacuation Council.[74]

The slippage between evacuation and deportation was the product of both operational similarities and shared objectives. As suggested above, the operations overlapped both temporally and spatially. There was a significant overlap even in the zones of resettlement: evacuation plans initially projected the resettlement of evacuees primarily in central Russia, but the Evacuation Council soon extended the zone of resettlement to Siberia, Central Asia, and Kazakhstan, prime regions in the geography of exile. Like deportation, moreover, evacuation became a convenient tool of population redistribution. In the most notable case, evacuations were actually initiated in Orel oblast with the explicit aim of repopulating the Volga regions that had been depleted by the recent deportation of the area's ethnic German population.[75]

More fundamentally, both operations involved an attempt to maintain social order and state security through policing and selected population transfer. The German invasion gave new urgency to the Soviet leaders' long-standing fears about the formation of a fifth column, enemy infiltration, and spies. With an external enemy penetrating deep into Soviet territory, opportunities for collaboration and treachery were rife. Moreover, the advent of war introduced new concerns about the dissolution of social order through disorganized flight and panic.

Evacuation was conceived, in part, as a response to these fears. It was designed to organize and direct civilian displacement and thus to avoid the disruption that would surely follow a mass exodus from the front. The operation was to ensure the efficient transfer of civilians while controlling access

[72] N. A. Lomagin, *Neizvestnaia blokada (Dokumenty, prilozheniia)*, vol. 1 (St. Petersburg: Neva, 2002), 23–25.

[73] See, for example, GARF, f. 6822, op. 1, d. 481, l. 151.

[74] Ibid., d. 482, ll. 1–2.

[75] RGASPI, f. 17, op. 22, d. 2080, l. 199; RGAE, f. 5675, op. 3, d. 14, ll. 89, 91–93. The Evacuation Council was involved in the operation despite the objections of Shvernik, who claimed that the resettlement of collective farmers did not fall within the purview of the council. GARF, f. A-259, op. 40, d. 3053, l. 39.

to the rear. This was the meaning of the shift from refugee to evacuee in the policy debates of the 1930s. Even though Soviet authorities did not, in the wake of the invasion, mandate the establishment of special detachments aimed at preventing the flight of civilians, as proposed by the Commissariat of Transportation some years earlier, policing functions were nonetheless considered an important component of the operation. One of the final points in a July 5 decree "on evacuating the population during war" instructed the NKVD to supervise the formation of evacuee echelons and entrusted state and military authorities with ensuring that only those who had proper authorization boarded the trains heading east.[76] Evacuation policy was elaborated, moreover, in conjunction with other restrictions on internal circulation. Most important among these was the declaration of martial law on June 22, 1941, which gave authorities the right to prohibit movement into and out of individual regions in the western and central parts of the country.[77] In addition, new restrictions on travel were introduced for the Soviet Union as a whole, which required the permission of the NKVD for travel between any two points in the country.[78] Combined with the labor laws introduced the previous year, which forbade, under penalty of imprisonment, "willful" departure from work, these measures served both to criminalize and to curtail unauthorized departures.[79]

Regulations on circulation aimed to limit both the number and the nature of the people heading east. They were directed against peasants and others whose departure threatened to clog essential transit routes and against "elements" of the population deemed dangerous to social order and state security. Soviet authorities were particularly wary of the populations of the newly annexed territories, where cleansing operations directed against bourgeois and enemy elements remained incomplete at the time of the invasion. Hailing from regions that were not yet fully Sovietized, in which nationalists and other armed groups were active and in which "anti-Soviet" sentiments were

[76] GARF, f. 6822, op. 1, d. 221, ll. 104–5.

[77] The declaration of martial law applied to the Baltic, Moldavian, Belorussian, and Ukrainian republics as well as Karelia, the Crimea, and a host of oblasts in the Russian Federation extending from the western border as far east as Rostov in the south, Ivanov in the center, and Arkhangelsk and Murmansk in the north. See Bukov, Gorinov, and Ponomarev, *Moskva voennaia*, 36.

[78] See V. M. Kuritsyn, "Prava i svobody grazhdan v gody Velikoi Otechestvennoi voiny," *Sovetskoe gosudarstvo i pravo* (May 1987): 129.

[79] See V. P. Popov, "Pasportnaia sistema v SSSR," *Sotsiologicheskie issledovaniia*, no. 9 (1995): 6. In December 1941, longer sentences were introduced for defense industry workers. According to the new statute, the "willful departure" of these sectors of the population would be treated as "desertion" and those charged would be tried in military courts and could be accorded prison sentences of anywhere between five and eight years. A new statute in 1942 put additional categories of industry, including transportation, coal, and gasoline, on a similar footing. See ibid. and Sheila Fitzpatrick, "War and Society in Soviet Context: Soviet Labor before, during, and after World War II," *International Labor and Working-Class History* 35, (Spring 1989): 44.

thought to run deep, people from these territories were routinely singled out in NKVD directives.[80] Their movement was restricted both by martial law and by the maintenance of controls along the preannexation borders of the Soviet Union. Directives issued in 1940 by the NKVD, which made passage across the old border dependent on police authorization, seem to have remained in place in the wake of the invasion.[81] Indeed, the only evidence I have found of a change to the border regime stipulated a stiffening of border controls rather than the obverse. Two weeks after the invasion, the central committee of the Moldovan Republic forbade crossing the Dniester River as well as travel by train without the specific authorization of the republic's NKVD.[82] As a resident of a town in the region later recalled, "a special permit was required . . . to cross the Dniester on the Russian-Bessarabian border.[83]

The residents of these new, not fully Sovietized regions, however, were not the sole cause of concern. The control of population flow was furthermore intended to keep escaped criminals and spies from penetrating the Soviet interior.[84] To this end, NKVD units were instructed to verify the documents of those en route and detain "suspicious elements."[85] Further measures were designed to protect specific spaces, namely Moscow and Leningrad. As the most important productive centers of the country and the symbolic centers of Soviet power, authorities were particularly concerned to control access to these cities. NKVD agents were thus instructed to assume positions at strategic junctures along the railway lines and roads leading to Moscow to prevent evacuees from entering the capital.[86] Regular reports were dispatched to members of the Evacuation Council detailing the number of attempts to penetrate the capital and the numbers of people detained, arrested, or redirected further east. Similar measures were introduced in Leningrad.[87]

In fact, prisons themselves were subjected to evacuation in an effort to prevent hostile elements from escape and possible collaboration. Organized by the NKVD, the evacuation of prisoners began immediately after the inva-

[80] See V. P. Iampol'skii et al., *Organy gosudarstvennoi bezopasnosti v Velikoi Otechestvennoi voine*, vol. 2, bk. 2 (Moscow: Rus', 2000), 31. Suspicion was particularly strong with regard to the Baltic populations. See ibid., bk. 1 (Moscow: Rus', 2000), 526; and "Iz istorii Velikoi Otechestvennoi voiny," 204.

[81] See V. P. Iampol'skii et al., *Organy gosudarstvennoi bezopasnosti v Velikoi Otechestvennoi voine: Sbornik dokumentov*, vol. 1, bk. 1 (Moscow: Kniga i biznes, 1995), 300–301.

[82] The only exception was for those called up by the military for work in fortification. RGASPI, f. 17, op. 22, d. 1717, l. 195.

[83] Quoted in Dov Levin, *The Lesser of Two Evils: Eastern European Jewry under Soviet Rule (1939–41)*, trans. Naftali Greenwood (Philadelphia: Jewish Publication Society, 1995), 283.

[84] Thus the NKVD issued a directive on July 4, 1941, "on preventing the attempts of enemy elements to penetrate into the Soviet rear with echelons of evacuated Soviet citizens." See Iampol'skii et al., *Organy*, vol. 2, bk. 1, 178.

[85] Ibid., vol. 2, bk. 1, 511–12.

[86] GARF, f. A-259, op. 40, d. 3022, l. 34.

[87] Sal'nikov, Stepashin, and Iangol, *Organy vnutrennikh del Severo-Zapada Rossii*, 151–53.

sion. Soon, however, it became clear that, as the deputy people's commissar of the NKVD put it to Beria in a letter of July 4, 1941, the "further removal of prisoners from prisons in the frontline regions, whether involving the newly arrested after the evacuation of prisons or as part of the extension of the zones of evacuation, is inexpedient given the extreme overcrowding of prisons in the rear and the difficulties with railway cars." The letter proposed instead that only prisoners still under investigation should be evacuated. The rest should be either released, if not "socially dangerous," or shot.[88] The evacuation of prisoners highlights the complexity of the evacuation. Evacuation was conceived both to protect human lives and state resources and to assure the integrity of Soviet space by guarding against internal dissolution and removing "dangerous elements" beyond enemy reach.

• • •

In early July 1941, authorities on the Brest-Litovsk railway line reported a "foolish, anarchical" incident on their line. One of the railway employees had "burst into the locomotive brandishing a revolver with the demand that they take only people, and that the remaining things (documents and valuables) be abandoned."[89] This incident, a "foolish" deviation from the norm, underscores the limits of the evacuation as conceived by central authorities. These limits are nowhere more marked than in regard to the question of the Jewish evacuation. German Einsatzgruppen reports from 1941, observing that increasing numbers of Jews had departed, suggested that the Soviet government had explicitly evacuated the Jewish population.[90] While a string of publications, both Soviet and Western, made similar claims at the end of the war, no archival evidence has surfaced to support them.[91] Among the thousands of papers of the Evacuation Council, not one makes specific mention of Jews, let alone instructs that they be evacuated. It seems safe to conclude that Jews—although evacuated in substantial numbers as party members, workers, writers, and the like—were not evacuated as Jews.

The Soviet state's failure to adopt specific measures to protect the Jewish population stemmed in part from the government's reluctance to pursue a policy that might encourage "defeatism" among the population.[92] As we will see, the notion that Hitler was only after Communists and Jews was a main-

[88] Aleksander Gurianov and Aleksander Kokurin, "Evakuatsiia tiurem," *Karta*, no. 2 (www.hro.org/editions/karta/nr6/evaku.htm).

[89] RGAE, f. 1884, op. 31, d. 3811, l. 3.

[90] See Raul Hilberg, *The Destruction of the European Jews*, vol. 1 (New York: Holmes and Meier, 1985), 295.

[91] Such claims were apparently first made by the Jewish Anti-Fascist Committee and subsequently repeated by Western scholars. See Levin, "Attitude of the Soviet Union," 159–61.

[92] A similar thesis is advanced by Il'ia Al'tman, *Zhertvy nenavisti: anatomiia kholokosta* (Moscow: Sovershenno sekretno, 2002), 387. On official policy regarding the rescue of Jews and other civilians by Soviet partisans in occupied territory, see Kenneth Slepyan, "The Soviet

stay of defeatist rumor both before and after the invasion. The absence of a specific program to evacuate Jews was also a product, however, of the official conception of the operation. Although civilians were subject to evacuation, the operation was primarily geared to protect resources rather than people. "People," moreover, were evacuated in accordance with a prewar hierarchy that determined whose lives the government was concerned to protect. The practices of the enemy, although familiar to Soviet authorities, did not enter into this equation.[93] Hence the absence of a specifically "Jewish" evacuation—and the relative neglect of the rural population.

The "official mind of the evacuation" shaped the priorities and conception of the operation but not the way in which it transpired on the ground. In practice, evacuations differed substantially from the organized transfer envisaged by authorities in the Kremlin. Moreover, the twin objectives of safeguarding human resources and maintaining social order proved only partially compatible. The tension between these objectives would shape the evacuation process, as would the actions of local authorities.

Partisan Movement and the Holocaust," *Holocaust and Genocide Studies* 14, no. 1 (2000): 1–27.

[93] According to Al'tman, "by mid-August 1941, the Soviet leadership had precise information on the mass murder of the Jewish population." *Zhertvy nenavisti*, 385–87.

3

EVACUATIONS IN PRACTICE

In early July 1941, a former official of the Minsk regional party committee (obkom) wrote to Stalin, asserting that the "evacuation [of Minsk] . . . took place in such a disorganized fashion that one is forced to reflect, and pose the question, why did it happen this way?" According to the former official, "until 10 P.M. on the evening of the twenty-fourth, nobody knew that the city was to be evacuated. Even we, responsible members of the obkom, did not know." At ten that evening a selection of party secretaries and other leading workers "got in their cars" and left. "A heavy bombing of the city began. The population fled in panic." The author of the letter, who was forced to find his own ride out of the city, concluded that "really, this could have been prevented had the secretaries of the obkom not shamefully fled the city but directed the evacuation."[1]

The evacuation of the Belorussian capital could not have been more different from the carefully crafted plans of the Evacuation Council. To be fair, the evacuation of Minsk was carried out in extreme circumstances: evacuations began only two days after the German invasion; and the city was subjected to heavy bombardment from the first day of the war and was occupied by enemy forces in under a week. On the face of it, Minsk was thus an exceptional case. In many ways, however, it was all too typical. The scene described by the Minsk obkom official was repeated, in its essentials, throughout the summer and fall of 1941. Time and again, reports highlighted the same three phenomena: the "flight" of officials, the flight of the population (sometimes referred to as "spontaneous self-evacuation"), and "panic." The terms themselves reflect the gulf separating developments on the ground from the dictates of the Evacuation Council.

---

[1] RGASPI, f. 17, op. 122, d. 10, l. 16.

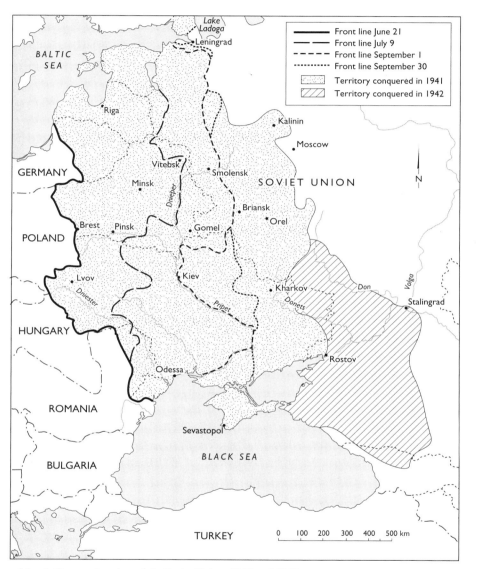

Map 1. German invasion of the Soviet Union, 1941 and 1942

Legend:

- Front line June 21
- Front line July 9
- Front line September 1
- Front line September 30
- Territory conquered in 1941
- Territory conquered in 1942

BALTIC SEA

Lake Ladoga

Leningrad

Riga

Kalinin

Moscow

GERMANY

Vitebsk

Smolensk

SOVIET UNION

Minsk

Dnieper

N

Brest

Pinsk

Briansk

Orel

Gomel

POLAND

Lvov

Dniester

Kiev

Pripet

Kharkov

Donets

Don

Volga

Stalingrad

HUNGARY

Rostov

Odessa

ROMANIA

Sevastopol

BULGARIA

BLACK SEA

TURKEY

0 100 200 300 400 500 km

This is not to say that the Evacuation Council was without effect or that the operation was a failure. By the end of 1941 some 12 million Soviet citizens had been evacuated, to be followed by approximately 4.5 million the following year.[2] "Evacuation," however, could encompass many different things, from the organized procedure envisaged by the Evacuation Council to the disorderly departures described by the Minsk obkom official. The way the operation unfolded is emblematic of the tragic beginnings of the Soviet-German war and encapsulates both the strengths and weaknesses of the Soviet system.

FLIGHT AND SPONTANEOUS SELF-EVACUATION

Just over a month after the German invasion, the political division of the Red Army reported on "signals" received from frontline units "concerning the unworthy behavior of certain leading party and Soviet cadres in the frontline regions. Saving their own skins, they abandon the population to the mercy of fate."[3] Similar reports poured in from across the front lines: the "evacuation of the population is going poorly," observed one official on the Northwestern front. "Local soviet and trade organizations leave first."[4] From the Southwestern front, the head of the political-propaganda division reported in mid-July that a "number of local party and Soviet cadres, as well as members of the police and state security organs, instead of aiding the army in their struggle against saboteurs and nationalist groups, fled in panic before the evacuation and abandoned districts, villages, and enterprises to the mercy of fate."[5] Ac-

---

[2] At the end of December 1941, Pamfilov estimated that approximately ten million people had been evacuated to the east. GARF, f. 259, op. 40, d. 3014, l. 24. This figure seems to be based on data provided by the Commissariat of Transportation, which would not include an additional two million people who were evacuated the same year by boat. See I. V. Kovalev, *Transport v Velikoi Otechestvennoi voine (1941–1945)* (Moscow: Nauka, 1981), 87. Unfortunately, similar statistics are not available for 1942. Soviet and Russian scholars have generally put the total number of evacuees either at seventeen or eighteen million or at twenty-five million but have failed to explain how they arrived at these numbers. See, for example, G. A. Kumanev, "Evakuatsiia naseleniia SSSR: dostignutye rezul'taty i poteri," in *Liudskie poteri SSSR v velikoi otechestvennoi voine*, ed. Rostislav Evdokimov (St. Petersburg: Russko-Baltiiskii informatsionnyi tsentr BLITs, 1995), 145; Iu. A. Poliakov et al., *Eshelony idut na vostok: iz istorii perebazirovaniia proizvoditel'nykh sil SSSR v 1941–1942 gg. Sbornik statei i vospominanii* (Moscow: Nauka, 1966), 13. The economic historian Mark Harrison has estimated that there were a total of 16.5 million evacuees, based on a calculation of the difference between the actual and expected populations of the unoccupied parts of the Soviet Union in 1942. *Soviet Planning in Peace and War, 1938–1945* (Cambridge: Cambridge University Press, 1985), 72. I have used Harrison's more conservative estimate as a point of reference and have combined it with available data to offer a rough breakdown of the number of evacuees each year.

[3] RGASPI, f. 17, op. 122, d. 10, l. 30.

[4] P. N. Knyshevskii et al., *Skrytaia pravda voiny: 1941 god* (Moscow: Russkaia kniga, 1992), 126.

[5] Ibid., 266.

cording to a report from the Southern front, "the evacuation of the population from the frontline regions is poorly organized. The leaders of party and
Soviet organs evacuate their families in panic, leaving the rest of the population to the mercy of fate."[6] The phenomenon was so widespread that a political officer on the same front summed up the situation in early August with the
observation that "as a general rule, the leaders of villages and districts flee to
the rear in panic, leaving their posts early."[7]

From north to south, observers thus noted one and the same phenomenon: the "flight" of officials. The term, with its connotations of cowardice,
desertion, and disorganization, was inimical to the very concept of evacuation. The practice it denoted, moreover, seemed to constitute not simply a
transgression of official evacuation procedure but a threat to the entire process. This was certainly the implication of a report penned by the political
administration of the Southern front in early August 1941:

> In the Shpolianskii district the evacuation has turned into disorderly flight as
> a result of a loss of leadership over the population by district organizations.
> The director of the mill and the head of the fire brigade took flight first, aban-
> doning all valuables and printed matter. Many collective- and state-farm
> chairmen have also taken flight, seizing collective and state resources. Mem-
> bers of the city soviet fled (only the chairman remained), the district commit-
> tee of the Komsomol fled.[8]

In this account, the flight of officials transformed what might have been an
organized evacuation into "disorderly flight."

Although reports from the political administration of the army tend to
focus on villages, the phenomenon of official flight was by no means an exclusively rural phenomenon, as the case of Minsk makes clear. Reports on the
evacuation of cities such as Minsk, Brest, and Pinsk differed little in their
essentials from the accounts of the evacuation of collective and state farms.
Nor were such scenes confined to the first few months of the war. The evacuation of the midsize city of Kalinin, for example, was hardly more organized,
although it took place in October. As a military procurator reported, the "required order during the evacuation was not, it would seem, maintained."
The evacuation of the families of workers and employees was begun at the
behest of oblast authorities on October 9 and 10, as the front line drew
nearer to the city. Instead of the organized evacuation of a select sector of
the population, however, the "majority of directors of institutions and enterprises started to evacuate not only the families of workers and employees,
but the workers themselves." At the same time, "certain directors of oblast
institutions left the city themselves. As a result, on the night of October 12

[6] RGASPI, f. 122, d. 10, l. 45.
[7] Ibid., f. 17, op. 122, d. 10, l. 51.
[8] Ibid., l. 46.

to 13 two-thirds of the population of Kalinin spontaneously self-evacuated in various directions."[9]

What began as an organized evacuation thus quickly devolved into the disorganized mass flight of both authorities and the population at large. Among the responsible figures who "fled the city" (in the words of a report by a member of the military soviet) were not only "certain directors" of oblast-level organizations, but the "entire police, all NKVD officers, and the fire brigade."[10] No reports on the evacuation of Kalinin appear to have made it into the files of the Evacuation Council, but it seems fair to conclude that the council members would have judged it a failure, which is not to say that nobody was evacuated from the city. The problem, rather, was that everybody was. More aptly, what transpired was not evacuation but, as the procurator put it in his report, "spontaneous self-evacuation."

Like the flight of officials, the phenomenon of "self-evacuation" was the subject of numerous reports over the summer and fall of 1941. In late July 1941, for instance, the officer in charge of the political division of the southern railway line reported that "alongside the organized evacuation by convoy, a wave of evacuees lacking both permission and direction has recently grown, in the form of spontaneous self-evacuation."[11] The term, improvised by officials on the ground, denoted a process driven by "individual initiative" rather than state action. Self-evacuation transpired outside the realm of the official evacuation, circumscribed by the directives of the military and the Evacuation Council. It described the action of those who, "lacking permission," simply departed on their own. Like the flight of officials, "spontaneous self-evacuation" was in itself a form of transgression: it violated, in addition to official evacuation procedure, a whole web of laws regulating population circulation, according to which the very act of "departing on one's own" (samostoiatel'no) was by definition unlawful. The term itself conveyed the illicit nature of unauthorized departures even as it acknowledged a breakdown in official evacuation procedure.

As a mass phenomenon, self-evacuation was sparked by signs or portents of imminent enemy occupation. These came in various forms, one of which was the sight of Red Army soldiers in retreat. According to a report from the Northwestern front, "the retreat of soldiers in groups and individually after battle, usually on roads that pass through villages, has a somewhat demoralizing effect on the population and is the source of the spontaneous flight of peasants to the rear, even from villages and countryside located further from the front."[12] The flight of local authorities could have a similar effect, as could the evacuation of factories or goods. Thus, in the city of Vitebsk,

[9] Knyshevskii et al., Skrytaia pravda, 173–74.
[10] Ibid., 169.
[11] GARF, f. 6822, op. 1, d. 422, l. 53.
[12] "Iz istorii Velikoi Otechestvennoi voiny: nachalo voiny," Izvestiia TsK KPSS, no. 7 (1990): 204.

Figure 1. Evacuees leaving their homes, July 1941, Leningrad oblast (courtesy TsGAKFFD SPb).

the "alarm" and "panic" of the population was initially sparked by the evacuation of the city's industries. It was exacerbated, however, by the news "that responsible members of the oblast organizations were evacuating their own families and belongings."[13]

The scale of self-evacuation was a function of both the limited scope of evacuation and the breakdown of official evacuation procedure. Many of those who departed on their own hailed from sectors of the population that were either left off the official evacuation lists or had not yet been granted permission to depart. Not infrequently, however, the line between evacuee and self-evacuee was far from clear. Take the case of Tamara Kokoshkina, who recalled the conditions of the evacuation of Kalinin in an interview with a local newspaper many years later. On the eve of the evacuation, Tamara worked as the head of a boiler shop in the Kalinin rubber-sole factory. She recalled, "As soon as the front approached Kalinin, an order was issued to evacuate the factory to the Urals, and everything that it was not possible to evacuate, to destroy." In practice, this meant that "I had to figure out how to leave by myself. . . . On October 13, having been unable to catch the designated fire truck, I gathered my family and we departed by foot on the Moscow highway. My son—in my hands, my daughter could by that time walk

[13] Knyshevskii et al., *Skrytaia pravda*, 118.

Figure 2. Children awaiting their train, June–July 1941, Leningrad (courtesy TsGAKFFD SPb).

on her own, my mother we transported in a cart, and my aunt . . . and father walked slowly on their own."[14]

THE ORGANIZED EVACUATION

As many of these cases suggest, the flight of officials and the population at large almost invariably took place in the midst of what was, at least initially, an organized evacuation. Flight, in other words, is only one side of the story. If we turn from party and procuracy reports to the files of the government authorities responsible for organizing the evacuation, a very different picture of the operation emerges. Consider the following form, drawn up in the summer of 1941: "The district evacuation commission requires you and your children to leave Leningrad for the duration of the war as part of the evacuation. In preparation for your departure you will be given three days. Within this time frame you are required to come to the district evacuation commission to receive an evacuation certificate and a boarding pass."[15] Cer-

[14] Boris Ershov, "Kak trudno my vyzhivali," interview with Tamara Kokoshkina, *Tverskoi oblastnoi ezhenedel'nik Karavan*, 29 November 2000 (www.karavan.tver.ru/html/n308/article4.htm).
[15] TsGASPb, f. 330, op. 2, d. 11, l. 150.

tificates, permits, vouchers, and passes—such were the mechanisms through which the directives of the Evacuation Council were translated into practice. These documents constitute the bureaucratic trappings of the organized evacuation. They attest to the existence of an organized procedure and make it clear that the dictates of the Evacuation Council were not without effect.

In Leningrad, where the form cited above originated, the evacuation was organized by a specially designated commission that was established within days of the invasion.[16] This body stood at the head of a network of district commissions, which were responsible, among other things, for notifying evacuees of their upcoming departure and issuing them with the appropriate forms. Every day, anywhere from five to fifteen thousand people were evacuated from the city. The total number of evacuees rose accordingly: in just under six weeks, officials could boast of the evacuation of over half a million urban residents.[17] Even so, the evacuation was far from an unmitigated success, as the tragic fate of some of the city's evacuated children attests. Although children constituted a majority among evacuees in the summer of 1941, many were transported not to the rear but to the surrounding countryside.[18] The prospect of German troops reaching the outskirts of the city was simply not entertained. As Harrison Salisbury wrote of this period, "the great Nazi blitz of London was the horror which filled the minds of most Leningraders, official and unofficial."[19] By late July, however, German troops were sweeping northward, advancing on the city and its hinterland. The result was that some children found themselves in the path of the enemy. Desperate parents besieged the district commissions, requesting information and immediate action.[20] Although most of the children in the areas in question were returned to the city, not all made it back alive.[21]

An even greater tragedy lay ahead. By mid-August, when it dawned on authorities that the city itself could be under threat, orders were issued to evacuate a further seven hundred thousand women and children from the city.[22] By then it was already too late: within less than two weeks, the railway line between Leningrad and Moscow was severed, and by September 8, 1941, the remaining railway lines linking the city to the rest of the country were cut off. Of a population of over three million, only half a million had

[16] V. M. Koval'chuk, "Evakuatsiia naseleniia Leningrada letom 1941 goda," *Otechestvennaia istoriia*, no. 3 (2000): 16.
[17] TsGASPb, f. 330, op. 2, d. 11, l. 14.
[18] GARF, f. 6822, op. 1, d. 409, l. 56.
[19] Harrison E. Salisbury, *The 900 Days: The Siege of Leningrad* (New York: Harper and Row, 1969), 143.
[20] TsGASPb, f. 7384, op. 17, d. 443, l. 376.
[21] TsGASPb, f. 330, op. 2, d. 11, l. 14.
[22] TsGASPb, f. 7384, op. 17, d. 665, l. 20.

Figure 3. Evacuees departing Leningrad by airplane, October 1941 (courtesy TsGAKFFD SPb).

been evacuated.[23] The remaining 2.5 million were trapped in a city with rapidly dwindling supplies.

For the next few months, the only escape from the city was by air, and evacuation efforts were consequently sharply constrained. Departures by airplane were generally reserved for the political and cultural elite: among those who were accorded seats on planes that fall was the poet Anna Akhmatova. It was only when winter set in that evacuations resumed on a larger scale. Desperate to secure food for the starving city, authorities opened up a supply route across the frozen expanses of Lake Ladoga. The ice road simultaneously served as a conduit for much needed supplies and a new route out of the city for the remaining population. During the winter of 1941–42, a further half million residents were evacuated along this makeshift route.[24]

The evacuation of Leningrad was not marked by the mass flight that characterized the evacuation of so many other places. In part, this reflected the fact that there was nowhere to run: by the time it was clear that the city

[23] Although just over 800,000 people were evacuated that summer, this number included almost 150,000 refugees from the Baltic states and Karelia, as well as 175,000 children who were re-evacuated to Leningrad when the areas to which they had been originally evacuated came under threat. TsGASPb, f. 330, op. 2, d. 18, l. 1. See also Koval'chuk, "Evakuatsiia naselenia Leningrada," 22.

[24] GARF, f. 5446, op. 59, d. 12, l. 7.

was under imminent threat, the most obvious exits from the city were no longer open. Both authorities and the population were stuck. But it also reflected a degree of organization and discipline that was notably lacking in Minsk. These traits notwithstanding, the evacuation of Leningrad was hardly a success. It was marred by both misfortune and mistakes, and when all was said and done, it saved only a fraction of the population from a desperate struggle to survive in the city under siege.

A somewhat more successful operation was mounted in the Black Sea city of Odessa, one of the country's most important ports. Odessa was one of a handful of Soviet cities subject to aerial attack on the first night of the invasion. The evacuation of the city began only a few weeks later. Every day, anywhere between two hundred and fourteen hundred people were evacuated, some by their factories, others by the city soviet, and others still by district soviets, each of which established its own evacuation commission.[25] Prior to leaving, evacuees were issued with certificates affirming that they had permission to depart. In keeping with the directives of the Evacuation Council, the operation targeted various sectors of society: Sophia Abidor was evacuated as the mother of an infant child, the ten-year-old Leonid Averbukh and his mother as the family of an officer, and Saul Borovoi as a distinguished historian.

This is not to say that the directives of the Evacuation Council were translated seamlessly into a corresponding evacuation on the ground. The compilation of the lists, the distribution of the relevant documents, and the allocation of transport constituted moments when official priorities could be modified or subverted. In Odessa, as elsewhere, there were multiple opportunities for nepotism, bribery, and favors. An investigation into the "willful" departure of several high-ranking oblast officials revealed that the flight of the officials in question had been facilitated by none other than the head of the oblast evacuation point, who, "taking advantage of his official position, gave [them] boarding tickets on the ferry." Under questioning, the evacuation official further disclosed that he had given out other tickets "at his own discretion."[26]

Despite such instances, the operation was by and large successful. Even when the city was encircled in mid-August 1941, evacuation continued by boat. According to obkom officials, by the time the city was occupied in mid-October 1941, some 350,000 people had departed, a good proportion of them through the evacuation center.[27] All told, this accounted for approximately half of the city's prewar population. The contrast between the

---

[25] GAOO, f. P9, op. 3, d. 347, ll. 1–8. On the district commissions, see, for example, GAOO, f. P22, op. 5, d. 3, l. 174.

[26] See GAOO, f. P9, op. 3, d. 342, l. 37 and d. 341, l. 120.

[27] According to the report, 216,500 people had been evacuated through the evacuation center, 60,000 of them citizens of Bessarabia who had sought refuge in Odessa. Another 135,000 had reportedly left the city by other means. GAOO, f. P11, op. 1, d. 1822, l. 19.

report from Minsk and the report from Odessa is striking. Instead of an angry letter to central authorities, oblast officials from Odessa could proudly proclaim that "even though there were negative moments, the evacuation proceeded in an organized fashion."[28]

The relative success of the evacuation of Odessa was in part a function of timing. Odessa was not occupied until mid-October, giving authorities there ample time to organize an orderly evacuation from the city. Officials from Belorussia, comparing the evacuations in various locales, accounted for the differences in the way the operation unfolded in precisely these terms. Noting the relative success of the evacuation of the midsize town of Gomel, they reflected that the evacuation of Gomel took place "in a more organized and planned manner" than the evacuation of Vitebsk because Gomel "found [itself] in a more favorable situation."[29] The "more favorable situation" inhered mainly in the date of occupation: while Vitebsk was occupied in early July and was evacuated under heavy enemy fire, Gomel was not occupied until the latter half of August. The contrast between Gomel and Vitebsk, Odessa and Minsk, would seem to suggest that evacuations became substantially more successful as the summer progressed. Whereas this is certainly true in terms of the percentage of the population evacuated, it does not account for the striking similarities in the way evacuations played out. For while evacuations frequently began in organized fashion, they often ended in the same disorganized fashion decried by the Minsk obkom official. What was true of Kalinin, where an organized evacuation quickly devolved into disorderly flight, was true of a host of other places. Nowhere was this dynamic more visible or dramatic than in Moscow, the Soviet capital, which embodied both the organized evacuation and the phenomenon of flight.

THE EVACUATION OF THE CAPITAL

The evacuation of Moscow began almost immediately after the invasion. Within days, the city's train stations were crowded with people.[30] Tens of thousands departed each day: by the middle of July almost 1 million Muscovites had been evacuated, and by the end of August the number had risen to well over 1.5 million.[31] The majority of those who departed that summer were evacuated collectively. Olga Boltianskaia, for instance, whose husband worked in the film industry, was evacuated with other film workers.[32] Lydia

[28] Ibid., l. 20.

[29] "Iz istorii Velikoi Otechestvennoi voiny," *Izvestiia TsK KPSS*, no. 8 (1990): 216.

[30] GARF, f. 259, op. 40, d. 3023, l. 60.

[31] GARF, f. 6822, op. 1, d. 409, l. 86; GARF, f. 259, op. 40, d. 3064, l. 44.

[32] Diary of O. A. Boltianskaia, RGALI, f. 2057, op. 2, d. 29, l. 87, entry of August 4, 1941.

Chukovskaia, the daughter of the renowned children's writer and literary critic Kornei Chukovskii and a writer in her own right, was similarly evacuated by the Litfond, the body responsible for funding writers. The same organization evacuated the poet Marina Tsvetaeva and her son Georgii Efron.[33] Others were evacuated in what authorities referred to as an "individual order" (that is, not as part of the organized echelons assembled by district organizations or workplaces). They too, however, were furnished with evacuation papers and accorded space on trains, albeit at their own expense. Zinaida Stepanishcheva and her infant son, for example, having decided to depart, were issued tickets at the evacuation center for Chkalov and evacuated from Moscow in late July 1941.[34] The actor Solomon Mikhoels dispatched his daughters to Sverdlovsk a few weeks later.[35]

By and large, the early evacuation of Moscow was an orderly affair. Although there were invariably instances of unauthorized flight, most people seem to have heeded the dictates of authorities.[36] When the writer Kochetkov, who would later be evacuated to Tashkent, sought to obtain tickets for Turkmenistan in late July, he was unable to secure a ticket for his mother and hence did not depart.[37] Moreover, when another writer "willfully departed for Tashkent," he was recalled to Moscow by the Union of Soviet Writers and branded a traitor.[38]

In mid-October 1941, however, the character of the evacuation changed. The German assault on Moscow, launched at the end of September, seemed poised to succeed. One by one, the towns separating enemy forces from the capital had fallen: Orel, without even a battle; Briansk; Vyazma. The Germans were approaching Moscow. In response, evacuation efforts, which had tapered off considerably since the height of the summer, were stepped up: orders were issued on October 9 to evacuate an additional three hundred thousand women and children; a request by the Union of Soviet Writers to evacuate elderly and infirm writers as well as the families of writers on the front lines was approved a few days later.[39] On October 15, Stalin convened a meeting in his office. Fearful that the capital itself could not hold out against the enemy, he ordered the evacuation of the government, all foreign embassies, and the Commissariats of the Navy and Defense. Molotov was to lead the government to its new capital of Kuibyshev, while Stalin

[33] On the evacuation of Tsvetaeva and Efron, see Georgii Efron, *Dnevniki (1940–1941 gody)*, vol. 1, ed. E. B. Korkina and V. K. Losskaia (Moscow: Vagrius, 2004), 478–90.

[34] Z. G. Stepanishcheva, "Vot tak i zhizn' proshla," TsDNA, f. 422, l. 6.

[35] Nataliia Vovsi-Mikhoels, *Moi otets Solomon Mikhoels: vospominanie o zhizni i gibeli* (Moscow: Vozvrashchenie, 1997), 142.

[36] RGASPI, f. 17, op. 22, d. 1811, l. 66.

[37] Efron, *Dnevniki*, vol. 1, 471.

[38] The writer in question was Pavel Nilin. See K. Chukovskii, letter of September 29, 1942, in Kornei Chukovskii and Lidiia Chukovskaia, *Perepiska: 1912–1969*, ed. E. Ts. Chukovskaia and Zh. O. Khavkina (Moscow: Novoe literaturnoe obozrenie, 2004), 314.

[39] GARF, f. 259, op. 20, d. 3035, l. 94; f. 6822, op. 1, d. 48, l. 14.

would, in the words of the decree, "evacuate himself tomorrow or later, depending on the circumstances."[40] Unlike previous evacuation orders, which aimed to clear the city of excess mouths and protect civilians from bombardment, the evacuation order of October 15 was predicated on the possibility of withdrawal. Provisions were included to blow up factories and warehouses that could not be evacuated as well as the electrical equipment of the Moscow Metro should enemy troops break through to the gates of the city. At the same time, the heads of each of the people's commissariats and of other major organizations were summoned to the Kremlin and instructed to organize the evacuation of the factories and institutions under their jurisdiction.

The days of mid-October witnessed a flurry of activity as tens of thousands of people were evacuated from the capital. Among the range of evacuated enterprises and institutions were the Academy of Sciences, the Commissariat of Milk and Meat, the Union of Soviet Writers, the Stalin car factory, the State Jewish Theater, and the predatory animals of the Moscow Zoo. Large numbers of people were evacuated within days, sometimes hours. On October 14, 1941, Kosygin reported to Molotov, Mikoian, and Kaganovich that over fifteen hundred "artists, writers, and scholars" had been evacuated from the city.[41] Among them was Maria Belkina, who was evacuated as the wife of a literary critic serving on the front lines. Belkina later recalled how she had been summoned to the Writers' Union on October 12: "I spent the whole day [there] in line for tickets and was issued my evacuation documents."[42] Such were the mechanisms through which the evacuation was organized and ordered. The personal file of the poet Iosif Utkin still contains the certificate given him by the Union of Soviet Writers on October 14, 1941, indicating that he was being evacuated with the union.[43] The writer Vladimir Lugovskoi was issued a similar certificate: "The following is given to Comrade Lugovskoi and attests to the fact that he is being evacuated by the Union of Soviet Writers of the USSR together with his family."[44] The distribution of these documents was carried out on the basis of lists, which were compiled by various institutions in conjunction with the decrees of the Evacuation Council. The compilation of the lists, the distribution of the relevant documents, and with it, the means of transportation were the essential processes of the organized evacuation. State, party, and personal archives contain a wealth of such documentation. The various resolutions, graphs, lists, and certificates stand as material evidence of

---

[40] The decree is titled, "On the Evacuation of the Capital of the USSR, City of Moscow." RGASPI, f. 644, op. 1, d. 12, l. 155.

[41] GARF, f. 6822, op. 1, d. 468, l. 4.

[42] Maria Belkina, *Skreshchenie sudeb*, 2d ed. (Moscow: Blagovest Rudomino, 1992), 291.

[43] RGALI, f. 1717, op. 1, d. 8, l. 1.

[44] The certificate is reproduced in N. A. Gromova, *Vse v chuzhoe gliadiat okno* (Moscow: Sovershenno sekretno, 2002), 22.

the success of the Soviet state in organizing the evacuation. Statistics corroborate the general impression: during the three days between October 15 and October 18 alone, almost a thousand railway cars departed from the city's stations carrying the employees of people's commissariats and other institutions.[45]

What began as an organized procedure, however, quickly spun out of control. As in the cases examined above, the fracture point in Moscow was not the population at large but the Soviet managerial and political elite. The following account, addressed to the NKVD shortly after the events it describes, is typical: "On October 15, 1941, at 1 P.M. the director of aviation factory X, Perovskii, departed in his car . . . , leaving the factory without leadership. The factory was supposed to be evacuated to Sverdlovsk, but Perovskii, instead of organizing the evacuation, took 10,000 rubles from the cash box of the factory, loaded three barrels of gasoline into his car, and left, claiming he had been summoned by the district party committee. In addition, he signed documents authorizing the release of 20,000 rubles to the main engineer, 10,000 rubles to the assistant head engineer, and 2,000 rubles" to an assistant director. "The heads of the factory's shops and departments, witnessing the panicky flight of the director, themselves departed with the first echelon, abandoning 80 percent of the qualified workforce to the mercy of fate." If this were not enough, the "secretary of the party organization likewise deserted, leaving his party card behind."[46]

This report was drawn up by the director's assistant. Judging from the fact that he was not on the list of those who received money from the director, we can surmise that perhaps they had had conflicts, and that this report, really more of a denunciation, constituted an attempt to settle scores. Whatever the politics informing the report, however, the basic story it presented was echoed in numerous and diverse sources including the memoranda of the NKVD, interviews conducted by the Commission on the history of the Great Patriotic War, the protocols of district party committee meetings, the diaries of individual Muscovites, correspondence intercepted by the censors, and memoirs penned both by ordinary citizens and state functionaries. Only the cast of characters changed: in one case a factory manager, in another the director of a medical institute, who "succumbing to panic, took his deputies . . . and fled Moscow by automobile, leaving the hospital without leadership." (Like Perovskii, he helped himself and his subordinates to generous sums of money.)[47] Among the other stock characters guilty of flight and the embezzlement of state assets were the directors of state stores and party

---

[45] GARF, f. 6822, op. 1, d. 461, ll. 21–25.

[46] The report also notes that "the director took the factory stamp with him, did not turn over responsibility to anyone, . . . and did not pay workers their wages." See K. I. Bukov, M. M. Gorinov, and A. N. Ponomarev, eds., *Moskva voennaia, 1941–1945. Memuary i arkhivnye dokumenty* (Moscow: Mosgorarkhiv, 1995), 122–23.

[47] Ibid., 123, 725.

members. The director of a fashion house "succumbing to the panicky mood about the unavoidable surrender of Moscow," allegedly started selling state goods at a profit.[48] In at least four of the capital's districts, the first secretaries of the district party committees were charged with desertion and expelled from the party.[49] In all, according to the incomplete data of the Moscow commandant's office, 779 high-level personnel fled from 438 different enterprises, stealing a total of 1,484,000 rubles; squandering as much as 1,000,000 rubles worth of valuables and property; and taking, in the process, one hundred cars and trucks.[50] Nine hundred and fifty people were expelled from the party, many of them for "cowardice and desertion."[51] On October 16 and 17 alone, as many as one thousand party and party candidacy cards were destroyed.[52]

The results of this flight were a breakdown of order and a mass, disorganized, "spontaneous" flight of the population at large. On October 16 Georgii Efron noted in his diary, in his second entry of the day, that an "enormous number of people depart *n'importe ou* [any which where], overloaded with bags and trunks. . . . It seems that 50 percent of Moscow is evacuating itself."[53] The historian P. N. Miller made a similar observation in his diary entry of the same day: "People walk in all directions, loaded with luggage—obviously the vast majority reckon on traveling by foot. Even evacuated factories and institutions are doomed to travel thus."[54]

Descriptions of this period frequently focus on the Highway of the Enthusiasts, the city's principal artery to the east. As one Muscovite later described it: "The entire highway was a continuous wave of people heading east. Carriages, wheelbarrows, carts. The majority carried their belongings on their shoulders."[55] According to a member of the Komsomol, who was standing just south of the entrance onto the Highway of the Enthusiasts, there were "tens of thousands of people" making their way east.[56]

In these conditions, the boundary between the evacuee and the self-evacuee was often difficult to discern. This lack of clarity could have damaging repercussions, particularly for those in positions of responsibility, as self-evacuation, depending on the circumstances, could easily be construed as "desertion." For example, a district procurator was fired by the city's military procurator

---

[48] TsAGM, f. 819, op. 2, d. 46, l. 161.

[49] RGASPI, f. 17, op. 22, d. 1798, l. 96.

[50] "Iz istorii Velikoi Otechestvennoi voiny," *Izvestiia TsK KPSS*, no. 4 (1991).

[51] K. I. Bukov, "Ne tol'ko panika (oktiabr' 1941 g. v Moskve)," in *Neizvestnaia Rossiia: XX Vek*, vol. 3 (Moscow: Istoricheskoe nasledie, 1993), 179.

[52] M. M. Gorinov, V. N. Parkhachev, and A. N. Ponomarev, eds., *Moskva prifrontovaia, 1941–1942: Arkhivnye dokumenty i materialy* (Moscow: Mosgorarkhiv, 2001), 264.

[53] Georgii Efron, *Dnevniki (1941–1943 gody)*, vol. 2, ed. E. B. Korkina and V. K. Losskaia (Moscow: Vagrius, 2005), 49.

[54] Gorinov, Parkhachev, and Ponomarev, *Moskva prifrontovaia*, 290.

[55] Bukov, Gorinov, and Ponomarev, *Moskva voennaia*, 112.

[56] Bukov, "Ne tol'ko panika," 183.

for "leaving the city without my permission." In his defense, the district procurator claimed that he had been "evacuated from Moscow" "on the recommendation of the district party organization and the military procurator himself."[57] In a similar case, an employee in the central telegraph office, a certain Mokhriakov, was likewise charged with "willful departure from work" in mid-October. According to the accused, he had been told on October 15 by the same individual who now accused him that "there would be no evacuation of the enterprise, rather it would be liquidated, and that it was not recommended for Communists to remain in the region and each should make his way out of Moscow as he likes." The next day, he was provided with an evacuation certificate by the second in command and he left the city shortly thereafter.[58] Although the charges against Mokhriakov were ultimately dismissed on the grounds that he had indeed left the city as part of the evacuation, the case demonstrates the degree of disorder that characterized even the "organized" evacuation.

The case of Moscow stands as a striking example of both the successes and the failures of evacuations in practice. On one hand, the state succeeded in organizing the transfer of select sectors of the population to the rear in a timely fashion and on a large scale: in late December 1941 Beria, Shcherbakov, and Pronin reported to Stalin that 2.2 million Muscovites had been evacuated since the beginning of the war.[59] The success was in some sense systemic: a mobilizational state that was organized in a semicorporatist fashion and owned most of the means of transportation was optimally suited to effect and control the timely transfer of people. On the other hand, the evacuation highlighted the weaknesses of the Soviet system: instead of a resolute response, the local political and managerial elite simply "deserted" their posts, abdicating their responsibilities and defying central directives. We are thus left with the question posed by the Minsk obkom official, who wrote of the evacuation of his city that the evacuation "took place in such a disorganized fashion that one is forced to reflect, and pose the question, why did it happen this way?"[60]

PANIC ON THE FRONT LINES

If we turn to contemporary accounts, the answer is clear-cut: evacuation efforts were invariably foiled by the "flight" and "panic" of the very people who were supposed to organize the operation. This was certainly the conclusion of the Minsk obkom official, whose rhetorical question regarding

[57] TsAGM, f. 2842, op. 5, d. 4, ll. 8, 37.
[58] Ibid., d. 5, ll. 26, 32.
[59] TsAOPIM, f. 3, op. 52, d. 10, l. 157.
[60] RGASPI, f. 17, op. 122, d. 10, l. 16.

the causes of the disorderly evacuation had a seemingly simple response: "really, this could have been prevented had the secretaries of the obkom not shamefully fled the city but directed the evacuation."[61] It was also the conclusion of the political administration of the army, whose reports on the evacuation are almost formulaic. These reports present a standard scenario that is both highly condensed ("party leaders leave first") and cast in moralizing terms ("Saving their own skin," local party and Soviet cadres "abandon the population to the mercy of fate"). Even more formulaic were the proceedings of oblast and republican party organizations, which decreed the dismissal of thousands of party members in the first several months of the war on the charge that they had "deserted their posts before the evacuation began." In the protocols of the party committees, flight, and by extension the failures of evacuation, were presented as the product of personal failings. The secretary of the party committee of the city of Klintsy, for example, V. F. Tokarev, was expelled from the party and fired from his job not only for "abandoning the city significantly before the arrival of the enemy," but for "displaying cowardice and weakness of spirit unworthy of a party leader and a Communist."[62]

The charges leveled against Tokarev differed little from those leveled at hundreds of officials over the late summer and fall of 1941.[63] Typically, the charges were not limited to a single individual but extended, in separate rulings, to what appears to have been significant portions of the ruling elite: in the case of Klintsy, this included not only Tokarev, the party secretary, but also the second secretary of the party committee, the secretary in charge of industry, the head of the city soviet, and the head of the municipal NKVD.[64] For the most part, the proceedings were brief and, as suggested above, formulaic. By chance, however, central archives have preserved another, much richer source on Tokarev's behavior and the evacuation of the town of Klintsy, a report penned on August 25, 1941, by a plenipotentiary of the Evacuation Council and the Commissariat of Textiles who had been dispatched to the town, one of the country's principal sites of cloth production on the eve of the war, to oversee the evacuation of its textile factories. His report, which discusses developments in the city until shortly before Tokarev is said to have deserted it, provides revealing insights into the complex of conditions that obstructed the evacuation and precipitated flight.

The plenipotentiary arrived in the city on the evening of August 15, as units of the German Army Group Center, led by Colonel General Heinz

---

[61] Ibid.

[62] RGASPI, f. 17, op. 22, d. 2080, l. 195.

[63] For other examples, see the protocols of the bureau meetings of the Karelo-Finnish SSR, Moldavian SSR, Kalinin gorkom, Kursk obkom, Kiev obkom, Dnepropetrovsk obkom, Poltava obkom, and Odessa obkom in, respectively, RGASPI, f. 17, op. 22, d. 1203, 1717, 759, 1589, 3244, 3106, 3374, and 3339.

[64] RGASPI, f. 17, op. 22, d. 2080, ll. 204, 205, 196; d. 2081, l. 8.

Guderian, were swinging southward toward the city. The evacuation of Klintsy's industry had begun that evening, on the orders of the deputy chairman of the oblast executive party committee. The plenipotentiary, after "familiarizing myself with the situation regarding the evacuation of the city's industry," concluded that a "full evacuation" was no longer possible due to the "unsatisfactory" situation on the front.[65] Clearly, the evacuation had begun too late. According to one of the plenipotentiary's sources in the town, the head of the Klintsy cloth trust, the "uneasy situation in the sector of the front adjoining Klintsy was felt as early as August 5 or 6." Why, then, had nothing been done? The same source reported that he had, at that time, "raised the question of a partial evacuation of machinery that was not being used. The secretary of the city's party committee Comrade Tokarev," however, "forbade the evacuation." Two days later, the trust head "raised the question of a partial evacuation to the party committee secretary for a second time." The response? "Tokarev suggested that he not raise this question, for there had been no decision on evacuation." The head of the cloth trust received a similar response from representatives of the oblast who paid a visit to the town a few days later. When presented with the question of a partial evacuation, they informed the trust head "that there was no threat to Klintsy, and for this reason there should be no discussion of evacuation."[66]

As a result of this policy of "no discussion," the evacuation of Klintsy was delayed until it was too late. When oblast authorities finally authorized an evacuation of the city's industry on August 15, there was neither the time nor the means to fulfill the plans. As the plenipotentiary reported, "we didn't get any train cars until the seventeenth, as they were all occupied with the evacuation of hospitals and heavy artillery. . . . On the seventeenth we were given eighteen platforms on which we evacuated motors, heavy metals, appliances . . . and on the eighteenth, at three o'clock, they were dispatched on the last locomotives, on which the head of the railway station of Klintsy and all his staff were also evacuated." The plenipotentiary's subsequent request for automobiles was refused, but he was promised seven hundred horses to complete the evacuation of the city's textile industry by five that morning. "Instead of 5 A.M., the horses arrived at noon, and instead of seven hundred, there were only twenty-eight." Of the remaining equipment and material, they were thus able to evacuate only the coat cloth from the Lenin factory.[67]

The situation was particularly dire for Klintsy's civilian population. While the Evacuation Council did authorize the evacuation by train of ten thousand women and children from the town, the decree was issued only on August 19.[68] By that time, in the words of the plenipotentiary, the "railway

---

[65] GARF, f. 6822, op. 1, d. 354, l. 125.
[66] Ibid., l. 123.
[67] Ibid., l. 122.
[68] The evacuation order is in GARF, f. A-259, op. 40, d. 3063, l. 9.

did not work, there was no motor transport, no animal-drawn transport since the collective farm horses had also been evacuated, and thus all the paths . . . were cut off."[69]

Taken together, the plenipotentiary's report and the Evacuation Council's decision point to two key factors that shaped the way evacuation transpired in Klintsy. First, there is the shocking ignorance of local and oblast authorities about developments on the front. The poor state of information is an essential context for understanding the phenomenon of "panic" that figures so prominently in contemporary reports on the evacuation. Equally striking is the reluctance of authorities at all levels to initiate evacuation. In the case of Klintsy, not only did local and oblast level authorities refuse to consider a partial evacuation as a precautionary measure, but the Evacuation Council authorized the evacuation of the town's civilian population only when it was already too late. The poor state of information and the reluctance to initiate evacuation were not, however, factors unique to Klintsy. Rather, they shaped the evacuation process across the front lines.

THE SOURCES OF PANIC: THE STATE OF INFORMATION

The foremost cause of flight, in the reports of Soviet authorities, was panic. Panic, from the standpoint of Soviet authorities, invariably stemmed from cowardice or, in a more sinister interpretation, from saboteurs.[70] In the language of political administration, prosecutor, and party reports, "panic" frequently figures as a criminal indictment rather than a psychological phenomenon. Read closely, however, these reports and others furnish valuable insight into the sources of "panic" and its impact on evacuation.

Panic was first and foremost a product of uncertain information coupled with devastating military setbacks. A letter from authorities in the town of Elna, in Smolensk oblast, points to the conditions that made panic possible. Addressing themselves to the Politburo, the authors reported that it was difficult to quell the "panic sown by evacuees, . . . for even the narrow circle of leading cadres does not have even approximate information about the situation on the nearest fronts. With the evacuees, of course, come provocateurs, who consciously sow panic, crying that Minsk is taken, that enemy troops approach Orsha, and in addition you see how people flee from Smolensk. . . . Meanwhile, the oblast authorities remain silent and it becomes difficult to orient oneself and to distinguish truth from provocation."[71]

---

[69] GARF, f. 6822, op. 1, d. 354, l. 122.

[70] Thus a procurator from the Rechitskii district suggested that the panic created by the disorganized evacuation of the town "was, obviously, purposefully carried out by enemy elements". RGASPI, f. 17, op. 122, d. 10, l. 15.

[71] Ibid., ll. 12–13.

The task of distinguishing "truth from provocation" was rendered particularly difficult in the face of an official policy of evasion with regard to concrete developments on the front. Local and regional authorities depended heavily on the press for up-to-date information. As the head of the party's organizational-instructional division reported at the end of September 1941, "at present the secretaries of oblast and city party committees derive their information principally from the newspapers."[72] During the first two months of the war, however, the Soviet press did not report the surrender of a single city.[73] On the day Minsk fell, for example, the press reported that "in the direction of Minsk, Red Army troops continue their successful struggle with the tanks of the enemy, opposing his movement to the east."[74] Military developments, moreover, were frequently related in generic terms, divested of both geographic specificity and meaningful content. Thus readers were routinely informed of "stubborn battles" that had taken place "on the front" in which "nothing important" had happened.[75]

With the official state news agency releasing only limited, and for the most part tardy, information about developments on the front, local authorities were forced to rely on oblast networks for even the most general information. All too often these proved woefully inadequate. Smolensk oblast, for example, issued only one directive to local authorities in the first week of the war, a request for "information on the state of churches and houses of prayer in the region."[76] In many cases, oblast authorities were themselves ill informed. As the plenipotentiary dispatched to Klintsy reported of the Orel oblast committee, the "obkom did not properly assess the situation on the front near Klintsy until the very last minute, as it was somehow unaware of what was happening on the front in its oblast." The situation was all the more grievous because the NKVD actually possessed information that it failed to pass on to the relevant oblast authorities.[77] The ignorance of oblast authorities was

[72] Ibid., d. 5, l. 203.

[73] It was only at the end of August that the press began to report the loss of individual cities. On the wartime press, see L. D. Dergacheva, "Istochnikovedcheskie problemy sovetskoi zhurnalistiki voennogo vremeni (1941–1945)," *Vestnik Moskovskogo universiteta, Seriia 8: Istoriia*, no. 2 (1999): 3–19.

[74] Quoted in Jeffrey Brooks, "*Pravda* goes to War," in *Culture and Entertainment in Wartime Russia*, ed. Richard Stites (Bloomington: Indiana University Press, 1995), 12. As Brooks suggests, in the absence of further reports on Minsk, readers "surmised what happened from reports of battles 'in the direction of Mogilev-Podolskii,' well to the east." Ibid.

[75] A notable exception to this trend was the publication on October 14 of a report on the loss of Viazma and the direct acknowledgment of a threat to Moscow.

[76] RGASPI, f. 17, op. 122, d. 10, l. 12.

[77] The plenipotentiary reported that he was told by the obkom secretary on August 15, while en route to Klintsy, that the situation on the front had not changed. When he reached Pochep, however, the head of the district NKVD, who was in a military meeting discussing the unstable situation in the district, advised him to avoid Unecha, and instead to take the somewhat more roundabout route through Starodub. According to the plenipotentiary, Unecha fell to the Germans on August 17 and Pochep and Starodub fell sometime later. On his return trip,

thus the product not only of a lack of useful information in the press but also of poor communication with other authorities in the region, most notably the military and NKVD. Justifying the unauthorized departure of authorities from the city of Brest, the oblast secretary shifted the blame to military headquarters, reporting that "many commanders and political cadres, instead of organizing the evacuation, fled the city in panic, saving their families as a first priority." Just as significant, however, was the fact that the military authorities "did not establish a link with the obkom. Thus, not knowing the situation, having no communication with the military command, and not counting on the battle-worthiness of the combat units, we were forced to leave Brest."[78]

Given the poor state of information and communication, local authorities were particularly vulnerable to rumors. The war created an environment that was ripe for the spread of rumor, which always thrived in times of crisis.[79] Not surprisingly, rumor quickly became a prime concern of Soviet authorities. According to the head of the People's Commissariat for State Security, "anti-Soviet elements, in connection with the war, are attempting to sow various malicious rumors with the aim of provoking panic and confusion among the population." Special measures to "cut off such rumors"—namely, prison terms of between two and five years—were proposed within a week of the invasion.[80] In addition, in at least some regions, evacuees were forbidden from spreading "any information on the progress of the war that could foster panic and defeatist attitudes."[81] Although central authorities explicitly forbade the spread of rumor and made it a criminal offense, they were incapable of shutting down the flourishing rumor mill.

The spread of rumor was facilitated by the mass of people heading east. Within weeks of the initial invasion, there was not a town west of the Urals that could not count among its population at least a few new arrivals from the front. Evacuees, who were concentrated in particularly high numbers in the regions adjacent to the front lines, bore tales of Red Army defeats, German atrocities, and as yet unreported occupations. In Elna, they spoke of the fall of Minsk; in the Ukrainian city of Zhitomir, they "spread rumors about the supposed total destruction of the cities of Lvov, Lutsk, Rovno, and others."[82] According to a party member in Kursk oblast, the mere arrival of

---

however, the secretary knew nothing of what had happened. GARF, f. 6822, op. 1, d. 354, ll. 120–21.

[78] "Iz istorii Velikoi Otechestvennoi voiny: nachalo voiny," *Izvestiia TsK KPSS*, no. 6 (1990): 205.

[79] On rumors during the collectivization campaign, see Lynne Viola, "The Peasant Nightmare: Visions of Apocalypse in the Soviet Countryside," *Journal of Modern History* 62, no. 4 (1990): 747–70.

[80] V. P. Iampol'skii et al., *Organy Gosudarstvennoi bezopasnosti v Velikoi Otechestvennoi voine*, vol. 1, bk. 1 (Moscow: Rus', 2000), 204, 113.

[81] Ibid., 218.

[82] Ibid., 94.

evacuees "had a strong impact on the workers of the district party committee," who, "throwing themselves into a panic, started to tie their bundles."[83] Despite the official equation of "rumormongers" with provocateurs, even the most zealous local authorities were in some measure captive to rumor, for in conditions of uncertainty and lack of information, as the report from Elna put it, "it becomes difficult to orient oneself and distinguish truth from provocation."

Panic was further fed by rumors about the fate that awaited authorities should they fall into enemy hands. It was well known that Communists would be targeted by the Germans, and they had every reason to be afraid. In the recently annexed territories, moreover, authorities had reason to fear the local population as well as the occupying forces. As an NKVD official from Riga related to Emma Gershtein and her family in Moscow later that summer, "'From every window they shot at us, in the back!'"[84]

The environment of uncertainty and the stunning rapidity of German advances constitute an essential backdrop to both the onset of panic and the flight that it engendered. Given the uncertainty and contradictory reports, it seems almost beside the point whether or not, in the smug tone with which one report on the Briansk front concluded, "the majority of these places are not occupied and do not look like they will be." How, after all, were local authorities to know? Moreover, the truth of the matter is that most of "these places" were in fact occupied. With enemy troops advancing at a rapid rate, vast areas of the country were in German hands by the end of September. Indeed, even the author of the previous comment tacitly acknowledged that the flight of local officials frequently preceded German occupation by only "several days."[85] In the dark as to the whereabouts of enemy troops and wary of the possibility of holding out, local authorities frequently fled, opting to "save their own skins" rather than fulfill their official responsibilities and risk capture by the enemy.

THE SPECTER OF PANIC: OFFICIAL AMBIVALENCE

Contemporary accounts notwithstanding, it is important to emphasize that the failures of evacuation did not stem exclusively from the flight and panic of local authorities. If we recall the case of Klintsy, Tokarev "deserted" only after the evacuation had already derailed. The flight of local authorities was, at least in this case, not the cause of a breakdown in evacuation but the result. Authorities too often found themselves in situations that were nothing short of hopeless, in which the means of transportation required to effectively

[83] RGASPI, f. 17, op. 122, d. 18, l. 9.
[84] Emma Gershtein, *Memuary* (Moscow: Zakharov, 2002), 415.
[85] RGASPI, f. 17, op. 122, d. 10, ll. 65, 64.

evacuate people and goods were no longer available. In large part, this was the result of the sheer rapidity of German advances and the enemy's success in incapacitating the railways, by far the most effective vehicle of evacuation. It was also a matter of timing. Evacuations were routinely initiated too late to be effective. This was the result not only of the poor state of information but also of political considerations—namely, the specter of panic and official ambivalence with regard to evacuation.

Let us return for a moment to the case of Klintsy, where Tokarev refused to initiate even a partial evacuation on the grounds that there had been "no decision on the matter." Tokarev was bound by the directives of the oblast. According to the plenipotentiary, he had been expressly forbidden to carry out an evacuation by the obkom in mid-July, when the town had first come under threat of occupation and the question of the region's evacuation had first been posed.[86] The refusal of oblast authorities to authorize an evacuation in either mid-July or mid-August stemmed in part, as the plenipotentiary suggested, from a "lack of knowledge" about the situation on the front. It also stemmed, however, from a tendency to put off evacuation until it was absolutely, and irrefutably, necessary. This approach emanated from the pinnacle of Soviet power, from the State Defense Committee and the Evacuation Council.

Central policy with regard to the timing of evacuation is aptly demonstrated in the case of Rostov oblast, in southern Russia, which came under threat in the late summer of 1941 when German Army Group South advanced on the Caucasus. In early September 1941 the secretary of the Rostov obkom wrote to Shvernik explaining:

> the population [of Taganrog] is afraid that we will be late with the evacuation. Fall is on its way, and it will not be possible to leave the town on anything but a train. The city of Taganrog is (1) an out-of-the-way blind alley, and (2) there can be movement in only one direction—toward Rostov. Such terrible congestion could result (as there is already), that much might be lost. I request that you resolve the question of the removal of children and their mothers from the cities of Taganrog and Rostov. Either way—whether the enemy advances or not—it will have to be done, the question is only when.[87]

The only immediate response to the request of the obkom secretary appears to have been an order to *cease* evacuations *to* Rostov oblast. The requested authorization for evacuations *from* the region came over a month later, in an Evacuation Council decree dated October 9 sanctioning the evacuation of thirty thousand women and children from Taganrog and thirty thousand from Rostov.[88] Taganrog was occupied shortly thereafter.

---

[86] GARF, f. 6822, op. 1, d. 354, l. 121.
[87] Ibid., d. 508, ll. 34–35.
[88] GARF, f. A-259, op. 40, d. 3070, ll. 1, 4.

Advance preparation of the kind proposed by the Rostov obkom secretary was inconsistent with key aspects of the Kremlin's approach to the war. With the exception of Moscow, Leningrad, and a handful of other cities, evacuations were routinely initiated only in conditions of a direct threat of occupation. Thus in Briansk, located southwest of Moscow, the evacuation of civilians was initiated on October 6, 1941, and the city was occupied on October 9. When German Army Group South once again threatened Rostov, moreover, in July 1942, women and children were evacuated on July 18, only four days before German forces reached the outskirts of the city. The late date of evacuations was a product not only of a lack of knowledge, but of a reticence to authorize evacuations in the interests of stemming panic and hardening resolve.

The specter of "panic" imposed real constraints on the realm of legitimate political action. "Panic" denoted at once both a state of mind and a category of action. Indeed, panic-mongering (*panikerstvo*) was a criminal offense. A directive issued to party and Soviet organizations in the frontline regions one week after the invasion instructed local and regional leaders to "organize a merciless struggle against all disorganizers of the rear, deserters, panic-mongers, and rumormongers" and to "hand over, without respect of persons, all those who, by their panic and cowardice, hinder defense work."[89] Panic thus functioned as a political construct as well as a psychological phenomenon.

. In a situation in which "rumors about the approach of German troops" were cast as "panicky," "aimed at introducing disorder amid the population," it became risky even to suggest that a particular region was in danger.[90] Indeed, there was a marked reluctance among military and civilian authorities alike to admit or even countenance the possibility of further retreat or surrender. This, at least, was the analysis offered by the secretary of the Latvian Central Committee, who claimed that it would have been possible to evacuate twenty to thirty thousand civilians instead of the five thousand actually evacuated had the "headquarters of the Baltic Special Military District" not "made calming statements until the last minute and misinformed us about the real situation on the front."[91] The choice of words is revealing. According to the Central Committee, the army was not itself misinformed about developments on the front but chose to withhold crucial information in the interests of "calming" civilian authorities and, presumably, forestalling panic. Any action predicated on a future retreat could potentially be construed as panic. In this climate, it is not surprising to learn that local authorities in the Brest-Litovsk region, according to the testimony of railway authorities there,

---

[89] V. A. Zolotarev et al., *Velikaia Otechestvennaia voina, 1941–1945: surovye ispytaniia* (Moscow: Nauka, 1998), 500–501.

[90] This is from an NKGB (state security organs) directive issued on June 26, 1941. See Iampol'skii et al., *Organy*, vol. 2, bk. 1, 86.

[91] "Iz istorii Velikoi Otechestvennoi voiny," 212.

forbade evacuation, for they "regarded raising the question of evacuation as the creation of panic, as a violation of state discipline."[92]

Indeed, evacuation decisions were frequently subjected to criticism on precisely these grounds. The prosecutor of the Rechitsa region, in western Belorussia, reported that he "doubted the correctness of [the evacuation] order [for Rechitsa], as it was not yet necessary." He concluded that "this invention of evacuation [*vydumka s evakuatsiei*] introduced great panic and was evidently undertaken with this objective by hostile elements."[93] An order to evacuate the city of Rostov in mid-October, issued by the North Caucasus Military Soviet only shortly after the Evacuation Council had initiated the civilian evacuation there, was likewise criticized for being issued "without sober calculation of the situation." Although not attributed to "hostile elements," it was nonetheless denounced as a "crude mistake," even though the city was subsequently occupied by German forces, albeit only for a week.[94] In Smolensk oblast, the prosecutor criticized local authorities for authorizing the evacuation of women and children, viewing the order as a manifestation of panic. Although the charge was later dismissed, the fact that it was leveled in the first place is nonetheless telling.[95] An evacuation order in the Moldovan Republic met with a similar response.[96]

Even the evacuation of those categories of the population specifically targeted by the Evacuation Council was sometimes subjected to criticism. A military prosecutor in Vitebsk was sharply critical of the evacuation of the wives of oblast soviet, party, and NKVD officials, whose departure, although forbidden by their workplaces, had "allegedly been authorized by the Central Committee of Belorussia."[97] Clearly, the prosecutor was skeptical that directives had indeed been issued by the Belorussian Central Committee, although such directives would have been entirely consistent with official evacuation policy. Authorities from the town of Elna, several hundred kilometers east of Minsk, displayed a similar disdain for a similarly defensible decision. In a letter to the Kremlin, they reported with evident disgust that "[t]he first bombs had barely fallen on Minsk before the wives of the commanding staff . . . were evacuated to Elna."[98]

The repeated critiques point to a crucial tension in the Soviet approach to evacuation. The most important directive dispatched to party and Soviet organizations across the front lines in the wake of the invasion, issued on

[92] G. A. Kumanev and Iu. A. Poliakov, "Voina i zheleznodorozhnyi transport SSSR, 1941–1945," in *Bor'ba narodov protiv fashizma i agressii* (Moscow: Nauka, 1988), 77.

[93] RGASPI, f. 17, op. 122, d. 10, l. 15.

[94] Ibid., op. 88, d. 79, l. 26.

[95] Vadim Dubson, "On the Problem of the Evacuation of Soviet Jews in 1941 (New Archival Sources)," *Jews in Eastern Europe* 3, no. 40 (1999): 37–56.

[96] Party authorities launched an investigation "into the correctness of the evacuation of the city of Soroki" within weeks of the invasion. RGASPI, f. 17, op. 22, d. 1717, l. 22.

[97] Bukov, "Ne tol'ko panika," 118.

[98] RGASPI, f. 17, op. 122, d. 10, l. 11.

June 29 and reprinted in *Pravda*, did not contain a word about the evacuation of the population. Instead, local authorities were enjoined to remain in place, to conduct a vigorous struggle against panic-mongers, and "to defend every inch of Soviet land, to fight to the last drop of blood for our cities and villages." Tellingly, the word "evacuation" is absent from the text. The only instructions regarding the removal of goods are set forth in a section on measures to be taken "during the forced retreat of Red Army units." Finally, the measures themselves, essentially a restatement of the policy of scorched earth, stipulate the removal of heavy metals, grain, and fuel, and make no mention of either the "population" or even "men of serving age."[99]

This directive points to a larger, fundamental ambivalence with regard to evacuation, one that emanated from the Kremlin but was manifest at all levels of authority, both military and civilian. The injunction to "fight to the last drop of blood" was in many ways incompatible with a policy of civilian evacuation. This was certainly the conclusion drawn by authorities in Elna, who concluded their letter to the Kremlin with the assertion that the "task before us is not evacuation but a rapid counteroffensive, for we don't have the right to evacuate ourselves."[100] To be sure, the merits of a civilian evacuation had been a matter of debate since the Soviet state began preparations for war. None other than the General Staff had argued as recently as 1937 that the "major political and industrial centers" on the front lines "should not be evacuated," but should "serve as moral buttresses for our troops."[101] While the creation of the Evacuation Council seemed to put the old debate to rest, the June 29 directive suggested that the issue was far from resolved. In a war that was conceived, from the outset, as a "people's war," all civilians were cast in the role of defenders of the motherland. Those not eligible for service in the army were conscripted into civilian defense units or dispatched to frontline regions to build trenches. Attuned to the spirit of official directives, the popular rumor mill came up with its own conclusions: in the suburbs of Leningrad it was rumored that "they are not letting people out of the city, that it is doomed to be a 'fortress and a bulwark of the people's spirit against the fascist aggressors,' that we will fight for it 'to the last breath' . . . that the population itself must defend this 'bulwark.' "[102]

While evacuations were ultimately authorized and carried out in Leningrad and elsewhere, the rumors were not completely without foundation. The notion of "spontaneous self-evacuation" made sense only insofar as evacuation itself was regarded as a regulated and restricted operation. As we have seen, moreover, Soviet authorities went to considerable lengths to

[99] The directive, issued jointly by Sovnarkom and the Central Committee, was also issued to the state security organs. See Iampol'skii et al., *Organy*, vol. 2, bk. 1, 122–23.

[100] RGASPI, f. 17, op. 122, d. 10, l. 11.

[101] GARF, f. 8418, op. 12, d. 470, l. 7.

[102] N. A. Lomagin, ed., *Neizvestnaia blokada (Dokumenty, prilozheniia)*, vol. 2 (St. Petersburg: Neva, 2002), 442.

keep people in place. "Leaving work," one Jewish woman later recalled, "was punishable under martial law . . . and we weren't released from our jobs."[103] Time and again, moreover, people who sought permission to depart were accused of "sowing panic."[104] The irony of Soviet evacuation policy was that the same rationale underpinning restrictions on mass movement threatened to destabilize the entire operation. In the name of forestalling panic, not only "spontaneous self-evacuation" was curtailed but authorized evacuations as well. How else to explain the repeated critiques of the evacuation of the very categories of people who were designated for departure by the Evacuation Council?

Ultimately, as the rumors from Leningrad suggest, the official commitment to evacuation was undercut by its perceived symbolic cost—a belief by authorities at all levels that it would undermine the will to fight. In this vein, evacuation efforts were consciously curtailed. As Stalin explained in a directive to Khrushchev several weeks into the war, extending the zone of scorched earth and evacuation would "demoralize the population, elicit dissatisfaction with Soviet power, disorganize the rear of the Red Army, and create a mood within the army and among the population of compulsory withdrawal instead of determination to repulse the enemy." As a result, he halved the projected territory from which scorched earth and evacuation would be carried out to within 75 kilometers [46.6 miles] from the front and decreed that the operation should be initiated "only in the case of the retreat of the army."[105] A similar note was sounded from the battlefield. For example, a senior battalion commander informed Mekhlis, the head of the army's political division, that the evacuations were interfering with the work of the army. "Local organs of power evacuate material valuables before the arrival of the Germans. They do not explain the reasons for the evacuation. As a result, the population believes that the settlements will undoubtedly be surrendered to the Germans and therefore the population does not conduct an organized struggle against the German invaders, considering it useless."[106] Evacuation, on this account, fed defeatism; it seemed to belie the assertions that Kiev, Leningrad, or, most famously, Stalingrad, "will not be surrendered to the enemy."

The tendency to conflate evacuation with retreat and to see both as a form of defeatism would have particularly tragic consequences in August

---

[103] Quoted in Mordechai Altshuler, "Escape and Evacuation of Soviet Jews at the Time of the Nazi Invasion: Policies and Realities," in *The Holocaust in the Soviet Union: Studies and Sources on the Destruction of the Jews in the Nazi-Occupied Territories of the USSR, 1941–1945*, ed. Lucjan Dobroszycki and Jeffrey S. Gurock (Armonk, N.Y.: M. E. Sharpe, 1993), 94.

[104] See, for example, the account in Dov Levin, *The Lesser of Two Evils: Eastern European Jewry under Soviet Rule (1939–41)*, trans. Naftali Greenwood (Philadelphia: Jewish Publication Society, 1995), 283.

[105] "Iz istorii Velikoi Otechestvennoi voiny," 207.

[106] RGASPI, f. 17, op. 122, d. 10, l. 64.

1942 in Stalingrad, where, under the rallying cry of "not one step back," Stalin refused to authorize the city's evacuation until it was too late. As the head of the Stalingrad Committee of Defense later put it, the "issue of evacuating [the inhabitants of Stalingrad] was not resolved, for 'Stalingrad will not be surrendered to the enemy.' "[107] Although livestock were evacuated from the region as early as mid-July, the first evacuation of the city's population was authorized only on August 15, and even this was only partial. It approved the evacuation of some twenty-five thousand nonworking women and children, a mere fraction of the city's population, which was estimated at around four hundred thousand in mid-July.[108] By the time an additional evacuation order, also limited to women and children, was issued on August 24, the city was already under heavy attack.[109] A report on the work of an evacuation hospital during this period, penned in early October 1942, gives a sense of what conditions were like: "To speak about evacuation in this period it is essential to underline that it took place in exceptionally difficult conditions. The whole city was enveloped with fumes and constituted a colossal blazing bonfire; in places the asphalt burned. . . . The fascists bombed the river crossings and the embankment with particular ferocity. . . . On August 24 by six P.M. the whole bank was enveloped in a sea of fire, the piers, warehouses, ferries, barges, and moors all burned." The evacuations were carried out with great loss of life. To give but one example, of some 1,200 civilians leaving the burning city on the night of August 24, 1942, aboard the ship *Joseph Stalin*, only 150 survived the crossing.[110]

• • •

Across the front lines, evacuations were carried out in extraordinarily difficult conditions. Although circumstances varied from one place to another, and success rates depended at least in part on date of occupation, in many ways there was no marked progress in the handling of evacuations as the war progressed. The way the evacuation transpired in Kalinin, in mid-October 1941, differed little from what happened in countless other regions in the initial weeks of the war. In a sense, this is not surprising. Each case was handled by local authorities who confronted the problem of evacuation

---

[107] A. S. Chuianov, "V trudnye dni," in *Eshelony idut na Vostok*, 238.

[108] TsDNIVO, f. 113, op. 12, d. 62, l. 344. The prewar population of the city was 325,000, but the population rose substantially in the first year of the war, as the city was one of the principal reception sites for evacuees.

[109] The resolution "On the Evacuation of Women and Children to the Left Bank of the Volga" was issued by the Stalingrad City Soviet "in conjunction with the difficulties that have been created in supplying the population with food." The order did not require the authorization of the Evacuation Council as the evacuation was to take place to other regions within the oblast. TsDNIVO, f. 171, op. 1, d. 6, l. 30.

[110] TsDNIVO, f. 113, op. 12, d. 83, l. 19. On the same evening, four hundred people died in a similar manner crossing the Volga on a sanitary ferry carrying seven hundred patients.

and the specter of occupation for the first time and under similar political constraints.

It is easy to criticize the legions of regional officials who succumbed to "panic" and "fled." Authorities, however, found themselves in a difficult position. With only limited access to information about developments on the front, they were almost invariably captive to rumor. They were enjoined, moreover, to remain in place "until the retreat of Red Army units," at the same time as they were assured priority in the evacuation process for both themselves and their families. Those who left too early, or fled, were expelled from the party and sometimes from their jobs. Those who "willfully remained" in enemy territory, by turn, were subject to grueling interrogations in the wake of the reconquest. The middle ground, the realm of legitimate political action, was narrow indeed.

Authorities were not the only ones confronted with difficult decisions in the face of the evacuation. The mass phenomenon of "self-evacuation" was also the product of choices. As the flight of Soviet citizens suggests, the evacuation was never the controlled process conceived by officials on the Evacuation Council. Even the Soviet state proved unable to completely regulate the process of displacement. Ultimately, the evacuation was shaped not only by the party and state authorities who oversaw it but by the countless individual decisions made by individual Soviet citizens.

4

POPULAR RESPONSES

Reflecting on her experiences during the war, Irina Ehrenburg observed: "The perspective of evacuation revealed the division in the population. Many civilians were not at all determined to depart. To the contrary, they were waiting for the Germans, were persuaded that the invaders would save the country."[1] Lydia Osipova, one of Ehrenburg's contemporaries, echoed her assessment. In a diary entry of mid-August 1941, Osipova, a resident of one of Leningrad's suburbs, recorded that the "boundary between 'defeatists' and 'patriots' has taken shape with unusual precision. The patriots strive to evacuate themselves as quickly as possible, while the others, like us, attempt by all means possible to hide from the evacuation."[2] The accounts of these two women, who stood on opposite sides of the divide, treat the evacuation in strikingly similar terms: the evacuation exposed divisions and sharpened boundaries. In reality, the boundaries were substantially less sharp than either Ehrenburg or Osipova imagined. Whereas some saw evacuation as an act of patriotism, others perceived it as a form of flight. Few, however, did not ascribe some meaning to the process. The evacuation compelled individual Soviet citizens to reflect on their place in the polity and their role in the war. In the process of evacuation, they attempted to come to terms with their loyalties and duties not only as citizens but also as working people and as family members—husbands and wives, parents and children.

Reactions to evacuation constitute an important chapter in the history of popular responses to the war. Scholarship on this topic, mimicking the questions posed by wartime intelligence agencies, has generally focused on the

---

[1] Irina Ehrenbourg, "Entretien avec Irina Ehrenbourg," interview by Catherine Gousseff in *Moscou, 1918–1941: de l'homme nouveau au bonheur solitaire*, ed. Catherine Gousseff (Paris: Éditions Autrement, 1993), 315.
[2] Diary of L. Osipova, in *Neizvestnaia blokada (Dokumenty, prilozheniia)*, ed. N. A. Lomagin, vol. 2 (St. Petersburg: Neva, 2002), 443, entry of August 17, 1941.

level of support for the regime.[3] By narrowing the field of inquiry to the question of resistance and support, it has tended to present a one-sided picture of Soviet civilians at war. At the same time, more general scholarship on the worldview, values, and attitudes of Soviet citizens typically deals with the 1930s only, terminating abruptly before the war.[4] Yet, as Amir Weiner has pointed out, the war was a "watershed" in individual autobiographies. It "forever divided Soviet history and life into two distinct eras."[5] The war created new categories of exclusion from the body politic at the same time as it opened up new avenues of integration. Like the revolution more broadly, it demanded the active participation of each and every citizen.

Individual responses to the moment of decision open a window onto the moral universe of Soviet citizens during the first year of the war. Although material concerns were a constant preoccupation, the decision to stay or to go was rarely a simple calculus of survival. Notions of duty and loyalty shaped popular responses to the war and the evacuation and informed the way in which the dilemma—to stay or to go—was articulated and understood.

Evacuation was a moment not only of individual reflection but of popular protest. Soviet citizens openly defied state directives on evacuation and, on several occasions, even took to the streets. The terms of popular protest reveal the prevailing conceptions of evacuation. Evacuation was alternately viewed as a rescue operation and a form of expulsion. It could be cast as an act of cowardice and panic, in some cases even of treachery. In referring to the evacuation of others, it was frequently presented as a story of privilege and nepotism. These perceptions could be subversive: evacuation was perceived as abandonment and the abdication of responsibility, as a marker not only of enemy conquest but of breakdown from within.

Evacuation gave rise to resentment, directed against the world of officialdom and against Jews, who were widely perceived to have taken flight en masse. This perception contributed to the tendency to see Jews as alien to the Soviet body politic, thus feeding the flames of popular antisemitism.

[3] John Barber, "Popular Reactions in Moscow to the German Invasion of June 22, 1941," *Soviet Union/Union soviétique* 18 (1991): 5–18; Richard Bidlack, "The Political Mood in Leningrad during the First Year of the Soviet-German War," *Russian Review* 59, no. 1 (2000): 96–113; M. M. Gorinov, "Muscovites' Moods, 22 June 1941 to May 1942," in *The People's War: Responses to World War II in the Soviet Union*, ed. Robert W. Thurston and Bernd Bonwetsch (Urbana: University of Illinois Press, 2000), 108–34.

[4] For a sample of such literature, representing different approaches, see Sarah Davies, *Popular Opinion in Stalin's Russia: Terror, Propaganda, and Dissent, 1934–1941* (Cambridge: Cambridge University Press, 1997); Jochen Hellbeck, *Revolution on My Mind: Writing a Diary under Stalin* (Cambridge, Mass.: Harvard University Press, 2006); Stephen Kotkin, *Magnetic Mountain: Stalinism as a Civilization* (Berkeley: University of California Press, 1995); Lynne Viola, ed., *Contending with Stalinism: Soviet Power and Popular Resistance in the 1930s* (Ithaca, N.Y.: Cornell University Press, 2002).

[5] Amir Weiner, *Making Sense of War: The Second World War and the Fate of the Bolshevik Revolution* (Princeton, N.J: Princeton University Press, 2001), 7, 366.

More broadly, the war simultaneously shook the population's confidence in Soviet power and became a powerful source of integration into the polity, shoring up support for the regime.

"TO GO OR NOT TO GO"

On August 20, 1941, Maria Konopleva was approached by a former colleague at the Hermitage Museum in Leningrad with an offer to join some of the museum's staff in evacuation in Sverdlovsk. In her diary, she recorded her reaction: "For a long time I couldn't fall asleep, considering which decision to take—to go or to remain?"[6] The writer Emma Gershtein, faced with the prospect of evacuation from Moscow, passed a similar night of anxious indecision. She remembers the eve of her attempted (and failed) evacuation as one of the most anguished of her life: evacuation meant abandoning her parents.[7] For Konopleva and Gershtein, the period of indecision lasted one night. For others, it was much more extended. The diary of the literary critic Leonid Timofeev records over three months of oscillation: on as many as six different occasions between July and mid-October 1941, he was confronted with a decision—to stay or to go. Twice he decided to depart, only to change his mind.[8] Alexander Boldyrev, a resident of Leningrad, was more decisive— on February 11, 1942, he recorded in his diary that he was "as before, firm in my position—'not to go.' "[9]

As these cases suggest, evacuation confronted many Soviet citizens with a choice, even if it sometimes proved illusory. Individuals were compelled to take a position on what quickly emerged as one of the most pressing issues of the day. As Timofeev observed in late July, "people talk, in the main, about evacuation."[10] According to the Leningrad artist Ostroumova-Lebedeva, "everyone is worried by one and the same question: should we go?"[11] In bread lines, on the factory floor, and late at night around kitchen tables, the dilemma was discussed: "To go or not to go." It was debated, according to Emma Gershtein, "in every house, in every family."[12] It was, in Olga Friedenberg's words,

[6] M. S. Konopleva, "V blokirovannom Leningrade (1941–1942): zametki," OR RNB, f. 368, op. 1, d. 1, l. 44, entry of August 20, 1941.

[7] Emma Gershtein, *Memuary* (Moscow: Zakharov, 2002), 417.

[8] L. I. Timofeev, "Dnevnik voennykh let," *Znamia*, no. 6 (2002): 141, 143, 150, 154, 156, 157, entries of July 14 and 23, September 22, October 8, 12, and 13, 1941.

[9] Aleksandr Nikolaevich Boldyrev, *Osadnaia zapis': blokadnyi dnevnik*, ed. V. S Garbuzova and I. M. Steblin-Kamenskii (St. Petersburg: Evropeiskii dom, Evropeiskii universitet v Sankt-Peterburge, 1998), 56, entry of February 11, 1942.

[10] Timofeev, "Dnevnik voennykh let," 143, entry of July 23, 1941.

[11] A. P. Ostroumova-Lebedeva, *Avtobiograficheskie zapiski*, ed. N. L. Priimak (Moscow: Tsentrpoligraf, 2003), 253, diary entry of August 16, 1941.

[12] Gershtein, *Memuary*, 414.

"an agonizing problem!"[13] The poet Marina Tsvetaeva, in Moscow during the bombardment of the city, reportedly "asked everyone one and the same question: to go or not to go? Is it necessary to evacuate, or not? . . . This became an idée fixe for her, or rather," reflected Maria Belkina, "we were all afflicted at this time with this 'idée fixe'!"[14] It was the burning question of the day, posed in conversations, diaries, and correspondence. "Are you planning to go anywhere?" Elena Dobychina, a resident of Leningrad, inquired of her sister in Moscow in a letter of late July 1941. "After an agonizing period of thought and doubts, I decided to remain here."[15]

The choice was clearly seen as momentous. Alexander Boldyrev recorded the day he made public his decision to remain in the besieged city of Leningrad as a "historic day—I announced to the Leningrad State University my full refusal to evacuate." The significance of the deliberations stemmed from the commonly held conviction that, as Boldyrev put it in his diary, "it is terrible to go. It is also terrible to remain."[16] Only in the conditions of starvation that prevailed in Leningrad during the first winter of the blockade was evacuation displaced from the realm of decision and debate to that of fantasy. It was, in young Yuri Riabinkin's words, a "sweet dream." In the final diary entries before his untimely death, he wrote repeatedly of the evacuation as a longed-for salvation. "If only we could be given an evacuation, now!" he lamented. A few lines further down, he issues a plea to God: "save me, give me an evacuation, save all three of us, Mama, Ira, and me!"[17]

Although some struggled with the dilemma alone, evacuation was frequently decided on collectively. According to the young Dima Afanasiev, evacuation was a matter of debate for the entire family.[18] Emma Gershtein, in her memoirs, recounts how a resident of her building conferred with family, neighbors, and friends to debate the weighty question.[19] Dmitrii Kargin and his wife convened a "family council."[20] In many cases, house managers and acquaintances joined the fray, as did family members from afar, dispatching letters to offer their advice. "Are you going anywhere?" Nikolai Chuk-

---

[13] Letter of July 12, 1941, in *The Correspondence of Boris Pasternak and Olga Friedenberg*, ed. Elliott Mossman, trans. Margaret Wettlin (New York: Harcourt Brace Jovanovich, 1982), 206.

[14] Maria Belkina, *Skreshchenie sudeb*, 2d ed. (Moscow: Blagovest Rudomino, 1992), 288.

[15] OR RGB, f. 420, op. 12, d. 1, l. 8.

[16] Boldyrev, *Osadnaia zapis'*, 61, 58.

[17] Diary of Iu. Riabinkin, in *Blokadnaia kniga*, ed. Ales Adamovich and Daniil Aleksandrovich Granin (Leningrad: Lenizdat, 1989), 387, 443, entries of November 29, 1941 and January 4, 1942.

[18] Diary of D. Afanas'ev, in *Vechnye deti blokady: dokumental'nye ocherki*, ed. Tamara Staleva (Moscow, 1995), 15.

[19] Gershtein, *Memuary*, 415.

[20] D. I. Kargin, *Velikoe i tragicheskoe: Leningrad, 1941–1942* (St. Petersburg: Nauka, 2000), 144.

ovskii wrote his father in mid-October. "In my opinion, you should go [*vam nado ekhat'*]."[21]

Not surprisingly, gatherings to discuss the evacuation were frequently the scenes of arguments. Valentina Chemberdzhi later wrote: "I remember—of course, very dimly—how arguments broke out in the family: Grandma Varia and her son Tasia didn't want to go and didn't go. They were later shot by the Germans. Aunt Lialia with her daughter Masha, Mama and I, and Aunt Tania—we all quickly departed for Moscow."[22] Evacuation was likewise a source of tension between Olga Boltianskaia and her husband. As she recalled in her diary some weeks later, "Grisha hinted that we [she and her son] should go to Tashkent. I turned on him: 'Do you want to get rid of us?' "[23] In the home of Elena Kochina, evacuation was the cause of her and her husband's "first quarrel." Kochina was to be evacuated with her institute, but her husband, who was working in Leningrad, did not, in her words, "want me to leave. We argued. Offensive and unfair words flew back and forth between us." Even when they made up, a few hours later, "something continued to stand between us. We were no longer who we had been before the quarrel, and no longer who we had been before the war."[24]

A CALCULUS OF SURVIVAL

In late September 1941, Leonid Timofeev reflected in his diary: "Which of us will be better off, those who depart or those who remain, is difficult to say." Timofeev perceived the dilemma as a calculus of survival—the difficulties of the decision inhered in weighing the respective risks. On October 13, 1941, he noted in his diary, "now I must either remain, risking my head, or subject myself to all the misfortunes of evacuation."[25]

The risks of remaining were, first, subjection to bombardment. It is surely no coincidence that in Moscow the wave of departures from the city intensified in the wake of the first aerial attacks in late July 1941. As Olga Boltianskaia observed, "[a]fter the first bombardments the flight from Moscow began."[26] Although the casualties of the air war over Moscow were modest by the standards of the time, the repeated attacks took their toll on peoples'

[21] Letter of October 15, 1941, in Nikolai Chukovskii, *O tom, shto videl*, ed. E. N. Nikitina (Moscow: Molodaia gvardiia, 2005), 593.

[22] Valentina Chemberdzhi, "Nash dom," *Druzhba narodov*, no. 3 (2000): 170.

[23] Diary of O. A. Boltianskaia, in RGALI, f. 2057, op. 2, d. 29, l. 87, entry of August 4, 1941.

[24] Elena Kochina, *Blockade Diary*, trans. Samuel C. Ramer (Ann Arbor, Mich.: Ardis, 1990), 36.

[25] Timofeev, "Dnevnik voennykh let," 151, 156, entries of September 24 and October 13, 1941.

[26] Diary of O. A. Boltianskaia, in RGALI, f. 2057, op. 2, d. 29, l. 87, entry of August 4, 1941.

nerves.[27] Another Muscovite, Olga Grudtsova, described her paralyzing fear in the face of the repeated bombardment of the city in her memoirs:

"To leave! If only I could leave. At Mosfilm the film director Golub objects: 'Olga Moiseevna, you don't know what evacuation means, you don't know what it means not to live at home! I will never leave Moscow!' Oh, it's all the same to me, where to live and how to live, provided that there are no bombs and blackouts, which I do not have the strength to endure!"[28] In a similar vein, Marina Tsvetaeva was persuaded that "it was better to go to Tataria, to who knows what, than to remain in Moscow under bombardment."[29] When Tsvetaeva's son, Georgii Efron, found himself back in Moscow after his mother's suicide in evacuation, his decision to depart once more was likewise driven, at least in part, by fear of both bombardment and the suffering that would surely be inflicted on a city under siege.[30]

Remaining also raised the specter of subjection to enemy occupation. Saul Borovoi later wrote: "for some reason I was not afraid of dying under bombs. I was more worried by something else: should I leave or wait—wait for what?"[31] As subsequent events would attest, what awaited those who remained was a brutal occupation regime. Hitler waged a war of annihilation in the East. He sought to eradicate both Communists and Jews and to enslave the Slavic masses in newly founded German colonies. At the time, however, Soviet citizens were poorly apprised of Hitler's plans, and what occupation would entail was a matter of debate. Timofeev, for example, was altogether uncertain about what to expect of the Germans. On September 19, 1941, after hearing the news of the fall of Kiev, he recorded in his diary: "They say that the letters from refugees are very agitated and advise addressees in every way possible to flee from Moscow while there is still time. I don't know to what degree the theory of mass terror ascribed to the Germans is correct. They are, after all, interested in the attitudes [*raspolozhenie*] of the population." Later, on October 10, he wrote: "In general I don't see anything terrible with staying in a big city. Here the possibility of excesses is improbable. But that would be the case if I were a modest clerk. However, as I am, albeit in highly relative terms, a figure, they could treat me harshly."[32] As these reflections suggest, the terms of debate heightened

[27] See Rodric Braithwaite, *Moscow 1941: A City and Its People at War* (New York: Knopf, 2006), 185.

[28] Ol'ga Grudtsova, "Dovol'no, ia bol'she ne igraiu . . . : Povest' o moei zhizni," *Minuvshee* 19 (1996): 58.

[29] Georgii Efron, *Dnevniki (1940–1941 gody)*, vol. 1, ed. E. B. Korkina and V. K. Losskaia (Moscow: Vagrius, 2004), 481, entry of August 5, 1941.

[30] Georgii Efron, *Dnevniki (1941–1943 gody)*, vol. 2, ed. E. B. Korkina and V. K. Losskaia (Moscow: Vagrius, 2005), 44, entry of October 15, 1941.

[31] Saul Borovoi, *Vospominaniia* (Moscow: Evreiskii universitet v Moskve, 1993), 238.

[32] Timofeev, "Dnevnik voennykh let," 150, 156. Timofeev appears to have derived his image of the danger facing intellectuals from a draft of Ilya Ehrenburg's *The Fall of Paris* (ibid., 153, entry of October 8, 1941).

consciousness of the divisions within Soviet society and compelled people to evaluate their chances of survival in terms that were established, at least in part, by the invaders. This applied to no group more fully than the Soviet Union's Jewish population.

Soviet Jews were divided about the treatment they could expect under enemy occupation. Although antisemitism had been a long-standing and well-publicized component of the Nazi program, the shift from a policy of systematic discrimination to all-out genocide occurred only in the aftermath of the invasion. As a result, even the Soviet government failed to apprehend Hitler's murderous intentions until August 1941.[33] The picture Soviet authorities presented in the press, moreover, was notoriously incomplete. Although the Soviet press contained some information about German anti-semitism and the fate that awaited Jews in occupied territories, Soviet tales of German atrocities generally presented the victims in generic terms: atrocities were almost invariably committed against "peaceful Soviet citizens," and Jews were rarely singled out.[34] In some cases, reports of atrocities were explicitly modified to erase any mention of Jews.[35] The silence surrounding the specifically anti-Jewish measures of the occupying forces was motivated in part by a desire to combat German propaganda that sought to "Judaize" the Bolshevik regime. It was also the product of an attempt to quell defeatism among the population at large.[36] None other than Ilya Ehrenburg, a Soviet Jewish writer and prominent wartime propagandist, proposed that "in my opinion, it would be good to have an article by a well-known Russian (Sholokhov or Tolstoy) about the Jews, unmasking the fiction that Hitler's wrath is directed only against the Jews."[37] The logic underpinning the Soviet denial of the specificity of Jewish suffering is evident in the following case, reported by the party secretary of Moscow's Red Seamstress factory in late September 1941: "in discussions we explain that Hitler does not only destroy Communists and Jews, he wants to destroy all humanity, to destroy our construction, to strangle the whole people."[38]

As a result of this policy, some among the Soviet Union's Jewish population had little inkling of what lay in store. Sophia Abidor, a young Jewish woman from Odessa, was surprised when a fellow student, a Russian, urged her to leave the city as soon as possible. When she asked him why he didn't

[33] See Il'ia Al'tman, *Zhertvy nenavisti: anatomiia kholokosta* (Moscow: Sovershenno sekretno, 2002), 387.

[34] See Mordechai Altshuler, "Escape and Evacuation of Soviet Jews at the Time of the Nazi Invasion: Policies and Realities," in *The Holocaust in the Soviet Union: Studies and Sources on the Destruction of the Jews in the Nazi-Occupied Territories of the USSR, 1941–1945*, ed. Lucjan Dobroszycki and Jeffrey S. Gurock (Armonk, N.Y: M. E. Sharpe, 1993), 83–91.

[35] See G. B. Kostyrchenko, *Tainaia politika Stalina: Vlast' i antisemitizm* (Moscow: Mezhdunarodnye otnosheniia, 2001), 229.

[36] For a similar interpretation, see Al'tman, *Zhertvy nenavisti*, 387.

[37] Il'ia Erenburg, *Na tsokole istorii . . . Pis'ma, 1931–1967*, ed. B. Ia. Frezinskii (Moscow: Agraf, 2004), 291.

[38] RGASPI, f. 17, op. 22, d. 1811, l. 77.

prepare to leave as well, he replied, "I'm Russian—they won't touch me."[39] Although few could imagine precisely what lay in store, the sense that Jews would be singled out by the invaders was widespread, as the advice of Abidor's classmate attests. The Soviet press, after all, was only one source of information. Just as important was the always active rumor mill.

Rumor assumed a privileged place among the range of information networks in the wake of the invasion, growing in amplitude and, arguably, in importance. "We don't know anything," noted Leningrad resident Ostroumova-Lebedeva in her diary. "Various rumors are circulating. You can't believe everything, but there are no official reports."[40] Workers in the Stalin automobile factory in Moscow similarly reported: "since fascist aircraft started bombing Moscow, official discussions [in the shop] have stopped. We don't have a radio. We ... live only by rumors [*fakticheski zhivem odnimi slukhami*]."[41]

The silence of official information networks such as the radio and the press on a range of key questions gave rumor free rein. In addition, the war fostered the growth of spaces that were conducive to the spread of rumor. Foremost among these were the food lines that formed in the wake of the invasion. As a report from Zhitomir noted, "since the beginning of the war in Zhitomir, as in other cities, there are long lines for bread, flour, groats, and so on."[42] The role of lines in the spread of rumor was noted by a variety of people in the initial weeks of the war. An anonymous letter to Zhdanov from an inhabitant of Leningrad regarded the lines for foodstuffs as one of the central problems facing the city: "I think that the police should simply chase away the lines [*goniat ocheredi*], for as it is, a state of total panic is developing; in lines one can hear all sorts of provocation."[43]

Rumors about life under enemy occupation drew on information about enemy forces spread by letters from the front, soldiers on leave or en route to new postings, and refugees from regions already occupied by German forces. They were nourished, moreover, by a powerful current of prewar defeatist rumor, which projected the beginning of a better life with a Soviet defeat at German hands.[44] One of the leitmotifs of rumor was that the Germans targeted only Jews and Communists. The notion that Hitler "is after only Jews and Communists" was a mainstay of defeatist rumor in the im-

---

[39] Sophia Abidor, interview by Ella Levitskaya, April 2003, in *Jewish Witness to a European Century*. Russian transcript provided by Centropa.org.

[40] Quoted in N. A. Lomagin, *Neizvestnaia blokada (Dokumenty, prilozheniia)*, vol. 1 (St. Petersburg: Neva, 2002), 220.

[41] RGASPI, f. 17, op. 88, d. 69, l. 12.

[42] V. P. Iampol'skii et al., *Organy gosudarstvennoi bezopasnosti v Velikoi Otechestvennoi voine*, vol. 2, bk. 1 (Moscow: Rus', 2000), 95.

[43] Lomagin, *Neizvestnaia blokada*, vol. 1, 217.

[44] On prewar defeatist rumor, see Nicolas Werth, "Rumeurs défaitistes et apocalyptiques dans l'URSS des années 1920 et 1930," *Vingtième siècle* 71 (July–September 2001): 25–35.

mediate prewar period.[45] Such rumors continued well into 1941 and possibly 1942, bolstered by German propaganda pamphlets that claimed "we are fighting not the Russian people but Jews and Communists." According to a recent article on popular sentiment in Leningrad during the first year of the war, "it was widely presumed that if the city fell, the occupiers would liquidate Jews and party personnel, but opinions were divided over what would happen to the rest of the population."[46] Similar attitudes were expressed in Moscow. In early July, a worker in a garment factory, a party member no less, told a group of workers that "Hitler won't do anything to the Russians; he will kill only the Jews."[47]

Given the widespread currency of the rumors, one would think that Soviet Jews would have felt a strong compulsion to depart. Many, however, chose to remain. In part, their decision stemmed from an incapacity to imagine the true extent of Nazi policy. Lydia Osipova was aware of Hitler's antisemitism but was convinced that "Hitler is not the beast that our propaganda paints . . . and he does not kill all the Jews to a person, but there will probably be some kind of limits on them, and that is disagreeable." Among her Jewish friends, some chose to depart, but others remained: "many Jews say: 'Why should we go off somewhere? Well, maybe we will be sent for some time to a camp, but then we'll be released. It won't be worse than now."[48] Emma Gershtein later recalled how she reassured herself that her parents, both Jews, would survive: "They were left to the care of my sister with her husband and children. Her husband was Russian, a native of Vologda. I repeat, we were still naïve, thinking that this relationship would help my Jewish family survive under the Nazis."[49]

Disbelief stemmed not only from a failure of imagination (altogether understandable, given the circumstances) but from memory. Evgenia Galina, a young Jewish girl living in Zhitomyr when the war broke out, recalled that her grandfather "refused to go with us. He said that he had seen the Germans during World War I and didn't think they could do Jews any harm."[50] Deborah Averbukh recounted a similar story: "My father said we didn't have to evacuate because the Germans were highly civilized people; he remembered them from the occupation in 1918."[51] The notion that the Germans were civilized appears to have been fairly widespread among the

[45] Ibid., 34.

[46] Bidlack, "The Political Mood in Leningrad," 101.

[47] P. G. Grigor'ev, ed., "Moskva voennaia. 1941 god . . . (novye istochniki iz sekretnykh arkhivnykh fondov)," *Istoriia SSSR*, no. 6 (1991): 111.

[48] Diary of L. Osipova, in Lomagin, *Neizvestnaia blokada*, vol. 2, 443.

[49] Gershtein, *Memuary*, 417.

[50] Averbukh notes that one month later, having realized that there was a difference between the Germans her grandfather had encountered during World War I and the Nazis, he, too, departed and joined them in evacuation. Deborah Averbukh, interview by Ella Orlikova, December 2001, in *Jewish Witness to a European Century* (www.centropa.org).

[51] Ibid.

older generation. Alexander Kovarskii writes that his grandfather, Benjamin Katz, decided not to leave his native village: "'you members of the Komsomol need to go, but the Germans won't do anything bad to me. I know them, I was a prisoner during World War I. Germany is a cultured, civilized country.' These were his parting words."[52] Positive interactions with Germans also shaped the actions of a woman in Novorossiisk whose son-in-law was German. Her granddaughter later described how, despite the rumors that were then circulating about the German treatment of the Jewish population in occupied territories: "Grandma didn't believe in the atrocities of the Germans; she considered it Soviet propaganda. She had no trust in the Soviets."[53]

As the previous example suggests, evaluations of the risks were informed by attitudes toward Soviet power as well as assessments of the Germans. Jews and non-Jews alike reacted with skepticism to what they read in the paper about the atrocities committed by the invaders. In Moscow at the Red Rosa industrial complex a worker reportedly "did not believe the reports in Soviet papers about the Germans' brutal treatment of workers. He says that under Hitler we will work just as we work now."[54] In another factory, a worker reportedly claimed that "everything printed in the announcements of the Soviet Information Bureau is simply nonsense. The announcements aren't even worth talking about; it's all lies, there's no reason to believe the papers. . . . The fascists aren't going to shoot women and children."[55]

Images of occupation, however, were only one part of the equation. Saul Borovoi recalled how a fellow Jew from Odessa advised him: "don't go anywhere—under the Germans it will be very, very bad for us; we will live in degradation, suffering, and so forth. But we will have a chance of surviving. To become a refugee—this means certain death."[56] As a calculus of survival, the evacuation dilemma compelled people to evaluate both the risks of remaining and the dangers of departure. Many were afraid of what lay ahead. Departure was regarded, in the words of Ksenia Polzikova-Rubets, as a "leap into the unknown."[57] The teenage boy Dima Afanasiev in the town of Gatchina near Leningrad recorded his family's deliberations in his diary. His mother, worried by the sudden departure of other families, decided: "we need to gather our things and go to the rear. Grandma and Ania said that without signing up with anyone, we couldn't just go to an unknown destination."[58] A similar note was sounded by the classicist Olga Friedenberg in

[52] Aleksandr Kovarskii, "Detstvo na ulitse chempiona," *Zhurnal Mishpokha*, no. 14 (2004) (www.mishpoha.org/nomer14/a18.htm).

[53] Greta Ionkis, *Maalot* (St. Petersburg: Aleteiia, 2004), 99.

[54] M. M. Gorinov, V. N. Parkhachev, and A. N. Ponomarev, eds., *Moskva prifrontovaia, 1941–1942: Arkhivnye dokumenty i materialy* (Moscow: Mosgorarkhiv, 2001), 139.

[55] Grigor'ev, "Moskva voennaia," 116.

[56] Borovoi, *Vospominaniia*, 240.

[57] Kseniia Vladimirovna Polzikova-Rubets, *Dnevnik uchitelia blokadnoi shkoly* (St. Petersburg: Tema, 2000), 51, entry of March 19, 1942.

[58] Staleva, *Vechnye deti blokady*, 15.

a letter to her cousin Boris Pasternak. "The day before yesterday we underwent a serious crisis when the question arose as to whether we should leave Leningrad with the university or whether I should resign my post. The problem was not, of course, one of work, but of setting out for nowhere." As Friedenberg wrote in her diary:

> We were terrified by the thought of having to leave Leningrad. After the initial tragic and disorganized evacuation of children alone, parents no longer wished either to leave the city themselves or give up children who had not yet been taken away. Everybody wanted desperately to stay where he was. Neither the intelligentsia nor the broad masses believed in the good things to be found in faraway places, and the very thought of being transported in lice-infested freight cars struck terror in their hearts.[59]

Alexander Boldyrev expressed similar doubts. "What awaits there? Is it better than here? And what if it's worse? How can one make sense of anything in this dark chaos of questions?"[60]

People's conceptions of life in evacuation were informed by the letters they received from those who had already departed and by rumor, that all-important source of information during the war. Maria Konopleva noted in her diary in August 1941:

> in general people leave unwillingly. Everyone is afraid of the possibility of getting laid off somewhere far away in an unknown city—finding themselves without living space or a salary while food prices are rising sharply, as my colleagues who left earlier for Sverdlovsk reported. P., who departed on first priority, writes that she has to waste several hours a day in search of food, that sugar at the market costs 100 rubles a kilogram, since a mass of refugees from the west have arrived in the city. The price of a room per month is reaching 500 rubles. Many still live in tents.[61]

According to Ostroumova-Lebedeva:

> Women don't want to go. Their husbands are either fighting or employed. They have to go alone. Even if you have money, you can't get more than 200 rubles from the bank. It is impossible to stock provisions, as everything is sold by ration cards. There are hundreds of thousands of people who have nothing except what they receive because their husbands are at the front. And you have to admit, these are very modest sums. And then, news arrives from every quarter that in the cities and villages everything has been eaten and people are

[59] Letter of July 12, 1941, and diary entry in Mossman, *The Correspondence of Boris Pasternak and Olga Freidenberg*, 206, 205.

[60] Boldyrev, *Osadnaia zapis'*, 63, entry of February 20, 1942.

[61] Konopleva, "V blokirovannom Leningrade," OR RNB, f. 368, op. 1, d. 1, l. 45, entry of August 20, 1941.

starving. Many refugees from Minsk, Smolensk, Moscow, Pskov, and elsewhere have descended on the Volga, the Urals . . . and everything is devastated
along the railway lines.[62]

As these diary entries suggest, many people regarded evacuation as the
greater danger. In Leningrad in particular, the policy of evacuation met with
open defiance on the part of the population. Individually and in groups,
people refused to leave. A typical confrontation between the district authorities responsible for implementing the evacuation and the women slated
to depart is described by the artist Ostroumova-Lebedeva in a diary entry of
mid-August 1941: "They told them at the district soviet, 'We will take away
your food cards.'—'Go ahead. We will live without them.'—'We will take
away your passports and . . . deprive you of your living space.'—'Go ahead,
all the same we're not going anywhere.' In the end, the women left [the
meeting], determined not to depart."[63] Even the next summer, after a devas-
tatingly harsh blockade winter, many were reluctant to leave. According to
a party report, "there is a substantial portion of the city's population that is
slated for obligatory evacuation but does not want to depart." There were
allegedly almost eighty people from sixteen buildings in the Kuibyshev district alone who "absolutely refuse to leave."[64] People were particularly wary
of the organized evacuation. In early August, large groups of women reportedly gathered outside the district executive committee offices after hearing
news of the imminent evacuation of women and children. "Many ask, 'can
we go to the Vologda and Kirov oblasts, to our relatives?' When they are
told that they will all depart in an organized fashion to a set destination, it
incurs mass discontent. Two women in the Petrograd district announced
that in that case they won't go anywhere as each of them has three young
children and 'we're not going to go to a hungry death.'" One woman even
threatened to kill herself.[65]

The intransigence of the population stemmed from a lack of faith in the
state's capacity to provide for the population. The prospect of evacuation,
particularly to an "unknown" place, invariably raised the specter of hunger
and destitution. In addition, not all regarded evacuation as the caring policy
of a magnanimous state.

In the spring of 1942, the Leningrad party organization reported a
"marked change in the population's relationship to evacuation." According
to the report, "people are beginning to better understand the necessity of
leaving and to prepare for it. Refusals to evacuate have become significantly
rarer and, in most cases, after corresponding discussions with citizens who
earlier refused, they accept the necessity of leaving. Many say: 'now we un-

---

[62] Quoted in Lomagin, *Neizvestnaia blokada*, vol. 1, 221–22.
[63] Ibid., 222.
[64] TsGAIPD SPb, f. 25, op. 5, d. 188, l. 51.
[65] Ibid.

derstand that we are not being expelled. There is concern for us and we understand that we must leave.'"[66] This report is notable less for the changes it purports to chart than for its exposition of the way the population had thus far apprehended the evacuation. As the report suggests, reluctance to depart grew in part out of suspicion that the evacuation was a form of expulsion. The equation of evacuation with expulsion appears to have been widespread. In the Volodarskii district, for example, nineteen elderly people announced: "we're not going anywhere, we have nowhere to go. Our children are in the army, we have worked our whole lives. Can it really be that all we have earned is to be expelled from Leningrad?"[67]

The perception that evacuation was tantamount to expulsion was particularly incendiary when children were concerned. Party reports contain numerous examples of confrontations between state authorities and parents, most notably mothers, over the evacuation of their children. According to one party report in Leningrad, "in the shops of the Svetlana factory, female workers appealed to the leadership in tears requesting permission to go home, or else 'they will take away our kids without us, and we won't know where they took them.'" Officials occasionally encouraged the notion that the state was taking away children. According to the same report, "when several mothers of building 64 on Kirovskii Boulevard gathered in front of the house manager with questions about evacuation, he informed them, 'Whether you howl or not, we are still going to take the kids from you.'" Rumors spread that the children "will be assigned to families on collective farms."[68]

As these examples attest, some regarded the evacuation with suspicion. Reflecting on the evacuation in his diary, Nikolai Punin compared the evacuation to the terror of the 1930s. "Why didn't they evacuate anybody during the 'Ezhov days' [the terror]? After all, it was equally terrible."[69] Punin's comment points to the ambiguities of the evacuation as perceived by members of the intelligentsia. The same state that stigmatized and arrested them in 1937–38 now proclaimed its desire to protect them. For the population at large, moreover, for whom expulsions had become a routine dimension of urban life, evacuation was easily equated with deportation. In addition to concerns about the forced nature of the operation, there were persistent fears that it was conceived as a permanent transfer, not as a temporary measure. In a state in which residence rights were strictly controlled, return to the country's major cities could easily be denied by the state. Evacuation thus presented special risks.

Individual assessments of the risks were informed by attitudes toward Soviet power, manifest in popular skepticism toward the Soviet press as well

[66] TsGAIPD, f. 25, op. 5, d. 188, l. 17.
[67] Ibid., l. 51.
[68] Ibid., ll. 51–52.
[69] N. Punin, *Mir svetel liuboviu: dnevniki, pis'ma*, ed. L. A. Zykov (Moscow: Artist. Rezhisser. Teatr, 2000), 344, diary entry of August 26, 1941.

as suspicion of the state and its promises. Risk, however, was only one term in the evacuation dilemma. At stake were not simply self-preservation and survival, but the relationship between citizen and state as well as conceptions of duty, loyalty, and patriotism.

CITIZEN AND STATE

The evacuation compelled people to define and declare their loyalties. Irina Ehrenburg later commented of the evacuation, "I discovered in this period that many Muscovites were actually anti-Soviet and this was true even of certain writers." Describing the division among the population, she recounted: "I was particularly sensitive to this division among Muscovites because it was manifest within my own family. Our maid was the most openly pro-German. She was a woman from the countryside, a former collective-farm worker who had gone through a hard time during collectivization and who had long thought that there could be no regime worse than that installed by Stalin." As for Ehrenburg's parents, who were divorced, her father, the prominent Jewish writer Ilya Ehrenburg, wanted to remain to defend the capital. Her mother, in contrast, "by origin part German and part Russian, . . . had decided not to leave Moscow and I think I can say that she was favorable to the Germans."[70] Like Ehrenburg's maid and mother, Lydia Osipova and her husband hoped that the arrival of the Germans would signal the beginnings of a better life. As Osipova noted in her diary in her first entry of the war, "whatever the Germans are like, they won't be worse than what we have."[71]

Osipova saw evacuation as a choice between "liberation" by the Germans and continued subjection to the current "damned regime."[72] Similar perspectives can be found in other sources. The writer Vsevolod Ivanov, for instance, had no doubt that some of his acquaintances had "waited for the Germans." "Perhaps it is a coincidence," his wife ruminated on their return from Tashkent, "but all our acquaintances who are religious did not leave Moscow."[73] Another Muscovite later reflected that "many were fed up with Soviet power. . . . There was a feeling that, thank God, communism was coming to an end."[74] In a similar vein, Valentina Bogdan, a Cossack resident

---

[70] Ehrenbourg, "Entretien avec Irina Ehrenbourg," 315–16.

[71] Diary of L. Osipova, in Lomagin, *Neizvestnaia blokada,* vol. 2, 441.

[72] Ibid., 441–42.

[73] Vsevolod Ivanov, *Dnevniki* (Moscow: IMLI RAN, Nasledie, 2001), 200, entry of November 19, 1942. According to Ivanov, Ekaterina Peshkova also had friends who had waited for the Germans, in her case an older woman. Ibid., 234, entry of January 2, 1943.

[74] According to this source, the situation changed only "when people saw that the Germans were far from saviors." Alla Andreeva, *Plavan'e k nebesnomu kremliu* (Moscow: Uraniia, 1998), 102.

of Rostov, recalls rejoicing at the news of the German invasion. "This is the beginning of the end of Soviet power!" she mused.[75]

Further evidence that evacuation was conceived as a choice between political regimes can be found in rumors. The notion that the Germans would target only Jews and Communists was, as we have seen, a staple of the rumor mill. These rumors both conveyed information and ascribed meaning. Consider the following case. In September 1941, a worker in a Moscow factory claimed that the Germans kill only the Jews. When a fellow worker retorted that the "Germans kill not only the Jews but also activists and Communists," the initial worker responded, the "Germans get rid of our leaders, but they leave us, the simple people, alone."[76] As this exchange demonstrates, the rumor that the Germans would target only Communists and Jews was at once an item of information and a message of subversion: one need not worry, need not flee or fight, for the enemy will do us no harm. Moreover, many of the rumors projected the beginning of a better life under German occupation. The following rumor, reported among peasants, was in many ways typical: The "Germans are conducting a war against Jews and Communists—they are an educated and clean people, they respect Orthodoxy and want to break up the collective farms."[77] Rumors about life under German occupation drew on the principal streams of discontent with Soviet power. Among peasants, the dismantling of the collective farm was a recurrent theme, while workers fixated on the elimination of the hated labor laws of the previous year.[78]

The rumors provide further confirmation of Irina Ehrenburg's claim that "the perspective of evacuation revealed the division of the population." It would be a mistake, however, to view the war merely as a window onto existing tensions and divisions. For even as the war revealed divisions, it sharpened some, muted others, and brought new ones into focus.

In many ways, the war ushered in a new chapter in the history of Soviet citizens' relations with the state. In the first place, as Amir Weiner has suggested, the war offered those who had been excluded from the polity the possibility of reintegration.[79] This is nowhere better expressed than in the memoirs of Rimma Neratova:

---

[75] Valentina Bogdan, "Memoir of an Engineer," trans. Yuri Slezkine, in *In the Shadow of Revolution: Life Stories of Russian Women from 1917 to the Second World War*, ed. Sheila Fitzpatrick and Yuri Slezkine, 416.

[76] Nicolas Werth and Gael Moullec, eds., *Rapports secrets soviétiques: la société russe dans les documents confidentiels, 1921–1991* (Paris: Gallimard, 1995), 228.

[77] Kostyrchenko, *Tainaia politika Stalina*, 225.

[78] Grigor'ev, "Moskva voennaia," 118–19.

[79] Weiner, *Making Sense of War*, chap. 1. To be sure, rehabilitation was dependent on service in the army and reintegration was only ever partial: rehabilitated kulaks, for instance, were not entitled to reclaim their previous dwellings. See Mark Edele, "A 'Generation of Victors?' Soviet Second World War Veterans from Demobilization to Organization, 1941–1956" (Ph.D. diss., University of Chicago, 2004), 111, 122. Moreover, as Lynne Viola points out, when the remaining kulaks were endowed with the rights of other Soviet citizens in recognition

At the beginning of the war, Papa said that in one way the war was good for all those who were under suspicion or who had prerevolutionary secrets, that their old sins would now fall away: the war cut off the old life. Now, the reckoning of sins would begin anew: they would now examine how a person conducted himself during the war, what he did, how he acted, what he said, thought. Our new wartime biography was completely clean.[80]

The war wiped the slate clean in more ways than one. Just as it erased the stigma of past offenses in the eyes of the state, it also dimmed the memory of oppression on the part of individual Soviet citizens.[81] The writer Olga Berggolts had been tormented before the war by memories of the prison where she had been held for several months in 1938. In the fall of 1942, however, in the besieged city of Leningrad, she wrote:

> And so, on June 22, 1941, when war was declared, the prison receded and took its leave. Not altogether—I hid these diaries, and one of my first thoughts was that they could deport me or arrest me only because I had already been arrested without cause, but this quickly passed. I plunged into my work, other massive thoughts and feelings possessed my soul, my prewar depression disappeared; . . . The prison took its leave—that is, it stopped hurting, as it was replaced by a different, new, sharper pain that was also common to the whole people.[82]

In this case and others, the war facilitated reconciliation with the regime, even if it did not produce enthusiastic support. Ilya Ehrenburg later recalled how, early in the war, he and his daughter Irina's husband, Boris Lapin, "started to recall the year 1938." Lapin, according to Ehrenburg, had been deeply shaken by the terror of 1937–38. The war, however, resolved his sense of bewilderment and alienation. In the late summer of 1941, "Lapin said: 'You know, when all's said and done, it's easier now; things have somehow shaken down.'"[83] Emma Gershtein expressed a similar sentiment in her memoirs. Describing her realization in the first months of the war that Moscow could fall to the Germans, she wrote: "only from that day did I stop

---

of their contribution to the war, they were still not granted permission to leave the special settlements. *The Unknown Gulag: The Lost World of Stalin's Special Settlements* (Oxford: Oxford University Press, 2007), 178.

[80] Rimma Neratova, *V dni voiny: semeinaia khronika* (St. Petersburg: Zvezda, 1996), 87.

[81] Amir Weiner makes a similar point with regard to the party leadership. He refers to the "erasing of the terror from the political memory of the Vinnytsia party elite." "The Making of a Dominant Myth: The Second World War and the Construction of Political Identities within the Soviet Polity," *Russian Review* 55, no. 4 (1996): 657.

[82] O. F. Berggol'ts, "Iz dnevnikov O. Berggol'tsa," *Zvezda*, no. 5 (1990): 180, entry of October 28, 1942.

[83] Ilya Ehrenburg, *Men, Years, Life: The War, 1941–45*, vol. 5, trans. Tatiana Shebunina (London: Macgibbon and Kee, 1964), 24.

thinking about our camps and stop imagining the suffering, grief, hunger, and cold that were endured there."[84]

At the same time, the war was also a source of new uncertainties. *Pravda* had confidently assured its readers only days before the invasion that there was nothing to fear. Had the Soviet regime made an error in its dealings with Germany? If this were not enough to induce doubt among certain sectors of the population, there was the hard fact of Soviet defeats. Faith in the forward march and historical destiny of the country was deeply shaken by the failures of the Red Army and the seemingly inexplicable advances of the enemy. Ilya Ehrenburg later wrote of this initial period of the war, "it is impossible to assess the confusion, bitterness, and alarm felt by each one of us."[85] The spectacle of defeat introduced doubts that profoundly unsettled accepted worldviews. The army that had for so long been touted as "invincible" was in retreat. A war that was supposed to be fought on enemy soil was extending further and further into the Soviet interior, engulfing huge swathes of the country. The rumor mill offered up an array of explanations: it was rumored that Timoshenko had gone over to the side of the Germans; that Levanevskii, a hero of the Soviet Union who had disappeared in a flight over the North Pole, had participated in German air attacks on Moscow; that Stalin had sold Smolensk.[86] The retreat was even blamed on kulaks in the newly annexed territories: "In the western oblasts kulaks probably remained, and they handed over our cities and villages. Our old border was impassible, but they [the Germans] passed through it nonetheless, which means that there was spying involved."[87] The rumors were in many ways products of the previous decade, a decade in which the most trusted members of the polity were unmasked as foreign spies and class enemies allegedly forged alliances with foreign foes. They were also products, however, of the unease produced by Soviet defeats. The recurring rumors of betrayal sought to explain what to many appeared inexplicable—the repeated retreats of an army that was supposedly invincible.

In the most extreme cases, the doubts produced by this unexpected turn of events shattered the foundations of individual support for the regime. Amir Weiner describes the case of a young Ukrainian woman, a member of the Komsomol, whose faith was so shaken by the spectacle of defeat that she defected to the Organization of Ukrainian Nationalists. In a piece written for submission to the organization near the end of the war, she described how her first encounter with German troops undermined her commitment to Soviet power: "The belief in the invincibility of the Soviet Union collapsed,

---

[84] Gershtein, *Memuary*, 412.

[85] Ehrenburg, *Men, Years, Life*, vol. 5, 11.

[86] See Grigor'ev, "Moskva voennaia," 111–12, 118. The Timoshenko rumor appears to have enjoyed wide circulation. On a variation of the rumor in Kamenets-Podolsk, see Liliia Shchupak, *Nichto ne prokhodit bessledno* (New York: Effect Publishing, 1997), 31.

[87] Grigor'ev, "Moskva voennaia," 118.

the gilded facade fell away, and falsehood showed its real face. What was the point in fortifying the defense for such a long period and all the talk about the invincibility [of the Soviet Union], when everything collapsed in one month?"[88]

While such reactions were likely more the exception than the rule, developments on the front shook the confidence of even (or perhaps especially) the most resolute Soviet citizens. If they did not undermine support for Soviet power, they nonetheless eroded belief in the ultimate victory of Soviet troops. The Leningrad artist V. I. Vladimirov, in his commemorative booklet on the war, recorded his anxiety on learning of the evacuation of the Hermitage and the State Russian Museum: "The vexing, oppressive news tormented me—this means that we are afraid that the enemy is so strong that we cannot be sure that we will not permit him to reach our city and we are afraid that works of art . . . could suffer. Of course, caution is a wonderful thing, but it unintentionally provokes doubt in our strength."[89]

Vladimirov, as the above citation suggests, wanted desperately to believe in the strength of the Red Army and the capacity of the Soviet Union to repel the aggressor. In this respect, he was not unlike Ilya Ehrenburg, who later wrote, "I believed in victory, not because I relied on our resources or on the Second Front, but because I needed to believe: for me in those days, as for all other Soviet citizens, there was no alternative."[90]

The tension between confidence and doubt runs through Soviet citizens' written record of the war. It figures nowhere more prominently than in discussions of evacuation. Indeed, the question "to stay or to go" was frequently cast as a matter of faith. Timofeev, for example, attributed the departure of a friend for Tashkent to the fact that "in his opinion, the war was supposed to have begun in 1942."[91] The integral role of confidence and doubt in structuring the terms of the evacuation dilemma are clearly revealed in a diary entry made by Leningrader Maria Konopleva. Describing the general evacuation, she noted:

> not all, however, leave. Many old Leningrad artists remain in Leningrad, those who believe that the city will not be surrendered to the Germans. I personally share this conviction . . . although I can't, of course, substantiate it. I believe it, like Anna Akhmatova, who came out not long ago with this quatrain: "The enemy banner will vanish like smoke, truth is on our side, we will be victorious." For the moment, however, this faith is difficult to corroborate.[92]

[88] Quoted in Weiner, *Making Sense of War*, 373.
[89] I. A. Vladimirov, "Pamiatka o Velikoi Otechestvennoi voiny: zametki," OR RNB, f. 149, op. 1, d. 4, l. 5.
[90] Ehrenburg, *Men, Years, Life*, vol. 5, 11.
[91] Timofeev, "Dnevnik voennykh let," 156, entry of October 13, 1941.
[92] Konopleva, "V blokirovannom Leningrade," OR RNB, f. 368, op. 1, d. 1, ll. 42–43, entry of August 17–18, 1941.

As this entry suggests, confidence in a Soviet victory was in many ways a matter of faith rather than reasoned reflection. It was also a source of pride. The war elevated confidence and faith to cardinal virtues, essential attributes of the upstanding Soviet citizen. The case of Vladimirov is instructive in this regard. In his notes, he contrasted the "tremendous number of people who have thrown themselves at the station," desperate to depart, with the calm resolve of his family:

> All this time, my family members have conducted themselves like genuine Soviet citizens. My daughters have continued to work calmly, full of fervor for their tasks, and my son, my sweet son, has honestly and selflessly worked as a military electrical engineer in Petrozavodsk. He wrote me and I felt with pride that there was not even a shadow of faintheartedness in any of his words.
>
> Many of my friends, seeing my unbending, unwavering calm and the courage of my family, calmed down and agreed with me that there is nothing to worry about . . . and that it is best to remain in Leningrad and calmly live through whatever happens.[93]

A similar sentiment is evident in the diary of Georgii Kniazev, head archivist for the Leningrad Academy of Sciences. Proclaiming his decision to remain in Leningrad, he proudly affirmed: "But our city—I firmly believe this—will not fall into the hands of the enemy."[94]

In subsequent years, those who remained frequently described their decision as a sign of their faith in Soviet forces and confidence in the country's final victory. Igor Manevich, in a volume on Jewish participation in the war, portrayed his father as adamantly resolved against departure. Prompted by his wife to evacuate the family, he reportedly responded "we're not going anywhere; the Germans won't take the city. Perhaps there will be street fighting, but we will not surrender the city."[95] The Leningrad physiologist Maria Petrova likewise presented her decision to remain as an act of faith. Her comments on the topic reveal with particular precision how faith was transformed into a hallmark of good citizenship and the very fact of remaining into an act of patriotism. "I deeply believed," she wrote in 1944: "in the power and strength of our Red Army, in Stalin, . . . in . . . popular patriotism, and thus I stuck firmly to my decision. . . . In spite of the very difficult conditions of daily life, to which I was completely unaccustomed, in spite of the . . .

---

[93] Vladimirov, "Pamiatka o Velikoi Otechestvennoi voiny," OR RNB, f. 149, op. 1, d. 4, ll. 6–7, entry of July 1941.

[94] Diary of G. A. Kniazev, in *Blokadnaia kniga*, ed. Ales Adamovich and Daniil Aleksandrovich Granin (St. Petersburg: Pechatnyi dvor, 1994), 208, entry of July 17, 1942.

[95] L. A. Aizenshtat, *Kniga zhivykh vospominaniia evreev-frontovikov, uznikov getto i kontslagerei, boitsov partizanskikh otriadov, zhitelei blokadnogo Leningrada* (St. Petersburg: Akropol, 1995), 9.

success of the German invaders, not for a minute did I lose faith or drop my spirits, and I even supported others in this direction."[96]

Petrova thus inscribed herself into the pantheon of wartime heroes through the simple act of faith. As the above examples suggest, the evacuation dilemma was about much more than "which of us will be better off." It turned on notions of patriotism, duty, and loyalty.

DUTY

The dilemma of evacuation forced people to reflect on their obligations. Ksenia Polzikova-Rubets expressed a not uncommon sentiment in her reaction to the departure of a friend. In her diary, she wrote, "I feel that they shouldn't leave. After all, the mother is a surgeon and she is needed here."[97] In letters to friends, Polzikova-Rubets repeatedly reaffirmed her commitment to remain in the besieged city, despite the hardship of daily life and her sense of isolation. As Tatiana Lozinskaia reported to Nikolai Antsiferov, both friends of Polzikova-Rubets, "now she writes that she has been offered the opportunity to leave, but she refused, as 'I want to fulfill my duty to the end.'"[98] In a letter to Antsiferov several months later, Polzikova-Rubets herself wrote: "I very much want to live, so I can work. I am needed by the children in the school. And I won't go anywhere, even though I miss many people terribly."[99] A similar sense of commitment to work underwrote the Leningrad physiologist Petrova's decision to remain. As she wrote in a piece penned in 1944, "only by remaining in Leningrad could I complete my work" and fulfill "my duty as a scientist before the motherland."[100]

As these examples suggest, "duty" (*dolg*) was a key term in the lexicon of the evacuation dilemma, as were normative terms such as "should." The prevalence of notions of civic duty is underscored by the sense of shame felt by those who abrogated such duties in the name of personal commitments. Emma Gershtein recalled the evacuation of one of her colleagues at the Moscow Literary Museum. "Where? To Kazan, to his family. We bid each other farewell. He was unbearably ashamed [*nevynosimo stydno*]."[101]

[96] M. K. Petrova, "V osazhdennom i svobodnom Leningrade," OR RNB, f. 576, op. 1, d. 5, l. 2.

[97] Polzikova-Rubets, *Dnevnik uchitelia*, 59, entry of April 12, 1942.

[98] T. B. Lozinskaia to N. P. Antsiferov, February 3, 1942, OR RNB, f. 27, op. 1, d. 279, l. 5.

[99] K. V. Polzikova-Rubets to N. B. Antsiferov, August 9, 1942, OR RNB, f. 27, op. 1, d. 332, l. 1.

[100] Petrova, "V osazhdennom i svobodnom Leningrade," OR RNB, f. 576, op. 1, d. 5, l. 2.

[101] Gershtein, *Memuary*, 414. Note that while such actions were frequently encouraged when mothers were concerned, the departure of fathers to remain with their families was typically regarded as an evasion of responsibility.

Duties could be fulfilled either by remaining or departing, depending on individual circumstance and the eye of the beholder. Although civic duty frequently underwrote decisions to remain, it was also invoked in decisions to depart. Thus the Jewish historian Saul Borovoi recalled that "for me personally the period of oscillation—to go or not to go—lasted for a short time only. When it became clear that the seizure of Odessa was almost inevitable, I firmly decided that I should not, I did not have the right to, remain in fascist hands. Of course, the instinct for self-preservation was primary, but the sense of a social duty also played a role."[102] Anastasia Sorokina, a senior laboratory assistant in one of the Academy of Sciences institutions before the war, likewise conceived of evacuation as a duty. Asked to lead a group of children into evacuation in Kazakhstan, she responded: "I will not decline. As a Komsomol member I will try to warrant your trust." Her choice of a poster for the first page of her recollections of the evacuation, which she wrote up in an album that was part memoir and part scrapbook, is telling. The poster, one of the most famous of the war, featured a peasant woman, her arm stretched forward holding an enlistment oath, and the caption: "The motherland calls" (*Rodina mat' zovet*).[103] By inserting an army recruitment poster into her chronicle of evacuation, Sorokina made the point that she, too, was heeding the call of duty and serving her country, if not on the front lines.

Civic duties, however, frequently competed with duties of another kind. The Leningrad journalist Frida Vigdorova, who had enrolled in a course to become a frontline nurse after the German invasion, felt compelled to withdraw when she found out she was pregnant. Although she was reportedly unsure about how to proceed, she ultimately decided that the "child must live," and she was subsequently evacuated to Tashkent, although not without regrets.[104] In a similar vein, Maria Belkina yearned to join her husband on the front.[105] Left to her own devices, she might well have remained in Moscow. As the mother of an infant son and the daughter of elderly parents, however, she was chastised for her desire to remain. "Everyone told her that the Germans would be in Moscow, if not today then tomorrow, that she was a bad mother and daughter, not thinking about her child and her parents."[106] As this example suggests, the evacuation dilemma was conceived as a matter of both civic and familial duty. Individuals—or, more properly, women—were expected to be not only "genuine Soviet citizens" but also "good mothers" and "good daughters."

[102] Borovoi, *Vospominaniia*, 239.
[103] A. V. Sorokina, "Tri goda na vsiu zhizn'," TsDNA, f. 18, op. 1, d. 21, ll. 11, 1.
[104] Kena Vidre, "Kakaia ona byla, Frida Vigdorova," *Zvezda*, no. 5 (2000): 111.
[105] N. A. Gromova, *Vse v chuzhoe gliadiat okno* (Moscow: Sovershenno sekretno, 2002), 18.
[106] Ibid., 15.

Maternal duties in particular shaped how the evacuation dilemma was debated and conceived. The Muscovite Zinaida Stepanishcheva—who, like Belkina, would end up in Tashkent—recalled in her memoirs:

> my husband and I decided: we lived together and we would die together. I planned to go nowhere. But our house manager—a very dependable and good old man . . . , who had known me since I was a child, began to call on me every day: "Well, you're letting me down," he said. "All women with small children have been ordered to leave Moscow, and you dig your heels in. You have a young child, and you and your Sviatoslav have decided to die together. But did you ask your child? Did you consider that he might not want to die?"

She was also urged by her mother, who lived in Tashkent and wrote: "Come right away! What are you waiting for?" In the end, it was Stepanishcheva's husband who convinced her, himself persuaded by the house manager. "Well, if they kill us all together, fine. But what if they kill us, and our son becomes an orphan or is maimed?"[107]

Stepanishcheva's and Belkina's experiences highlight the extent to which the dilemma "to go or to remain" was conceived as a matter of duty. As the mothers of young children, both women were expected to depart. Familial duties, however, could also underwrite individual decisions to remain. Countless people refused evacuation on the grounds that they could not abandon elderly parents. As Tatiana Lugovskaia, faced with the possibility of evacuation, wrote to a friend in September 1941, "I have many people here who would die without me."[108] Olga Grudtsova likewise recalled in her memoirs that despite her desperate desire to leave the capital, "I couldn't permit myself to leave while my parents were still in Moscow."[109] Others felt a duty to remain close to their husbands on the front. Thus two sisters later recalled that whereas they were evacuated from the city in early July, their aunt "flatly refused to send her children with us, as she believed that the Germans would never get to Leningrad. She thought that they [the children] should stay with her husband, who as an engineer was mobilized for the construction of fortifications around the city."[110] Kornei Chukovskii felt a similar sense of obligation to his children. "If you ask me whether I will stay in Moscow," he wrote to his daughter Lydia, who was in evacuation in Chistopol, "I would say that I am not sure. It seems to me that I am obliged to remain for you, Marina, Boba, Kolia."[111]

---

[107] Z. G. Stepanishcheva, "Vot tak i zhizn' proshla," TsDNA, f. 422, ll. 5–6.

[108] Letter to L. Maliugin, September 11, 1941, in Tat'iana Lugovskaia, *Kak znaiu, kak pomniu, kak umeiu. Vospominaniia, pis'ma, dnevniki* (Moscow: Agraf, 2001), 252–53.

[109] Grudtsova, "Dovol'no, ia bol'she ne igraiu," 59.

[110] Anna Uspenskaia and Natalia Uspenskaia, "Literaturnaia kritika. Liudi, idei, knigi. Brat'ia Uspenskie," *Neva*, no. 7 (2002): 199.

[111] Marina was Chukovskii's daughter-in-law, who was already in evacuation in Perm; Boba (Boris) and Kolia (Nikolai) were his two sons. Letter of mid- to late September, in Kornei

The significance attached to familial duty, particularly to the young and the old, is nowhere more apparent than in the propensity to criticize those who abrogated these duties. As suggested above, Belkina and Stepanish-cheva were both roundly criticized for their reticence to depart. In Leningrad, a woman who refused to depart with her young children was publicly branded an "egoist" by a group of women in her district and was accused of thinking "only of herself; the interests of the city don't concern her."[112] Others were admonished and cajoled by neighbors, family members, and friends. Particularly forceful criticism was reserved for those who departed on their own, abandoning either children or elderly parents. Sofia Unkovskaia, a schoolteacher in Kalinin, was nothing short of appalled by some acquaintances who "in this terrible time abandoned their own mother to the mercy of fate."[113]

While conceptions of familial duty thus shaped the terms of the evacuation dilemma, the nature and limits of these duties were a matter of debate. The currency of "family obligations" as a justification for departure, as well as the sometimes cynical reception they met, are aptly conveyed in the diary entry of a Moscow doctor on October 14, 1941. According to the doctor, "people are leaving Moscow in droves. Some of those who depart claim that they are jealous of those who remain, but that they have 'other obligations,' for instance, a son (thirty-six years old!)."[114]

TANGLED LOYALTIES

Lisa Kirschenbaum, in a study of wartime propaganda, has pointed to "the centrality of the local and the private in wartime conceptions of public duty." The war poster that Sorokina inserted into her evacuation album is a perfect example. "Mothers functioned in Soviet propaganda," Kirschenbaum contends, "both as national symbols and as the constantly reworked and reimagined nexus between home and nation, between love for the family and devotion to the state." She argues that "during the war . . . native place (*rodina*), home, and family emerged as key constituents of Soviet patriotism."[115] The seamless connections among family, home, and fatherland forged in wartime propaganda were much more strained, however, in the corpus of works penned by individuals about their own subjective experiences.

Chukovskii and Lidiia Chukovskaia, *Perepiska: 1912–1969*, ed. E. Ts. Chukovskaia and Zh. O. Khavkina (Moscow: Novoe literaturnoe obozrenie, 2004), 310.

[112] TsGAIPD, f. 25, op. 5, d. 188, l. 21.

[113] Sofia Alekseevna Unkovskaia, "Moia zhizn'. Vospominaniia uchitel'nitsy," OR RNB, f. 576, op. 1, d. 5, ll. 1035–36. See also Polzikova-Rubets, *Dnevnik uchitelia*, 59.

[114] Gorinov, Parkhachev, and Ponomarev, *Moskva prifrontovaia*, 285.

[115] Lisa A. Kirschenbaum, "'Our Cities, Our Hearths, Our Families': Local Loyalties and Private Life in Soviet World War II Propaganda," *Slavic Review* 59, no. 4 (2000): 825, 828.

Very often, as Maria Belkina was all too aware, it was simply not possible to fulfill one's duty to the motherland and one's duty as a mother at the same time. Nonetheless, diaries and letters present evidence that such connections were made by individuals as well, who strove in the spaces of their own writing to weave family, home, and fatherland into a seamless narrative.

One of the central patriotic idioms in diaries and correspondence was attachment to one's native home. For Tatiana Lugovskaia, for example, the decision to remain was based on loyalty not only to family but to place. As she wrote to a friend in September 1941, "I don't have the strength to leave Moscow—this city has displayed more endurance and calm than I could have imagined. For me, as an old Muscovite, this is especially dear."[116] Olga Friedenberg expressed her commitment in strikingly similar terms. In a letter to her cousin Boris Pasternak she wrote, "We are staying. I haven't the strength to forsake my beloved city, and Mother hasn't the strength to make the trip."[117] Attachment to place figures particularly prominently in the writings of the Soviet intelligentsia and the elderly. Maria Konopleva, recently retired, expressed her choice in her diary as a decision to "remain in Leningrad, where I was born and spent my whole life."[118] Georgii Kniazev, after an afternoon spent admiring "the majestic panorama of my native city," resolved in his diary that "I'm not leaving it for anywhere. Should some misfortune occur, better that I die here, somewhere on the embankment or in the waters of the Neva."[119]

Such outpourings serve as an important reminder that even in the "quicksand society" of the Stalinist 1930s, individuals felt a strong attachment to the cities and villages in which they had spent a good portion of their lives.[120] What they tell us about the nature of wartime patriotism, however, is more difficult to decipher. In his memoirs on the war, Ilya Ehrenburg described a conversation with a foreign journalist. "Trying to understand [the steadfastness of the Russians], he asked me a lot of questions and said that apparently there was a great feeling for our native soil. I said that we were attached both to our Russian soil and to the Soviet regime, even though life was not easy."[121] The journalist's question and Ehrenburg's response point to one of

[116] Letter to L. Maliugin, September 11, 1941, in Lugovskaia, *Kak znaiu*, 252–53.

[117] Letter of July 12, 1941, in Mossman, *The Correspondence of Boris Pasternak and Olga Freidenberg*, 206.

[118] Konopleva, "V blokirovannom Leningrade," OR RNB, f. 368, op. 1, d. 1, l. 44, entry of August 20, 1941. See also Kipitonova, who wrote, "I firmly decided not to abandon suffering Leningrad in which I had already lived fifty-seven years." "V osazhdennom i svobodnom Leningrade," OR RNB, f. 576, op. 1, d. 5, l. 1.

[119] Diary of G. A. Kniazev, in Adamovich and Granin, *Blokadnaia kniga*, 207, entry of July 7, 1941.

[120] The phrase "quicksand society" is Moshe Lewin's in *The Making of the Soviet System: Essays in the Social History of Interwar Russia* (New York: Routledge, 1985), 221.

[121] Ehrenburg, *Men, Years, Life*, vol. 5, 15. The passage continues: "(At the time I could not tell Caldwell about all our difficulties, my pride would not let me. But though our people knew

the difficulties in defining the nature of wartime patriotism. Since the middle of the 1930s, Soviet propaganda had sought to forge a popular patriotism that would combine national sentiment and attachment to the Soviet regime, what the historian David Brandenberger has termed "national Bolshevism."[122] The attempt to fuse national and political allegiances, however, was not always successful. Consider the case of Valentina Bogdan. Like Lydia Osipova, Bogdan welcomed the German invasion as the beginning of the end of Bolshevism. When her brother Alesha urged her to evacuate, she refused, pinning her hopes instead on a German victory in the war. When she, in turn, urged her brother, a soldier in the Red Army, not to fight, he "looked at me in total disbelief. 'What are you telling me? To surrender to the enemy? To give up my country without a fight?!'" "Your country has been in enemy hands for twenty-three years now," Valentina replied, "and it is them, not your country, that you will be defending!"[123] Both brother and sister had a strong sense of patriotic duty, but their understanding of the "motherland" and how best to serve it led them to diametrically opposite conclusions. Alesha was driven to the front lines, to battle with the Germans, whereas his sister was driven into the arms of the invaders, whom she cast as liberators of the Russian land.

Valentina Bogdan's motherland stood in stark contrast to the Soviet regime. In most cases, however, the contours of the motherland were more difficult to chart. Indeed, where "native soil" ended and socialism, Stalin, or the Soviet system began was not always clear. Ostroumova-Lebedeva, an elderly member of the Leningrad intelligentsia who forswore the possibility of evacuation, repeatedly professed her commitment to "my motherland and my people" in her diary.[124] Her frequent references to the "Russian people" would seem to suggest that her motherland was an exclusively national one. But it was also one in which Stalin occupied an important place. As she recorded in her diary on the occasion of Stalin's July 3 address to the Soviet population: "today I listened to Comrade Stalin's wise speech with heartfelt emotion [*serdechnoe volnenie*]. His words instill calm, courage, and hope in my soul."[125]

Although the nation and, to a lesser degree, Stalin dominate the patriotic register of the war years, these were not the only patriotic idioms in play. The twenty-one-year-old David Samoilov, for instance, understood patriotic duty as a quintessentially socialist virtue, something that he and others like him, members of the intelligentsia, had attained only through a painful process of

---

a lot they did not go out to face death because they were ordered to—for when death is close at hand discipline alone is not enough: self-sacrifice is needed.)"

[122] David Brandenberger, *National Bolshevism: Stalinist Mass Culture and the Formation of Modern Russian National Identity, 1931–1956* (Cambridge, Mass.: Harvard University Press, 2002).

[123] Bogdan, "Memoir of an Engineer," 418.

[124] Ostroumova-Lebedeva, *Avtobiograficheskie zapiski*, 254, entries of August 31, 1941.

[125] Ibid., 254, 250, entries of August 31 and July 3, 1941.

"tearing out the rusty roots of decadence from our hearts and our blood." At a time when the motherland—which was sufficiently expansive to encompass the national, socialist, and Stalinist idea—dominated patriotic discourse, Samoilov invoked terms with much more specific socialist referents. In his early wartime musings on his generation, he reflected that the "impersonal words: shock brigade, plan, agitation, struggle for socialism" had, over the preceding years, "acquired flesh" and "unity" and he now regarded them as the "truth, the real truth."[126]

These few examples underscore the complexities of wartime patriotism. Although Ehrenburg was undoubtedly right that popular patriotism often represented a fusion of the Soviet and the national idea, this was clearly not always the case. Sometimes, as in the case of Osipova or Bogdan, the two came into conflict. Much more frequently, however, they coexisted in a relationship that could be, depending on the individual and the moment, mutually reinforcing or markedly lopsided, seamless or strained. In some cases, they simply receded in importance as other ideas, such as socialism, assumed center stage. The socialist ideal could reinforce attachment to the Soviet state or the nation, but it could also undermine it. Likewise, attachment to place—which could function as one link in a larger chain joining home town, nation, and Soviet state together—could also serve as an alternative patriotic register that allowed those who were wary of both the national and the Soviet idea to join the common cause.

While the nuances of wartime patriotism defy easy generalization, the presence of a patriotic imperative does not. Nikolai Punin is in some sense the exception that proves the rule. Punin's refusal to be evacuated grew out of his reluctance "to be drawn into the war, to fall into its rhythm, its muzzle."[127] Much more common, however, was the impulse to participate. Nadezhda Mandelstam, who fervently hoped that "this war will be the end of Hitler and of Fascism," wrote to her friend Boris Kuzin that "I need to be closer to the war, to somehow help the soldiers—not somehow, but every which way that I can."[128] Mandelstam, whose husband had been executed and who had little reason to support the Soviet state, nonetheless rallied to the common cause and saw it as her duty to contribute.

The impulse to inscribe individual actions and motivations into a framework of patriotic duty is underscored by a diary entry made by Ksenia Polzikova-Rubets about a fellow Leningrader:

I sincerely would like aunt Lela to receive a medal. It seems to me that Lev Tolstoy wrote about her, as about many of us: "With half of Russia in enemy

[126] David Samoilov, *Podennye zapisi* (Moscow: Vremia, 2002), 148, 146, entry of November 3 or 4, 1941.

[127] Punin, *Mir svetel liuboviu*, 344, diary entry of August 26, 1941.

[128] Letter of between June 22 and August 3, 1941. Nadezhda Mandel'shtam, *192 pis'ma k B. Kuzinu*, ed. N. I. Kraineva and E. A. Perezhogina (St. Petersburg: Inapress, 1999), 657.

hands, and the inhabitants of Moscow fleeing to distant provinces, with one levy after another being raised for the defense of the Fatherland, we, who were not living in those times, cannot help imagining that all Russians, great and small, were solely engaged in immolating themselves, in trying to save their country or in weeping over its downfall. All the stories and descriptions of those years, without exception, tell of nothing but the self-sacrifice, the patriotic devotion, the despair, the anguish and the heroism of the Russian people. Actually, it was not at all like that. It appears so to us because we see only the general historic interest of the period, and not all the minor personal interests that men of that day had. Yet, in reality, private [*lichnye*] interests of the immediate present are always so much more important than the wider issues that they prevent the wider issues which concern the public as a whole from ever being felt—from being noticed at all, indeed. The majority of the people of that time paid no attention to the broad trend of the nation's affairs, and were influenced only by their private concerns. And it was these very people who played the most useful part in the history of their day."[129]

Polzikova-Rubets concluded her lengthy citation from Tolstoy's classic *War and Peace* with the comment that the "word 'personal' [*lichnoe*] has a negative connotation now; I would like to replace it with 'dependably and honestly fulfilling their daily tasks [*delo*].'"[130] Thus, even as Polzikova-Rubets invoked the authority of Tolstoy to make a case for the disjuncture between patriotism and individual motivation, she simultaneously sought to close the gap, as it were, by downplaying the "personal" or "private" character of individual motivation and infusing such motivation with notions of selflessness and duty. As this particular case suggests, historians should be wary of neatly dividing personal motivations into "private" or "personal" and "patriotic." Individuals repeatedly sought in their own writings to collapse the two and to inscribe their actions into a framework of patriotic duty. Lydia Ginzburg commented of Leningrad during the blockade that "only in talk of the war does the language of the people merge with that of the newspapers."[131] As striking as the turn to the personal in state propaganda, described by Kirschenbaum, was the emphasis placed by individual citizens on civic and patriotic duties. As David Samoilov observed of his generation in October 1941: "no one repudiated the war. If I write about this some day, I will write about how the category of duty became a reigning concept for us.

[129] Polzikova-Rubets, *Dnevnik uchitelia*, 190, entry of August 20, 1943. The translation of the passage from Tolstoy is taken from Leo Tolstoy, *War and Peace*, trans. Rosemary Edmonds (London: Penguin, 1982), 1116.

[130] Ibid.

[131] Lidiya Ginzburg, *Blockade Diary*, trans. Alan Myers (London: Harvill, 1995), 56. Lisa Kirschenbaum, who cites the same passage, seems to suggest that the confluence in language was a product of a personalization of official rhetoric. "'Our Cities, Our Hearths, Our Families,'" 829. Even though the words of the grandmother cited by Ginzburg contain a personal referent (the woman refers to her husband on the front), what is striking is the degree to which popular press slogans were integrated into the daily life of ordinary Soviet citizens.

It is the only feeling that should inspire people from the cradle: duty."[132] The evacuation was not only a moment of patriotic rallying, however. For a start, not all regarded evacuation as the magnanimous policy of a caring state. Moreover, just as individuals became more conscious of their duties, they became more prone to judge.

POPULAR PROTEST

Evacuations were sharply contested both on the streets and in the home. The spectacle of evacuation was, moreover, a source of anger and resentment, vented in a wave of denunciations, widespread public protest, and in the relative intimacy of individual diaries and correspondence. People contested both the policy of evacuation and the way it was carried out. The challenges expressed by individuals and groups underscore the complexity of the population's attitudes toward Soviet power. They betray an admixture of strident expectations coupled with both skepticism and suspicion. They further point to the explosive and divisive character of the evacuation, and the way in which evacuations, widely touted as a sign of the state's care for its citizenry, threatened to undermine Soviet power.

"We Will Be Left without Work"

On October 17, 1941, workers in the central Russian town of Ivanovo arrived at work at the usual hour of 6 A.M. The previous day had been a day off, but there had likely been little respite for the largely female workforce that made its way to the factory that morning. Since the outbreak of the war, the workday had increased to ten hours. Wages, moreover, had steadily declined. Over the course of only a few months, they had fallen by as much as 50 percent: people previously earning 800 rubles a month found their salaries reduced to a mere 400; those lower on the pay scale confronted cuts of similarly staggering proportions. Many of the women had families to support, a task made increasingly difficult with their husbands at the front. There were lines, and days off would have been occupied with attempts to procure basic but much needed food items—even potatoes were nowhere to be found in the state stores that served the town's population.

Those who entered the factory that morning were greeted by an unusual sight: the machinery was partially dismantled. No word of an impending evacuation had been uttered, but the evidence was there for all to see. The sight provoked an outburst. As one group of workers proclaimed: "they are taking away the machinery, and we will be left without work." Rumors that

[132] Samoilov, *Podennye zapisi*, 140, entry of November 3 or 4, 1941.

bread was being evacuated and that the bank had already left merely fed the flames of popular discontent. Amid the uproar, cries sounded that "our directors together with Chastukhin (the director of the industrial complex) sent their families off, but they don't send ours and they want to leave us without work." Others cried that "all the directors fled the city, and we remain alone."[133] The protests reflected fears that the factory would be evacuated and workers left behind. The evacuation thus struck at the heart of one of the central promises of Soviet power—work. Rumors circulated that the whole factory was slated for destruction together with the workers, in keeping with the policy of scorched earth.

According to the report, the "wildest rumors and cock-and-bull stories, not founded on anything, spread. Moreover, all these fables apparently had a common source, as their content was identical (the destruction and mining of factories, the removal of flour, the evacuation of the bank, the flight of responsible figures, etc.)."[134] What the obkom secretary put down to conspiracy most likely had more prosaic roots. The unity of the rumors was a function not of a common source but of a shared set of assumptions and fears, a shared mental and material universe. It matters little whether the families of the NKVD remained in place, as the report claimed, or had in fact been evacuated, as rumors suggested. After all, it was well known that bureaucrats in the textile industry had evacuated their families: once one set of authorities had been shuttled out of the city to the presumed safety of the interior, it was only reasonable to expect that others would follow. Quite naturally, rumors singled out the NKVD and the factory management. These, together with the ministry, constituted the backbone of the local elite. In many places, moreover, they had indeed been evacuated alongside ministry and other officials. If they were not in this particular case, the claim to the contrary was nonetheless both reasonable and believable.

The rumors were further informed by Soviet policy pronouncements. The textile workers of Ivanovo, like their compatriots across the front lines, were undoubtedly aware of the Soviet policy of scorched earth. It was, after all, a key element in Stalin's speech of July 3, 1941, the contents of which were eagerly discussed by workers across the country. Given the popular equation of evacuation with retreat, it was only reasonable to assume that food and other valuables would soon follow the factories en route to the east. The notion that the factory would be blown up also had its origins in the proclaimed policy of the regime. The mantra to "leave nothing to the enemy" was emblazoned on the front pages of *Pravda*. Finally, the rumors took hold in the vacuum created by a lack of information. As the report

[133] N. Werth et al., "Smiatenie oseni sorok pervogo goda: dokumenty o volneniiakh ivanovskikh tekstil'shchikov," *Istoricheskii arkhiv*, no. 2 (1994): 119.
[134] Ibid., 124.

from Ivanovo put it, the evacuation "began on October 17, on the factory's day off. No explanatory work . . . regarding evacuation was undertaken in advance."[135]

The disturbances in Ivanovo eventually petered out. The advancing armies were stopped on the outskirts of Moscow and the city was not subjected to a full-scale evacuation. The disturbances underscore, however, the destabilizing potential of evacuation. The evacuation, conceived by the state as an essential aspect of the war effort, threatened to deprive the population of its livelihood. As such, it was met with resistance not only in Ivanovo but in cities and towns across the front lines. The intensity of these disturbances varied considerably depending on the region and the immediate circumstances surrounding the onset of evacuation. Perhaps the most fierce resistance to evacuation was mounted in the Donbass, where mine workers attacked and sometimes killed managers attempting to evacuate the region. According to a report penned by the procuracy division of the Red Army, workers in the mines of the Donbass region actively demonstrated against the evacuation and destruction of the mines. Their objective, in the words of the report, was "to impede the dismantling and destruction of the mines, to restore the running of the mines, to change the leadership of the mines in order to organize their protection." The organizers of one such demonstration allegedly told the workers that "we don't care which regime we have, but they shouldn't suspend the operation of the mines." In the Donbass, unlike Ivanovo, the protests against the evacuation of factories were also accompanied by what authorities classified as "counterrevolutionary" pronouncements. Some among the protesters praised Germany.[136]

As the example of the Donbass suggests, protests against the evacuation of factories were concerned with more than livelihood. If the reports of the Red Army are to be trusted, those demonstrating against the evacuation of factories on the Don were also demonstrating against Soviet power. Similar incidents, with even more explicit politics, were reported in the recently annexed territories. In the Brest region, for example, where the equipment of the Mikopevicheskii plywood factory was being evacuated, the person in charge had to summon ninety armed infantry to put down popular resistance to the evacuation.[137] In Pinsk, authorities were shot at as they left the city; and in Riga, where the evacuation of the families of party and Soviet cadres was left "to the very last minute," it took place "when the so-called 'fifth column' was already active and there was rifle and machine-gun fire on the streets of the city."[138]

[135] Ibid., 119.
[136] GARF, f. 5446, op. 81a, d. 347, ll. 54, 58.
[137] RGAE, f. 1884, op. 31, d. 3811, l. 2.
[138] "Iz istorii Velikoi Otechestvennoi voiny: nachalo voiny," *Izvestiia TsK KPSS*, no. 7 (1990): 212.

In most cases, however, the political meaning of the disturbances was much less clear. The workers of Ivanovo, as we have seen, agitated in favor of their livelihood, not the invader. The protests nonetheless posed a threat to the regime. Not only did the evacuation elicit protests, and in some cases outright opposition, but it unleashed a wave of resentment against the Soviet leadership. In the process, the polity was redefined and the legitimacy of the Soviet state was called into question. Nowhere was this process more significant or more visible than in Moscow, the Soviet capital, in mid-October 1941.

"Soviet Power Has Abandoned Us": Moscow, October 16, 1941

The evacuation of the capital in mid-October 1941 quickly became known by a shorthand—October 16, 1941, "the day," as one Muscovite put it years later, "that I will never forget."[139] It was, in Georgii Efron's words, an "infamous day when, at the approach of the enemy, those who should have been among the foremost defenders of the red capital shamefully fled, destroying their communist party membership cards." According to Efron, the impact of October 16 could not be underestimated: as he noted in his diary a few weeks after the events themselves, "for an enormous number of committed Communists and simply for an enormous number of people, the day of the 16th was a revelation."[140] What, however, was revealed? What was the meaning of the "unforgettable," "infamous" day?

October 16 was perceived, most immediately, as a breakdown of order, the first signs of which were a disruption of the rhythms of everyday life. This perception is aptly conveyed in the diary entry of the Muscovite P. N. Miller, a historian by training:

> October 16. Thursday. Everything has sharply and suddenly changed. *Izvestia* was not issued: they say it was evacuated. The Soviet Information Bureau, for the first time approaching the truth, reports that on the western sector the situation has sharply deteriorated. . . . On the streets there is disorder: the janitors have not cleaned the frozen sidewalks. The transportation is in complete disorder. The Metro is closed.[141]

The perception of breakdown was immediate and widespread: Timofeev began his diary entry on that day in remarkably similar terms: "And so, breakdown. There is still no newspaper and I don't know if there will be."[142] The Metro closure in particular made a deep impression on contemporaries. As

---

[139] Labas, "Chernyi sneg na kuznetskom," 37.
[140] Efron, *Dnevniki*, vol. 2, 94, entry of November 6, 1941.
[141] Diary of P. N. Miller, in Gorinov, Parkhachev, and Ponomarev, *Moskva prifrontovaia*, 290.
[142] Timofeev, "Dnevnik voennykh let," 159.

one Muscovite later recalled, "this was the only day in all these years that the Moscow Metro did not work."[143]

More disturbing still, as factories across the city were evacuated, or closed down in the absence of management, workers were laid off en masse, sometimes with pay and more often without. In one Moscow factory, workers arrived on the designated day of evacuation to find, in the words of one employee, "the absence of the management: they had all left. A racket arose. Workers made their way to the accountant's office for their wages: according to the law we were to be paid two months' wages. The cashier was not there. The management was not there. Nobody was there. A disturbance broke out."[144] Commissar of Aviation A. I. Shakhurin witnessed a similar scene. Arriving at one of the city's aviation factories on October 16, "I found workers in the midst of an agitated discussion. I asked what the matter was. They were silent. Then they said: 'The director left and took the money. There was not enough to give us our pay.'" In fact, as Shakhurin related to Stalin later that afternoon, the state bank was out of money. Why? As Molotov was forced to explain to Stalin, the commissar of finance, the person responsible for the bank, had been evacuated and was now in Gorkii.[145]

All these events fed the font of popular resentment. Disturbances broke out in factories across the city. In addition to protests, the unrest involved pillage and outright physical attacks on management. Although the NKVD described the disturbances as "anarchic manifestations," these "manifestations," however disorderly, followed definite patterns. Typical was the sequence at one of the capital's shoe factories: workers began pillaging the factory's stocks only after the failure of authorities to pay them their promised discharge salary. Attacks on management, moreover, consistently targeted those who attempted to depart. The NKVD reported that in one Moscow factory, the assistant director, "filling his car with a large quantity of food items, tried to leave the factory. He was stopped, however, and beaten up by workers."[146]

As suggested earlier, the immediate cause of such actions was the failure to provide severance pay. They were further fueled, however, by anger and fear occasioned by the very fact of evacuation. As discussed in relation to Ivanovo, the closure of factories signaled a loss of livelihood for workers. As factories were shipped off to the east, workers lost their jobs as well as the benefits that they conferred. Anger over the evacuation of factories was augmented by rumors about the possible destruction of factories and other elements of the city's infrastructure, as prescribed by the policy of "scorched

[143] Gorinov, Parkhachev, and Ponomarev, *Moskva prifrontovaia*, 266.
[144] G. V. Reshetin, in *Moskva voennaia, 1941–1945. Memuary i arkhivnye dokumenty*, ed. K. I. Bukov, M. M. Gorinov, and A. N. Ponomarev (Moscow: Mosgorarkhiv, 1995), 111.
[145] Ibid., 109.
[146] Gorinov, Parkhachev, and Ponomarev, *Moskva prifrontovaia*, 262.

earth." In one factory, a manager was beaten up after notifying workers that their barracks would be blown up.[147]

Finally, the attacks were informed by a powerful current of moral critique. Although workers generally targeted the goods that management carried with them, only rarely are we told that they engaged in theft. Take the following account: a fifteen-year-old boy made his way to the Highway of the Enthusiasts: There, he later recalled, "I was a witness to robbery." This is what he wrote in his diary: "they stopped a big black car . . . and pulled out some manager or another and his family—his wife, an old man, and two teenage boys. They were about to start beating the manager, calling out that he had stolen property, but he broke loose and fled into the woods following his family. They broke into the trunk, where there were food items."[148] The crowd did not steal the food, however—they discarded it. For the attack was not primarily an act of theft but a settling of scores and a punishment of those whom many considered thieves and traitors to the fatherland. As one Muscovite put it in a letter to his son in the army: "When all the directors and heads fled, sowing panic, shaming themselves in the face of the workers and honest humankind, they became traitors."[149]

The attacks against goods were not incidental: the evacuation elicited a critique not only of cowardice but of self-interest and hypocrisy. The flight of authorities violated popular conceptions of patriotism and of justice. Consider, for example, the following diary entry by Verzhbitskii: "Who thrust this date upon us, this disgrace? The people who first trumpeted the themes of heroism, staunchness, duty, honor. . . . The Highway of the Enthusiasts, along which the cars of yesterday's 'enthusiasts' rushed toward the east—filled with nickel-plated beds, leather suitcases, rugs, caskets, bulging wallets, and the fatty flesh of the masters of all this junk—is defamed."[150] This critique sounded a theme that was repeated in multiple and diverse sources: it was echoed, for example, in a collective denunciation submitted to the NKVD by a group of factory personnel against the head of their factory who, rather than organizing the transfer of the factory's machinery and personnel, "was exclusively occupied with loading his personal property onto the factory's train cars, such as his upright piano, grand piano, mirror, dressers, sideboards, beds, mattresses, goat, dog, bicycles, and friends of his who have no relation to the factory."[151] The "nickel-plated beds," "grand pianos," and "mirrors" stood in flagrant violation of the collective ethos of sacrifice imposed by the war: these useless, bourgeois items, figured as symbols of decadence and of the privileging of personal over public interest.

[147] Ibid.
[148] Aleksandr Aleksandrovich Kuznetsov, "Oktiabr' i noiabr' 41-ogo," *Nash sovremennik*, no. 12 (2001): 147.
[149] Bukov, Gorinov, and Ponomarev, *Moskva voennaia*, 160.
[150] Ibid., 478.
[151] Gorinov, Parkhachev, and Ponomarev, *Moskva prifrontovaia*, 263.

They were key elements in the moral critique of authorities elaborated in the wake of the evacuation.

In an interview many years later, a former worker of Moscow's Hammer and Sickle factory recalled that "all sorts of bureaucrats fled Moscow along [the Highway of the Enthusiasts], abandoning their enterprises and workers to the mercy of fate. They fled with suitcases and all their furniture. . . . How did the workers apprehend this: What's this [*kak zhe tak*]? The authorities flee and abandon us here without leadership?"[152] As these recollections suggest, the panic of mid-October was intimately connected in the popular imagination with a sense of betrayal and moral outrage. Diarists did not fail to note the sharp change in the mood on the street: Georgii Efron noted on October 19 that "in the city there are enormous lines, disorder. People speak openly about things that would have been unimaginable only a few days earlier. . . . They criticize the government."[153] According to David Samoilov, "on the trams people openly cursed Soviet power."[154] The tenor of popular resentment and the sense of moral outrage is captured in the diary entry made on October 16 by Timofeev: "In lines and in the city in general there is a sharp and hostile attitude toward the 'ancien regime': they betrayed us, abandoned us, left us."[155] Verzhbitskii recorded similar popular outbursts in his diary entry of the same day:

Besides the newspapers, no wall literature has appeared. Instead, everywhere there is bubbling indignation, people speak loudly, they cry about betrayal, about the fact that the "captains jumped ship first," seizing valuables while they were at it. You hear conversations that three days ago would have landed one in front of a tribunal. Lines, lines without end: clamorous, nervous, pugnacious, agonizing. . . . People begin to recall and enumerate all the offenses, oppression, injustices, suppression, the bureaucratic mockery by state functionaries, the conceit and self-assurance of party members, the draconian decrees, the deprivation, the systematic deception of the masses, the newsprint lies of the toadies, the glorification. . . . It is terrible to hear.[156]

The criticisms were both pointed and forceful. They reprised and amplified key elements of a critique of evacuation elaborated in the summer and early fall. The evacuation of cultural institutions and elites had been contested from the outset. As a school teacher wrote to *Pravda*:

[152] Artem Drabkin and Nikolai Iakovlevich Zheleznov, "Nikolai Iakovlevich Zheleznov (iz arkhiva N. Ia. Iakovlevich)" (http://iremember.ru/tankers/zheleznov/zheleznov1_r.html).
[153] Efron, *Dnevniki*, vol. 2, 59.
[154] Samoilov, *Podennye zapisi*, 149, entry of November 3 or 4, 1941.
[155] Timofeev, "Dnevnik voennykh let," 159.
[156] Bukov, Gorinov, and Ponomarev, *Moskva voennaia*, 478. Timofeev likewise wrote on October 17: the "population does not hide its hostile and contemptuous attitude toward the leadership, which established a model of mass irresponsibility and, so to speak, untimely flight. The masses will not forgive them for this." "Dnevnik voennykh let," 160.

an altogether unpleasant picture of the so-called evacuation has developed. . . . Every central directorate . . . considers it its duty to evacuate itself somewhere. At breakneck speed, people stop working, abandon the affairs of the state literally to the mercy of fate, and depart. This happens mostly as a result of the cowardice of people running one or another institution. You must be aware of numerous cases in which, during the especially rapid progress of the Germans in the initial days of the war, several so-called managers, influenced by assorted dark rumors propagated by the enemy, made it their sacred duty to quickly flee Moscow, literally flee.

The writer concluded that "we must put an end to this type of excursion" and admonished that organizations should be made to work "in the manner called for during war."[157] Another letter to the newspaper from one of the capital's female residents echoed similar themes. "Is it right," she asked,

to evacuate the families and relatives of employees of the Commissariat of Aviation such that . . . they left for Saratov with trucks full of goods and petrol? Can we really waste petrol on such things? If such transports were somehow centralized, controlled, state-directed, it would undoubtedly be possible to economize. . . . Perhaps I am mistaken, but I consider such exceptional privileges incorrect in a situation that is so difficult for the masses.[158]

As both letters suggest, the sense of civic duty discussed in relation to the evacuation dilemma was equally manifest in citizens' expectations of party and Soviet authorities. Citizens both expected and demanded "correct" behavior from their leadership. When this was not forthcoming, as it was not at several key junctures during the first several months of the war, the party, soviet, and managerial elite were branded as cowards and even as traitors.[159] Their propensity to "save their own skins" made them the objects of a powerful current of moral critique which threatened to undermine the legitimacy of Soviet power.

Antisemitism

"State functionaries" and "party members" were not the only targets of popular resentment. The other principal target was Jews. This is how one individual later described the scene on the square leading to the Highway of the Enthusiasts: "Here and there people stopped the cars heading toward the

[157] GARF, f. 6822, op. 1, d. 52, l. 42.
[158] Ibid., l. 43.
[159] Similar critiques were voiced in Leningrad, where authorities were likewise charged with flight and cowardice. See, for example, Kargin, *Velikoe i tragicheskoe*, 22 and I. V. Vladimirov, "Pamiatka o Velikoi Otechestvennoi Voiny. Zametki," OR RNB, f. 149, op. 1, d. 4, ll. 6, 19, entries of June or July 1941 and September 6, 1941.

highway. They dragged the passengers out, beat them up, grabbed their things, and threw them on the ground. Cries rang out: beat the Jews." As striking as the actual event is the author's sense of surprise: "I would never have believed it had I not seen it myself." Although he had gone to school with Jews, he noted: "I can't recall any clear and open examples of antisemitism. There was some mockery, but it was mild, more like a joke, and nothing more. That's why this savage reprisal against the Jews, and not only against them, on October 16 . . . had such a strong impact on me."[160]

Antisemitism was not a novel phenomenon in Soviet Russia. However, the comments of contemporaries suggest that the evacuation marked a turning point in the openness with which such sentiments were expressed. While the individual cited above was shocked by what he saw on October 16, 1941, public expressions of antisemitism had in fact been on the rise in Moscow since the war and the evacuations had begun. NKVD Chief Lavrenti Beria reported to Stalin in September 1941 that "according to the data of the NKVD, there has been a rise in manifestations of antisemitism in recent days."[161] The phenomenon was noted by Timofeev as well.[162] Information collected through party channels, moreover, points in a similar direction. At a factory canteen in Moscow in early September, for example, a party member began a fight with a Jewish saleswoman when she refused to give him more than his allocation of beer. He called out, "I know! Your pockets are full, you're going to make off to the Urals." Receiving encouragement from those around him, he continued, "The Germans will mow them down (pointing to the Jewish vendor), and all the Jews will be kaput."[163] The preceding passage points to the key assumptions underpinning wartime antisemitism, namely that the "Jews," according to yet another party member, "are all cowards" and, in the words of an unnamed engineer, "are hiding from the war, saving their skins."[164] In Moscow's Red Seamstress factory, according to the report of a party committee secretary in late September 1941, "people were saying that the Jews flee" and even several Communists "attempt to support" this line of argument. Interestingly, popular perception bore little relation to reality, at least in this particular factory: when the party secretary compiled the data on those who had left, "it turned out that, in all, three hundred workers had left with their children, of whom there were eight Jews, also with their children."[165]

[160] Bukov, Gorinov, and Ponomarev, *Moskva voennaia*, 111–12.
[161] Gorinov, Parkhachev, and Ponomarev, *Moskva prifrontovaia*, 629.
[162] Timofeev, "Dnevnik voennykh let," 153, entry of October 7, 1941.
[163] Grigor'ev, "Moskva voennaia," 117–18. At this juncture, another person interjected that the "'Germans kill not only Jews but Communists and activists as well.' Boldyrev responded, 'I know, they kill only the upper echelons, but us, the rank and file, they don't touch.'" Ibid., 118.
[164] Grigor'ev, "Moskva voennaia," 117; Gorinov, Parkhachev, and Ponomarev, *Moskva prifrontovaia*, 629.
[165] RGASPI, f. 17, op. 22, d. 1811, ll. 77–78.

Popular antisemitism was further predicated on the notion that the war was the fault of the Jews and that the Soviet war effort was conceived in their defense. According to one report, "at a Moscow factory in early September a blacksmith announced 'I have been called up for service, I'm off to defend the kikes.'"[166] Some argued that the Jews had "organized the war." Others went so far as to claim that the "USSR is not a Russian country, it's a Jewish [*zhidovskaia*] country, let them defend it."[167] Together, these examples highlight the effectiveness of Nazi propaganda in singling Jews out from the population at large. To be sure, many of the antisemitic statements drew on old tropes.[168] They were shaped in crucial ways, however, by the specific nature of the war and the evacuation in particular. Despite the studied avoidance of tales of the murder of Jews in the Soviet press, the Soviet population was apprised of the antisemitic nature of the invading forces. If they were not aware of its full extent, rumor—nourished by German propaganda, Soviet press announcements, and prewar conceptions—nonetheless ensured that Jews became a distinct object of consideration in discussions of the war.

Although Soviet authorities continued their "struggle against antisemitism," manifest most concretely in a series of arrests for antisemitic remarks, there was a palpable sense that something had changed. To many, it seemed that antisemitism had become acceptable. It is surely not coincidental that the insults hurled at the canteen worker, discussed above, were made by a party member. In a similar case, when a party member claimed that Hitler would attack only Jews, workers were reportedly "shocked to hear this claim from a party member." It was telling, moreover, that according to the report, the "party organization has thus far not responded to this fact."[169]

If antisemitism arose in the early stages of the evacuation, it was amplified in conjunction with the events of October 16, 1941. P. N. Miller noted in his diary the next week that "antisemitism has appeared."[170] There were numerous reports of antisemitic actions during this period. Alexander Kuznetsov, for example, later recalled a boyhood friend inviting him to join in as he watched the crowds on the Highway of the Enthusiasts "catch Jews." "'What?' I didn't understand. 'They're making off, and people are catching them there. Let's go and have a look.'"[171] The NKVD reported that a group of workers at a motorcycle factory attempted to incite a pogrom, calling on workers to "kill the Jews."[172] Like some of the observers cited above, moreover,

---

[166] Grigor'ev, "Moskva voennaia," 119.

[167] Gorinov, Parkhachev, and Ponomarev, *Moskva prifrontovaia*, 629.

[168] Jews were also accused of shirking military service during World War I. See Eric Lohr, "The Russian Army and the Jews: Mass Deportation, Hostages, and Violence during World War I," *Russian Review* 60, no. 3 (2001): 406.

[169] Grigor'ev, "Moskva voennaia," 111.

[170] Gorinov, Parkhachev, and Ponomarev, *Moskva prifrontovaia*, 291.

[171] Kuznetsov, "Oktiabr' i noiabr' 41-ogo," 147.

[172] Bukov, Gorinov, and Ponomarev, *Moskva voennaia*, 118.

the NKVD observed a rise in antisemitism in connection with the evacuation. Letters detained by the censors in late October and November 1941 contained a plethora of antisemitic remarks: "I resent the Jews. Until the war they had living space, they had everything, and just when it comes to defending Moscow, they scatter." A serviceman wrote, in an astonishing misrepresentation of the size of Moscow's Jewish population: "in Moscow you won't see a Jew. They all fled, beginning with the big bosses. . . . If anyone, Jews should be the ones defending Moscow first. The USSR is the only country in the world that makes allowances for them. After all, Jews made up 75 percent of the inhabitants of Moscow, and the majority were engaged in high-level work. . . . Our government will be making a big mistake if it lets them back into Moscow."[173]

The perception that Jews had taken flight was widespread. Miller observed in his diary that "hardly any members of the intelligentsia remain, and the Jews have fled. They are not at all visible in lines."[174] In a similar vein, a resident of the capital wrote to friends or family in evacuation that "we wanted to go, . . . but there are no trains. Only Jews are leaving Moscow."[175] Even Georgii Efron recorded in his diary on October 16, in the second entry of the day, that "Communists and Jews are leaving the city."[176] The perception that Jews were fleeing in disproportionately high numbers did have some basis in fact. Statistical data compiled by Soviet authorities in 1941 make it clear that Jews were substantially over-represented among the overall evacuee population.[177] To some extent, this was a function of a general over-representation of Jews among those sectors of the population designated for evacuation by the Soviet state, namely the political, managerial, and cultural elite. It was also a function, however, of the nature of the war, a war in which Jews had been singled out by the enemy, thus increasing their proclivity to depart and further heightening public awareness of the phenomenon, as suggested above. At the same time, assessments of the Jewish character of those in flight were grossly exaggerated. The people who streamed out of Moscow on October 16 and the following days included many non-Jews. Not all, moreover, were managers

[173] Ibid., 160.
[174] Gorinov, Parkhachev, and Ponomarev, *Moskva prifrontovaia*, 291.
[175] Ibid., 151.
[176] Efron, *Dnevniki*, vol. 2, 50.
[177] According to data compiled on December 12, 1941, 26.94% of evacuees were listed as Jews. RGAE, f. 1562, op. 20, d. 249, ll. 67–68. This percentage undoubtedly exaggerates the proportion of Jews within the overall evacuee population, as official statistics during the evacuation generally took much better account of the urban population than the rural one, and the vast majority of Soviet Jews (86.9%) lived in urban areas on the eve of the war. On the population distribution of Jews before the war, see Mordechai Altshuler, *Soviet Jewry on the Eve of the Holocaust: a Social and Demographic Profile* (Jerusalem: Centre for Research of East European Jewry, Hebrew University of Jerusalem; Yad Vashem, 1998), 34.

and political secretaries: many ordinary people departed, some determined not to fall into enemy hands, others fearful of being cut off from family further to the east. We might well pose the question asked by the Red Seamstress party secretary discussed above. Faced with a clear discrepancy between the reality of departures and popular perceptions, he asked the workers "why they don't speak about all those who left, why do only the Jews grab their attention?"[178] In the Red Seamstress factory, this question, together with the data on departures, allegedly "completely put an end" to antisemitic discussions in the factory. For the most part, however, such "explanatory work" was not undertaken. The participation of Jews on the front was passed over in silence, and popular rumblings about Jews taking flight were never publicly refuted. The image of Jews in flight left a lasting impression on the capital's residents, and those of other cities as well.[179] The popular post-war joke that Jews had served on the "Tashkent front" merely underscores the degree to which the association between Jews and flight fostered a new wave of popular antisemitism that became a staple of the post-war period.

If the perception of Jewish flight had a clear and lasting legacy, the legacy of the perceived flight of officials was more ambiguous. Within days, October 16 had become a shorthand for the events of mid-October, which quickly became the talk of the town. According to Verzhbitskii, "People talk about all this openly and loudly in lines. One supplements another." The regional censors reported that in the first two weeks of November alone, 1,670 letters discussing the events of that day had to be confiscated. The day became a historical landmark and a symbol. Verzhbitskii predicted that "October 16, 1941, will become a most infamous date in the history of Moscow, a date of cowardice, confusion, and betrayal."[180] Timofeev went so far as to compare the day to Bloody Sunday, when tsarist troops fired on a peaceful demonstration, delegitimizing tsarist rule and igniting the Revolution of 1905.[181]

The chaos of the day was deemed a "provocation." It was blamed by some on General Timoshenko, whom Verzhbitskii speculated had been removed from his post, and by others on the former commandant of Moscow, Reviakin, who, according to rumor, had been shot. Verzhbitskii ruminated in his diary: "It is possible that they were both the authors of October 16."[182] In fact, both had simply been transferred to posts elsewhere. Neither had

---

[178] RGASPI, f. 17, op. 22, d. 1811, ll. 77–78.

[179] Party reports in Leningrad point to a similar rise in antisemitism in conjunction with the evacuation. On expressions of antisemitism in Leningrad, see TsGAIPD, f. 25, op. 5, d. 180, l. 134.

[180] Bukov, Gorinov, and Ponomarev, *Moskva voennaia*, 476, 159, 478.

[181] Timofeev, "Dnevnik voennykh let," 160, entry of October 17, 1941.

[182] Bukov, Gorinov, and Ponomarev, *Moskva voennaia*, 479.

played a significant role in the events of October 16. The tendency to attribute the collapse of October 16 to betrayal, however, served to limit the scope of delegitimation. In articulating charges of treachery and betrayal, the capital's residents not only deflected criticism from the regime itself but also forged a link between themselves as individuals and the community and cause that was betrayed.

Perhaps the most common sentiment expressed in conjunction with October 16 was shame, not anger. In a novel written some twenty years later, the Soviet writer Konstantin Simonov attempted to come to grips with the meaning of October 16 through the eyes of his protagonist, Sintsov. "Later, when all this belonged to the past, and somebody recalled that 16th of October with sorrow or bitterness, he [Sintsov] would say nothing. The memory of Moscow that day was unbearable to him—like the face of a person you love distorted by fear."[183] Similar sentiments were expressed at the time. "October 16. This day—I don't have the strength to recall it . . ." one woman mused in her diary. "The evacuation of factories. . . . Everything blends together in the terrible grief of the entire people, which is difficult to describe."[184] David Samoilov, too, was deeply disturbed by the events of that day, "a day," as he put it in his diary, "of anarchy, a day which I will write about in good time. I left Moscow with pain and bitterness in my heart."[185] Another woman, in a letter to a friend she had recently seen off to Tashkent, maintained that "what we went through from October 15–18 we will never forget. Such shame, such indignation, and such disappointment."[186] The sense of shame and humiliation merely underscores the degree to which Muscovites, on the whole, identified with the political community whose image, in their eyes, had been so badly tarnished. To be sure, some among the capital's inhabitants were only too glad to see the leadership depart. Moreover, the spectacle of flight profoundly unsettled accepted worldviews. For one young woman, the events of the sixteenth were a source of "moral crisis."[187] That said, the wellspring of anger, the repeated cries that "Soviet power has abandoned us," and the deep sense of shame all suggested that most of the capital's residents were not eager to see Soviet power go: rather, they counted on Soviet authorities to remain and defend the capital. Finally, the rapidity with which the event was memorialized suggests just how quickly order was reestablished: within days,

---

[183] Quoted in Alexander Werth, *Russia at War, 1941–1945* (London: Barrie and Rockliff, 1964), 238.

[184] Bukov, Gorinov, and Ponomarev, *Moskva voennaia*, 400.

[185] Samoilov, *Podennye zapisi*, 149, entry of 3 or 4 November, 1941.

[186] Quoted in Gromova, *Vse v chuzhoe gliadiat okno*, 21.

[187] This is how Georgii Efron describes how his friend Valia experienced this period. *Dnevniki*, vol. 2, 64, entry of October 21, 1941.

October 16 was already relegated to the domain of history. Muscovites did not anticipate a repeat.

· · ·

The demonstrations and protests of the summer and fall of 1941 were among the most serious public disturbances since the collectivization and dekulakization campaigns some ten years earlier. They were all the more noteworthy in that they occurred while the country was at war. Nonetheless, they did not shake the foundations of Soviet power: contrary to German expectations, the Soviet population did not rise up en masse against the country's leadership. The demonstrations were localized, scattered, and, for the most part, disorganized. More important, although the protests by their very nature constituted a challenge to Soviet power, few among them can properly be qualified as acts of resistance.[188] With some notable exceptions, particularly in the annexed territories and on the Don, demonstrators sought to preserve Soviet power, not to dismantle it. The leadership was criticized not for excessive intervention in the lives of its citizens but for withdrawal. The popular mantra that "Soviet power has abandoned us" points to the limits of defeatism among the population at large. The disturbances were the product of popular contestations of Soviet wartime policy, specifically the policy of evacuation. Far from fifth columnists, those who manifested their discontent on the street, in letters, and in diaries expressed disappointment and shame: they had been let down by a power that they expected to maintain order and protect the motherland, however conceived.

Perhaps paradoxically, the evacuation of Moscow thus presents a snapshot of the Soviet state both at its most vulnerable and at its strongest. For the war and the evacuation simultaneously challenged the authority of the Soviet state and drew the Soviet population closer together. As Andrei Sakharov later reflected, "the war made us a *nation* once again."[189] Among those for whom the war forged a firmer sense of belonging was a relation of Sakharov's whose husband had been killed in the terror and who remarked during a bombing raid early in the war that "for the first time in years I feel that I am Russian."[190] This woman's impulse to declare herself was in many ways typical. The war compelled people to define their loyalties and their communities—whether understood in national, ideological, or familial terms. In confronting the evacuation dilemma, moreover, individual Soviet citizens reflected on the nature of duty and on their obligations as citizens, family

[188] On the category of resistance see Lynne Viola, "Popular Resistance in the Stalinist 1930s: Soliloquy of a Devil's Advocate," *Kritika* 1, no. 1 (2000): 45–69.

[189] Andrei Sakharov, *Memoirs*, trans. Richard Lourie (New York: Knopf, 1990), 41.

[190] Ibid., 40.

members, and friends. The ultimate decision taken—to stay or to go—would have far-reaching implications. Those who opted to remain would suffer through the travails, depending on their location, of enemy occupation, siege, or bombardment. Those who opted to depart, by turn, would embark on a journey into the unknown.

5

THE JOURNEY EAST

"All of Russia was on the move," Aleksander Wat recalled.[1] In city after city, settlement after settlement, residents took leave of their homes, their things, their former lives. The daughter of the poet Dmitrii Kedrin later recalled how "Mama distributed our things among neighbors and friends: to one—the wardrobe, to another—the tea kettle and wash basin, to another—our room. Taking only the most necessary items, we departed for the Kazan station."[2] They were embarking, as Sergei Eisenstein put it, on a journey into the "unknown."[3]

THE STATION

There was no more emblematic point of departure for the journey into evacuation than the railway station. Descriptions of railway stations abound in memoir literature on the war and the evacuation. As Irina Ehrenburg later remarked, "the memory of Evacuation is first and foremost that of the station."[4] The Kazan station, Moscow's primary gateway to the east, was in

---

[1] Aleksander Wat, *My Century: The Odyssey of a Polish Intellectual*, trans. Richard Lourie (New York: New York Review of Books, 2003), 307.
[2] Dmitrii Kedrin and Svetlana Kedrina, *"Vkus uznavshii vsego zemnogo—"* (Moscow: Vremia, 2001), 537.
[3] Memoirs of S. M. Eisenshtein, in K. I. Bukov, M. M. Gorinov, and A. N. Ponomarev, eds., *Moskva voennaia, 1941–1945. Memuary i arkhivnye dokumenty.* (Moscow: Mosgorarkhiv, 1995), 156.
[4] Irina Ehrenbourg, "Entretien avec Irina Ehrenbourg," interview by Catherine Gousseff in *Moscou, 1918–1941: de l'homme nouveau au bonheur solitaire*, ed. Catherine Gousseff (Paris: Éditions Autrement, 1993), 317.

many ways the archetypal wartime station.[5] From the Kazan station trains departed for the Volga, the Urals, Kazakhstan, and Central Asia. Friends and family took leave of one another, unsure of whether and when they would meet again.

The war transformed the Kazan station into a veritable encampment. Within days, there were three thousand people in the station. In little over a week, the number had increased over fivefold, to twenty thousand.[6] There was, as one report put it, a "tremendous accumulation of people." They sat on makeshift seats of luggage, waiting for a train to carry them east, "unable to obtain tickets for two or more days."[7] One woman recalled that she and her parents "sat for almost two days" in the Kazan station simply waiting for their train.[8] The writer Kornei Chukovskii, who departed from the Kazan station during the panic of mid-October, described the station in his diary: the "square in front of the station was darkened with people; in the station itself there were at least fifteen thousand people."[9] According to Maria Belkina, the station was "crammed full of people and things."[10] The overcrowding merely added to the chaos. One traveler recalled entering the Kazan station on October 16, 1941. "The huge, high-ceilinged waiting rooms hummed with thousands of voices, punctuated by the piercing cries of children. Men and women, young and old, many in unfamiliar dress, as though headed for the North Pole—felt boots, quilted jackets, sheepskin coats, sheets, and three-tiered fur hats, dragged out of God knows what closet. All this was scrambled up with parcels, bales, suitcases, boxes, trunks, and children's bathtubs."[11]

"What went on at the Kazan station defies description . . . ," Ilya Ehrenburg later wrote.[12] Merely boarding a train proved to be a major challenge. Kornei Chukovskii noted in his diary that "it was impossible . . . to get to my railway car. If it hadn't been for Nikolai Virta [a fellow writer], I would have gotten stuck in the crowd and not gone anywhere."[13] The historian Militsa Nechkina likewise recalled: "at the station there was a terrible crush of people. It was impossible to board the train. If it were not for a deft stu-

---

[5] The Kazan station was one of four Moscow stations from which evacuees departed for the rear. During the most intense period of evacuation in mid-October 1941, it was the departure point for almost half of all trains leaving the capital. See GARF, f. 6822, op. 1, d. 461, l. 9.

[6] GARF, f. A-259, op. 40, d. 3042, ll. 75–76.

[7] Ibid., l. 76.

[8] Kedrin and Kedrina, *"Vkus uznavshii vsego zemnogo—,"* 537.

[9] Kornei Chukovskii, *Dnevnik, 1930–69* (Moscow: Sovremennyi pisatel', 1995), 158, entry of October 19, 1941.

[10] Maria Belkina, *Skreshchenie sudeb,* 2d ed. (Moscow: Blagovest Rudomino, 1992), 291.

[11] Gennady Andreev-Khomiakov, *Bitter Waters: Life and Work in Stalin's Russia. A Memoir,* trans. Ann Erickson Healy (Boulder, Colo.: Westview, 1997), 177.

[12] Ilya Ehrenburg, *Men, Years, Life: The War, 1941–45,* vol. 5, trans. Tatiana Shebunina (London: Macgibbon and Kee, 1964), 17.

[13] Chukovskii, *Dnevnik,* 158, entry of October 19, 1941.

dent in our department, who managed to throw me and all my bundles into the railway car, I would not have been able to leave."[14] Inna Shikheeva Gaister, the adolescent daughter of convicted enemies of the people, received no such assistance. She later recalled: "the boarding was terrible. We pushed our way into the railway car with difficulty. We had two suitcases and two sacks with things, but we couldn't get the sacks onto the train."[15]

The railway station was a site not only of separation but of loss. In his memoirs, Ilya Ehrenburg recalled how, at the Kazan station, "I lost my small suitcase containing the manuscript of the third part of *The Fall of Paris*. Later I felt very sad about it, but at the time my thoughts were on anything but literature and I was more worried by the loss of my razor—how was I going to shave?"[16] The Russian composer Dmitrii Shostakovich similarly lost his suitcases, and with them his as yet unfinished seventh symphony. Shostakovich, however, was somewhat more fortunate than Ehrenburg— the suitcases were found in an adjoining railway car.[17] In some cases the luggage made it on, but its owners did not. The daughter of Dmitrii Kedrin recounts how, when her family's train was finally announced, "my parents seized our suitcase, an enormous bundle of things, and they ran to the train, threw our things into the fifth car and ran back—for us. But at that moment in front of their very eyes the doors of the enormous gates closed, and they remained on the platform while the train began to slowly depart."[18] Like Ehrenburg, Kedrin lost his poems as well as his material possessions.

Writers lost their manuscripts, parents their children. As one Moscow resident put it in an appeal to authorities in Uzbekistan to help reunite his family: "last year my family and I were evacuated from Moscow to Tashkent. While boarding the train, we lost one another, and as a result one daughter came to Tashkent, my wife and I ended up in Orsk, and our second daughter went missing."[19]

ORDER IN CHAOS: HIERARCHY, PATRONAGE, AND PRIVILEGE

The chaos on the streets and in the station seemed to some the signs of a system and society in the process of disintegration. The center of Soviet power

---

[14] M. V. Nechkina, "V dni voiny," in *V gody voiny: stat'i i ocherki*, ed. Aleksandr Mikhailovich Samsonov (Moscow: Nauka, 1985), 33.

[15] Inna Shikheeva-Gaister, *Semeinaia khronika vremen kul'ta lichnosti, 1925–1953* (Moscow: Niudiamed-AO, 1998), 62.

[16] Ehrenburg, *Men, Years, Life*, vol. 5, 17. Lugovskaia also lost her luggage here. Letter to L. Maliugin, January 30, 1942, in Tat'iana Lugovskaia, *Kak znaiu, kak pomniu, kak umeiu. Vospominaniia, pis'ma, dnevniki* (Moscow: Agraf, 2001), 255.

[17] Mikhail Ardov, *Shostakovich v vospominaniiakh syna Maksima, docheri Galiny i protoiereia Mikhaila Ardova* (Moscow: Zakharov, 2003), 12.

[18] Kedrin and Kedrina, "*Vkus uznavshii vsego zemnogo—*," 537.

[19] TsAGT, f. 10, op. 18, d. 31, l. 112.

was being divested of its principal functions and stripped of its symbols. Calls to the Kremlin went unanswered—there was no one there to answer them. The very paper on which the power of the regime was inscribed was being dispersed and in some cases destroyed. Aleksander Wat later recalled how, during the evacuation of Moscow's notorious Lubianka prison, the NKVD walked among the prisoners carrying documents: "They threw the dossiers haphazardly into trucks, the personnel dossiers of millions of people, the dossiers on which all the force of Stalinist power rests."[20] That which could not be evacuated was destroyed. P. N. Miller recorded in his diary that "as a result of yesterday's panic, all the house registers, all kinds of lists, charts, and so on were destroyed on somebody's orders, and thus information about people has completely disappeared."[21] Archives went up in flames. As Andrei Sakharov wrote in his memoirs, the "wind lifted up darkened pieces of paper: everywhere, official archives and documents were being burned."[22] Despite the breakdown in public order and the unprecedented dislocation of people and things, however, the social order was still very much intact. This was nowhere more apparent than in the long line of trains slowly making their way east.

At first glance, the trains presented a perfect picture of disorder: as one railway director remarked in a conversation a few years later, "there was a motley collection of passenger trains."[23] According to another official, "people were evacuated on just about anything: in buses, trolleybuses, freight cars, on open platforms. . . . People even departed in Metro cars."[24] Indeed, Anna Akhmatova sighted the "blue carriages of the Moscow Metro, buried under the snow," as far away as Novosibirsk.[25]

The trains were packed, overflowing with people and goods. Olga Boltianskaia, en route to Tashkent, recorded the conditions on the train in her diary as she pulled away from the Kazan station: "There are so many people crowded into the railway car that all the benches, the passages, and the platforms are occupied."[26] Zinaida Stepanishcheva likewise recalled that "there were people or things everywhere."[27] Overcrowding was endemic. While official norms stipulated a maximum of thirty-five people to a railway car, they invariably carried many more. The historian Nikolai Druzhinin later wrote that his railway car "was stuffed: it carried more than the official norm (fifty

[20] Wat, *My Century*, 37.

[21] Diary of P. N. Miller, in M. M. Gorinov, V. N. Parkhachev, and A. N. Ponomarev, eds., *Moskva prifrontovaia, 1941–1942: arkhivnye dokumenty i materialy* (Moscow: Mosgorarkhiv, 2001), 290, entry of October 17, 1941.

[22] Andrei Sakharov, *Vospominaniia* (New York: Izdatel'stvo imeni Chekhova, 1990), 63.

[23] Bukov, Gorinov, and Ponomarev, *Moskva voennaia*, 378–79.

[24] Gorinov, Parkhachev, and Ponomarev, *Moskva prifrontovaia*, 281.

[25] Lydia Chukovskaya, *The Akhmatova Journals*, trans. Milena Michalski and Sylva Rubashova (London: Harvill, 1994), 192, entry of November 2, 1941.

[26] Diary of O. A. Boltianskaia, RGALI, f. 2057, op. 2, d. 29, l. 89, entry of August 4, 1941.

[27] Z. G. Stepanishcheva, "Vot tak i zhizn' proshla," TsDNA, f. 422, l. 8.

passengers)."[28] Moreover, there was an extraordinary quantity of baggage. According to one traveler, "there were so many bags and so many people in each compartment that it was impossible either to get in or to sit down. The platforms at the backs of the cars were loaded with boxes, small bathtubs, and certain bucket-like pots—evidently, treasures with which it was impossible to part."[29]

There was, however, an order to the chaos. Amid all the confusion, there were nonetheless discernible patterns in the distribution of people and things. Seats were distributed on the basis of institutional affiliations, so central in the mediation of relations between citizen and state. Andreev-Khomiakov describes his train as it pulled out of the Kazan station: "In the forward car was some academic institution or other; the People's Commissariat of River Transportation was in the next car; behind us was what looked to be some kind of theatrical society, or maybe it was an agricultural academy."[30] The organization of passengers reflected the corporate structure of Soviet society. Individuals were evacuated with the specific organizations that employed them (workers with their factories, for example) or, more broadly, by profession. Consider, for example, the linguist Dmitrii Ushakov's description of another train that set out for Central Asia from the Kazan station that October. "On our train one railway car was for academics, the others: 'writers,' people in the film industry . . . , the university . . . , and others."[31] The film director Sergei Eisenstein, who traveled on the same train, later wrote of his journey into evacuation, a "bomb in one railway car, and there would no longer be any Soviet directors. Almost all of us, having worked side by side for twenty years, were now side by side in one railway car."[32]

This basic organization was further structured by family relations. Consider the writers' car on the train described above. While a good portion of the passengers were in fact writers, the train also carried a substantial number of family members. The poet Vladimir Lugovskoi traveled with his ailing mother and his sister Tatiana, a painter, and even with their housekeeper, who was accorded a seat on the train as his aunt.[33] An angry letter to authorities denouncing abuses in the evacuation made specific mention of the managers who "under the guise of evacuation, try to take not only the apparatus of their organization, but their relatives right up to the tenth degree."[34] While these charges were clearly somewhat exaggerated, familial relations did play

---

[28] N. M. Druzhinin, "Evakuatsiia iz Moskvy v 1941–1943 godakh: vospominaniia," *Istoriia SSSR*, no. 5 (1981): 111.

[29] Andreev-Khomiakov, *Bitter Waters*, 183.

[30] Ibid.

[31] Letter of December 22, 1941, in O. V. Nikitin, ed., "Poslednie pis'ma D. N. Ushakova G. O. Vinokuru," *Izvestiia RAN. Seriia literatury i iazyka*, no. 1 (2001): 67.

[32] Bukov, Gorinov, and Ponomarev, *Moskva voennaia*, 156.

[33] N. A. Gromova, *Vse v chuzhoe gliadiat okno* (Moscow: Sovershenno sekretno, 2002), 20.

[34] GARF, f. 6822, op. 1, d. 52, l. 42.

an important role in determining the distribution of seats. The family had become a central category of Soviet social policy. Although decrees setting out the conditions of the evacuation took the nuclear family of husband, wife, and children as the basic unit, the examples examined above suggest that the extended family remained an operative category in practice, if not in policy.[35]

Superimposed on the basic structure of corporate status and family relations were networks based on personal connections and patronage. Anna Akhmatova, for example, acquired a seat on a train from Kazan to Tashkent not only as an important writer but as a friend of the Chukovskii family.[36] Similarly, the Soviet photographer Moisei Nappelbaum secured his family's evacuation from Moscow by calling on a patron. His daughter later wrote that her father "had recently taken a photograph of Molotov and his family, which he had printed and presented to Molotov, refusing to be paid. Now he had to repudiate the nice gesture. He called [Molotov's] secretary, explained his situation, and requested help. He was given a thousand rubles and an official trip to Nalchik."[37] The trains thus presented a patchwork. Affiliations based on family, personal, and patronage networks were layered over those based on work.

The railway-car interiors, moreover, bore the clear imprint of the hierarchies that structured Soviet society. Diplomats, at the top of the pyramid, were provided with first-class cars, equipped with restaurant cars and sleepers. Distinguished writers, scholars, and cultural figures traveled in only slightly more modest compartments: Kornei Chukovskii described his train as an "international car, with separate compartments."[38] International cars were, as Lydia Chukovskaia, who traveled in a normal car, put it, "warmer, softer, and more spacious."[39] The less privileged journeyed east in commuter cars and cargo trains. A worker in the Stalin automobile factory recalled that "our train was composed of electric railway cars designed for suburban travel."[40] Zinaida Stepanishcheva, who was evacuated from Moscow "in individual fashion," similarly recalled that the train on which she traveled east was, "in normal times, used for the transportation of livestock and cargo."[41]

As revealing as the railway-car interiors were the items that people carried with them. The stratification of Soviet society was clearly inscribed in

---

[35] In Leningrad, the executive committee of the city Soviet instructed that relatives who lived in different regions of the city be allowed to be evacuated together. This is one of the few instances in which policy formulations took the extended family into account. TsGASPb, f. 7384, op. 17, d. 447, l. 137.

[36] Chukovskaya, *The Akhmatova Journals*, 189–90, entry of October 28, 1941.

[37] RGALI, f. 3113, op. 1, d. 24, l. 165.

[38] Chukovskii, *Dnevnik*, 158, entry of October 15, 1941.

[39] Chukovskaya, *The Akhmatova Journals*, 192, entry of October 30, 1941.

[40] TsAGM, f. 415, op. 16, d. 293, l. 24.

[41] Stepanishcheva, "Vot tak i zhizn' proshla," l. 8.

the baggage allowances. A decree on the evacuation of people employed by government ministries stipulated a limit of 150 kilograms per employee, and an additional 50 kilograms for each family member who went along. Among the permitted items were "clothes, linen, shoes, bedding, dinner plates, tea sets, and pots and other household items, with the exception of furniture."[42] The very next decree issued by Sovnarkom, on the evacuation of workers, stipulated one hundred kilograms per head of family, with an additional forty kilograms accorded to family members.[43]

Those with the requisite political clout circumvented official regulations altogether. A director of the Lenin railway line recalled: the "appetites of each people's commissariat were very big. Each people's commissariat, each factory demanded the maximum and therefore came to us and announced: give me some railway cars for my own use, for Sidor Ivanovich, for my wife! They arrived with pianos, couches, tables, and so on." To be sure, the director assured his interviewer that, despite numerous scandals, "appetites were cut down." Nonetheless, only a few moments later, he stated that "*in some cases* we took no person, no privileges, into account."[44] The phrasing suggests that the complete disregard of person and privilege was more the exception than the norm. If "appetites" were indeed "cut down" to size, privileges were not, in general, cast aside. Furniture, particularly luxury items such as pianos and coffee tables, figures prominently in descriptions of the railway stations where people boarded the trains heading east. The daughter of Dmitrii Kedrin later wrote of their two-day sojourn in the Kazan station in mid-October, "We could see, through the ranks of soldiers, women in fur coats leading luxurious dogs, followed by people carrying inlaid coffee tables."[45]

The "inlaid coffee tables," armoires, and pianos constitute a topos in accounts of the evacuation. Evacuation was a moment of disclosure. Privileges that were in normal times concealed behind closed doors, in buildings that were off-limits to the general public, were laid bare for all to see. Mikhail German tellingly recalls his childhood journey into evacuation as his first encounter with the word *blat*, which designates a system of reciprocal favors. "The adults who were not of high rank [*ne iz chinovnykh*] simply traveled in platform cars. But the clever people [*liudi ushlye*] and those 'with position' took up space, traveling with their entire families, their housekeepers, and an enormous quantity of goods. Wasn't it then that I first heard the word *blat*?"[46]

[42] GARF, f. 6822, op. 1, d. 221, l. 1.
[43] Ibid., d. 423, l. 1.
[44] Bukov, Gorinov, and Ponomarev, *Moskva voennaia*, 376. Italics mine.
[45] Kedrin and Kedrina, "*Vkus uznavshii vsego zemnogo—*," 537.
[46] Mikhail German, *Slozhnoe proshedshee* (St. Petersburg: Iskusstvo SPb, 2000), 86.

JOURNEY FROM THE FRONT LINES

The conditions of departure depended not only on status and connections but also on circumstance. Muscovites, once again, were in a relatively privileged position. Despite persistent fears and rumors of bombardments, there were relatively few casualties as the capital's residents set out on their journey east.[47] Not so in other cities. Stalingrad was perhaps the most extreme example of a systematic German policy of bombing transport, but such incidents occurred in many other places as well. In Leningrad in mid-July, for instance, an official reported of an evacuation train carrying children that "enemy aircraft bombed the train, as a result of which many children were killed or wounded."[48] In the westernmost parts of the country, which were evacuated only when the cities were already under heavy bombardment, losses were particularly heavy. Alexander Kovarskii, a child at the time, later recalled how the train on which he traveled east with his mother and aunt from Vitebsk to Tashkent was forced to stop several times en route as enemy planes bombed the railways.[49] Raisa Yasvoina, traveling east from Kiev with her mother and her younger brother, had a similar experience. "I remember," she later recounted, "how the bombing started. . . . We got out of the train, and everybody was screaming and crying. It was terrible, a nightmare . . . and I somehow lost my mother."[50] Fortunately for Raisa, they soon found each other, and continued on their journey together. Thirteen-year-old Tania Aizenberg, who was evacuated from Kiev in late August 1941, was not so lucky. Several months later, in Tashkent, she recounted her experiences to Lydia Chukovskaia. The train on which she and her mother were traveling had stopped and she was playing outside while her mother prepared lunch in the railway car. All of a sudden, planes appeared overhead. "I ran into the fields. The fields were very wide. The wheat was already lying in sheaves. I hid in the sheaves. I looked up from under the wheat: the train was on fire, as was the railway car, where Mama was." Aizenberg made the rest of the journey to Tashkent on her own.[51]

The journey by boat could be equally treacherous. In Odessa, boat became the sole means of evacuation in August 1941. As Sophia Abidor later recalled, the "Germans had surrounded Odessa from all sides, and it was no longer possible to leave by train." Memories of the evacuation are invari-

---

[47] On the rumors, see L. I. Timofeev, "Dnevnik voennykh let," *Znamia*, no. 6 (2002): 157, entry of October 14, 1941; and Georgii Efron, *Dnevniki (1941–1943 gody)*, vol. 2, ed. E. B. Korkina and V. K. Losskaia (Moscow: Vagrius, 2005), 38, entry of October 14, 1941.

[48] TsGASPb, f. 7384, op. 17, d. 443, l. 310.

[49] Aleksandr Kovarskii, "Detstvo na ulitse chempiona," *Zhurnal Mishpokha*, no. 14 (2004) (www.mishpoha.org/nomer14/a18.htm).

[50] Raisa Yasvoina, interview in *Jewish Witness to a European Century*. Russian transcript provided by Centropa.org.

[51] Lidiia Chukovskaia and Lidiia Zhukova, *Slovo predostavliaetsia detiam* (Tashkent: Sovetskii pisatel', 1942), 25.

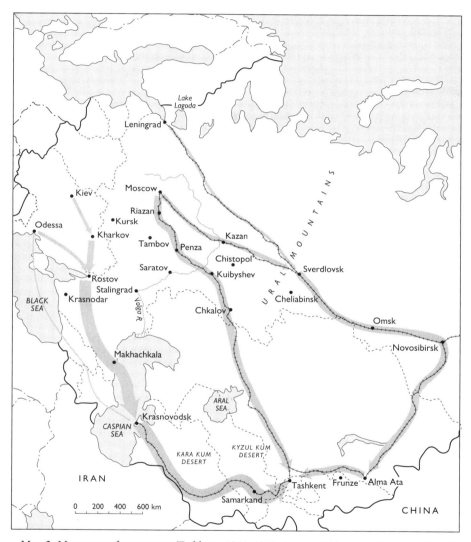

Map 2. Movement of evacuees to Tashkent, 1941–1942. Arrow width is roughly proportional to the number of evacuees from each city.

ably associated with bombardment. Sophia Abidor recalled how her boat was bombed en route from Odessa to Sevastopol. Fortunately, the fire was extinguished.[52] Less fortunate were those traveling on the ship *Lenin* on the fateful day when it hit a mine shortly after leaving Odessa. In his memoirs, Saul Borovoi recounts how an acquaintance had offered to secure him a spot on the *Lenin*, but he had declined: the "thought that I would have to ask something of someone was unbearable to me." Instead, Borovoi traveled on the less comfortable *Voroshilov*, from which he observed the tragedy firsthand. The *Lenin* sank, and only a fraction of the ship's four thousand passengers survived. Borovoi, who participated in the rescue effort, recalled one survivor in particular: a young man whom he pulled out of the water, "almost naked, but in his hands he had his Komsomol membership card. He was terrified of losing it."[53]

In other cases, people traveled by car or truck. In this respect, the military, managerial, and political elite were particularly well provisioned. Despite directives issued in Belorussia forbidding the requisitioning of state cars to this end, the practice was widespread, particularly among military officers who regularly requisitioned cars to evacuate their families. A command issued to the troops of the Western Front in early July noted that "at the same time as active units at the front have a desperate need for motor transport, a significant number of cars settle in the rear and are used in a most disorderly manner."[54] Party members and factory directors likewise requisitioned cars to evacuate either themselves or their families. In Kursk, for example, the manager of an alcohol trust "decided to take his family from Kursk to Cheliabinsk oblast, illegally procuring documents for their departure, even though an evacuation of Kursk oblast and the city of Kursk was not underway. Using his position, he departed with his family in a car belonging to the trust, which he filled with 425 kilograms of petrol."[55]

Given the scarcity of transportation, many traveled by foot. In the town of Klintsy, where evacuations were left until it was already too late, the civilian population had little choice. The writer Mark Friedkin set down the following account of his family's evacuation based on his father's reminiscences: The family, including his father Solomon and his father's paralyzed mother Genessia, had gathered at the train station to wait for a train that was rumored to be en route. "When they arrived at the station, the coaches were not there yet. . . . They waited for the coaches until the evening, and when it had already gotten dark, it became clear that there would, of course, be no trains, and moreover that it was no longer possible to travel by rail-

[52] Sophia Abidor, interview by Ella Levitskaya, April 2003, in *Jewish Witness to a European Century*. Russian transcript provided by Centropa.org.

[53] Saul Borovoi, *Vospominaniia* (Moscow: Evreiskii universitet v Moskve, 1993), 247–48.

[54] P. N. Knyshevskii et al., *Skrytaia pravda voiny: 1941 god* (Moscow: Russkaia kniga, 1992), 159.

[55] RGASPI, f. 17, op. 22, d. 1589, l. 105.

way because the Germans had cut it off. At that moment, following the announcement, the station came under heavy bombardment and fire. There was terrible panic and confusion." When the bombing stopped, Solomon could no longer find his mother. "Meanwhile, it was impossible to wait any longer—the last of our forces had already left and the Germans could appear at any moment. Solomon wept, pulled his hair, and cried that he could not leave, abandoning his mother he was not even sure where. [A friend] told him that if he stayed, he would save neither his mother, himself, nor his son. . . . In sum, they left." According to Freidkin, they walked for forty days, until they reached the city of Kursk, and from there boarded a train, which took them to the interior.[56] Solomon's predicament was not unusual. Fifteen-year-old Liuba Bulgakova from Gomel told Chukovskaia how the city's railway station had been bombed during the evacuation, and how "our children's home had to leave by foot. We walked 400 kilometers by foot."[57] Evacuation by foot even became one of the officially ordained methods of organized evacuation. A standard evacuation order in Odessa, for instance, stipulated that the evacuation of members of the Odessa Academic Opera Theater and their families (a total of 150 people), take place "by foot." They were to be followed by three trucks with their things and two cars.[58] Whether the journey began by boat, by automobile, or by foot, however, most evacuees eventually ended up on one and the same mode of transport—the train.

IN TRANSIT

Over the course of several weeks, the Soviet Union had been transformed. Railway stations had become settlements in which the resident population changed daily. Aleksander Wat recalled that in Saratov, on the middle Volga, there were "peasant men and women, whole families, middle-class people, workers, intellectuals, all on the miserable floor of the train station. . . . There were permanent camps during the war, entire families with their bundles waiting a day, two, three."[59] The government had established an extensive network of evacuation centers where those en route would be fed, receive medical aid, and temporary shelter.[60] By early 1942, there were sixty-seven of them in the Russian Republic alone, and dozens more in Central Asia, Kazakhstan and the Caucasus.[61] However, many of these had not been established until the flow of evacuees had already reached flood-like

---

[56] Mark Freidkin, *Opyty* (Moscow: Carte blanche, 1994), 315–17.
[57] Chukovskaia and Zhukova, *Slovo predostavliaetsia detiam*, 75.
[58] OIKM, D. 11189.
[59] Wat, *My Century*, 309
[60] On the responsibilities of the evacuation centers, see GARF, f. A-327, op. 2, d. 4, l. 12.
[61] Ibid., ll. 32, 38–39.

Figure 4. Evacuees board a train at the Finland Station for Lake Ladoga, March 1942, Leningrad (courtesy TsGAKFFD SPb).

proportions.[62] Moreover, while designed to accommodate as many as twelve hundred people each, these centers were nonetheless unable to provide for the masses of people heading east. In Kharkov, one of the first cities to be flooded by the rapid influx of people, authorities estimated that over ten thousand people were crowded into the city's stations and its only evacuation center.[63] Lilia Shchupak recalls arriving in the former Ukrainian capital: The "evacuation center had been set up not far from the station in a school. There were already many people there, who had come from different places: they sat on suitcases, bundles, and simply on the floor."[64]

The sheer volume of people passing through individual stations on a daily basis overwhelmed authorities and the facilities at their disposal. During the most intense period of evacuations, as many as seventeen or eighteen thousand people passed through the Sverdlovsk evacuation center each

[62] In Novosibirsk, for example, where evacuees began to arrive in the middle of July, an evacuation center was not established until September. See Kristen Elizabeth Edwards, "Fleeing to Siberia: The Wartime Relocation of Evacuees to Novosibirsk, 1941–1943" (Ph.D. diss., Stanford University, 1996), 87.

[63] GARF f. A-259, op. 40, d. 3068, l. 19.

[64] Liliia Shchupak, *Nichto ne prokhodit bessledno* (New York: Effect Publishing, 1997), 50.

Figure 5. Evacuated residents of Leningrad awaiting transportation after crossing Lake Ladoga, April 1942, Kobon (courtesy TsGAKFFD SPb).

day.[65] During the war, "passing through" could take anywhere from a couple of hours to a couple of weeks. As Aleksander Wat explained in his memoirs, "when changing trains you had to have your ticket validated again at the window, and it always turned out that there were no seats for the next two, three, four days. Since there were no hotels, there was no choice but to camp out at the station."[66] If a new ticket was required, the wait could be even longer. Inna Shikheeva-Gaister and her small circle of traveling companions moved from their apartment in Ufa "to live at the train station, to make it more convenient to stand in line for tickets."[67] They reached their turn in line after one week.

The primary cause of delays was the acute shortage of railway cars. As a report from Kuibyshev put it, "railway authorities do not provide the required number of railway cars for the dispatch of evacuees."[68] The transportation of millions of people and goods posed a formidable challenge, which tested the limits of the country's infrastructure. By November 20, 1941, 914,380 railway cars had been sent east carrying raw materials, industrial goods, machinery, and people.[69] One year later, the number had risen to more than a million and a half. This represented a substantial proportion of the country's overall transportation capacity. In July 1941, almost half of the existing stock of railway cars was involved in the evacuation.[70] Evacuee transport was significantly complicated by the seemingly limitless needs of the front. In the eastern Ukrainian Republic, for example, officials noted that the "directors of the stations are incapable of sending the evacuees anywhere due to the lack of passenger trains and the absence of covered rolling stock, used only for the needs of the front."[71] A similar problem was reported on the Black Sea during the evacuation of the Crimea in August 1941, when repeated requests for boats were refused on the grounds that it would simply not be possible "until the freeing up of ships from Odessa."[72] The shortage of railway cars had a dramatic impact on both the efficiency of the overall process and on the conditions in which people traveled.

The situation was particularly dire in Stalingrad. In late November, a special commission was dispatched to Stalingrad to investigate reports of problems in evacuee transit. They found "two hundred thousand evacuated people, not only on the trains but at the stations, evacuation centers, and harbors, on the streets, in the stadium, on city squares, and . . . on the out-

[65] GARF, f. A-327, op. 2, d. 33, l. 211.

[66] Wat, *My Century*, 308.

[67] Shikheeva-Gaister, *Semeinaia khronika*, 66.

[68] RGASPI, f. 17, op. 22, d. 1559, l. 31.

[69] G. A. Kumanev and Iu. A. Poliakov, "Voina i zheleznodorozhnyi transport SSSR, 1941–1945," in *Bor'ba narodov protiv fashizma i agressii* (Moscow: Nauka, 1988), 96.

[70] I. V. Kovalev, *Transport v Velikoi Otechestvennoi voine (1941–1945)* (Moscow: Nauka, 1981), 83.

[71] GARF, f. A-259, op. 40, d. 3053, l. 20.

[72] GARF, f. 6822, op. 1, d. 43, l. 4.

skirts of town."[73] The city on the lower Volga that was to become the site of the most famous battle of World War II was, in the first year of the war, one of the primary reception points for evacuees. In the first seven months of the war, 438,500 people passed through the city's evacuation center.[74] According to monthly reports from the center, not a single evacuee spent fewer than two full weeks waiting for connections.[75]

Predictably, such conditions sparked bursts of outrage. In mid-November 1941, Shvernik received an irate letter from a Communist stranded in Stalingrad on his way from the Donbass to Novosibirsk. Describing in vivid detail the general disarray, he charged: "I didn't see such disorder, chaos, and helplessness in all the years of the revolution. The people move east at will, literally starving, enduring unbelievable suffering. And what is really bad is the inability of authorities on the railway line and in cities to organize the mass distribution of food, hot water, and warm clothes for living people."[76] Provisioning a population on the move posed enormous logistical challenges. In principle, the evacuation centers provided evacuees with food and hot water. An evacuation center in Gorkii oblast boasted an impressive menu, which included, according to a report to Shvernik: noodle soup with or without meat, cutlets, meatballs, goulash, coarse barley kasha, and tea.[77] Such delicacies, however, with the possible exception of the tea, are nowhere to be found among the varied descriptions of food en route in memoirs, diaries, and correspondence. In region after region, authorities complained that the evacuation points "work poorly."[78] In Stalingrad, it was reported that only one of the city's five evacuation centers had hot food.[79]

How one traveled depended, in no small measure, on who one was. The linguist Dmitrii Ushakov later wrote to a friend, "how did we travel? Badly, it seemed (it was crowded, we had to take turns sleeping, etc.); now it seems that we traveled in splendid style." He further recounted that "twice en route, in Kuibyshev and then in Orenburg [Chkalov], we were issued enormous pieces of bread on somebody's orders. Compare that to the mass of sorrow, suffering, and sacrifice that has fallen to the lot of thousands and thousands of others!"[80] Given the standards of the day, this was indeed high style. As Maria Belkina, on the same train as Ushakov, later wrote, "I was lucky, I ended up in a privileged echelon."[81] It should be noted that, with the exception of the movie star Liubov Orlova, who was reportedly brought

---

[73] Ibid., d. 510, l. 57.

[74] Of those, 40% had gone on to settle in other oblasts.

[75] GARF, f. 327, op. 2, d. 33, l. 167.

[76] GARF, f. 5466, op. 59, d. 4, l. 105.

[77] GARF, f. 6822, op. 1, d. 422, l. 78.

[78] RGASPI, f. 17, op. 22, l. 31.

[79] GARF, f. 6822, op. 1, d. 510, l. 56.

[80] Letter to G. O. Vinokur, December 22, 1941, in Nikitin, "Poslednie pis'ma D. N. Ushakova," 67.

[81] Belkina, *Skreshchenie sudeb*, 344.

food by star-struck admirers en route, even the most distinguished of people were, as individuals, no more able to secure food at evacuation centers than ordinary citizens. When Kornei Chukovskii stood in line for bread at a stop by the Aral Sea, he got nothing.[82] What set Chukovskii and his traveling companions apart, rather, was the willingness and ability of higher authorities to intervene on their behalf. Writers, the "engineers of human souls," traveled with candles and sausage procured for them before their departure from Moscow by Alexander Fadeev, the secretary of the Writers' Union.[83] Telegrams requesting preferential treatment, moreover, were dispatched on their behalf to stations en route.[84] The relative comfort of the intellectual and cultural elite was ensured not only by the likes of Fadeev, who stood at the head of the literary establishment, but by the highest levels of the political establishment. No less than Kosygin saw to it that the evacuated "artists, writers, and honored scientists" were adequately provisioned. "The two echelons dispatched from the Kazan station have one 'soft' railway car and one restaurant car," he reported to Molotov, Mikoian, and Shvernik in mid-October. "The two passenger cars dispatched from the Paveletsk station have also been supplied with food for the journey."[85]

This is not to say that writers traveled in comfort: the writers' echelon with which Georgii Efron traveled, for example, received no bread for over six days. Echoing the conclusions of the Communist stranded in Stalingrad, the writers Derzhavin and Kochetkov reportedly claimed that "even in 1917–18, in the years of collapse and terrible disorder, there was greater order on the railways." Even so, when the writers arrived in Syzran they were given 250 grams of bread each. Apparently a group of academics had gone on ahead to Kuibyshev with the aim of "easing our situation." Once the echelon reached the country's temporary capital, moreover, a group of writers succeeded in getting goulash and bread from the NKVD, while the "academics succeeded in provisioning the entire echelon with bread (in the quantity of approximately 1 kilogram per person), butter (200 grams, it seems), sugar (400 grams), a jar of eggplant caviar, semolina wheat."[86]

Self-evacuees, by contrast, were cut loose from the institutionally based webs through which Soviet citizens gained access to housing, food, and other goods. Zinaida Stepanishcheva, who traveled east unaffiliated with her six-month-old child, enjoyed no such help. They received adequate provisions while still in European Russia, but conditions deteriorated considerably once they crossed the Ural Mountains. "Even in major cities there was not only not

---

[82] Chukovskii, *Dnevnik*, 159, entry of October 22, 1941.

[83] RGALI, f. 631, op. 15, d. 565, ll. 159, 175.

[84] For example, Fadeev sent telegrams to Cheliabinsk, Sverdlovsk, and the heads of the Omsk and Tashkent railway lines to ensure that writers on their way to Tashkent were not held up en route. RGALI, f. 631, op. 15, d. 565, ll. 174, 177, 187, 188.

[85] GARF, f. 6822, op. 1, d. 468, l. 4.

[86] Efron, *Dnevniki*, vol. 2, 120–21, entry of November 13, 1941.

enough boiling water, but there was insufficient cold boiled water. And nobody among us resolved to drink unboiled water."[87] Conditions were so bad that, as Stepanishcheva recalled, "my milk began to disappear." In several cases, those who lacked appropriate documentation were simply refused food outright.[88]

Making one's way through the hurdles required companions. As Georgii Efron, contemplating his upcoming evacuation to Tashkent, noted in his diary: "I'm not going alone—that is already very significant."[89] In this sense, the collective really had become a basic unit of Soviet society. As in Soviet life more generally, travel on one's own made the journey significantly more difficult.[90] One person was required to stand with the luggage while another stood in line. Companions were essential. Stories of the railway journey frequently revolve around the new and transitory communities that formed en route. The adolescent Shikheeva-Gaister and her younger siblings banded together with another young woman whom they met on the journey east.[91] Stepanishcheva's whole railway car banded together under the leadership of one particularly enterprising individual. And Nikolai Druzhinin recalled how a "distinctive 'commune' formed en route, which existed until the end of our journey."[92]

At the same time, evacuees set about reconstituting the communities that had only recently been rent apart. They sought to reestablish contact with those they had left behind and to bridge the widening gulf that separated them from their loved ones. Evacuees sent hurried letters to family and friends informing them of the progress of their journey and in some cases of their departure. Kornei Chukovskii dispatched a telegram to his daughter Lydia, evacuated earlier that summer to Chistopol, from Penza: "Going to Tashkent." He urged her to join them there.[93] Elena Dobychina wrote to her sister on August 4, "I don't know if this postcard will reach you. . . . I am on the train. I am going to Tashkent."[94]

THE TOPOGRAPHY OF REFUGE

Within weeks of the German invasion, evacuees were dispersed across the country. Data from the Central Statistical Bureau charting the flow of evacuees

[87] Stepanishcheva, "Vot tak i zhizn' proshla," l. 10.

[88] This happened, for example, in Samarkand. GARF f. 327, op. 2, d. 56, l. 42.

[89] Efron, *Dnevniki*, vol. 2, 71, entry of October 26, 1941.

[90] In Leningrad, a group of elderly people asked if they could be evacuated together "as on their own they don't have the strength to travel and will get lost somewhere." TsGAIPD SPb, f. 25, op. 5, d. 188, l. 20.

[91] Shikheeva-Gaister, *Semeinaia khronika*, 62.

[92] Druzhinin, "Evakuatsiia iz Moskvy," 111.

[93] Telegram of October 15, 1941, in Kornei Chukovskii and Lidiia Chukovskaia, *Perepiska: 1912–1969*, ed. E. Ts. Chukovskaia and Zh. O. Khavkina (Moscow: Novoe literaturnoe obozrenie, 2004), 315.

[94] E. E. Dobychina to N. E. Dobychina, August 4, 1941, OR RGB, f. 420, op. 12, d. 1, l. 7.

east suggests that by October 1941, there was not a single oblast or autonomous republic that did not count evacuees among its numbers.[95] The data would seem to belie the existence of selected regions of evacuee reception— evacuees were everywhere. Yet, in both the prewar evacuation guidelines and in the more concrete plans elaborated in the wake of the invasion, authorities clearly envisaged a specific topography of refuge. The evacuation, after all, had been designed to distribute and order rationally the displaced population. The objective had been to avoid the mass chaos that had engulfed the country in World War I. The resettlement of evacuees was further designed to maintain industrial production and to replenish the rural labor force, depleted by the recent conscription.[96] To this end, the Evacuation Council had drawn up graphs charting exactly how many trains from which destinations would go where.[97] For example, the families of workers and employees in the Leningrad region, a projected total of one hundred thousand evacuees, were to be evacuated to Kirov oblast (twenty thousand), Iaroslavl oblast (forty thousand), and Ivanovo oblast (forty thousand). Those from western Ukraine would be directed to Stalingrad, Rostov, and Aktiubinsk oblasts, Krasnodar and Ordzhonikidze krais, and Kazakhstan.[98] This information was relayed both to organizations subject to evacuation and to individual evacuation centers, which determined the destination of those traveling "in an individual order."

Neither Tashkent nor, for that matter, Uzbekistan even figured among the designated reception sites for evacuees drawn up by the Evacuation Council in the immediate aftermath of the invasion.[99] From the perspective of early July 1941, authorities in Moscow could hardly imagine that the

---

[95] RGAE, f. 1562, op. 20, d. 249, l. 34.

[96] The Evacuation Council sought to use the evacuation to deal with labor shortages in both urban and rural regions. Specialized workers were in theory directed to cities in which their skills were in demand, and the bulk of evacuees were directed to the countryside, where the shortage of labor was more acute than in the cities. In addition, authorities attempted to use the evacuation to meet the drastic shortage of labor created by the deportation of entire peoples as "enemy nations." Evidence of state attempts to funnel evacuees into the regions formerly occupied by the Volga Germans can be found in GARF, f. 6822, op. 1, d. 74, l. 76.

[97] The first such chart, drawn up in early July, set out the number of people to be evacuated from each of the areas subject to evacuation at the time and how many were to be dispatched to which destinations. GARF, f. A-259, op. 40, d. 3028, ll. 67–68.

[98] Ibid.

[99] The designated reception sites listed in a plan dated July 3, 1941, included the Kazakh Republic, the Uvash, Tatar, and Komi Autonomous Republics, and Archangel, Vologda, Iaroslavl, Gorkii, Stalingrad, Saratov, Kuibyshev, Tambov, and Penza oblasts. GARF f. A-259, op. 40, d. 3028, l. 57. In the July 5 Decree on the Evacuation of the Population during War, the designated regions were considerably expanded. A draft of the decree instructed authorities to "permit the resettlement of evacuees from the frontline regions as a first priority in cities, workers' settlements, and villages in Gorkii, Penza, Kirov, Kuibyshev, Saratov, and Stalingrad oblasts and the Mordvin, Chuvash, Udmurt, Tatar, and Bashkir ASSRs. As a second priority in Chkalov, Molotov, Sverdlovsk, Cheliabinsk, Omsk, and Novosibirsk oblasts and Altai krai and the Kazakh SSR." Ibid., d. 3022, l. 14.

Central Asian republics, located thousands of kilometers from the front lines, would be required for resettlement. Although Siberia, Kazakhstan, and the Urals quickly appeared in evacuation plans, the most important initial reception sites of the civilian evacuation were the central oblasts of Saratov, Tambov, Riazan, and Penza.[100] In some cases, the designated reception areas for evacuees were so close that evacuees found themselves effectively on the front lines. The most notorious example of this was in the Iaroslavl region, which served as a designated reception site for evacuated children from Leningrad.

Given both the rapid collapse of the front and the obvious dangers of resettling civilians in its vicinity, the zones of evacuee reception were substantially enlarged, and both Uzbekistan and its capital city became important centers of the organized evacuation. Over the course of several months, a wide variety of institutions, factories, and enterprises were evacuated to Tashkent, ranging from textile and machine-tool construction factories from the major industrial centers of both Russia and Ukraine to the Leningrad Conservatory. Tashkent was a privileged reception site for a whole range of institutes of the Soviet Academy of Sciences and emerged as a particularly important center of the cultural evacuation.[101] Kosygin himself ordained the evacuation to Tashkent of some four hundred "elderly and infirm writers and the families of writers on the front."[102] The Moscow State Jewish Theater, the Theater of the Revolution, and a number of film directors were all evacuated to Tashkent. The city also became the primary reception site of the country's artistic community.

In theory, travel to Tashkent was open only to those who had been sent there. In keeping with the state's goals of controlling evacuee distribution, individuals were not, with some exceptions, at liberty to choose their own destinations. Stepanishcheva recounts in her memoirs how she was unable to procure a ticket to Tashkent at the evacuation center in Moscow. "They had their own agenda—to gather a sufficient number of Muscovites to help reap the harvest in Sverdlovsk and Chkalov oblasts. Whether or not I would be able to earn much there with a nursing baby didn't interest anyone. And they gave me papers for Chkalov oblast. When my husband went to get the ticket and once again began talking about Tashkent, no one listened to him and they gave him a ticket for Chkalov."[103] Olga Boltianskaia's efforts to procure a ticket to Tashkent were no more successful. "There was

---

[100] These areas appear repeatedly in evacuation plans and had the greatest concentration of evacuees as of September 1, 1941. RGAE, f. 1562, op. 20, d. 249, l. 22.

[101] The following Academy of Sciences institutes were evacuated to Tashkent: the Institute of Language and Letters, the Institute of Philosophy, the Institute of Law, and the Institute of History. Three other institutes were initially designated for Tashkent, but their destination was later changed. GARF, f. 6822, op. 1, d. 52, l. 58.

[102] GARF, f. 6822, op. 1, d. 48, l. 14.

[103] Stepanishcheva, "Vot tak i zhizn' proshla," l. 6.

a resolution," she recounted in her diary, ". . . to transport everyone only 200 to 300 kilometers from Moscow."[104]

In practice, however, the charts and graphs of the Evacuation Council were but pieces of paper, with little real effect. The Evacuation Council's efforts to order evacuee resettlement rationally were stymied by logistical problems of mammoth proportions. As a report to the Uzbek Sovnarkom put it, the "dispatch of contingents to republics, oblasts, and districts in the Central Asian republics is not organized correctly."[105] For a start, each train had to go through a variety of stations on its route, any of which could redirect it. A representative of the division responsible for the settlement of evacuees complained that regional bureaus in Sverdlovsk, Omsk, and Novosibirsk were taking matters into their own hands, and had "redirected the railway cars to regions where there was no planned reception of evacuees."[106] In many cases, local authorities were less concerned with the ultimate destination of the railway cars than they were with clearing out their own stations. The Georgian Republic proposed sending evacuees who had arrived in the coastal towns of Batumi, Sukhumi, and Poti on to Central Asia,[107] and Turkmen authorities almost systematically redirected evacuees onward to Uzbekistan.[108] The difficulties confronting local station masters are evident in the following case from Penza: despite having received a telegram prohibiting the use of railway cars for those who had already reached their destination, the head of the Penza railroad station, in the face of the "accumulation of thousands of people", "was compelled to find ten to twenty railway cars to transport them elsewhere."[109]

Many trains traveled without any indication of their final destination, leaving railway stations with little guidance. Authorities in Rostov, for instance, reported on "the need to draw attention to the following serious deficiencies in the organization of the evacuation: not all echelons have lists of evacuees, and many don't have a final destination."[110] In the prevailing chaos, there were even cases of trains returning to the places they came from with their passengers still on board. Over only a month and a half, twelve trains carrying evacuees had been turned around at Kuibyshev, Valuik, and Penza.[111] The situation

---

[104] Diary of O. A. Boltianskaia, RGALI, f. 2057, op. 2, d. 29, l. 87, entry of August 4, 1941. It was only when her husband, who worked in the film industry, managed to get her name on a list of film workers being evacuated to Tashkent that she procured a ticket to the city. Ibid., ll. 87–88.

[105] TsGARUz, f. 837, op. 32, d. 2894, l. 62.

[106] GARF, f. A-327, op.2, d. 56, l. 119.

[107] GARF, f. A-259, op. 40, d. 3037, l. 20.

[108] TsGARUz, f. 837, op. 32, d. 2894, l. 88.

[109] GARF f. 6822, op.1, d. 40, l. 1.

[110] Ibid., d. 422, l. 23. Authorities in Penza, noting a similar phenomenon, blamed the Council of People's Commissars and the People's Commissariat of Transportation, which were invariably late in assigning destinations. Ibid., l. 53.

[111] Ibid., l. 53.

was so disorderly that authorities on the receiving end were compelled to take action: the Uzbek Sovnarkom, for example, decided to send representatives to Penza, Kuibyshev, and Krasnovodsk to regulate the flow of people.[112]

Even if a train made it to its designated destination, there was no guarantee that its passengers would. Everywhere, authorities echoed the conclusion of two Uzbek officials dispatched to the station of Arys to assess the situation: "There are no commandants to accompany echelons who might organize the movement of masses of people. As a result, some people disembark en route at various stations."[113] When the Leningrad City Soviet received a complaint from central evacuation authorities suggesting that they had authorized such behavior, they replied that "evacuees from Leningrad are sent only to those oblasts indicated by the government: evacuees disembark at stations en route at their own discretion." While officials promised that the district executive committees would "take measures to warn evacuees that those who willfully disembark will not be accepted," such warnings, if issued, appear to have had little effect.[114] The head of an echelon from Leningrad reported in early August 1941 that of his echelon of 1,825 people, only 480 were left when the train arrived at its destination.[115] Those who remained, moreover, all wanted to go to Tashkent, "and thus our echelon was sent to Tashkent."[116]

As the example above suggests, some disembarked en route, whereas others continued on to places beyond their designated destinations. "Many evacuees do not remain in the places they have been sent and travel further," complained one official. "Thus, for example, I saw evacuees in collective farms in the Krasnodar region who traveled from there on to Tashkent."[117] The memoirs of Zinaida Stepanishcheva offer a glimpse into the mechanics of such a journey. Stepanishcheva had been given a ticket for Penza, but on departure from Moscow, she had joined an unofficial, collectively formed echelon bound for Tashkent. When the group reached Penza, the same enterprising individual asked each of the "Tashkenters" for a bit of money, and secured their passage to Chkalov by bribing the coupler to simply attach their car to the outbound train. "In Chkalov," Stepanishcheva recalled: "he did the exact same thing and we were attached to a train that went to Tashkent. . . .

[112] TsGARUz, f. 314, op. 1, d. 37, l. 6.
[113] TsGARUz, f. 837, op. 32, d. 2894, l. 62.
[114] TsGASPb, f. 7384, op. 17, d. 448, l. 193. The files of the Leningrad Evacuation Council suggest that they did in fact condone the practice, provided that evacuees remain within the designated areas. Those with relatives in other regions were permitted to disembark en route and make their way to their families on their own. See the decision of the Executive Committee of the Leningrad Soviet of August 16, 1941, in TsGASPb, f. 7384, op. 17, d. 665, l. 20. Similar allowances were made, at least in theory, in Moscow. See GARF, f. A-259, op. 40, d. 3058, l. 65. As Stepanishcheva's case suggests, however, such directives were not always followed.
[115] TsGASPb, f. 330, op. 2, d. 3, l. 10.
[116] Ibid.
[117] GARF, f. 6822, op. 1, d. 40, l. 1.

We traveled from Penza to Tashkent without tickets. Everyone had documents from the evacuation center, designating various destinations, but we all went to Tashkent. In the chaos that prevailed in the country, nobody checked either our tickets or our documents."[118] A representative on the Penza railway line reported that the "evacuated population travels in a disorganized fashion, in all manner of trains, and frequently without tickets."[119] Stepanishcheva and her traveling companions were clearly no exception.

Central authorities were well apprised of the chaos on the ground. A report from late September 1941 on the "abnormalities" in the evacuation insisted that "these useless free journeys around the Soviet Union need to come to an end."[120] The sentiment was echoed by many others, who insisted that the Commissariat of Transportation "immediately put an end to this disorder in the advancement of evacuees."[121] The repeated efforts to bring order to evacuee movement met with limited success. A report from the summer of 1942 on the country as a whole noted that "only a third of the population (not including schools, kindergartens, etc.) arrives at its designated destination."[122] The problem was not simply one of logistics. Rather, the Evacuation Council's grand resettlement scheme was further foiled by the refusal of the population to perform "in accordance with the plan" (*po planu*).

If central officials had a logic to their distribution plans, evacuees followed a logic of their own. As a report in early August 1941 put it, "significant groups of evacuees move from place to place, in search of the best place to settle."[123] The "best place" was in many ways defined in the eye of the beholder. At the most general level, evacuees sought out places where they had family or friends. This appears to account for the large number of Leningraders, discussed above, who "disembarked en route" and were the source of so much consternation. As the head of an echelon evacuated from Leningrad in August 1941, reported, "many members of my echelon left and set out on their own for their relatives."[124]

In addition, evacuees tended to opt for cities over villages. Rural regions were notably unpopular among evacuees, who went to considerable lengths to avoid being settled in the countryside. "The evacuated population from the cities of our old border . . . aim to settle in cities, trying in every way to escape settlement on a collective farm," one report complained. A similar report was filed in the Rostov region, where authorities drew attention to the "tendency" among certain evacuees "not to remain in rural places."[125]

---

[118] Stepanishcheva, "Vot tak i zhizn' proshla," ll. 7, 9–10.
[119] GARF, f. 6822, op. 1, d. 40, l. 42.
[120] Ibid., l. 1.
[121] Ibid., l. 42.
[122] GARF, f. A-327, op. 2, d. 36, l. 77.
[123] GARF, f. A-259, op. 40, d. 3053, l. 21.
[124] TsGASPb, f. 330, op. 2, d. 3, l. 35.
[125] GARF, f. 6822, op. 1, d. 422, l. 23.

Evacuees, claimed yet another official, "attempt in all ways possible to settle only in cities and worker settlements."[126] Among the dozens of cities that drew evacuees in such large numbers, one in particular stood out.

DESTINATION TASHKENT

"Everyone wanted to go south," recalled Aleksander Wat. "Where? Everyone wanted to go to Tashkent. Why Tashkent? Because Tashkent was a 'city of bread.' . . . That's the power of a title: *Tashkent, City of Bread*. Magic words. The book had been published in Russia, but it had been translated into Polish. The Poles didn't know about it, but all the Jews, even the ones who didn't read, had heard about it from others. *Tashkent, City of Bread*."[127] Tashkent was indeed one of the most popular wartime destinations. Although no one commented on the phenomenon quite as lyrically as Wat, he was but one of many to describe it. "A great number of evacuees are headed for Tashkent," reported one official in Penza in the fall of 1941. "There is reason to fear that an excessive number of people will accumulate there and that it will be necessary to transfer them to other regions."[128] A report from the Kazakh city of Arys likewise noted that "significant masses of people move haphazardly [*samotekom*] to Uzbekistan and, as a first priority, to Tashkent."[129] According to Saul Borovoi, who journeyed across the Caspian Sea from Makhachkala to Krasnovodsk, "the majority of refugees sought to go to Tashkent."[130] Whether in Moscow, Penza, Kazakhstan, or on the shores of the Caspian Sea, observers repeatedly noted the same phenomenon: in the words of an official in Uzbekistan, "everyone is headed for Tashkent."[131]

As Aleksander Wat's comments suggest, Tashkent's appeal was, in no small measure, the product of a fictional account, Neverov's *Tashkent, City of Bread*. Written in the early 1920s, it was adapted into a popular children's book and was translated into a host of other languages including Polish, Yiddish, and Hebrew.[132] The novel, set during the famine of 1921, followed a young boy on his journey from the famine-stricken Volga region east to Tashkent in search of bread for himself and his family. The title notwithstanding, the author spends little time describing the city itself. Rather, most

[126] GARF f. A-259, op. 40, d. 3024, l. 72.
[127] Wat, *My Century*, 310–11.
[128] GARF, f. 6822, op. 1, d. 40, l. 1.
[129] TsGARUz, f. 837, op. 32, d. 2894, l. 62.
[130] Borovoi, *Vospominaniia*, 258.
[131] TsGARUz, f. 314, op. 1, d. 116, l. 18. Tashkent was one of two cities singled out by Moscow municipal authorities in a report on increased demand on specific railway routes. The other city was Novosibirsk. GARF, f. A-259, op. 40, d. 3042, l. 68.
[132] The children's book, adapted from the novel, was entitled *Mishka Dodonov* and published in 1925.

of the novel is taken up with descriptions of the voyage. The title alone, however, helped forge an image of the Uzbek capital in the popular imagination. References to the novel are ubiquitous in memoir literature on the evacuation. The Muscovite Maria Belkina, for example, invoked the title to explain the influx of refugees into the city: "'Tashkent—city of bread'! There was a novel of that name by Neverov, written in 1923."[133] The novel was reportedly mentioned by a large number of Lithuanian Jews in testimonies about their wartime experiences in the Soviet Union.[134]

Tashkent was placed on the mental map of the displaced population not only by Neverov but by the thousands of others like him who had made the trek to Tashkent during the cataclysm of World War I, the Civil War, and the famine. By 1941, the path to Tashkent in times of trouble was well trodden. The first wave of refugees to reach the city came during the famine of 1891, when thousands of migrants descended on Turkestan in search of food and arable land. Tashkent subsequently served as a refuge for displaced people during World War I, and as Neverov's novel suggests, it became a particularly sought after destination during the famine of 1921.[135] By the outbreak of World War II, through Neverov's novel and the memory of the events it described, Tashkent had entered popular consciousness as a land of plenty and a place of refuge, untouched by the ravages of war. Jack Pomerantz, a refugee from Poland, recalled in his memoirs that he and his unknown traveling companions "held onto Tashkent as we would a dream, envisioning it as a place where we might begin to make our lives better."[136] Vladimir Petrov wrote of Central Asia that "here, it was said, life was still good, almost prewar: you could buy anything and even find a room."[137] Timofeev, weighing a possible evacuation to the Volga city of Saratov or Tashkent, praised the latter's "distance."[138]

Tashkent's appeal stemmed from its southern location as well as its almost legendary food supply and distance from the front. Although evacuees would later complain bitterly about the inhospitable climate, many were originally drawn there on its account. Georgii Efron, who was of two minds

[133] Belkina, *Skreshchenie sudeb*, 345.

[134] See Dov Levin, *Baltic Jews under the Soviets, 1940–1946* (Jerusalem: Centre for Research and Documentation of East European Jewry, Avraham Harman Institute of Contemporary Jewry, Hebrew University of Jerusalem, 1994), 192 n. 32.

[135] See Jeff Sahadeo, *Russian Colonial Society in Tashkent, 1865–1923* (Bloomington: Indiana University Press, 2007), 115–16, 165–66, 224–25.

[136] Jack Pomerantz and Lyric Wallwork Winik, *Run East: Flight from the Holocaust* (Urbana: University of Illinois Press, 1997), 55.

[137] Vladimir Petrov, *My Retreat from Russia* (New Haven: Yale Univesity Press, 1950), 38.

[138] Timofeev, "Dnevnik voennykh let," 162, entry of October 23, 1941. While some evacuees sought to remain within striking distance of their homes, settling in the fertile Volga region, many evacuees sought to move as far as possible from the front. Officials in the Rostov region noted, "there are many demands from evacuees to send them further—to the East." GARF, f. 6822, op. 1, d. 422, l. 24.

about leaving Moscow, reasoned in his diary that "at least one need not fear the cold in Tashkent and its surrounding area."[139] In Leningrad, where evacuees were sometimes informed about the climactic conditions in different parts of the country by an onsite geographer, Tashkent seemed like an indisputably better choice than Novosibirsk, Cheliabinsk, Sverdlovsk, or one of the many other northern cities that also served as important reception sites for evacuees.[140] As one Polish refugee explained, "the moderate climate, with its mild winters, was attractive to many refugees, who were poorly prepared for the severe winters in other regions of the Soviet Union."[141] Evgenii Pasternak later recalled his mother's thinking when presented with the possibility of going to Tashkent: among other considerations, she had felt that "Tashkent always seemed a wealthy, well-fed city, and in winter it was warm there."[142] Likewise, Vladimir Petrov recalls that the passengers in his train heading south from Novosibirsk to Tashkent "were very pleased to be going south."[143]

Other factors drew people to the city as well, most notably the presence of family or friends. Evacuation authorities were literally inundated by what one official in Saratov described as evacuees' "mass applications, requests, to be sent to places where they have relatives."[144] Although Tashkent was not the most sought-after city in this regard, the Uzbek capital did have a substantial Russian population. Between the establishment of Soviet Uzbekistan in 1924 and the eve of the Nazi invasion, Tashkent had welcomed a steady stream of migrants from Russia. In addition, the city had emerged as one of the prime destinations in the region for exiles, second only to Alma-Ata.[145] As one Leningrader who found refuge in the city described it, Tashkent was a city where "members of the intelligentsia, exiled from the capital, lived."[146] Evacuees with friends or family in the city were almost invariably drawn there. The Leningrad historian Boris Romanov expressed a typical sentiment when he wrote in a letter, "I would like to go to Tashkent, I have friends there."[147] As Stepanishcheva recalled in her memoirs, "if I was going to go anywhere, we thought, then of course it would be to Tashkent, to my

[139] Efron, *Dnevniki*, vol. 2, 72, entry of October 26, 1941.

[140] TsGAIPD SPb, f. 25, op. 5, d. 188, l. 20.

[141] Shchupak, *Nichto ne prokhodit bessledno*, 42.

[142] Boris Pasternak and Evgenii Pasternak, *Sushchestvovania tkan' skvoznaia: Boris Pasternak perepiska s Evgeniei Pasternak, dopolnennaia pis'mami k E. B. Pasternaku i ego vospominaniiami* (Moscow: Novoe literaturnoe obozrenie, 1998), 422.

[143] Petrov, *My Retreat from Russia*, 38.

[144] GARF, f. A-259, op. 40, d. 3023, l. 50.

[145] On migration in the interwar period, see Paul Stronski, "Forging a Soviet City: Tashkent, 1937–1966" (Ph.D. diss., Stanford University, 2003), chaps. 2, 5. Although by far the most substantial number of exiles were the Koreans, deported in 1937, there were also an unidentified number of political exiles.

[146] A. E. Levitin-Krasnov, *"Ruk tvoikh zhar": 1941–1956* (Tel Aviv: Krug, 1979), 145.

[147] Quoted in V. M. Paneiakh, *Tvorchestvo i sud'ba istorika: Boris Aleksandrovich Romanov* (St. Petersburg: RAN Institut Rossiiskoi istorii S.-Peterburgskii filial, 2000), 191.

mother. I would need to work, and my mother would stay at home with the baby."[148] Olga Boltianskaia went there because of her relatives, Evgenia Pasternak because of friends "who can help us."[149]

The rapid influx of evacuated enterprises, institutes, and individuals into the city only augmented its appeal. Deborah Averbukh, for instance, started out for Vladivostok but changed direction midway. She chose Tashkent because the Kiev Polytechnic Institute, where she had been enrolled before the war, had been evacuated there and she hoped to continue her studies.[150] The Muscovite Timofeev, ever unsure of where and whether to go, was drawn to Tashkent by the presence of his evacuated institute, Lydia Chukovskaia by the presence of her evacuated father.[151] The relative importance attached to family or friends is evident in the following reflection made by Stepanishcheva of her traveling companions en route to Tashkent. "The Muscovites were all going to somebody, but the refugees from Vitebsk had no one to go to. What will happen to them? How will they be received by the Tashkent leadership? By the local population?"[152] These were indeed unsettling questions, but even the refugees entertained the hope of finding family or friends, if not in Tashkent itself, then in the station. As the Polish refugee Jack Pomerantz later wrote, "for refugees, a train station was like a headquarters. It was a meeting point, a place for news, a place to live, a place where anything could happen."[153] This was particularly true of the Tashkent station. As another refugee later put it, "everyone meets in Tashkent."[154]

Tashkent was also sought after by institutions. The city was a privileged destination, second only to a handful of cities, most notably Kuibyshev, the country's temporary new seat of power. Theaters and other cultural institutions regarded Tashkent as a desirable destination in part because of the large Russian-speaking population. As the chair of the Committee of the Arts explained in a successful bid to keep a Muscovite theater in Tashkent, "the Theater of the Revolution cannot work in Fergana, as the city has only an insignificant percentage of Russians. The transfer of the theater to Fergana will lead to its inevitable ruin."[155]

---

[148] Stepanishcheva, "Vot tak i zhizn' proshla," TsDNA, f. 422, l. 6.

[149] Boltianskaia's sister in law lived in Tashkent, while Evgenia Pasternak was good friends with the Kozlovskii family, who had been exiled to Tashkent several years earlier. Pasternak and Pasternak, *Sushchestvovania tkan' skvoznaia*, 421.

[150] Deborah Averbukh, interview by Ella Orlikova, December 2001, in *Jewish Witness to a European Century* (www.centropa.org).

[151] Timofeev, "Dnevnik voennykh let," 162, entry of October 23, 1941. Note that Timofeev never actually went to Tashkent, despite his ongoing consideration of the city. Instead, he remained in Moscow.

[152] Stepanishcheva, "Vot tak i zhizn' proshla," l. 14.

[153] Pomerantz and Winik, *Run East*, 63.

[154] Quoted in Levin, *Baltic Jews under the Soviets*, 175.

[155] GARF, f. 6822, op. 1, d. 52, l. 55.

For academics, Tashkent was equally attractive. As Druzhinin later recalled, members of the Academy of Sciences "energetically" sought "to remain in a major center, with institutions of higher education and libraries."[156] In both Leningrad and Moscow, academics actively petitioned for permission to be sent there. "I petition for the destination of Tashkent," wrote the pro-rector of the Moscow University in November 1941, "where there are all the necessary conditions for the development of research."[157] Such was the eventual concentration of scholars in the city that those who found themselves in less desirable locations referred to it enviously as "the Soviet Athens."[158]

• • •

The journey to Tashkent was long and arduous. Moreover, as Georgii Efron noted in his diary en route, the "routes that lead there are numerous."[159] Those traveling from the north tended to take the route through Chkalov, formerly Orenburg. The Orenburg-Tashkent line had been built in the early twentieth century, connecting the central Asian colony to the metropole.[160] Before the war, the journey usually took under a week. For those traveling east in 1941, however, the journey was almost always longer. Whereas Kornei Chukovskii traveled the distance in just over a week, Maria Belkina's train took eleven days, Zinaida Stepanishcheva's fifteen days, and Georgii Efron's over three weeks. Elena Dobychina, setting out from Leningrad, journeyed for twenty days, and Victor Zhirmunskii one month.[161] The railway lines were overburdened in both directions. On some lines in the region, trains were moving on average no faster than 200 kilometers per day.[162] Georgii Efron's diary contains a running chronicle of his echelon's progress: on the fourth day of the journey, he noted that "our train advances by 100 to 200 meters, then stops for a good half-dozen hours. It would be truly comical if it weren't so sad."[163]

[156] Druzhinin, "Evakuatsiia iz Moskvy," 112.
[157] GARF, f. 6822, op. 1, d. 49, l. 74. For other examples, see TsGASPb, f. 7384, op. 17, d. 442, l. 97; GARF, f. A-259, op. 40, d. 3085, ll. 43–44.
[158] Letter of September 6, 1942, in E. R. Kurapova, ed., "'Russkoi zemlei nikomu nikogda ne vladet!' Iz pisem k M. B. Nechkinoi. 1942 g.," *Istoricheskii arkhiv*, no. 2 (2005): 187.
[159] Efron, *Dnevniki*, vol. 2, 84, entry of November 1, 1941.
[160] Daniel Brower, *Turkestan and the Fate of the Russian Empire* (London: RoutledgeCurzon, 2003), 81–84.
[161] Chukovskii, *Dnevnik*, 158–59; Belkina, *Skreshchenie sudeb*, 344; Stepanishcheva, "Vot tak i zhizn' proshla," TsDNA, f. 422, l. 9; Efron, *Dnevniki*, vol. 2, 132; E. E. Dobychina to N. E. Dobychina, August 4 and August 28, 1941, OR RGB, f. 420, op. 12, d. 1, ll. 7, 9; and letter of February 3, 1942, in G. F. Blagovoi, ed., "Perepiska V. M. Zhirmunskogo s S. E. Malovym," *Izvestiia RAN. Seriia literatury i iazyka*, no. 2 (2002): 63.
[162] For the average speeds on a range of railway lines in the Urals, Siberia, and Central Asia, see GARF, f. 6822, op. 1, d. 481, l. 33.
[163] Efron, *Dnevniki*, vol. 2, 87, entry of November 3, 1941.

Although the train route through Chkalov was undoubtedly the most direct route to Tashkent, it was not the only one. Evacuees from Moscow and Leningrad often traveled the more roundabout northern route, setting out along the Trans-Siberian railway and then cutting south at Novosibirsk along the Turksib railway, built in the 1930s, through Alma-Ata and on to Tashkent. This was the route taken by Anna Akhmatova and Lydia Chukovskaia, who joined a writer's echelon headed for Tashkent in Kazan.[164] Polish citizens recently released from confinement in northern Kazakhstan likewise approached Tashkent from the north.

Most common among the "disorganized" population, however, was the far more arduous southern route. Former inhabitants of southern Russia and the Ukraine, as well as people who had been evacuated to these regions in the first several months of the war, frequently came via the Caspian Sea and the Turkmen desert. Tatiana Okunevskaia recounts how her mother-in-law, who lived in the town of Zaporozhe, in southern Ukraine, found her in Tashkent: "when the Germans entered the city, her son remained at work, but she ran from her house to the railway station and got on some kind of departing platform. . . . Finding out somehow that I was in Tashkent, she began making her way toward me. Her route was terrible: south across the Caspian Sea, across Turkmenistan, two months she was hungry, unwashed, lice-ridden."[165]

This was an improvised route, a route that was nowhere to be found in the fairly intricate plans of the Evacuation Council, which charted how many trains would leave which destination for where. Throughout the fall of 1941, and again during the Germans' spring and summer offensives of 1942, hundreds of thousands of people descended, unplanned and often by foot, upon the city of Makhachkala, on the shores of the Caspian Sea.[166] A report from the Dagestani NKVD in October 1941 warned that there were already "thirty thousand evacuees [in the city] who had come unplanned from Rostov oblast and others." Another seventy thousand were apparently en route.[167] On arrival, people slept, ate, and lived in the port by the harbor, waiting for the boat that would take them further east, jostling to secure a space on one of the ships that intermittently departed for the further shore.[168] As one observer, who was in the city on business, wrote to Stalin: "what I

[164] Chukovskaya, *The Akhmatova Journals*, 192–93, entry of November 2, 1941.

[165] Tat'iana Okunevskaia, *Tat'ianin den'* (Moscow: Vagrius, 1998), 99.

[166] Many Leningrad institutions that had been evacuated to the Caucasus were re-evacuated to Central Asia, including Tashkent, in the wake of the renewed German offensive in the summer of 1942. For a description of the difficulties encountered by these institutes in transit, see GARF, f. A-327, op. 2, d. 46, ll. 30–31. Those who were evacuated through Makhachkala and other ports on the Caspian Sea in the summer and fall of 1941 often traveled as many as 150 kilometers by foot simply to reach the port. GARF, f. 7021, op. 100, d. 83, l. 7.

[167] GARF, f. 6822, op. 1, d. 482, l. 9.

[168] The same report from the Dagestani NKVD noted that "ships for the transfer of evacuees by sea are not given." Ibid.

saw there exceeded my worst expectations. Refugees sit under the open sky for two to three weeks, waiting for a ship. . . . People are sick, they are hungry, and they are lice-ridden. Nobody is concerned with evacuating them in a planned manner."[169] Saul Borovoi, who traveled through the city on his journey from Odessa, later wrote that "Makhachkala presented a terrible picture."[170]

Those who managed the crossing to the Turkmen city of Krasnovodsk found themselves in equally deplorable conditions. There were reportedly as many as thirty thousand evacuees in Krasnovodsk in early November 1941, living "in squares, on the sidewalks, and in the streets of the city."[171] Krasnovodsk had nothing in the way of infrastructure to greet evacuees, feed them, and organize their journey to places equipped to accommodate them. As a report by a representative of the Uzbek Sovnarkom put it, "in Krasnovodsk the evacuated population is not subject to an organized resettlement; as nobody there is occupied with this question, there is no evacuation center."[172] Indeed, neither the city nor even the Republic of Turkmenistan were listed among the sites designated to receive evacuees. Many of those who took this route were accordingly pushed onward. According to the same report, "all the trains with evacuees are dispatched directly to Uzbekistan." The result was the "unplanned arrival of . . . evacuees in Tashkent."[173]

[169] GARF, f. A-259, op. 40, d. 3017, l. 30.
[170] Borovoi, *Vospominaniia*, 257.
[171] TsGARUz, f. 837, op. 32, d. 2894, l. 88.
[172] Ibid.
[173] Ibid.

6

SURVIVAL ON THE TASHKENT FRONT

"I am going to Tashkent," Maria Belkina, recently evacuated from Moscow, wrote to her husband en route. "That's it . . . I am beginning a new life, without illusions and hopes."[1] For Belkina, as for others, the journey into evacuation was a time of anxious contemplation. Those heading east pondered what the "new life" held in store. Georgii Efron, likewise en route to Tashkent, was tormented by questions, which he duly recorded in his diary: "What will I do in Asia? . . . What will it be like?" As his train approached the Uzbek capital, his companions were reportedly preoccupied with one and the same question: "what awaits us in Tashkent?"[2] Their collective unease stemmed from uncertainties regarding both the city and their status. As Olga Boltianskaia noted in her diary in the first entry of her trip, "we have found ourselves in the position of refugees."[3] It was only on arrival, however, that Boltianskaia and other evacuees would discover just what this "position" entailed.

The Soviet writer Alexei Tolstoi, evacuated to Central Asia in October 1941, allegedly christened Tashkent the "Istanbul of the poor."[4] Istanbul had served as a refuge some twenty years earlier for many of the aristocrats, Tols-

---

[1] Quoted in N. A. Gromova, *Vse v chuzhoe gliadiat okno* (Moscow: Sovershenno sekretno, 2002), 24.

[2] Georgii Efron, *Dnevniki (1941–1943 gody)*, vol. 2, ed. E. B. Korkina and V. K. Losskaia (Moscow: Vagrius, 2005), 130, entry of November 17, 1941.

[3] Diary of O. A. Boltianskaia, RGALI, f. 2057, op. 2, d. 29, l. 86, entry of August 4, 1941.

[4] Quoted in Gromova, *Vse v chuzhoe gliadiat okno*, 39. Eduard Babaev later wrote: "Anna Akhmatova once said that an elderly and clever writer referred to Tashkent during the evacuation as the 'Istanbul of the poor.' Perhaps, this was Alexei Tolstoi?" See Eduard Babaev, *Vospominaniia* (St. Petersburg: Inapress, 2000), 101. Akhmatova herself used the term some years later in a short written piece about the composition of her *Poem without a Hero*. See Anna Akhmatova, "My Half Century: Selected Prose," ed. Ronald Meyer (Ann Arbor: Ardis, 1992), 128.

toi included, who fled Russia during the Civil War. In some ways, it was an apt comparison. Those who gathered in Tashkent were, like their forebears in Istanbul, displaced from their homes by a political regime they sought to escape; they were, in Boltianskaia's words, "refugees." Moreover, Tashkent, like Istanbul, was an alien city, an Asian city. "It could have been Istanbul or even Baghdad," Anna Akhmatova wrote of an evening in Tashkent.[5] The similarities, however, end there. For Tashkent, unlike Istanbul or Baghdad, was not, in fact, a foreign city. The journey to Tashkent, though long and trying, traversed no international boundary. The "poor" who flocked to the city in such great numbers were, with the notable exception of Polish refugees, Soviet citizens in a Soviet city. Their plight was not that of the stateless. Rather, it was that of the uprooted in a society in which roots—spatial, institutional, and personal—determined both status and access to scarce state-supplied goods.

Displacement deprived evacuees of one of the key requirements for inclusion in the urban polity—a set residence. Although evacuees were not stateless, their rights were sharply constrained by administrative procedures that made residence dependent on official sanction. The gates to the cities of refuge were thus not open to all. Moreover, access to scarce state goods required inclusion in an official distribution network. Inclusion was mediated not by citizenship—Maiakovskii's famous and oft-repeated line, "I am a citizen of the Soviet Union," is nowhere to be found among the petitions of evacuees—but by corporate status and connections. In this regard, self-evacuees were in a particularly precarious position, for the act of self-evacuation effected a breach in the dense web of institutional networks that mediated relations between citizens and state. Evacuation also disrupted personal networks, which were almost as important as institutional ones in the struggle to survive.

Maria Belkina, in another letter to her husband en route, wrote that "all the bridges have been burned. . . . There is no return to the old life."[6] Networks had been disrupted, families rent apart, apartments left behind. Thousands of kilometers from their homes, evacuees set about repairing old bridges and establishing new ones.

THE GATES TO THE CITY

The Tashkent station was awash with people. Whether they came across the Caspian Sea, through the Kazakh steppe, or across the Kyzulkum desert, they came in large numbers. "The refugees kept coming and coming," Zinaida Stepanishcheva wrote, echoing countless other observers.[7] The first wave of

---

[5] Babaev, *Vospominaniia*, 36.

[6] Quoted in Gromova, *Vse v chuzhoe gliadiat okno*, 28.

[7] Z. G. Stepanishcheva, "Vot tak i zhizn' proshla," TsDNA, f. 422, l. 21. See also Maria Belkina, *Skreshchenie sudeb*, 2d ed. (Moscow: Blagovest Rudomino, 1992), 345.

evacuees descended on the city in the late summer and fall of 1941. It was followed by a second wave that arose late in the summer of the next year, in the wake of the renewed German offensives in the south. In August 1942 alone, fifty-five thousand evacuees were reported to have come through the city and station of Tashkent.[8] Of these, a full 40 percent arrived in an unorganized manner.[9] A veritable city of transients emerged, centered on the train station. Bernard Ginsburg, a refugee from the annexed territories of eastern Poland, later wrote that "the railroad station and the adjacent large square were clogged with refugees when I arrived. It was an unbelievable concentration of uprooted human beings, tired, hungry, sick, confused—a sea of thousands and thousands of homeless people."[10] According to Maria Belkina, a "whole tent-city, an enormous 'gypsy' encampment developed along the railway lines leading to Tashkent. Only in this encampment, the gypsies were all fair and flaxen-haired and the tents were clumsily assembled, made out of blankets and sheets, and women, obviously city dwellers, fumbled with bits of haloxylon and wood chips, trying, with a set of bricks, to cook food and boil a tea kettle. *These* Tashkent did not accommodate! They directed them to *kishlaki* (Central Asian villages), where they didn't want to go, or forced them to travel to other cities, but one needed a 'direction' to get into other cities as well."[11]

As Belkina's comments suggest, the gates to the proverbial "city of bread" were not open to all. Deborah Averbukh, who traveled east on her own initiative, later recalled that "we weren't allowed to go to Tashkent." She and her traveling companions jumped off the train at the outskirts of the city and made the rest of the journey by foot.[12] Averbukh was one of many who were barred from the city by a State Defense Committee decree prohibiting the registration of "refugees and evacuees from the frontline regions who arrive in an unorganized manner" in areas under martial law and in thirty-five designated cities, including Tashkent.[13] Central directives thus established a system of differential access for evacuees to the country's major cities: only those who had been earmarked for evacuation by the state and

[8] TsGARUz, f. 837, op. 32, d. 3523, l. 247.

[9] Ibid.

[10] Bernard L. Ginsburg, *A Wayfarer in a World in Upheaval* (San Bernardino, Calif.: Borgo, 1993), 37. Another refugee, Jack Pomerantz, described his first view of Tashkent in strikingly similar terms: "There, stretching before me . . . was an enormous human camp. Hundreds, perhaps thousands of people lay on the sidewalk and street in front of the train station." See Jack Pomerantz and Lyric Wallwork Winik, *Run East: Flight from the Holocaust* (Urbana: University of Illinois Press, 1997), 55.

[11] Belkina, *Skreshchenie sudeb*, 345.

[12] Deborah Averbukh, interview by Ella Orlikova, December 2001, in *Jewish Witness to a European Century* (www.centropa.org).

[13] RGASPI, f. 644, op. 1, d. 80, l. 95. This decree, issued in late September 1941 constituted a "partial elaboration and change" of earlier, less restrictive regulations, whereby the average evacuee was required to present only proof of living space to be registered. RGASPI, f. 17, op. 3. d. 1041, ll. 69, 225.

subsequently dispatched to a specific place were allowed to resettle in the country's most desirable urban centers.

There were, of course, exceptions. As in the evacuation itself, Muscovites and Leningraders were privileged: residents of these two cities, even if they traveled individually, were granted permission by the NKVD to settle in any city where they had relatives or friends, provided the latter could furnish them with living space.[14] Thus did the Muscovite Zinaida Stepanishcheva, whose mother resided in Tashkent, gain access to the city even though she had been officially evacuated to Chkalov. A similar dispensation was granted to the families of party and Soviet leaders as well as the families of officers of the Red Army, the Navy, and NKVD troops.[15] With time, however, even these groups were subject to restrictions. In November 1941, the Uzbek republican government limited access to the city to the families of those evacuated with their factories or enterprises and to "individual scientists, cultural figures, and others" who had been granted "personal authorization" by the heads of the Uzbek party apparatus and the government.[16]

The increasingly restrictive regulations were accompanied by a series of measures intended to enforce the new registration regime. Traditional police measures designed to weed out "socially harmful" and other undesirable elements were adopted and adapted. The same November 1941 decree that limited access to Tashkent stipulated that evacuees who were not entitled to reside in the city but who had "in one way or another" managed to secure registration be evicted and resettled in the provinces and on collective farms.[17] Verifications and evictions, targeting illegal evacuees as well as the usual suspects, henceforth became routine.[18] Raids were carried out "at markets, in the theaters, parks, and other places with an accumulation of people."[19] Deborah Averbukh, who entered the city illegally, later recalled that "every night I stayed in different dormitories, fearing police raids."[20] In addition, *troiki* (committees of three) were established to verify the urban population by residence, building by building. Police were instructed to identify "persons without a defined occupation, the criminal element, and violators of the passport regime." Within a month, "all those identified for expulsion on the basis of the verification" were to be "removed" and set up with work outside the city of Tashkent.[21]

[14] The directive in question barred residents of Moscow and Leningrad only from settling in frontline regions. GARF, f. A-259, op. 40, d. 3041, l. 8.

[15] Ibid., d. 3022, l. 40.

[16] GARF, f. A-259, op. 40, d. 3067, l. 136.

[17] Ibid. Those who did not comply were to be forcefully evicted.

[18] See, for example, GAGT, f. 10, op. 17, d. 14, l. 65.

[19] Ibid., d. 51, l. 211. On police raids, see Pomerantz and Winik, *Run East*, 55.

[20] Deborah Averbukh, interview.

[21] GAGT, f. 10, op. 17, d. 51, l. 211.

Measures designed to cleanse the city of economic and social "impurities" (speculators, the unemployed, suspect elements) were complemented and reinforced by prophylactic policies of a different sort. The mass and uncontrolled influx of people was seen as a harbinger not only of disorder and social pollution but of infection. Thus the introduction of a more rigorous document verification process at the Tashkent train station, intended to restrict settlement to those with the proper authorization, was championed in the name of "controlling the spread of infectious diseases" in one decree and of "combating crime and infringements of the law" in another.[22] The latter decree further extended the scope of the proposed operation from the Tashkent station to the railway line more generally. Authorities at stations en route were instructed to redirect evacuees to other destinations and "make the corresponding changes in their evacuation documents." In addition, the decree stipulated that destinations should be inscribed in individual passports.[23]

Taken as a whole, the range of measures proposed and put into place raised troubling questions about the status of evacuees. These measures were not simply inspired by a concern with crime or disease. Evacuees occupied a precarious position in Soviet wartime society simply by virtue of their displacement. As people lacking a fixed residence, they could easily be assimilated to a range of suspect categories, namely that of the homeless, the unemployed, and even the administratively exiled. To be sure, top Uzbek government officials were sharply critical of the tendency among party and state authorities to view all evacuees as "speculators, dark people, and spies."[24] In a decree on caring for evacuees, the Uzbek Council of People's Commissars insisted that the evacuated population was "overwhelmingly composed of honest Soviet citizens who have temporarily fallen on hard times."[25] The "vast majority of evacuees," the decree continued, "consist of workers, employees, engineers, and technical workers, among whom there are many of our country's distinguished figures, who were compelled to be temporarily evacuated and who strive while in evacuation to give of their labor, knowledge, and ability to reinforce the rear and the front."[26] Local authorities, however, could hardly be faulted for their mistake. For there was little precedent either in their prewar experience or in current government policy for treating the displaced and the dispossessed as "honest Soviet citizens."

[22] See ibid., ll. 9–10; l. 212. Similar decrees, drawn up by the NKVD and designed to "prohibit the entrance into Tashkent of people who do not have the right or the permission to reside in Tashkent," instructed railway authorities to establish a round-the-clock checkpoint at the exits from the station. Only those with a *propiska* (registration stamp) in their passports for Tashkent were to be permitted to leave the station. TsGARUz, f. 314, op. 1, d. 37, l. 11.

[23] GAGT, f. 10, op. 17, d. 51, l. 212.

[24] GARF, f. A-259, op. 40, d. 3067, l. 149.

[25] Ibid.

[26] Ibid.

Since the early 1930s and the introduction of the passport regime, residence and work had become the twin requirements for full inclusion in the
Soviet polity. People who lacked a "fixed residence" and were not engaged
in "socially useful labor" were routinely targeted in "cleansing" operations
designed to clear major cities of "socially undesirable elements."[27] In fact,
evacuees were technically distinct from the habitually homeless and unemployed, and those who were evacuated in organized fashion had papers to
prove it. Nonetheless, in the absence of clear and coherent signals from the
center regarding the status of evacuees, it was all too easy for authorities at
all levels to treat them as marginals.

This tendency was perhaps nowhere more apparent than in Azerbaijan,
where the republican NKVD, with the approval of the Council of People's
Commissars, listed evacuees among the categories of people to be expelled
from the capital city in a routine police cleansing operation. More specifically, the decree targeted two groups for resettlement: "people without a defined occupation and not engaged in socially useful labor" and "all citizens
who have arrived since the beginning of the war from territory temporarily
occupied by the enemy, frontline regions, and regions adjacent to the front
lines."[28] Both groups, moreover, were to have notes inserted into their passports restricting them to the region of resettlement. The decree was quickly
denounced by the Evacuation Council as an "incorrect" and "indiscriminate
approach to the problem of wartime displacement." Not only was the republic home to many people who had been sent there on the express orders
of the Evacuation Council, but the families of party and Soviet authorities
as well as of workers and employees had "evidently" sought refuge in the
republic with relatives and friends and "there are no grounds to expel or
resettle them."[29] The spirited defense of evacuees notwithstanding, the Azerbaijani decree reflected tendencies manifest at the highest levels of authority
in Moscow.

First, it revealed a view of evacuees as socially unproductive and unde-
serving members of the polity. An official in the Commissariat of Justice,
noting the "accumulation" of evacuees "in several places (Tashkent, Alma-
Ata, Stalinabad, and others)," complained in a report to Andrei Vyshinskii,
the chief prosecutor, that a "great number of these citizens are not engaged
in any form of socially useful labor." He presented evacuees as akin to deserters from both the labor and the military fronts. "Many," he wrote, "move from
one place to another, avoiding military service." "Meanwhile," he continued, "in enterprises and on collective farms there is a large shortage of labor
power." He proposed that the Commissariat of Justice "grant the Council of

[27] See Paul M. Hagenloh, "'Socially Harmful Elements' and the Terror," in *Stalinism: New Directions*, ed. Sheila Fitzpatrick (New York: Routledge, 2000), 286–308.
[28] Exempted from the resettlement were state pensioners and invalids. GARF, f. A-259, op. 40, d. 3067, l. 156.
[29] Ibid., l. 158.

People's Commissars the right to require evacuated citizens to work in enterprises, organizations, and on collective farms."[30] Shortly thereafter, Vyshinskii gave his backing to the draft decree.[31]

While obligatory labor assignments were clearly not commensurate with the expulsion proposed by Azerbaijani authorities, both decisions were based on a conception of evacuees as noncontributing members of society, and both saw them as essentially movable resources. The Evacuation Council, although it in some ways shared the latter view, was nonetheless critical of the decree's exceedingly narrow conception of "socially useful labor," which excluded both housekeepers and those "who do not work for a set wage, such as, for instance, artists, writers, handicraftsmen, and so on." More important, perhaps, council representative Pamfilov objected to the ease with which evacuees were being recategorized as unemployed. Surely those displaced from their homes should not de facto be classified among the jobless? "Clearly," he concluded his critique, "after arrival in an unknown place we must provide a time frame within which the arrivee is given the opportunity to find a job. Only after the expiration of this time frame . . . should the arrivee be regarded as nonworking."[32]

Pamfilov's reservations notwithstanding, the perception that evacuees were not "useful" members of society seems to have been widespread. "People from the frontline regions," reported one regional official in a fairly typical complaint, "refuse to work."[33] While authorities in another region claimed that most evacuees "go to work with pleasure," they nonetheless noted that there were some who "lodge big complaints, abandon their work, and go from one organization to another."[34] In the Kalinin district, officials drew attention to the case of one evacuee who quit her job after one day, stating "why should I work for 250 rubles and receive 500 grams of bread when I can not work and receive 300 grams?"[35] Such people, Pamfilov reasoned, should be given a week's worth of bread and told that they will be given no more thereafter.[36] The tendency among some evacuees to refuse work (many on the grounds that they would soon be returning to their homes) was seen as deeply problematic by officials on the ground and in Moscow. Evacuees were accused by evacuation authorities of displaying a "suitcase mood," of never really settling into their new abodes and becoming productive members of society.[37]

---

[30] Ibid., d. 3017, l. 4. The memo also stated that the "Commissariat of Justice considers it necessary to establish that the distribution of tickets for railway transportation and transportation by ship take place only with the permission of the organs of the police."

[31] Ibid., l. 5.

[32] Ibid., l. 7.

[33] GARF, f. 6822, op. 1, d. 422, l. 14.

[34] Ibid., l. 43.

[35] GARF, f. A-327, op. 2, d. 366, l. 50.

[36] Ibid., l. 52.

[37] Ibid., l. 52; d. 68, l. 11.

The second tendency evident in both the Azerbaijani decree and in directives issued from Moscow was the equating of evacuees with deportees. This link was particularly pronounced in a draft of the first decree on the registration of evacuees, prepared by none other than the Evacuation Council. Point 3 of the decree, as it was initially drawn up, stipulated that in the process of registration police insert a "note" into evacuee passports restricting their residence to a single city or settlement. It further called for the removal of the previous registration permitting residence in the evacuee's city of origin.[38] In this case, the criticism came from Vyshinskii. His response was unequivocal: "it is necessary to change the draft decree, excluding point 3 and correspondingly changing the form, for if we leave point 3 in this form then all evacuees will find themselves in the position of deportees [*ssylnye*], which, it stands to reason, would be entirely unacceptable."[39] Although the clause was removed, ambiguities surrounding the status of evacuees remained. German deportees were routinely counted among the evacuated population,[40] and authorities in a variety of regions appear to have done the "unacceptable" and confined evacuees to the regions of their resettlement.[41] This was the aim of one Uzbek official who, noting the "many cases of the departure of evacuees from their place of resettlement," called on all oblast authorities to "quickly put an end to such a practice."[42]

For individual evacuees, who were at best vaguely aware of the various decrees and decisions discussed above, the determination of their status effectively came down to one crucial document: the *propiska*, or registration stamp. Miryam Bar, who like many other Polish Jews traveled to Tashkent after her release from confinement in Siberia, describes the challenge of procuring the *propiska* in her memoirs:

It was impossible to receive work without having living space first; the stamp that was placed in one's identity papers in the police department was called a *propiska*, and hundreds of people, thousands of people, perhaps tens of thousands, wandered around Tashkent in search of a way to acquire a *propiska*. Only those who had already found work and already had a place to stay could get a *propiska*. There was not a person who knew precisely what was

[38] GARF, f. A-259, op. 40, d. 3041, l. 15.
[39] Ibid., l. 16.
[40] GARF, f. 6822, op. 1, d. 481, l. 151. Complaints were lodged with the Evacuation Council regarding the uncontrolled movement of both evacuees and deportees. The special settler division of the NKVD complained to the Evacuation Council: "taking advantage of the lack of a reliable count, German migrants [*pereselentsy*] willfully move from collective farm to collective farm, from district to district, and even to other oblasts." GARF, f. A-259, op. 20, d. 3032, l. 52. Similar complaints were repeatedly made about evacuees, despite the ostensibly clear refusal to impose the same restrictions on their movement. An example from Uzbekistan can be found in TsGARUz, f. 837, op. 32, d. 3519, l. 2.
[41] For example, authorities in Rostov oblast attempted to confine evacuees to their regions of resettlement. GARF f. 6822, op. 1, d. 422, l. 23.
[42] TsGARUz, f. 837, op. 32, d. 3519, l. 2.

written in the government's instructions, but according to the reports of the well informed, it was like this in reality: without a *propiska* they will not give you work, and you will not receive a place to live, but without work and a place to live, they will not give you a *propiska*. There were apparently some people who succeeded in breaking this vicious bureaucratic cycle, but of those whom I spoke to, not a person knew how it was done.[43]

Not surprisingly, the *propiska* occupies a central place in memoir litera-ture, diaries, and fictional treatments of the evacuation.[44] Acquiring a *pro-piska* proved to be a challenge not only for the disorganized population (for whom it was, at least in theory, off-limits in a city such as Tashkent) but for "organized" evacuees as well. Fadeev, the head of the Writers Union, took no chances. Within weeks of the evacuation, he dispatched a telegram to the Uzbek government requesting that a set list of writers be granted permits for the city.[45] His actions were well advised, for time and again, "organized" evacuees were refused registration by the local police. The head of a hospital administration, for example, appealed to none other than Lazar Kaganovich for help in securing the registration of eleven em-ployees whose previous requests the Tashkent police had refused.[46] In some cases, the refusals were the product of a conflict of interest between au-thorities in Moscow and those in Tashkent. Thus members of the Muscovite Theater of the Revolution, for example, were initially denied registration as part of a government strategy to, in the words of one critical account, "preserve the inviolability of local theaters."[47] In other cases, the motives were much less clear and perhaps reflected the general uncertainty regard-ing who exactly was entitled to registration.

Much more common than the refusal of "organized" evacuees, not sur-prisingly, was the refusal of the "disorganized" population. The search for registration on the part of individual evacuees has left an extensive paper trail. The archives of the Tashkent Evacuation Center contain countless re-quests by individuals seeking registration.[48] "I request registration in Tash-kent," began one typical request, "as the family of a serviceman consisting of three people, evacuated from Odessa. Living space has been given me by a relative."[49] Women requested the registration of their husbands, husbands their wives, and parents their children.[50] As one woman, requesting the reg-istration of her children, explained: "En route to Tashkent I lost my two

[43] Miryam Bar, *Lelot Tashkent* (Tel Aviv: Levin-Epshtin, 1970), 70.
[44] See, for example, Vasily Grossman, *Life and Fate: A Novel*, trans. Robert Chandler (Lon-don: Collins Harvill, 1985), 120–29.
[45] RGALI, f. 631, op. 15, d. 565, l. 176.
[46] GARF, f. 6822, op. 1, d. 50, l. 51.
[47] Ibid.
[48] See, in particular, GAGT, f. 330, op. 1, dd. 4, 5.
[49] GAGT, f. 330, op. 1, d. 5, l. 19.
[50] Examples of such requests can be found in ibid., ll. 1, 2, 6, 14, 22.

children. Now they have arrived barefoot and hungry. They sold everything they had en route."[51] After the war, there would be many stories of families separated by the war. But it was not simply the chaos of war that wrenched families apart. Once separated, it proved exceedingly difficult to get the paperwork necessary to reunite. Although some received authorization to register family members, others did not.[52] The Muscovite Abraam Ingman, whose family was separated while boarding the train to Tashkent, was granted authorization to join one of his daughters in Tashkent with his wife and grandson, but an application for the child's mother, the couple's second daughter, was refused.[53]

Those without family connections were even more likely to be turned away. A three-page letter requesting, "in the name of the Stalinist attitude toward living people," the registration of a woman and her two children evacuated from Kiev had "deny" scrawled across the top in purple ink.[54] Requests for registration, and their refusal, were so common that a standard rejection form was drawn up. "In conformity with the decree of the State Defense Committee of September 26, 1941, you have been refused registration in Tashkent. You are requested to go to the Evacuation Center at the train station without delay and to leave Tashkent."[55]

Miryam Bar had been told that living space was the key to successful registration. In many cases, however, living space alone was simply not enough. Stepanishcheva, in her memoirs, describes the scene outside a registration office in Tashkent. An acquaintance from Moscow, a German-Jewish refugee whose husband, by virtue of his German citizenship, had been sent to the camps as a German spy, was applying for permission to remain in Tashkent. Stepanishcheva's family gave her the required form stating that she had permission to be registered at their address, occupying part of their living space. She waited in line for hours, was finally received, and was given a stamp in her passport. Assuming that her requests had been fulfilled, she left the office and was immediately accosted by the crowd, asking where she had been sent. "With tears of happiness, she said, with complete sincerity, that she had been permitted to remain in Tashkent. 'That can't be,' some sober voices responded. 'So look at my passport,' and she herself had not yet glanced at it. And in her passport there was a stamp, 'registered in Kokand.'"[56] Even those who managed to secure both living space and employment could easily be turned away. As a young Jewish man who had fled Minsk protested in a letter to Stalin, "in Tashkent I was offered a job . . . as

[51] TsGARUz, f. 837, op. 32, d. 2728, l. 186.
[52] See, for example, GAGT, f. 330, op. 1, d. 9, l. 17.
[53] GAGT, f. 10, op. 18, d. 31, l. 112.
[54] TsGARUz, f. 837, op. 32, d. 2728, l. 206.
[55] Ibid., l. 7.
[56] Kokand is located in the Fergana Valley, southeast of Tashkent. Z. G. Stepanishcheva, "Vot tak i zhizn' proshla," l. 16.

a lab worker and the director granted me living space, of which I have documentation, but, despite all this, the police did not register me, why I don't know."[57]

Those who did not meet the official requirements were compelled either to leave the city or find their way around official strictures. Maria Belkina noted that although authorities sought to keep out the "disorganized population," "those who had both cunning and wealth might nonetheless settle in Tashkent by paying a bribe, a very substantial bribe."[58] Bribery was endemic. As Olga Boltianskaia was informed by her landlord, "here in Tashkent you can't take a single step without a bribe."[59] In Alma-Ata, in neighboring Kazakstan, an official in the city's passport division was accused of "systematically taking bribes to register evacuees from the frontline regions in the city."[60] Although no similar charges appear to have been leveled at authorities in Tashkent, there is ample evidence of abuse at all levels. Management in factories and other organizations appear to have played a particularly important role in securing registration for otherwise ineligible candidates. Verifications conducted in the industrial sector turned up numerous cases of individuals being registered to fill specific labor needs that they neither filled nor were remotely qualified to fill. For instance, the city's metal industry union registered an accountant under the guise that he was a blacksmith.[61] Given that the accountant was not subsequently employed in the metal industry, one can only assume that he either paid a bribe or was fortunate enough to have a connection in the industry in question.

Connections could be as effective as bribes in securing the necessary papers. Nadezhda Mandelstam, who had not, as she recounted in her memoirs, "been evacuated to Tashkent in organized fashion,"[62] nonetheless acquired permission to reside in Tashkent through the efforts of her brother. He acted, she speculated in a letter, "through Lydia Chukovskaia—Kornei's daughter."[63] When it appeared that Anna Akhmatova was going to be de-

[57] TsGARUz, f. 837, op. 32, d. 2895, l. 150. There are many cases of people being offered jobs and refused registration. In one interesting case, the registration of a number of workers employed by Military-Construction Sector no. 1 was refused by Tashkent evacuation authorities, in all likelihood because the list of employees consisted entirely of ethnic Germans. How these individuals managed to escape the deportations that had swept the western parts of the country is unclear. Ibid., d. 3253, ll. 49–50.

[58] Belkina, *Skreshchenie sudeb*, 345.

[59] Diary of O. A. Boltianskaia, RGALI, f. 2057, op. 2, d. 30, l. 81, entry of September 2, 1943.

[60] GARF, f. 5446, op. 81a, d. 362, l. 59.

[61] See, for this and other similar examples, RGASPI, f. 17, op. 43, d. 2239, ll. 169–70.

[62] Nadezhda Mandelstam, *Hope Abandoned*, trans. Max Hayward (New York: Atheneum, 1974), 596.

[63] N. Ia. Mandel'shtam to B. S. Kuzin, February 23, 1942. Nadezhda Mandel'shtam, *192 pis'ma k B. Kuzinu*, ed. N. I. Kraineva and E. A. Perezhogina (St. Petersburg: Inapress, 1999), 667. In her memoirs she states that she managed to secure registration, "thanks to Akhmatova." Mandelstam, *Hope Abandoned*, 597.

nied registration, the Chukovskiis again stepped in to help.[64] The role that Chukovskii appears to have played for a small circle of writers, Boris Grekov played for historians. When the Leningrad historian Boris Romanov, who had spent several years in the camps, was threatened with expulsion from Tashkent, it was only through Grekov's intervention that he was given permission to remain.[65]

Others simply evaded the police and lived in the city without papers, under the constant threat of eviction.[66] A former Gulag prisoner, the Moscow poet Kazarnovskii, was refused a residence permit for Tashkent but managed to find temporary shelter in the city with Nadezhda Mandelstam. Her neighbors, she recounts, "were pleased by the fact that I had not registered him with the militia. They hoped that, like all the evacuees, I would one day return home . . . and they would then come in for a little extra 'living space.' An unregistered tenant could have no claims on it."[67] The Polish-Jewish refugee Miryam Bar, who had no friends or family in Tashkent, likewise lived the life of an "illegal." Although she lived in constant fear of police checks, it was possible, she recalled, to circumvent them.[68] Bar and Kazarnovskii were certainly not the sole illegals walking the streets of Tashkent. Given their success in evading the police, however, we will never know just how many there were.

• • •

Despite the restrictions, the city was full of new arrivals. By the end of 1941, officials in the Resettlement Bureau put the number of evacuees living in Tashkent at just short of one hundred thousand.[69] This number would only

---

[64] When Chukovskaia heard that Akhmatova had been denied registration, she arranged for her father to go talk to M. I. Kichanov, the deputy head of the Uzbek Sovnarkom. In the end, it turned out that Akhmatova had not, in fact, been denied registration. Chukovskaia recounts the whole episode in her "Tashkent notebooks." See Lidiia Chukovskaia, *Zapiski ob Annoi Akhmatovoi, 1938–1941*, 5th ed., 2 vols. (Moscow: Soglasie, 1997), vol. 1, 352–53, entries of December 15 and 16, 1941.

[65] V. M. Paneiakh, *Tvorchestvo i sud'ba istorika: Boris Aleksandrovich Romanov* (St. Petersburg: Institut rossiiskoi istorii S.-Peterburgskii filial, Rossiiskaia akademiia nauk, 2000), 131.

[66] Verifications of local industry revealed dozens of people working without proper papers. TsGARUz, f. R-314, op. 1, d. 56, l. 135.

[67] Mandelstam, *Hope Abandoned*, 603.

[68] Bar, *Lelot Tashkent*, 73.

[69] Officials in the Tashkent City Soviet reported that as of January 1, 1942, 67,819 evacuees had been registered to live in Tashkent. GAGT, f. 10, op. 17, d. 10, l. 11. The Uzbek Resettlement Bureau, which kept its own statistics based on the number of people who had entered the city rather than the number that had been registered there, put the number on the same date at 97,936. RGAE, f. 1562, op. 20, d. 248, l. 10. Other sources put the number even higher, at 157,803. See Paul Stronski, "Forging a Soviet City: Tashkent, 1937–1966" (Ph.D. diss., Stanford University, 2003), 101.

increase the next year.[70] Isaak Bakhmatov, who had moved to Tashkent shortly before the war, wrote his family that "Tashkent is overflowing with refugees, overflowing with writers, overflowing with artists, overflowing with Muscovite factories, organizations, and educational institutions."[71] Maria Belkina described the city in similar terms. "The streets of Tashkent are full of Muscovites and Leningraders! People known to me in life, from film reels, from portraits in the papers—Tamara Makarova, a film star, with her husband the director Sergei Gerasimov; . . . Leningrad, Moscow!" Olga Boltianskaia recorded in her diary that "in general Tashkent is full of refugees from Moscow, Leningrad, Odessa, and so on."[72]

As these comments indicate, Tashkent's evacuees hailed from the most populous and important cities of the Soviet Union. They came from Moscow and Leningrad, Kiev, Kharkov, and Odessa. The populations of these five cities alone accounted for some two-thirds of Tashkent's registered evacuee population.[73] By far the most significant contributing city was Moscow. Almost thirty-eight thousand Muscovites were evacuated to Tashkent during the war, accounting for as much as 30 percent of the city's overall evacuee population.[74] In general, the southeastern and central regions of the Russian and Ukrainian republics were much better represented than the western borderlands. The arrivals were, moreover, almost exclusively urban. Those listed as coming from villages rather than cities accounted for a negligible percentage of the Tashkent evacuee population—0.1 percent.[75]

THE CITY

The city that greeted those displaced by the war struck most as foreign and unfamiliar. Tashkent did not yet boast the distinctively Soviet-style apartment blocks that would come to dominate its urban landscape after the earthquake of 1966. In 1941, plans to transform the city into a model Soviet city, a modern outpost in Central Asia, remained by and large paper projects.[76] Tashkent

[70] According to statistics on movement into and out of Tashkent, 23,179 people arrived in the city in 1942 from evacuated regions. RGAE, f. 1562, op. 20, d. 381, l. 2.

[71] I. M. Bakhmatov to E. M. Bakhmatova, November 25, 1941, TsDNA, f. 45, l. 6.

[72] Diary of O. A. Boltianskaia, RGALI, f. 2057, op. 2, d. 29, l. 99, entry of August 28, 1941.

[73] At the end of 1941, residents of these five cities accounted for three-quarters of the evacuated population. RGAE, f. 1562, op. 20, d. 248, ll. 10, 23. The next year, however, their proportion declined. Ibid., d. 381, l. 2.

[74] This number accounts for Muscovites who arrived in Tashkent in 1941 and 1942. Ibid., d. 381, l. 2. Second in importance was Odessa, which accounted for some fourteen thousand evacuees. Ibid.

[75] Ibid., l. 13.

[76] For an excellent treatment of urban planning in Tashkent before the war, see Stronski, "Forging a Soviet City," 35–46, 75–79.

was still a city of small one- and two-story houses and dirt lanes. It was divided between the Russian section of the city, built as a European colonial outpost in the late nineteenth century, and the Muslim district, or old town.[77] Nadezhda Mandelstam later recalled the "small, squat houses and tall trees—a contrast peculiar to Tashkent." The city was full of such contrasts. On the one hand, there were the "steep and narrow alleys." On the other, there were broad streets and European squares. Nadezhda Mandelstam recalls one particular square that she and Akhmatova christened L'Étoile, after the square of that name in Paris. "We conceived a fancy that General Kaufman, in laying out Tashkent, had indulged his nostalgia for Paris by making all the streets converge into this square modeled on the Étoile."[78]

Whatever pretensions to Europeanness the new city in particular might have had, however, Tashkent was, in the eyes of most evacuees, an inescapably Asian city. The journey into evacuation was conceived as a passage from Europe into Asia. The moment of passage figured as one of the few notable landmarks of the voyage.[79] Maria Belkina wrote to her husband, "We crossed the Volga, I gazed at the other side for a long time. . . . Kazan, we crossed the border."[80] Whereas for some the Volga figured as a clear dividing line, for others the divide lay further to the east. Kornei Chukovskii was in the Chkalov district, at the foot of the Urals, when he noted in his diary, "We are already in Asia."[81] Descriptions of the changing landscape figure as markers of the transition. Stepanishcheva later recalled the topographical transformation after crossing the Urals on the second week of her journey: "From Europe we found ourselves in Asia, and the endless Kazakh steppe with its unbearable heat and almost naked land began. . . . In places, it seemed as if the ground was covered with white snow and pieces of ice gleamed against the burning hot sun. In fact it was salt."[82] Chukovskaia also focused her descriptions on the animal life: "The desert . . . Camels in the distance. I've realized for the first time that they are beautiful, not ugly: the caravan is swaying along with a harmonious, stately motion."[83]

As Chukovskaia's comments suggest, some were enchanted by the new and foreign landscape. While the trip east was invariably remembered as arduous, there was a touristic element in many descriptions of the journey and

---

[77] On the construction of colonial Tashkent, see Jeff Sahadeo, *Russian Colonial Society in Tashkent, 1865–1923* (Bloomington: Indiana University Press, 2007), 22–56.

[78] Mandelstam, *Hope Abandoned*, 601–2.

[79] The other notable landmark was the first city along the way in which lights were not extinguished at night.

[80] Quoted in Gromova, *Vse v chuzhoe gliadiat okno*, 24.

[81] Kornei Chukovskii, *Dnevnik, 1930–69* (Moscow: Sovremennyi pisatel', 1995), 159, entry of October 21, 1941.

[82] Stepanishcheva, "Vot tak i zhizn' proshla," l. 10.

[83] Lydia Chukovskaya, *The Akhmatova Journals*, trans. Milena Michalski and Sylva Rubashova (London: Harvill, 1994), 193, November 8, 1941.

the final destination. Anna Akhmatova reportedly sat glued to the window for much of her trip from Kazan to Tashkent. "I'm glad to be seeing so much of Russia," she remarked to Chukovskaia.[84] Kornei Chukovskii, sick and preoccupied with the fate of his son on the front, noted, "I am nonetheless happy that I have gotten to see Tashkent, even if in old age." Indeed, Chukovskii was positively enchanted by the city, which he described as having a "special poetic quality, a melodiousness." "I walk the streets," he wrote in his diary,

> and it is as if I am listening to music—so wonderful are the rows of poplars. The canals and thousands of varied bridges across them, the views of single-story homes, which seem even lower in contrast to the high poplars—and the southern life on the street and the kind and courteous Uzbeks—and the bazaars, where there are raisins and nuts—and the abundant sun—why have I not been here before—why didn't I come before the war?[85]

A similar romanticization of the city is evident even in the writing of those who were otherwise very critical of the Uzbek capital. Tatiana Lugovskaia wrote to a friend who had disappointed her by not coming to Tashkent, "don't come, please. And you won't see Tashkent. You won't see the streets, planted with poplars, the distances, covered with dust, the camels—single and in whole caravans, the starry sky."[86]

Such descriptions of the city, although not altogether uncommon, are surprisingly rare in evacuee memoirs, diaries, and letters. Evacuation, after all, was no ordinary trip, and evacuees were not tourists, a fact of which they were all too aware. "It would have been nice," wrote an evacuee in Kazan, praising the architecture of the university, "to see all this as a tourist, and not as a refugee, which is what we are."[87] The tendency to romanticize the new and foreign setting was undercut by the hardships of daily life and by a persistent longing for the familiar. The cinematographer Boris Babochkin wrote to his wife on arrival in Alma-Ata from Tashkent: "The city is beautiful, you could fall in love with it. It is the opposite of Tashkent in every respect—the air is marvelous, there is no dust, it is an enormous park, not a city, there is asphalt everywhere, good houses, few people, no banditry, there

[84] Ibid., 189.
[85] Chukovskii, *Dnevnik*, 160, entry of October 24, 1941.
[86] Letter to L. Maliugin, 1943, in Tat'iana Lugovskaia, *Kak znaiu, kak pomniu, kak umeiu. Vospominaniia, pis'ma, dnevniki* (Moscow: Agraf, 2001), 275.
[87] T. B. Lozinskaia to N. P. Antsiferov, January 3, 1942, OR RNB, f. 27, op. 1, d. 279, l. 1. Another evacuee in Kazan, a historian, wrote to a friend in evacuation in Omsk: "I can't say anything bad about Kazan. It is probably even a nice city, but it is foreign, foreign. I can't bring myself to get to know it better—I simply don't see it, don't notice it; all my energy goes into my work and my thoughts. I have still not been to the Volga, and it is only 3 kilometers away." See the letter of September 6, 1941, in A. A. Svanidze, ed., "Pis'ma E. A. Kosminskogo E. V. Gutnovoi (1941–1959)," *Novaia i noveishaia istoriia*, no. 1 (2002): 120.

are no poor people altogether, and—most important—it is a Russian city. The first impression is charming."[88]

Babochkin's praise of Alma-Ata, after several months in Tashkent, underscores the prevailing vision of Tashkent among many evacuees. It was dusty and terribly overcrowded. Moreover, it was dangerous. There is not an account of the city from this period that does not at least mention the high levels of crime. "Banditry" preoccupied evacuees. Stepanishcheva later recalled the large number of swindlers who took advantage of ordinary inhabitants. She recounts how her mother bought two bottles of baked milk, "but it turned out that the milk was only in the neck of the bottle and the bottles themselves were filled with mashed potato. . . . Such things happened not only to my mother but to all our acquaintances. Everyone told each other the most unbelievable stories of deceit and swindling."[89] Rare was the evacuee who did not have something stolen. Alexander Kovarskii lost his new galoshes to a thief; Nadezhda Mandelstam was robbed of a ration of fish; Evgeniia Galina's mother had her purse stolen, Olga Boltianskaia's son his passport, and Olga herself some newly bought bread.[90]

Like crime, dirt and disorder pervade the writings of evacuees. Dmitrii Ushakov wrote in one of his first letters after arriving in the city that "Tashkent's misfortune is dust and dirt. When it is hot, the dust lies like powder, several centimeters thick; you come home all gray. It rains, and the dust turns into mud that one cannot get out of, fine, slippery, viscous enough that it pulls your galoshes off your foot."[91] Tatiana Lugovskaia described it in a letter to her friend Leonid as "wild"; "there is nothing here," she wrote, "besides dust."[92]

Moreover—and perhaps, to paraphrase Babochkin, "most important"—Tashkent was a foreign city. The city's urban layout, the flora and the fauna, seemed distinctly un-"Russian," and Russia itself seemed distant and removed. This sentiment was captured with particular poignancy in one of Lugovskaia's subsequent letters to her friend. Soon after her arrival in Tashkent she wrote:

> I've found myself in Tashkent, a city where even the water smells of dust and disinfectant, where in the summer water exposed to the sun begins to boil,

[88] Letter dated 24 August—2 September, 1942, in Boris Babochkin, *Vospominaniia, dnevniki, pis'ma,* ed. N. Babochkina and L. Parfenov (Moscow: Materik, 1996), 253.

[89] Stepanishcheva, "Vot tak i zhizn' proshla," TsDNA, f. 422, l. 26.

[90] Aleksandr Kovarskii, "Detstvo na ulitse chempiona," *Zhurnal Mishpokha,* no. 14 (2004) (www.mishpoha.org/nomer14/a18.htm); Mandelstam, *Hope Abandoned,* 354; Evgenia Galina, interview by Ella Levitskaya, April 2003, in *Jewish Witness to a European Century* (www .centropa.org); diary of O. A. Boltianskaia, RGALI, f. 2057, op. 2, d. 30, l. 33, entry of April 29, 1943.

[91] Letter of December 22, 1941, in O. V. Nikitin, ed., "Poslednie pis'ma D. N. Ushakova G. O. Vinokuru," *Izvestiia RAN. Seriia literatury i iazyka,* no. 1 (2001): 68.

[92] Letter to L. Maliugin, February 14, 1942, in Lugovskaia, *Kak znaiu,* 256.

where in the winter there is mud that has no equal anywhere else in the world (it more closely resembles a quick-drying carpenter's glue); a city where lady-bimbos (*damy-fify*) and grief have assembled from all over the Soviet Union, where on the streets, moving alongside the trams, there are camels and donkeys, where they for some reason call you *aga*, where they call your native Leningrad and Moscow Russia (!) . . . In this city, made for death, I have ended up. Why, for what—I cannot understand.[93]

If the urban landscape, the sights and sounds, almost invariably struck newcomers as foreign, there were some respects in which Tashkent was nonetheless familiar. The squat houses, winding alleys and caravans of camels masked what was an all-too recognizable feature of the urban landscape—its institutional architecture. Despite the continued frustration of authorities in both Moscow and Tashkent at the failure to make Tashkent a truly modern city, it was an undeniably Soviet city.[94] And what happened to evacuees once they arrived in Tashkent, their struggle to survive, is in many ways a typical Soviet story.

"TASHKENT, CITY OF BREAD"

The war led to a precipitous decline in living standards across the Soviet Union, and Tashkent was no exception.[95] In the first year of the war, the population of Tashkent grew by nearly 20 percent.[96] The city was, in Maria Belkina's words, "bursting at the seams."[97] Or, as Evgenia Pasternak put it, "Tashkent . . . has gone mad from the flood of evacuees."[98] The sheer number of people put an incredible strain on the city's resources. Tatiana Okunevskaia compared Tashkent to a "leech that has sucked its fill." It is "bursting," she wrote, "there is nowhere left to settle, nothing to eat."[99]

---

[93] Ibid.

[94] In describing Tashkent as a Soviet city, I have the institutional architecture of the city in mind and make no claims regarding the Sovietization of the city or its population. For a thoughtful treatment of this issue, see Stronski, "Forging a Soviet City." Although the institutional landscape of Tashkent largely mirrored that of other Soviet cities, it did have some distinctive features. For instance, red teahouses replaced the standard worker's club. Ibid., 80–81. In addition, within the standard raion (city district) authorities maintained the *mahalla* (Uzbek neighborhood).

[95] See John Barber and Mark Harrison, *The Soviet Home Front, 1941–1945: A Social and Economic History of the USSR in World War II* (London: Longman, 1991), 77–79.

[96] The population on July 1, 1941, based on the 1939 census and taking into account the administrative exclusion of two districts of the city, was estimated at 584,955. RGAE, f. 1562, op. 20, d. 244, l. 29. The population as of July 1, 1942, is recorded at 700,530 in ibid., d. 327, l. 101.

[97] Belkina, *Skreshchenie sudeb*, 345.

[98] Letter of December 1941, in Boris Pasternak and Evgenii Pasternak, *Sushchestvovania tkan' skvoznaia: Boris Pasternak perepiska s Evgeniei Pasternak, dopolnennaia pis'mami k E. B. Pasternaku i ego vospominaniiami* (Moscow: Novoe literaturnoe obozrenie, 1998), 431.

[99] Tat'iana Okunevskaia, *Tat'ianin den'* (Moscow: Vagrius, 1998), 98.

The struggle for survival on the Tashkent front fell disproportionately on the shoulders of women, who accounted for nearly two-thirds of the city's evacuee population.[100] As Nadezhda Mandelstam put it in a letter to a friend, "in general there are a lot of people, but they are all women."[101] Many women were faced with the task of supporting themselves, their children, and their elderly parents. Tatiana Lugovskaia wrote in a letter that "I have become the head of a fairly large family: two infirm—Mama and Volodia; Polia, who came with us; and Liubochka, whom I befriended here in Tashkent."[102] Daily life in Tashkent, moreover, was not easy. Olga Boltianskaia described her daily routine in her diary: "I have to walk a lot . . . to sell things at the market, purchase and lug home fuel from the market, stand in line for bread and at the cafeteria for soup and dumplings. I walk all day, covering terrible distances as the trams aren't running, and I come home, and it is like a cellar in our room—I have to heat the stove, prepare dinner, clean up, and so on. Toward evening I feel faint."[103] The heavy burden that fell on women's shoulders took its toll. Lugovskaia confided in a letter that "I never in my whole life felt like such a baba. I am very tired of this emancipation . . . and I want to lean my head on somebody's shoulder, but now, of course, is not a time to even dream about it."[104] It was, in Olga Boltianskaia's words, a "terrible period for women."[105]

Letters intercepted by the censors and excerpted for a report on the needs of the families of servicemen in Tashkent present a bleak picture of life behind the front lines. "I am living through difficulties the likes of which I have not yet encountered in my life," wrote one woman.[106] "Life is a full-blown nightmare," another wrote to her husband. "It would be better to live under bombardment than in these conditions. It is a slow death."[107]

Tashkent, which had seemed like an oasis from afar, now appeared to be, in Tatiana Okunevskaia's words, an "émigré hell."[108] Even the climate, one of the city's main attractions, was a source of seemingly endless misery. As one Muscovite complained in a desperate letter to authorities back in Moscow, "I cannot even describe how tormented I have been and continue to be at present. In the summer it became even more difficult because of the heat.

---

[100] According to statistics collected in December 1941, 72% of all adult evacuees in the Soviet Union were women. RGAE, f. 1562, op. 20, d. 249, l. 69. In Tashkent, the figure was somewhat lower, 64%. Ibid., d. 311, l. 109.

[101] N. Ia. Mandel'shtam to B. S. Kuzin, September 19, 1942, in Mandel'shtam, *192 pis'ma*, 684.

[102] Letter to L. Maliugin, January 30, 1942, in Lugovskaia, *Kak znaiu*, 255

[103] Diary of O. A. Boltianskaia, RGALI, f. 2057, op. 2, d. 29, l. 287, entry of December 30, 1942.

[104] Letter to L. Maliugin, February 14, 1942, in Lugovskaia, *Kak znaiu*, 257.

[105] Diary of O. A. Boltianskaia, RGALI, f. 2057, op. 2, d. 30, l. 18, entry of February 26, 1943.

[106] GAGT, f. 10, op. 17, d. 55, l. 1.

[107] Ibid., l. 216.

[108] Okunevskaia, *Tat'ianin den'*, 102.

I have malaria and my son is growing sickly thanks to the climate, which does not agree with him."[109] Olga Boltianskaia's doctor even recommended she leave Tashkent. "In the north," the doctor told her, "it would be easier for me."[110] The two most persistent causes of complaint, however, and the source of seemingly endless torment, were the daily struggle for food and the search for shelter.

Food was a constant preoccupation for evacuees, and hunger pervades their wartime writing. "Hunger torments and torments me," Georgii Efron noted in his diary in late January 1943, "I can think of nothing else."[111] Alexander Kovarskii, a child at the time, later observed that "hunger was the most powerful sensation during the war."[112] Food in Tashkent, while in plentiful supply, was not easy to attain. Olga Boltianskaia's first notation in her diary after arrival in the "city of bread" was that "it is very difficult here with bread; there is no sugar, no butter, and everything at the market is very expensive."[113] It is surely no coincidence that Boltianskaia's account of life in Tashkent began with prices at the market. The market figures prominently in almost every evacuee description of the city. Nadezhda Mandelstam later described the Alai Bazaar as a "wonderful Eastern marketplace with enormous vegetables and fruit in great piles and, hanging high up, tantalizingly out of reach, whole sheep's carcasses. Flat white loaves were offered at a staggering price by hucksters, and sun-blackened women traded in all kinds of cloying oriental sweet meats which stuck to the teeth."[114] Maria Belkina described it in equally colorful terms.[115]

The market figures in evacuee writing as more than a marker of Tashkent's "oriental" character, however; it occupies a central space in the topography of everyday life. "Absolutely everything comes from the bazaar," one evacuee explained in a letter to her father.[116] The centrality of the market underscores the degree to which it had supplanted the state as the principal provider of food to the population at large. "The solution to the problem of feeding the civilian population," William Moskoff writes of the wartime food supply, "was not to use the strength of the centralized Soviet planning system but to force the population to find the capacity to feed itself." The state provided only the most essential items, in quantities that were far from sufficient.[117] As Zinaida Stepanishcheva later wrote, "there was no state-

[109] RGALI, f. 962, op. 3, d. 1076, l. 3.
[110] Diary of O. A. Boltianskaia, RGALI, f. 2057, op. 2, d. 30, l. 44, entry of May 24, 1943.
[111] Efron, Dnevniki, vol. 2, 160, entry of January 27, 1943.
[112] Aleksandr Kovarskii, "Detstvo na ulitse chempiona."
[113] Diary of O. A. Boltianskaia, RGALI, f. 2057, op. 2, d. 29, l. 93, entry of August 11, 1941.
[114] Mandelstam, Hope Abandoned, 602.
[115] Belkina, Skreshchenie sudeb, 348.
[116] GAGT, f. 10, op. 17, d. 55, l. 39.
[117] William Moskoff, The Bread of Affliction: The Food Supply in the USSR during World War II (Cambridge: Cambridge University Press, 1990), 3. Rationing, which had been abolished

sponsored sale of foodstuffs or manufactured goods. All the stores were closed. Only rye bread was sold—800 grams for the working person and 400 grams for children and dependents."[118]

In these conditions, people were forced to shop at the bazaar, where, as Stepanishcheva put it, the "prices continuously rose."[119] "Prices have leaped by several times," Olga Boltianskaia noted in her diary. "Butter costs 100 rubles a kilo, ten eggs are 18 rubles, and so on."[120] The republican newspaper *Pravda Vostoka* complained about the excessively high prices, but despite the call to "bring order to the markets of Tashkent," the prices kept going up.[121] "Life in Tashkent," an evacuee remarked in a letter the following year, "is devilishly expensive."[122] Tatiana Lugovskaia, after hearing about a friend's sister in the nearby city of Chu, wrote that the place "seems to be a fable, for it cannot be that so close to Tashkent they can get food at prices ten times lower."[123]

Salaries, moreover, were comparatively low. The composer Yuri Tiulin, evacuated from Leningrad with the city's conservatory, described the situation in a letter in early 1942. "Potatoes," he wrote, "are already 16 rubles a kilo, rice is 42 and change, and with each day everything rises in price. I now receive a salary of not more than 750–800 rubles a month . . . for a household of five." In fact, Tiulin's salary was relatively high by Tashkent standards. As he himself acknowledged, "others are in a much worse situation, earning 150–300 rubles per month for a family of four to five people."[124] Tiulin was actually doubly fortunate. Not only was his salary good, but he had a stable job that had not been interrupted in the process of departure. Iakov Notkin, evacuated to Tashkent from Kiev, was in a similar situation. Even when Kiev's Industrial Institute, with which he had been evacuated, merged with the Central Asian Industrial Institute in Tashkent, Notkin retained his job as a teacher.[125] Although many evacuees had been evacuated with their workplace, many others were compelled to search out jobs on their arrival in Tashkent. Although the process was not easy, there were certainly jobs to be had. Raisa Yasvoina's mother found work in a rice factory, Alexander Kovarskii's

---

only several years earlier, was reinstituted during the war. Ration cards for bread and sugar were introduced in Tashkent, as in the rest of the country, on October 20, 1941. TsGARUz, f. 837, op. 32, d. 2594, ll. 1–3. In contrast to the previous rationing regime, however, which established a "guaranteed minimum at a certain fixed ration-price," the wartime rationing regime established maximum levels of consumption. Moskoff, *The Bread of Affliction*, 136.

[118] Stepanishcheva, "Vot tak i zhizn' proshla," l. 25.
[119] Ibid.
[120] Diary of O. A. Boltianskaia, RGALI, f. 2057, op. 2, d. 29, l. 123, entry of November 8, 1941.
[121] *Pravda Vostoka*, February 14, 1942.
[122] GAGT, f. 10, op. 17, d. 55, l. 278.
[123] Letter to L. Maliugin, February 14, 1942, in Lugovskaia, *Kak znaiu*, 258.
[124] RNB, f. 1088, op. 1, d. 154, l. 4.
[125] GARF, f. 8114, op. 1, d. 917, l. 33.

in a school, and Iania Chernina's in an armaments factory. Zinaida Stepanishcheva was given work in a laboratory, the elderly Aron Brukson found
work as a guard, and Nadezhda Mandelstam was hired as a teacher. By 1942,
evacuees could be found in every sector of the local economy and municipal administration.[126] Often, moreover, evacuees found work in their speciality. This
was true of the accountant Zinaida Levina, the saleswoman Hanna Galants-
Rusakovskaia, the nurse Khanna Brukson, and the tailors Khaim Rakhgendler and his wife.[127] It was also true of Malka Zaltsberg, who was hired by a
tuberculosis institute in Tashkent and even managed to complete her disserta-
tion while there.[128] Evgenia Galina's father, a clock repairman by profession,
also found work in his specialty but not without some hardship: the evacuation had not permitted him to bring his tools with him, and he had to set up
and equip a shop before he could begin earning.[129]

Either way, however, a salary alone was simply insufficient. "I had the
salary from my job," Nadezhda Mandelstam recalled, "but on this alone I
would have died of starvation."[130] As the actress Tatiana Okunevskaia explained, "I receive a salary for the film *Parkhomenko*, but what does it mean
on the market, if milk for my daughter costs 300 rubles a liter—that's a quarter of my salary."[131] Stepanishcheva went so far as to claim that the "size of
one's paycheck was no longer of great significance as it was practically impossible to live on it anyway. If I earned 250 rubles and my stepfather earned
400, and a kilogram of sugar cost 400 rubles, then the sugar was beyond
both my reach and his. The same went for other foods. One had to find other
means of surviving."[132]

In desperate straights, many evacuees were compelled, in the words of a
report on writers in the republic, to "sell their last possessions."[133] Georgii
Efron sold his suitcase, his boots (*valenki*), and various other possessions,
all of which secured him only a few measly meals at the market. As he noted
in his diary, "I have no stove, no oil, no bread, potatoes, pasta; and without
all that you can't prepare anything at home and you're forced to ruin yourself at the bazaar."[134] Twelve-year-old Iania Chernina traded in her dolls, the
sole possessions she had brought with her to Tashkent, to save her mother
and herself from starvation: her mother had lost her bread card and "we
didn't have any nice things that we could take to the market to trade or to

[126] GAGT, f. 10, op. 3, d. 130, ll. 33–41.
[127] See http://resources.ushmm.org/uzbekrefugees/getjpg.php/L/8849.jpg; G/3405.jpg; R/2215
.jpg; B/9711.jpg and R/2213.jpg.
[128] Leonid Averbukh, interview by Nicole Tolkachova, 2003, in *Jewish Witness to a European Century*, cassette 1, side A. Russian transcript provided by Centropa.org.
[129] Evgenia Galina, interview.
[130] Mandelstam, *Hope Abandoned*, 445.
[131] Okunevskaia, *Tat'ianin den'*, 98.
[132] Stepanishcheva, "Vot tak i zhizn' proshla," l. 25.
[133] RGALI, f. 962, op. 3, d. 1104, l. 25.
[134] Efron, *Dnevniki*, vol. 2, 160, entry of January 27, 1943.

sell." She managed to find an older Uzbek man who was willing to give her a month's worth of rice in exchange for the dolls.[135] Tatiana Okunevskaia, who was better provisioned and equipped, later recalled, "I brought my things, which I had just bought in Kiev at the commission shops and had not yet worn, to the market to trade them for food, and for the English dress I got 3 kilograms of flour. Hurrah! We are saved!"[136] Others, however, arrived in Tashkent with little more than the clothes on their back. "En route to Tashkent all my things were stolen," one evacuee from Stalingrad oblast wrote.[137] Some had lost their luggage along the way, others departed without it.[138] "Like many other evacuees," one family reported to the Tashkent Evacuation Center, "we were forced to depart in very difficult circumstances and we were thus unable to bring our things with us."[139]

Evacuees, uprooted from their homes and often alone, were in a particularly precarious position. Despite several high-profile articles in *Pravda* instructing authorities to "care for evacuees," evacuees as such received little in the way of help. In Tashkent and its environs, only evacuated children received aid as evacuees: a network of six cafeterias, established by the Republican Commission to Aid Evacuated Children, reportedly served as many as six thousand children a day, of whom nine hundred, or 15 percent, received their meals for free.[140] Notably, the subsidized meals were financed almost exclusively by donations and fund raisers organized by the commission's volunteers rather than by state institutions.[141] When it came to the state, money earmarked for the evacuated population was limited in quantity, directed to the "especially needy," and calculated as a one-time disbursement to aid in the search for a job.[142] Throughout 1942, the central

---

[135] Svetlana Aleksievich, *Poslednie svideteli (sto nedetskikh kolybel'nikh)* (Moscow: Pal'mira, 2004), 136.

[136] Okunevskaia, *Tat'ianin den'*, 101

[137] GAGT, f. 330, op. 1, d. 10, l. 32.

[138] Several such cases can be found in GAGT, f. 330, op. 1, d. 10, l. 2, and GARF, f. 7021, op. 100, d. 19, l. 4. Aleksander Wat had his luggage stolen from him at the Tashkent station. See Aleksander Wat, *My Century: the Odyssey of a Polish Intellectual*, trans. Richard Lourie (New York: New York Review of Books, 2003), 339.

[139] GAGT, f. 330, op. 1, d. 10, l. 35.

[140] TsGARUz, f. 837, op. 32, d. 3418, l. 53.

[141] According to a financial report drawn up by the Commission on August 31, 1942, state subsidization of the commission's work was negligible, amounting to only 5,000 rubles out of the more than 1,500,000 rubles that the commission received from across Uzbekistan. TsGARUz, f. 837, op. 32, d. 3418, ll. 54–55.

[142] Ibid., d. 2894, l. 121. In the fall of 1941, Tashkent municipal authorities, on the directives of Uzbek Party Secretary Iusupov, authorized "the allocation of 50,000 rubles from the local budget for December for the provision of aid to very needy evacuees from the frontline regions." GAGT, f. 10, op. 17, d. 14, l. 111. In February 1942, the executive committee of the Tashkent City Soviet requested additional funds from the Uzbek Sovnarkom, also for one-time aid disbursements, on the grounds that "at present the Executive Committee of the Tashkent City Soviet does not have funds for this purpose." TsGARUz, f. 837, op. 32, d. 3416, l. 182. Central authorities, however, stipulated that available funds be used exclusively to aid evacuees

government in Moscow issued only one decree on the provisioning of evacuees. That decree, moreover, applied only to evacuees from Leningrad, survivors of the first blockade winter.[143] As a procuracy report on the Commissariat of Trade put it, "evacuees are supplied from general sources."[144] Petitions to the Tashkent Evacuation Center yielded few results. In effect, "I am an evacuee," the repeated refrain in such petitions, was simply insufficient to secure access to scarce state goods.[145]

"A man alone cannot survive in the Soviet Union," wrote Aleksander Wat.[146] This was particularly true of evacuees. Nadezhda Mandelstam survived thanks to her sister-in-law, who gave her her ration card for use in the cafeteria of the Union of Artists, and her close friend and housemate Anna Akhmatova, who generously shared her own rations.[147] Mandelstam later reflected that, to survive, "one had to be entitled to draw proper rations at fixed state prices, not market ones."[148] "Fixed state rations," however, were not available to all. Maria Belkina describes the functioning of the state distribution system: "Tashkent already lived the life of other Soviet cities," she recalled. "Everything by ration cards and vouchers, closed stores converted into distributors [*raspredeliteli*], the distributors divided by category, the population divided by category. Some were accorded a Sovnarkom ration, some letter A, some letter B, and those without any letter—simply a bread card, a ration card, which entitled one to almost nothing—after all, what is 400 grams of cottonseed oil a month, or 500 grams of rice, or a piece of soap."[149]

Access to closed stores and special rations was dependent on what Timofeev, contemplating the evacuation while in Moscow, referred to as one's "juridical" status. Faced with the probable evacuation of his institute from Moscow to Tomsk, Timofeev decided to join the institute in evacuation, "as here, with the departure of the institute . . . I would cease to be a juridical

---

in the search for a job and noted that the republic's reserves were "almost completely depleted." TsGARUz, f. 837, op. 32, d. 2894, l. 121.

[143] GARF, f. 8131, op. 19, d. 62, l. 16. The decree, issued on May 24, 1942, stipulated that evacuees from Leningrad be accorded supplemental rations for two months from the date of their arrival in evacuation.

[144] Ibid. According to the report, there had been an initial decree on the provisionment of evacuees from both Moscow and Leningrad, but the Commissariat of Trade annulled the decree in mid-July 1941.

[145] There are entire files of requests sent to the Evacuation Division of the Uzbek Sovnarkom. See GAGT, f. 330, op. 1, d. 10.

[146] Wat, *My Century*, 307, my translation.

[147] N. Ia. Mandel'shtam to B. S. Kuzin, November 8, 1942, in Mandel'shtam, *192 pis'ma*, 687. Others survived thanks to family help from afar. Evgenia Pasternak and her son, for example, depended on the irregular sums sent by her former husband in Chistopol. E. V. Pasternak to B. L. Pasternak, August 22, 1942, in Pasternak and Pasternak, *Sushchestvovania tkan' skvoznaia*, 443.

[148] Mandelstam, *Hope Abandoned*, 445.

[149] Belkina, *Skreshchenie sudeb*, 348.

person, whereas in Tomsk, even in terrible conditions, I would still be a doctor of philology!"[150] As his reflections suggest, juridical status depended on membership in an officially recognized body—the Union of Soviet Writers, the Academy of Sciences, the Leningrad State Conservatory. These bodies, however, had been uprooted by the evacuation: the Academy of Sciences and the Union of Soviet Writers, for example, were now based in Kazan. Their members, moreover, were dispersed across the vast expanses of the Soviet rear. Academicians could be found in Tashkent, Alma-Ata, Syktyvkar, Sverdlovsk, and Frunze as well as Kazan.[151] Writers—though concentrated in the greatest numbers in Kazan, Tashkent, Kuibyshev, and Sverdlovsk—could be found in every republic, in towns large and small.[152] Networks had to be reconstituted, connections reestablished.

Those who were separated from their institutes faced innumerable problems. The mathematician Evgenii Slutskii, who received official authorization to go to Tashkent even though the Mathematics Institute was in Kazan, was inexplicably struck off the institute's official list shortly after his arrival in the Uzbek capital. He now found himself, as he put it in a desperate letter to the Academy of Sciences, in a "calamitous situation," able to find only a half-time job and making far less than he had.[153] Georgii Efron was in an even more precarious position. As the son of a deceased writer he received some aid from the literary fund, but he was not a member of the Writers' Union. As a result, when the union was giving out meat, he received none, for "I am not on the lists."[154] It was only when he succeeded in inserting himself into an alternative distribution network—for evacuated children—that he was able to secure a steady supply of food.[155]

It bears emphasizing that even those who were "on the lists" were not guaranteed relief from hunger. Maria Belkina, who later described the workings of the system, failed to note that, at least initially, she herself had only partial access to its privileges. The archives have preserved a report on her condition penned by Lezhnev, secretary of the Presidium of the Uzbek Union of Soviet Writers, in the middle of August 1942 in response to an inquiry by the all-union secretary Fadeev.[156] According to the report, Belkina's young child was well, but she herself "has lost a lot of weight, and complains about nervous exhaustion." Although Belkina "has access to the writer's cafeteria and to the general writer's distributors, the food provided

---

[150] L. I. Timofeev, "Dnevnik voennykh let," *Znamia*, no. 6 (2002): 141–42.

[151] GARF, f. 6822, op. 1, d. 45, l. 3.

[152] The principal concentrations of writers were communicated by the Union of Soviet Writers to newspapers and other journals. RGALI, f. 631, op. 15, d. 565, l. 173. There was also a substantial number of writers in Chistopol.

[153] ARAN, f. 2, op. 1, d. 140a, l. 2.

[154] Efron, *Dnevniki*, vol. 2, 152, entry of January 12, 1943.

[155] Ibid., 191, 209, entries of March 19, 1943 and April 16, 1943.

[156] RGALI, f. 630, op. 15, d. 603, l. 51.

is insufficient for an emaciated person." Belkina, it turns out, was not at the top of the writers' hierarchy. Although a group of writers did enjoy access to "better distributors" (which were generally reserved for the Soviet and party *aktiv*), Belkina was not among them. In fact, Lezhnev had requested the inclusion of a substantial number of writers in the elite distribution network, but, as he put it, his request had been "only partially fulfilled." The privilege was reserved for women who were married to laureates and order bearers. Thus Esther Markish, the wife of Perets Markish, gained access to the superior network, while women such as Belkina and Elena Bulgakova did not.[157]

"Juridical status" was clearly important but it was not always sufficient. As one desperate woman put it in a letter to the front, "one needs *znakomstvo* [acquaintances]."[158] Indeed, "contacts and connections," to use the historian Sheila Fitzpatrick's phrase, were crucial to survival.[159] There is no greater testament to the critical role played by contacts in the struggle for survival than the steady stream of letters that passed among evacuees, their families and friends, and authorities at all levels of government. The paper trail offers a weighty demonstration of the fact that "juridical status" alone could get one only so far. In Tashkent, as elsewhere, people looked after "their own." The Leningrad historian Boris Romanov, employed in Tashkent by an evacuated Muscovite institute, complained in a letter that "here everything is for 'one's own,' for Muscovites; for others there are only . . . words."[160] Evacuees were faced with the task of reconstructing networks—both personal and professional (categories that often overlapped). The reconstitution of old networks and the creation of new ones, and the role of both status and networks in the struggle for survival, are set into sharp relief by the allocation of housing.

THE SEARCH FOR SHELTER

If the flood of evacuees strained the city's food resources, it put an even greater strain on its housing stock. A report from 1943 concluded that "the housing stock [in Tashkent] does not meet even the most elementary demands that have been placed on it. At present each inhabitant has on average 2.6 square meters of living space."[161] Ambitious plans to construct an additional 56,000 square meters of living space in the republican capital to accommodate the influx of people yielded paltry results. As a December

---

[157] Ibid.

[158] GAGT, f. 10, op. 17, d. 55, l. 41.

[159] Sheila Fitzpatrick, *Everyday Stalinism: Ordinary Life in Extraordinary Times. Soviet Russia in the 1930s* (New York: Oxford University Press, 1999), 63.

[160] Paneiakh, *Tvorchestvo i sud'ba istorika*, 196.

[161] RGASPI, f. 17, op. 122, d. 37, l. 80.

1941 report on the progress of building put it, "not only has not a single square meter of living space been constructed, but the construction of barracks has not yet even begun."[162] The situation in the next year was not much better.[163]

As a result of the sluggish pace of new construction, most evacuees were housed in existing buildings, where a process of expulsion and "self-condensation" was initiated.[164] Local residents with suspect backgrounds or compromised family histories, the unemployed, and people of German descent were eligible for forcible removal from Tashkent to the surrounding countryside. A commission established for this purpose oversaw the compilation of lists of such people, who were subsequently expelled from Tashkent and whose permits to live in the city were revoked.[165] Displacement thus begat displacement. Those who were not expelled were forced to "self-condense" and share their "excess" living space. Isaak Bakhmatov described the housing situation in a letter to his relatives. Living space, he wrote, "has been reduced to four meters a person. . . . Every resident of Tashkent is now guessing who will be sent to them, will they end up with residents of good character, how many children will they bring, how lice-ridden will they be from the journey (it is unavoidable now)."[166] The headings used by officials in the Tashkent City Soviet to catalogue the requisitioned living space speak volumes. The space was categorized by the number of rooms, hallways, corners, and kitchens.[167]

In theory, those evacuated in an organized fashion were assigned housing by Uzbek authorities. Members of the Academy of Sciences, for example, were accorded a building in the center of town, at 84 Pushkinskaia. Boris Romanov, who was not fortunate enough to be given a room in the building, described it in positively glowing terms. It had, he wrote in a letter, "steam heat, electricity, lighting, someone who cleaned the floors, . . . billiards, pianos, telephones. It is divided into individual rooms with two to three windows, with furniture, [including] writing tables."[168] Indeed, the building's maintenance was overseen by none other than the deputy chairman of the Uzbek Council of People's Commissars.[169] The linguist Dmitrii Ushakov, who lived in the building, noted in a letter that it had been "taken from the NKVD. It is wonderful. The six of us occupy one very large room and another simply large room. . . . They have organized a cafeteria here, even a

[162] TsGARUz, f. 837, op. 32, d. 3716, l. 14.
[163] Housing construction in 1942 is described in a report dated September 10, 1942 in ibid., d. 3523, l. 44.
[164] GAGT, f. 10, op. 18, d. 26, l. 465.
[165] Ibid., op. 17, d. 22, l. 44.
[166] I. M. Bakhmatov to E. M. Bakhmatova, November 21, 1941, TsDNA, f. 45, l. 1.
[167] GAGT, f. 10, op. 17, d. 36, ll. 8, 32.
[168] Paneiakh, *Tvorchestvo i sud'ba istorika*, 193.
[169] TsGARUz, f. 837, op. 32, d. 3523, l. 107.

hairdresser. It is quiet and clean."[170] Among the building's other illustrious residents were Solomon Mikhoels, the actor and director of the State Jewish Theater, as well as a handful of respected writers, including Alexander Deich. Deich later described the building's residents as a "large colony of Moscow and Leningrad scholars and writers."[171]

Like members of the Academy of Sciences, writers occupied a privileged station before the war and had been evacuated to Tashkent in organized fashion. Authorities in Moscow, both in the government and on the Committee of the Arts, took a keen interest in their welfare, as did the Union of Soviet Writers, which was kept informed of their situation by a representative on the ground.[172] Union Secretary Alexander Fadeev sent numerous letters and telegrams on behalf of evacuated writers to Uzbek authorities, requesting that they "offer assistance to these writers, accommodate them, give them living quarters, and create conditions amenable to their literary and public-political work."[173] The reconstitution of writers' corporate status was further facilitated by the existence of an equivalent organization in Tashkent—the Uzbek Union of Soviet Writers. This organization served as an effective intermediary between the evacuated writers and Uzbek authorities as well as authorities in Moscow.[174] It should come as no surprise, then, that writers were accorded choice accommodations in the very center of town. In addition to the building at 84 Pushkinskaia, which they shared with other members of the cultural and intellectual elite, they were given buildings for their exclusive use at 7 Karl Marx Street and 54 Zhukovskaia.[175] Their residents included some of the most well-known and distinguished writers in the country.

Accommodation was not determined, however, solely by status. To secure a room, one also needed connections. Maria Belkina, who was given a

[170] Letter to G. O. Vinokur, December 22, 1941, in Nikitin, "Poslednie pis'ma D. N. Ushakova," 67.

[171] Aleksandr Deich, *Den' nineishii, den' minuvshii: literaturnye vpechatleniia i vstrechi* (Moscow: Sovetskii pisatel', 1969), 156.

[172] RGALI, f. 631, op. 15, d. 565, l. 173.

[173] Ibid., l. 6. See also ibid., ll. 176, 181. The Union of Soviet Writers was perhaps the single most important body in securing the livelihood of writers, but, like other organizations, its efficacy was undermined by displacement. In the fall of 1941, for example, the Writers' Union lost touch with the People's Commissariat of Finance, and thus found itself "without money." Ibid., l. 194. When a group of Tashkent writers requested a grant from the Literary Foundation in Moscow, moreover, it refused, citing insufficient funds. Union authorities did, however, serve as advocates on behalf of writers even in this case, appealing to the head of the Uzbek government to provide support for writers by financing publications. Ibid., d. 597, ll. 64–65.

[174] In October 1942, for example, the Uzbek Union of Soviet Writers appealed to the Committee of the Arts in Moscow requesting 150,000 rubles to be distributed as aid to evacuated writers in the republic. The author, describing the pitiful state in which writers were living, claimed that the "only real help for writers is help from the Literary Fund of the Uzbek Republic. Our Literary Fund is literally besieged with requests from writers for help." RGALI, f. 962, op. 3, d. 1104, l. 25.

[175] TsGARUz, f. R-2356, op. 1, d. 94, l. 35.

room in the building on Karl Marx Street, wrote her husband that "[Niko-lai] Virta helped me get it."[176] Evgenia Pasternak, who was initially housed in cramped conditions near the railway station with her son, likewise credited her acquisition of a room at 54 Zhukovskaia to friends in positions of authority. As she explained in a letter to her former husband, the poet Boris Pasternak, "everything good that we have here we owe to the Ivanovs. Kornei Ivanovich [Chukovskii] helped us move here."[177] Indeed, Kornei Chukovskii stood at the center of a small circle of people whose livelihood he secured through his good will and connections. Nadezhda Mandelstam, Anna Akhmatova, and Evgenia Pasternak all attributed their good fortune in finding housing to Chukovskii.[178] Chukovskii himself received his apartment through the former Uzbek people's commissar of enlightenment.[179] On other occasions, he appealed directly to Usman Iusupov, head of the Uzbek Communist Party. Thus did he go about securing the livelihood of thirteen-year-old Valentin Berestov, a budding poet and evacuee from Kaluga. Berestov later recalled that "Kornei Ivanovich not only 'made my life somewhat easier' [Chukovskii's own description of his aid to the young man], he saved it."[180] When Chukovskii's daughter, Lydia, sought to have Akhmatova transferred from the Karl Marx Street building to the greater comfort of the residence on Zhukovskaia, she noted in her diary that this would be "extremely difficult given that my father is not here, nor is Tolstoi."[181]

Alexei Tolstoi was even better placed than Chukovskii. As a deputy to the Supreme Soviet of the USSR and a member of the Uzbek Union of Soviet Writers, Tolstoi had direct access to Uzbek officialdom, and he emerged as an important patron for evacuated writers in Tashkent. Ekaterina Peshkova, the widow of the late Russian writer Maxim Gorky, later described the "spacious dining room" of Tolstoi's Tashkent home as a "center in which one would frequently meet Muscovites who had ended up in Tashkent and

[176] Quoted in Gromova, *Vse v chuzhoe gliadiat okno*, 42.

[177] Letter of Feburary 16, 1942, in Pasternak and Pasternak, *Sushchestvovania tkan' skvoznaia*, 437.

[178] N. Ia. Mandel'shtam to B. S. Kuzin, August 10, 1942, in Mandel'shtam, *192 pis'ma*, 680–81.

[179] Chukovskii, *Dnevnik*, 160, entry of October 30, 1941.

[180] Valentin Berestov, *Izbrannye proizvedeniia*, 2 vols. (Moscow: Izdatel'stvo imeni Sabash-nikovykh, 1998), vol. 2, 185–86. The archives in Tashkent have preserved evidence of Chuk-ovskii's intervention in the form of a report on Berestov's condition as one of several "particu-larly talented" children who were to be accorded aid "to set up the necessary conditions for the development of their creative capacities." "Berestov," the report begins, "has a poetic talent of enormous range, in the opinion of K. I. Chukovskii." TsGARUz, f. 94, op. 5, d. 4249, ll. 34–35. Chukovskii later wrote that he also involved Alexei Tolstoi in his efforts to aid Berestov. Be-restov, *Izbrannye proizvedeniia*, vol. 2, 186. The aid extended to Berestov as a youth with tal-ent rather than simply a youth in need serves as yet another indication of the special dispensa-tion afforded to the intellectual and cultural elite in the Soviet provisioning system.

[181] Chukovskaia, *Zapiski ob Annoi Akhmatovoi*, vol. 1, 473–74, entry of August 1, 1942.

make new friends."[182] Among Tolstoi's regular guests was Kornei Chuk-ovskii. Although Chukovskii and Tolstoi had known each other for years, they became friends only in Tashkent.[183] Tolstoi offered Chukovskii friend-ship, good company, and connections. When Chukovskii sought to help his daughter-in-law move to Tashkent, his first step was to seek out Tolstoi's intervention.[184] His daughter Lydia likewise turned to Tolstoi, albeit less directly, when she sought to secure aid for Akhmatova: she arranged for Tolstoi to visit Akhmatova so that he would see the horrid conditions in which she lived and send help. "And thus it happened," Chukovskaia re-corded in her notebook.[185]

Although Tolstoi and Chukovskii were without a doubt among the most "connected" of the Moscow writers, they were not the only ones with useful contacts. Lydia Chukovskaia, for example, managed to establish some con-nections of her own. While in Tashkent, she participated actively on the Commission to Aid Evacuated Children. There, she worked with Ekaterina Peshkova as well as the wives of high-placed members within the republican party organization. More than once she availed herself of these connections on Akhmatova's behalf.[186] Even Nadezhda Mandelstam, otherwise quite dependent on the contacts of others, managed to get one of her late husband's acquaintances, a "minor Moscow poet" who had arrived in Tashkent from Kolyma, into a hospital in Tashkent. She went through a cobbler she had be-friended, who went to a client "whose only pair of shoes he had mended all during the war."[187]

In many cases, given the lack of connections to people in the local and republican government, evacuees sought to mobilize support on their behalf in Moscow. The performer Ksenia Derzhinskaia, whose family's food status had been demoted after her return to Moscow, used her status or connec-tions in Moscow to get none other than the head of the office of Sovnarkom affairs to write to Abdurakhmanov, the head of the Uzbek government, to have her family reattached to a better distributor.[188] Solomon Mikhoels, as the head of the Jewish Anti-Fascist Committee and a prominent one-time

[182] E. P. Peshkova, "Vospominaniia ob A. N. Tolstom," in *Vospominaniia ob A. N. Tolstom,* ed. Z. A. Nikitina and L. I. Tolstaia (Moscow: Sovetskii pisatel', 1973), 26.

[183] Chukovskii, *Dnevnik,* 161, entry of January 21, 1942.

[184] Nikolai Chukovskii, *O tom, shto videl,* ed. E. N. Nikitina (Moscow: Molodaia gvardiia, 2005), 603.

[185] Chukovskaia, *Zapiski ob Annoi Akhmatovoi,* vol. 1, 373, entry of January 11, 1942. Akhmatova was apparently displeased. "I do not want to be bound to Tolstoi," she said. Akhmatova herself, however, appealed to Tolstoi on behalf of Georgii Efron. Ibid., 411, entry of March 10, 1942.

[186] Chukovskaia notes how she appealed to Peshkova to secure Akhmatova's entrance into a "privileged hospital." She further turned to A. I. Lomakina, the wife of a high-placed party member, to attempt to secure first-rank rations for Akhmatova. Ibid., vol. 1, 498, 481, entries of November 5 and September 16, 1942.

[187] Mandelstam, *Hope Abandoned,* 605.

[188] GARF, f. 5446, op. 70, d. 11, l. 32.

resident of Tashkent, also appealed to Abdurakhmanov, whom Mikhoels knew from his time in Tashkent, on behalf of a Jewish artist in need.[189]

While those with status or connections were able to secure decent accommodation, others of only slightly lesser stature found themselves in considerably worse conditions. The sharp differentiation among people of different status is evident in the conditions in which respected historians who were not members of the Academy of Sciences were housed. Although accorded a building in the center of town, the building consisted of "dormitories of ten to fifteen people of both sexes mixed up pell-mell with children of all ages and tempers. . . . In the dormitories there is insufficient lighting, the beds are terrible, . . . people's belongings are on windowsills or on the rare chair."[190] Members of the film industry, also evacuated in organized fashion, found themselves in an equally difficult situation. Employees of the Kiev film industry had still not been allocated housing three months after their arrival.[191]

Factory workers were even worse off. Typical, in this regard, were the living conditions of the young Valentin Berestov and his family when Chukovskii first met the young boy. Berestov's mother had found work in Tashkent as a janitor in an evacuated factory.[192] In the words of a report on her son's living conditions generated as a result of Chukovskii's intervention, the "conditions in which he lives are very bad. He lives in a common room in the dormitory of the Gosznak factory with his mother and younger brother and ten other people. The Berestov family has one bed for the three of them, one chair, and a corner of a common table. The residence is not heated."[193] Iania Chernina and her mother lived in similar conditions, in the corner of an auditorium below the factory dormitory.[194] The students of a trade school that had been evacuated from Moscow were no better off. According to a report from early 1942, "only half of them are provided with beds, more than one hundred sleep on the floor. They are short one hundred blankets, there are no pillows whatsoever, and they need two hundred sheets."[195]

Many evacuees ended up renting rooms from local residents. The families of Raisa Yasvoina, Alexander Kovarskii, and Sophia Abidor all found accommodation with Uzbek families. Uzbek living quarters loom large in evacuee descriptions of the city. For evacuees, the "oriental" character of the city inhered in its homes as much as its markets. Sophia Abidor noted that the house in which she lived in Tashkent was divided between a women's

---

[189] GARF, f. 8114, op. 1, d. 1122, l. 63.
[190] Paneiakh, *Tvorchestvo i sud'ba istorika*, 193.
[191] TsGARUz, f. 837, op. 32, d. 2892, l. 47.
[192] Berestov, *Izbrannye proizvedeniia*, vol. 2, 221.
[193] TsGARUz, f. 94, op. 5, d. 4249, l. 35.
[194] Aleksievich, *Poslednie svideteli*, 132–33.
[195] TsGARUz, f. R-314, op. 1, d. 56, l. 140.

section and a men's section.[196] Alexander Kovarskii, whose family was quartered with a well-off Uzbek merchant, commented on the "tall fence" that concealed the "white one-story residences of the landlord" and the "spacious courtyard" from the street, as well as the "domestic livestock" that was kept behind the house. He was also struck by the landlord's dining room: instead of a table and chairs, the floor was covered with thick rugs, and pillows were arranged around the "long, low table." While Kovarskii dwelled on the exotic "eastern" features of his landlord's home, he and his family were not housed in the "white one-story residences" at the center of the courtyard. Instead they occupied "something between an outbuilding and a shed" that boasted a clay floor, low ceilings, and plenty of holes.[197]

Like Kovarskii's family, most evacuees resided in much more modest buildings, and their view of Uzbek residential architecture was shaped accordingly. The Polish refugee Jack Pomerantz, who was quartered with a Tajik family during his brief period of employment in Tashkent, recalled: "I had never before seen such a house. Its walls were cement, and its roof was made of clay. In the middle of the house was a big pit, dug right into the floor. They cooked in that pit, and if it grew chilly, they kept a fire going in the pit for warmth. Smoke escaped through a chimney in the roof."[198] An evacuee writing to her husband on the front described her accommodation as an "Uzbek nomad tent [*kibitka*]; when it rains it drips from the roof, and if it rains just one more time, the whole roof will fall. . . . In general the room is damp, dangerous, and neither the children nor myself, with my health, should be living in it. It's like a cellar."[199] Tatiana Okunevskaia described her abode in Tashkent as a "basement without a single window, in an Uzbek home."[200] Complaints were plentiful enough that an oblast official was compelled to concede that evacuees "who have come from the European part of the union have difficulty enduring the living conditions in these buildings."[201] As evacuees on a collective farm in the region complained, the "living conditions of the Uzbeks are completely different from those of Russians."[202]

Although Abidor recalled her lodgings with gratitude ("at least we weren't on the streets," she remarked), evacuees were in a vulnerable position and could easily be taken advantage of.[203] A report on the resettlement of evacuees in Uzbekistan drew attention to the "abnormal situation" whereby evacuees in "Tashkent, Samarkand, Bukhara, and several other regions" are

[196] Sophia Abidor, interview by Ella Levitskaya, April 2003, in *Jewish Witness to a European Century*. Russian transcript provided by Centropa.org.
[197] Aleksandr Kovarskii, "Detstvo na ulitse chempiona."
[198] Pomerantz and Winik, *Run East*, 57.
[199] GAGT, f. 10, op. 17, d. 51, l. 6.
[200] Okunevskaia, *Tat'ianin den'*, 98.
[201] TsGARUz, f. R-314, op. 1, d. 57, l. 9.
[202] TsGARUz, f. 837, op. 32, d. 3517, l. 145.
[203] Sophia Abidor, interview.

asked to pay premium prices, bypassing city and district organizations. The report noted that in several cases people were being charged "from 50 to 100 rubles for a corner."[204] Evidence from letters and other sources suggests that such prices were by no means uncommon. One evacuee who reportedly paid 100 rubles for her accommodation described her living conditions as "nightmarish" in a letter to her father: "We occupy a corner of a room of 16 meters in which five people live: the landlady, her mother, her ten-year-old son and the two of us."[205] Olga Boltianskaia described her abode, where she lived with her husband and son, as a "half-dark kitchen room [*kukhon'ka*] of 10 meters square, without a floor, cold and dirty, but we had no other choice."[206]

Given the difficult living conditions and the shortage of space, people attempted to mobilize support from every quarter possible. Sheiva Berman, an evacuee from Odessa, appealed to her workplace in Tashkent, but they merely instructed her to contact her husband's former workplace, the whereabouts of which was anybody's guess. In desperation, she appealed to the People's Commissariat of Defense.[207] Another woman instructed her husband in a letter to "write wherever you need to [*kuda sleduet*] so that we get a room."[208] Those with family on the front urged their husbands and fathers to submit the paperwork required to entitle them to aid as the families of servicemen. Many women, however, did not know their husbands' whereabouts. This was the predicament of Tatiana Okunevskaia: "I am without Boris's military certificate; he is missing. I have no money, no apartment, no food."[209] Help from this quarter, moreover, even for those who procured the necessary paperwork, was not always forthcoming.[210] Sophia Abidor had a certificate from her husband, but it was still difficult to get by.[211] As one woman put it in a letter to her husband on the front, "as I write, I listen to an announcement on the radio about 'care for the families of servicemen.' I listen and tears begin to flow: where this care is and for which families I don't know."[212]

In short, those without connections were, as one woman put it, "completely helpless. Everywhere you need *blat*, and I don't have it; I am not one of those; you know me." Letters from evacuated women to husbands and

[204] GARF, f. A-327, op. 2, d. 52, l. 129.
[205] GAGT, f. 10, op. 17, d. 55, l. 39.
[206] Diary of O. A. Boltianskaia, RGALI, f. 2057, op. 2, d. 29, l. 287, entry of December 30, 1942.
[207] GAGT, f. 10, op. 17, d. 55, l. 202.
[208] Ibid., l. 6.
[209] Okunevskaia, *Tat'ianin den'*, 98.
[210] Municipal and district level divisions to supply the families of servicemen were established in Tashkent only in 1943, in conjunction with a Central Committee decree of January 22, 1943. TsGARUz, f. 837, op. 32, d. 4145, l. 1a.
[211] Sophia Abidor, interview.
[212] GAGT, f. 10, op. 17, d. 55, l. 18.

fathers on the front repeatedly lamented the fact that "there is no one to help." Another woman who sought help from the city district authorities was informed that "there is a very long line of people waiting for a room; people wait for years, so you may well die before you receive living space. Well Petia, I'll tell you straight," she concluded her letter to her husband, "you need to have *blat*, and I don't have it."[213] Although an examination of the files of the city soviet did not turn up any indictments of housing officials on charges of corruption, the Executive Committee of the Tashkent Soviet could not help but acknowledge that there were abuses in the system.[214] Indeed, it was common knowledge that, as one evacuee put it in a letter to her father on the front, "without *blat* in Tashkent you can't do anything."[215] According to the Leningrad composer Yuri Tiulin, Tashkent was rife with "self-provision, misappropriation, bribery, [and] swindling."[216] The general corruption led to a sense of desperation among many evacuees. As one Moscow woman put it in a letter to the front, "there is no sense in searching for justice or law in Uzbekistan."[217]

FINDING FAMILY AND FRIENDS

More important in the struggle to survive than the search "for justice or law" was the search for family and friends. As the cases considered above demonstrate, evacuees' networks of family and friends played a crucial role in securing their residence rights, food, and shelter—in short, the essentials required to survive. Nadezhda Mandelstam, to take but one example, lived in dire straights in southern Kazakhstan until she reestablished contact with her family. She owed her residence permit in Tashkent to the intervention of her brother, her meal card to her sister-in-law, and her supplemental rations to her close friend and onetime housemate Anna Akhmatova.[218] In addition to material support, friends and family offered indirect access to their own set of networks and connections. Mandelstam's brother did not himself have the required sway to secure his sister access to the city, but he had friends who did. For Mandelstam, as for many others, the intimate circle of family and friends was much more than a bedrock of emotional support. It stood at the nexus of the complex networks on which people depended for their

[213] Ibid., ll. 15; 9; 12.
[214] The executive committee of the city soviet criticized lower-level authorities for their failure to combat abuses in the distribution of living space. Ibid., op. 18, d. 38, ll. 134–36.
[215] Ibid., op. 17, d. 55, l. 39.
[216] Iu. N. Tiulin to V. A. Znamenskaia, February 10, 1942, RNB, f. 1088, op. 1, d. 154, l. 4.
[217] GAGT, f. 10, op. 17, d. 55, l. 170.
[218] See N. Ia. Mandel'shtam to B. S. Kuzin, February 23, 1942; June 10–June 12, 1942; and September 8, 1942, in Mandel'shtam, *192 pis'ma*, 667, 677, 687.

survival. As these circles became more important, however, they became more precarious.

The evacuation both separated families and disrupted channels of communication. As Dmitrii Ushakov wrote to a friend and colleague from Tashkent, "this is one of the dark sides of our life—knowing nothing about the people who are dear and close to us."[219] Old addresses were no longer valid. Families were often dispersed in multiple directions: some were on the front, their location ever changing, while others ended up scattered across the vast expanses of the Soviet rear. In October 1941, for example, Kornei Chukovskii and his wife were in Tashkent, their daughter Lydia in Chistopol, their daughter-in-law Marina in the Urals, one of their sons was missing, and the other, Nikolai, was in the Vologda region. Keeping one another apprised of their whereabouts was thus no small task, and many of their letters and telegrams aimed to do just that. "I beg you, inform me of Marina's exact address," Nikolai wrote to his father in early October 1941.[220] Some days later, he wrote again, instructing his father not to leave Moscow "without sending me a telegram, so that I know where you and mother are."[221] Nikolai need not have worried: even in the haste and panic of the mid-October evacuation, Chukovskii found the time to dispatch letters and telegrams to both Nikolai and Lydia informing them of his move.[222]

The Chukovskiis' concerted efforts to remain in touch were typical. As Saul Borovoi later wrote, "the first concern of all evacuees was to find their relatives [*blizkie*], find out something about their fate and let them know something about themselves, inform them of their address, and so on."[223] "Gradually," he recalled, "the 'geography' of my friends and fellow-countrymen-refugees became clearer."[224] The process of clarification could require considerable ingenuity. Nadezhda Mandelstam relied on her old friend Boris Kuzin, whose long-standing exile in Kazakhstan gave him a steady address, to reestablish contact with her family and friends. Her brief first letter to Kuzin after arriving in evacuation in southern Kazakhstan contained the essentials: she informed him of her new address, inquired about the whereabouts of his own family, and asked whether he had heard anything from her brother. As she explained a month later, "we agreed to find one another through you." Having still heard nothing, Mandelstam asked Kuzin to have his family in Moscow call her brother's apartment, and if nobody was there to call one of a

---

[219] Letter to G. O. Vinokur, February 19, 1942, in Nikitin, "Poslednie pis'ma D. N. Ushakova."

[220] Letter of October 6, 1941, in Chukovskii, *O tom, shto videl*, 593.

[221] Letter of October 15, 1941, in ibid., 594.

[222] Letter of October 17, 1941, in ibid.; Telegrams of October 15 and 17, 1941, in Kornei Chukovskii and Lidiia Chukovskaia, *Perepiska: 1912–1969*, ed. E. Ts. Chukovskaia and Zh. O. Khavkina (Moscow: Novoe literaturnoe obozrenie, 2004), 315, 316

[223] Saul Borovoi, *Vospominaniia* (Moscow: Evreiskii universitet v Moskve, 1993), 267.

[224] Borovoi, *Vospominaniia*, 268.

handful of other people who might be apprised of his whereabouts. Although it took some time, Mandelstam's efforts finally put her back in contact with her brother.[225]

For some, the process was relatively rapid. Kornei Chukovskii and his daughter Lydia, for instance, remained in touch throughout their respective displacements. The post, however, was not always reliable, and Chukovskii's contact with his son Nikolai was more precarious.[226] Their correspondence offers a telling picture of the prevailing state of affairs: despite the relatively active epistolary practice of both parties, father and son were unable to establish direct contact for months following the evacuation. "I am going to make yet another attempt, of I don't know how many, to write you," Nikolai began a letter to his father at the end of January 1942. Kornei evidently kept better count: "I am writing you a twelfth letter, but not one of them has reached you," he wrote a few weeks later. It was not until that spring that the two succeeded in establishing regular contact. A letter from father to son penned at the end of April or the beginning of May 1942 began: "Finally I can talk with you, having at least a minimal degree of confidence that the letter will reach you."[227] By the standards of the day, the two were relatively fortunate. Although their letters did not reach their destinations for several months, they never really lost each other either. At all times, they had news of one another through family and friends and an address to which to send their mail. This was more than many. Bella Khamut, who had been evacuated from Odessa to Tashkent in 1941 with her infant son, succeeded in locating her husband, who was serving in the army, only after four long years, and only with the help of some friends.[228]

As these examples suggest, personal networks of family and friends played an important role in maintaining contacts and locating loved ones who were "lost." When such networks failed or were unavailable, evacuees turned to the state. Shortly after the war began, state authorities had established a Central Information Bureau charged with the ambitious task of registering all evacuees and recording their location.[229] In addition to per-

---

[225] N. Ia. Mandel'shtam to B. S. Kuzin, September 30, 1941; December 29, 1941; and January 30, 1942, in Mandel'shtam, *192 pis'ma*, 658, 659–60, 663.

[226] The operation of the Tashkent post office was subject to criticism in the republican newspaper. One article noted that letters dispatched from Tashkent could take months to arrive at their destinations. *Pravda Vostoka*, October 17, 1943.

[227] N. Chukovskii to K. Chukovskii, January 30, 1942; K. Chukovskii to N. Chukovskii, February 21, 1942, in Chukovskii, *O tom, shto videl*, 598, 600, 608.

[228] GAOO, f. R1234, op. 7, d. 289, l. 240.

[229] At the outset, the bureau was run by the Resettlement Administration. The latter did not, however, prove up to the task. As one report on its work put it, the "Resettlement Administration does not have its own district branches which it can entrust with carrying out the registration." GARF, f. A-327, op. 2, d. 36, l. 56. A further discussion of the obstacles that confronted the Resettlement Bureau can be found in GARF, f. 259, op. 40, d. 3014, l. 23. In early January 1942, responsibility was transferred to the Administration for the Evacuation of the Population. See GARF, f. 259, op. 40, d. 3014, l. 31. By the end of the month, however, possibly

forming various economic functions, the bureau was intended to serve the public: to receive and answer queries by citizens searching for family and friends.[230] In theory, each adult evacuee was entered on two lists, the first compiled at the moment of departure, and the second at the moment of arrival.[231] The lists, however, were notoriously incomplete. By December 1941, when officials in Moscow estimated the total number of evacuees in the country at approximately ten million people, only two-thirds had reportedly been counted in the reception sites, and the Central Information Bureau had received the names of less than one-third.[232] In Uzbekistan, the state of affairs was even worse: as the head of the Uzbek statistical division reported to central authorities in Moscow in February 1942, "the compilation of bimonthly accounts has been conducted in an unsatisfactory manner and with great delays. In the lists of evacuees that have been compiled there are errors; there were not enough forms for the compilation of the lists. . . . As a result, as of January 1, 1942, the Evacuation Administration had lists for only one-quarter of the evacuees who had arrived by this date."[233]

The incomplete nature of the data and the dire consequences that could result from it are thrown into sharp relief by the case of Zazovskii, a writer from Leningrad who had been evacuated to Tashkent. Zazovskii's parents, learning of their son's presence in Tashkent, made their way to Central Asia to find him. Their trip, however, ended badly. As Zazovskii later recounted to Vsevolod Ivanov, although his parents had tried to contact him to warn him of their arrival, "their telegrams had not reached him, and at the information bureau they were told that 'no one by that name lives in Tashkent.' His parents lived for six days in the square beside the railway station. His mother died."[234]

---

in connection with the disbanding of the Evacuation Council, responsibility was once again transferred to the Main Administration of the Police under the NKVD, where it remained for the duration of the war. GARF, f. 9415, op. 3, d. 1419, l. 25.

[230] For various statements on the purpose of the registration process, see GARF, f. A-327, op. 2, d. 36, l. 77; and GAGT, f. 10, op. 18, d. 36, l. 1.

[231] As laid out in an instruction issued by the Administration for the Evacuation of the Population, the accounting process involved the compilation of the following information and documents: "(a) a list of the families and individuals dispatched in a particular echelon; (b) a list of the families and individuals who arrived in a particular district, city, or village; and (c) a personal card for each child evacuated without his or her parents." GARF, f. A-327, op. 2, d. 36, l. 67.

[232] GARF, f. 259, op. 40, d. 3014, l. 24. The precise figures are 6,570,000 counted in the reception sites and 3,074,000 whose names had been received by the Central Information Bureau.

[233] RGAE, f. 1562, op. 20, d. 316, l. 10. This, it should be noted, was a marked improvement from December 1941, when officials reported, "of the 603,000 people received, lists of names have been presented only for 43,000." GARF, f. 259, op. 40, d. 3014, l. 24.

[234] Vsevolod Ivanov, *Dnevniki* (Moscow: IMLI RAN, Nasledie, 2001), 165, entry of October 21, 1942.

Although Zazovskii's name should have been on the lists, delays and difficulties were only to be expected given the sheer enormity of the task and the shortages in staff.[235] To make matters worse, the Central Information Bureau had been evacuated to Buguruslan (in the Chkalov region), further disrupting its work. Over the course of 1942, however, matters improved markedly. In February of that year the state ordered a recounting, which required authorities to go to each and every house in the district and "establish whom of the people living there came as an evacuee after June 22, 1941."[236] By the end of the year, a report on the functioning of the bureau could proudly proclaim that "as a result of the re-registration 6,303,718 evacuees have been registered," a number that would increase only minimally over the course of the war.[237] Although this list was still far from complete, it nonetheless accounted for a substantial portion of the evacuee population.[238]

Given its mandate, and notwithstanding its many deficiencies, the bureau very quickly emerged as a key wartime institution. "Buguruslan" became a byword for the bureau's activities and a household term. In fairly typical fashion, an article on children in Uzbekistan noted that many Red Army soldiers had found their children in the republic "through Buguruslan."[239] As the article suggests, Soviet citizens actively availed themselves of the bureau's services. None other than the head of the Administration for the Evacuation of the Population, Pamfilov, convened a meeting with the editors of *Pravda* to ensure that the population was apprised of the appropriate protocol. Readers were to be informed of the bureau's new location in Buguruslan, and of the information that each inquiry should contain (full name and date of birth).[240] By December 1941, the bureau was receiving twenty to thirty thousand inquiries about the location of evacuees every day.[241] These numbers abated only slightly the following year: over the course of 1942, officials estimated that "twelve to fifteen thousand requests arrived per day."[242]

---

[235] According to a report on the work of the bureau over the course of the war, the bureau employed as many as 453 people at the height of its activity in 1942. That number dropped to thirty-two people at the end of 1946. GARF, f. 9415, op. 3, d. 1419, l. 26. In Uzbekistan, the staff in early 1942 consisted of twenty people. GARF, f. 259, op. 40, d. 3014, l. 28.

[236] RGAE, f. 1562, op. 20, d. 316, l. 15. The objective of the exercise, as explained in a directive issued in Uzbekistan, was to facilitate the "correct resettlement of evacuees, their work placement, as well as the distribution of information regarding the whereabouts of evacuees in response to inquiries by their families and relatives." Ibid., l. 13.

[237] GARF, f. 9415, op. 3, d. 1407, l. 3. At the war's end, the bureau's card catalogue contained 4,262,087 cards for 6,459,025 evacuees. This was the official count as of January 1, 1946. Ibid., d. 1419, l. 23.

[238] According to the estimate I have used of 16.5 million, it accounted for slightly less than 40% of the total.

[239] Vladimir Aleksandrov, "V gostiakh u detei," in *Pravda Vostoka*, November 14, 1943.

[240] GARF, f. A-327, op. 2, d. 36, l. 21.

[241] GARF, f. 259, op. 40, d. 3076, l. 10.

[242] GARF, f. 9415, op. 3, d. 1407, l. 3.

Initially, the bureau could not keep up with the volume of requests. In late December 1941, there were almost three hundred thousand unanswered queries. The percentage of inquiries that the bureau had thus far succeeded in providing a positive response to, moreover, was a paltry "5 to 7 percent of the number of people sought."[243] With time, however, these results, too, began to improve. In 1942, the bureau responded to over 3.5 million inquiries made regarding over 11 million people. Of those 11 million, the bureau was able to locate 1.75 million, almost 16 percent.[244] Subsequent years saw progressive improvements in the percentage of positive responses, which rose to a high of almost 29 percent in 1945. All in all, the bureau reportedly "responded to inquiries about the whereabouts of 17,072,868 people" and "established the whereabouts of 3,069,358 people."[245] This was a considerable number, and it is all the more impressive given that many of the inquiries received by the Bureau related to people who never made it into evacuation. The war correspondent Vasily Grossman, for instance, wrote to the bureau to inquire about the whereabouts of his mother, despite his certainty that she had been trapped in occupied territory. As he related in a letter to his father, "Mama is not on the lists of those evacuated. I knew that she hadn't managed to escape, but still my heart shrank when I read those typed lines."[246]

Despite the disappointments, the disorder, and the tremendous delays, the state apparatus could nonetheless boast numerous success stories. As a result of the efforts of thousands of people employed in local, oblast, and republican statistical sections as well as in the bureau in Buguruslan, real strides were made in putting friends and family members back in touch. Personal networks, when they worked, helped sustain evacuees both emotionally and materially. The reconstitution of networks, however, was both gradual and uneven. Those who had lost contact with their friends and family faced particular difficulties in evacuation. For none were these difficulties more pronounced than for arguably the most vulnerable sector of the evacuated population—children.

TASHKENT'S CHILDREN

Children made up a substantial percentage of the evacuated population.[247] In Uzbekistan, the sheer number of child evacuees prompted authorities to

---

[243] GARF, f. 259, op. 40, d. 3014, l. 22.

[244] GARF, f. 9415, op. 3, d. 1407, l. 3.

[245] These were the tallies at the end of 1946. Ibid., d. 1419, l. 25.

[246] Vasily Grossman, *A Writer at War: Vasily Grossman with the Red Army, 1941–1945*, ed. and trans. Antony Beevor and Luba Vinogradova (Toronto: Alfred A. Knopf Canada, 2005), 113.

[247] As of December 1, 1941, approximately 40% of registered evacuees were children up to age fifteen, and over half of these were aged seven or younger. RGAE, f. 1562, op. 20, d. 249, l. 69. Officials estimated that the proportion of children remained steady even as the number of evacuees officially accounted for rose. Ibid., l. 89.

Figure 6. Wards of a children's home evacuated from Kiev, Tashkent 1943 (courtesy Ts-GAKFFD RU).

establish a specially designated children's evacuation center, responsible for the twin tasks of reception and registration.[248] In November and December 1941, when the flood of evacuees reached its peak, an estimated two hundred children per day arrived at the Tashkent station.[249] By the summer of 1943, 33,921 children had been registered at the Tashkent evacuation center.[250] Well over half of these had arrived on their own or in groups with other children.[251] While many of these children—as many as half—were orphans, the other half had parents who would need to be informed of their location.[252]

[248] The evacuation center was established by a joint decree of the Uzbek Sovnarkom and party organization on November 15, 1941. See RGASPI, f. 17, op. 22, d. 2785, l. 229. For a further elaboration of its responsibilities, see TsGARUz, f. 837, op. 32, d. 2894, l. 132.

[249] TsGARUZ, f. R-314, op. 1, d. 56, l. 131.

[250] TsGARUz, f. 94, op. 5, d. 4439, l. 17.

[251] From November 1941 until mid-March 1942, of 22,000 evacuated children who arrived in Uzbekistan, 9,420 had come with children's homes, and the rest had traveled alone. TsGARUz, f. 837, op. 32, d. 3691, l. 23.

[252] These statistics apply to children who arrived on their own between November 25, 1941, and May 1, 1942, in Uzbekistan. Ibid., d. 4119, l. 72.

Enver Arifov, military commandant in Tashkent during the war, later wrote of the mass of unsupervised children: "one had gotten lost en route, another had been separated from her children's home, and a third did not know himself where he came from and how he ended up at the Tashkent station."[253] Tania Aizenberg, the young girl who was separated from her mother when their evacuation train from Kiev was bombed, was in many ways typical. Tania arrived in Tashkent on her own, having given her mother up for dead.[254] Tania, however, was lucky. In Tashkent she was interviewed by Lydia Chukovskaia, who published an account of her story in *Pravda*.[255] Tania's mother, who had survived the bombardment, read the story and subsequently made her way to Tashkent where she was reunited with her daughter.[256] Although theirs was a reunion of chance, it is possible that Tania's mother would have eventually found her daughter even without the article in *Pravda*. For Tania's particulars, including her new Tashkent address, had been carefully recorded for just that purpose.[257]

From the outset, evacuation authorities established a separate procedure for registering children.[258] Directives issued in Tashkent instructed authorities to collect the "surname, first name, patronymic, sex, age, echelon number, arrival time, arrival station, and final address" of the child. In addition, they were to enter "information that the child can give about his or her parents (the surname, first name, and patronymic of both parents, their place of residence and work, their physical appearance, etc.)." In Tania's case, the card simply contained her mother's name: Anna Naumovna Aizenberg. If the child was unable to describe his or her parents, the officials taking down the information were to provide a description of the child's appearance.[259]

Although the Central Information Bureau had a children's division, its deficiencies, coupled with the pressing nature of the task, attracted other parties to the process. Uzbekistan, and specifically Tashkent, led the way in this regard. The Commission to Aid Evacuated Children, established in the Uzbek

---

[253] Enver Arifov, *Zapiski voennogo kommendanta: dokumental'nye ocherki, vospominaniia, povesti* (Moscow: Sovetskii pisatel', 1990), 19. Although the vast majority of the children who arrived on their own were twelve years of age or older, there were younger children as well: over the five-month span from the end of November 1941 until the end of April 1942, an official tally of the number of children who arrived without supervision included 22 children under the age of three, 543 between ages three and seven, and 1,317 between the ages of eight and eleven. TsGARUz, f. 837, op. 32, d. 4119, l. 72.

[254] Lidiia Chukovskaia and Lidiia Zhukova, *Slovo predostavliaetsia detiam* (Tashkent: Sovetskii pisatel', 1942), 25.

[255] See Lidiia Chukovskaia, "Glazami detei," *Pravda*, March 25, 1942.

[256] Chukovskaia and Zhukova, *Slovo predostavliaetsia detiam*, 91.

[257] The card on which information about Tania was recorded can be viewed at http://resources.ushmm.org/uzbekrefugees/getjpg.php/A/3983.jpg.

[258] In addition to the two lists to be compiled for adult evacuees, authorities were instructed to fill out a "personal card for children evacuated without their parents." GARF, f. A-327, op. 2, d. 36, l. 67.

[259] GAGT, f. 10, op. 17, d. 14, l. 40.

capital by volunteers, created an information bureau of its own. As Lydia Chukovskaia later recalled, "the first task of the commission was to establish lists of children and their addresses. Sometimes, three- and four-year-old kids knew only their first names, not their family names. 'Kolya, what is your mother's name?' Silence. 'And your father's?' After a long silence: 'Papa.' 'And where did you live before?' "With my mother, my father, and Grandma."[260]

Kornei Chukovskii observed the workings of the information bureau firsthand. In a short publication put out in 1942 entitled "Uzbekistan and Children," he described the register in which the children's names were recorded. "In appearance, it is just an ordinary office ledger. On its blue pages is a seemingly boring list of names and surnames. But I never saw any other book arouse such strong emotions in people." Chukovskii himself witnessed a number of women find the names of their children in the book.[261] Although parents sometimes sought out their children in person, more common were written requests. Over the course of its first year, the commission received over four thousand letters from parents attempting to locate their children.[262] In the same time period, the commission located over four hundred children, or 10 percent of the total, and returned them to their families.[263] Thank-you letters to the commission were featured in the republican newspaper.[264] By the end of 1944, over one thousand children had been reunited with their families through the work of the Tashkent commission.[265]

Those who were not reunited with their families, the overwhelming majority, became wards of the state. Then Deputy Minister of Education Evgenia Rachinskaia later recalled how Uzbek Party Secretary Iusupov had instructed her that "not one child who arrives in our republic should be left without shelter."[266] Children who arrived at the Tashkent station alone or in groups were, depending on their age, either sent off to work in industry or on a farm, enrolled in a trade school, or put into children's homes.[267] Not surprisingly, the number and size of children's homes in the republic swelled in the wake of the evacuation.[268] Although accommodation was forthcom-

[260] Lidiia Chukovskaia, *Zapiski ob Anne Akhmatovoi*, vol. 2, 26–27.

[261] Kornei Chukovskii, *Uzbekistan i deti* (Tashkent: Gosizdat UzSSR, 1942), 17.

[262] TsGARUz, f. 94, op. 5, d. 4609, l. 14.

[263] Ibid., l. 15.

[264] See, for example, "Bol'shoe materinskoe spasibo," *Pravda Vostoka*, January 29, 1942.

[265] TsGARUz, f. 94, op. 5, d. 4414, l. 11.

[266] Quoted in G. Marianovskii, "Tashkentskii vokzal," in *Deti voennoi pory*, ed. E. Maksimova (Moscow, 1984), 28.

[267] TsGARUz, f. 837, op. 32, d. 4119, l. 42. Children aged fourteen and under were sent to children's homes, and children between the ages of fifteen and eighteen were either enrolled in a trade school or set up with work. Ibid., ll. 43, 46. The state also encouraged locals to take children in through adoption or foster care, both as individuals and as collectives. See ibid., d. 2894, l. 131.

[268] Between October 1941 and February 1942, sixty-four evacuated children's homes arrived in Uzbekistan. Of these, eleven were dissolved and the children distributed among the one hundred previously existing children's homes in the republic. While the number of chil-

ing, children's homes were notorious for their substandard conditions. Officials regularly noted the lack of such basics as heating and beds in the state-run institutions.[269] The reports on children's homes made by the commission's volunteers include one penned by Chukovskaia. After her return from one Tashkent children's home, Chukovskaia reported that the institution was sorely lacking in beds as well as bedding and that the children did not have such elementary items as pants, stockings, and slippers. She insinuated that the clothing the children had arrived in had been stolen from them at the city's receiving children's home run by the NKVD. She also noted the absence of any books—"the library does not exist"—as well as the inadequate heating and eating facilities.[270] Two years later, the situation had evidently not improved. A report penned in May 1943 noted that children were forced to share beds and "some of the children sleep on the floor."[271]

Food was a particularly pressing problem. A report sent to the chairman of the Uzbek government in mid-January 1942 noted that in one Tashkent home the children had not received any meat for four days.[272] Although the chairman was swift to act—a republican decree aiming to "improve the provisioning of children's homes with food" was issued in early February 1942—the decree seems to have had little effect.[273] A report on the implementation of the decree noted that the division responsible for food supply in the city of Tashkent had simply sat on the decree for almost two months. Those responsible apparently found it "unnecessary" to forward the decree to the district divisions, as the new norms, in their opinion, hardly differed from the old ones.[274] The extent of the discrepancies are evident in the provisioning of twenty-five children's homes in three districts of Tashkent in February and March 1942: although the homes received 95 percent of the sugar and candies they were supposed to, they received only 80 percent of the fat, 50 percent of the starch, and a meager 25 percent of the meat that central authorities had stipulated they should.[275] The results were predictable. The

dren's homes thus rose by approximately 50%, the number of caregivers in such homes doubled. TsGARUz, f. 94, op. 5, d. 4254, l. 120.

[269] See, for example, the report by a representative of the Uzbek Evacuation Administration in TsGARUz, f. 314, op. 1, d. 57, l. 179; and the report by Rachinskaia in TsGARUz, f. 837, op. 32, d. 3691, l. 13. Similar observations were made of the accommodations provided to teenagers who had been set up with work. See, for example, TsGARUz, f. 314, op. 1, d. 56, l. 132.

[270] TsGARUz, f. 94, op. 5, d. 4257, l. 87.

[271] TsGARUz, f. 837, op. 32, d. 3691, l. 43.

[272] Ibid., l. 13.

[273] The decree was issued on February 3, 1942, and stipulated an increase in the amount of basic food items to be accorded children in children's homes in the republic. Ibid., d. 4119, l. 7.

[274] Ibid., l. 10.

[275] The children's homes in question were located in the Stalinskii, Oktiabr'skii, and Kuibyshevskii districts. The figures were included in a report on the fulfillment of the government decree penned by the deputy minister of education. Ibid., l. 11.

directors of children's homes were forced to purchase food on the open market, where prices soared, and, in the absence of an increase in funds available for such purchases, the amount of food children received diminished.[276] Like the shortage of beds, the insufficiencies in the food supply persisted. In the summer of 1943, officials reported that in one children's home in Tashkent the children were fed nothing but bread (150 grams at breakfast, 100 grams at lunch, and 150 grams at dinner) and a bowl of soup at midday.[277] While this diet may have been worse than most, the majority of children's homes surveyed in the report were deemed "unsatisfactory" with regards to nourishment.[278]

The combination of poor conditions and meager food supplies could have devastating consequences. Illness was endemic, and death all too common. In the first quarter of 1943, in some seventy children's homes across Uzbekistan, authorities reported 1,258 sick children and 130 deaths.[279] Evacuees were particularly vulnerable, given the state in which they often arrived. The children in an evacuated home from Odessa reportedly arrived in Tashkent "weak and emaciated."[280] By early 1942, of the one hundred who had arrived in the city, fifteen had died.[281]

The case of children is instructive and reveals both the aspirations and the limits of the Soviet state. First, it seems clear that Soviet officials made a genuine attempt to provide for children in need. Many years later, Chukovskaia wrote that the "state, one must admit, supplied the children's homes generously with bread, milk, meat, blankets, clothing, even apples and grapes." In her words, however, the "generosity had its bad side: thieves set themselves up in the children's homes—one as a manager, another as a cook, and another as a director—and neither the teachers, who really cared about the children, nor the Commissariat of Education, nor the commission could cope with the wave of thefts." She cites as an example how construction material had been sent to one children's home "for the repair of the children's bedrooms." However, "all of it, in its entirety, went toward the construction of a new house: in the courtyard the personal house of the director emerged."[282] Another example is provided by Tamara Ivanova, who, like Chukovskaia, was active on the Commission to Aid Evacuated Children. Ivanova later recalled how a couple of volunteers working for the commission participated in a ring to skim off supplies from two of the cafeterias

---

[276] Ibid., l. 14.
[277] Ibid., d. 3691, l. 45.
[278] Ibid.
[279] Ibid., l. 46.
[280] TsGARUz, f. 94, op. 5, d. 4255, l. 139.
[281] Ibid., d. 4254, l. 3.
[282] Chukovskaia, *Zapiski ob Anne Akhmatovoi*, vol. 2, 27.

established for evacuated children.[283] Clearly, the state's capacity to provide for children was compromised not only by generally poor conditions, which only worsened with the war, but also by endemic corruption.

Given the conditions, it is perhaps not surprising that some children opted to flee the children's homes and take their chances on the street. According to one report, "in the second half of 1942 alone, 2,809 children left children's homes in the republic for 'unknown' reasons, including flight."[284] The result was a dramatic rise in the number of "homeless and neglected children," which the authors of the report attributed to the combination of lack of oversight and poor conditions.[285] Not since the days of the civil war had the problem of homelessness among the country's youth reached such dimensions.[286] Children who took to the streets were particularly vulnerable: while they often joined small groups of other youth and were thus not entirely alone, they had access neither to the state-sponsored system of supply nor to the formal and informal networks that helped secure the livelihood of many other evacuees.

DESTITUTION, DISEASE, AND DEATH

Children were not the only ones to end up on the streets of Tashkent. Although there are not even approximate estimates of the homeless, numerous people commented on the phenomenon. Olga Boltianskaia observed that "many sleep on the street as there is nowhere else to go."[287] A good portion of these people were undoubtedly refugees from Poland, non-Soviet citizens who had either fled the German advance or had recently been released from confinement in Siberia as a result of an amnesty declared after the invasion. Even though the Polish government in exile ultimately came to an agreement with the USSR whereby aid was funneled to former Polish citizens, these people had access to few of the paltry benefits available to evacuees. A group of Poles who appealed for aid to regional authorities in Kirov oblast were turned away on the grounds that they were "not evacuees, but *deportees*."[288]

---

[283] Tamara Ivanova, *Moi sovremenniki kakimi ia ikh znala: ocherki* (Moscow: Sovetskii pisatel', 1984), 371.

[284] TsGARUz, f. 837, op. 32, d. 3691, l. 46.

[285] The number of children detained by the police rose accordingly from 19,126 in 1941 to 35,219 in 1942 and 13,548 in the first quarter of 1943 alone. Ibid., l. 44.

[286] To be sure, evacuees were not alone among the growing ranks of homeless children. In Uzbekistan as elsewhere, the war put tremendous strains on families, and many local children also took to the street. See ibid. In addition, some proportion of the children on the streets were not evacuees but recent releases from children's labor colonies. TsGARUz, f. 314, op. 1, d. 56, l. 131.

[287] Diary of O. A. Boltianskaia, RGALI, f. 2057, op. 2, d. 29, l. 99, entry of August 28, 1941.

[288] GARF, f. 259, op. 40, d. 5250, l. 37.

More important, the Poles lacked both juridical status and connections. Those who remained in Tashkent lived the life of illegals and had little choice but to sleep on the streets. David Azrieli, a Polish-Jewish refugee, recalled that "every evening I made an effort to find a clean and comfortable place to sleep."[289] Miryam Bar also searched out a place to sleep each night, a task she suggested was made more difficult by the disappearance of city benches, which the city's residents, she heard, had stolen for firewood.[290]

People who lived on the streets, without rations or a job, were often reduced to begging. Levitin-Krasnov recalled how "in Tashkent, walking down the street, you could see a human mummy, lying impotent on the edge of the sidewalk. Occasionally people would throw a coin into his or her hat."[291] Vsevolod Ivanov evokes similar scenes in his diary. "Every day," he noted, "the ragged beggars stand not far from the cafeteria, by the poplars." His description of a funeral captures the state of utter destitution in which many of these people lived: "some destitute people appeared so covered in dust that it was impossible to tell whether they were men or women. They came up and asked, 'refugees, a kopeck.' It seems that they live here, at the cemetery."[292] Among those who were forced to rely on the generosity of others were Anna Matsueva and her two young daughters. Many years later, the younger one described how her mother "could no longer walk due to hunger and simply sat with her kids on the front steps. People who walked by would give them something. And that's how they lived." In desperate straights, Matsueva was persuaded to give the elder of her daughters into the care of another woman, a well-dressed stranger who approached her on the street.[293] In other cases, women were compelled to put their children into children's homes, unable to provide for them on their own.[294]

The large number of homeless and transient people coupled with a dramatic decline in sanitary standards created optimal conditions for the spread of disease.[295] Sanitation inspectors who were dispatched to remedy the situation were of little help, for, in the words of one report, they displayed a "particularly formal" attitude towards their work.[296] To make matters worse, supplies of soap were woefully inadequate, undermining the personal hygiene

[289] David J. Azrieli, Danna J Azrieli, and Leah Aharonov, *One Step Ahead: David J. Azrieli, Memoirs, 1939–1950* (Jerusalem: Yad Vashem, 2001), 84.

[290] Bar, *Lelot Tashkent*, 75.

[291] A. E. Levitin-Krasnov, *"Ruk tvoikh zhar": 1941–1956* (Tel Aviv: Krug, 1979), 139.

[292] Ivanov, *Dnevniki*, 102, entry of June 4, 1942.

[293] Einara Tomm, "Sestry," *Desnitsa*, December 18, 2002, no. 51 (194) (www.province.ru/publishing/index-izdanie.html).

[294] See the examples in Laurie Bernstein, "Communist Custodial Contests: Adoption Rulings in the USSR after the Second World War," *Journal of Social History* 34, no. 4 (2001): 845, 847.

[295] On the Uzbek health-care system during the war, see Stronski, "Forging a Soviet City," 172–81.

[296] TsGARUz, f. 837, op. 32, d. 3706, l. 23.

of even the most fastidious evacuees.[297] Tashkent thus became a breeding ground for infectious diseases.[298] Already in December 1941, city officials noted a rise in cases of typhus "and other infectious diseases," raising the specter of an epidemic.[299] In the first ten days of that month, there had been twenty-six registered cases of typhus in the republic.[300] By the next fall, in Nadezhda Mandelstam's estimation, there were "sick people all around."[301] Indeed, there were few evacuees who did not fall ill with something in Tashkent. Akhmatova contracted typhoid fever, along with two other women in the writer's residence in which she lived, as did Lydia Chukovskaia and the Ivanovs' two sons.[302] Olga Boltianskaia's husband fell ill with tuberculosis, and the writer Pavel German suffered from pneumonia.[303] Iakov Notkin was "continuously sick. . . . I have a stomach ulcer, angina pectoris, spasms in the vessels of the gonadal nerve tissue, and a number of other illnesses."[304]

Given the prevailing conditions, it is hardly surprising to find that the cemetery appears repeatedly in evacuee descriptions of the city. In a sense, Tashkent really was, as Tatiana Lugovskaia described it, a "city made for death," a place "where coffins are among the goods in greatest shortage."[305] The number of deaths was so great among the evacuated population that the city's existing European and Jewish cemeteries proved insufficient. As early as January 1942, the European cemetery had to be expanded.[306] And in late 1943, the city moved to establish a new Jewish cemetery, noting, "at present the burial of Jews who have died in the city of Tashkent has become extremely difficult."[307] Lugovskaia and Mandelstam buried their mothers in Tashkent, Boltianskaia her father, Raisa Yasvoina her younger brother, and

---

[297] A report from the summer of 1942 noted that the plan for soap production had fallen short by almost two-thirds. RGASPI, f. 17, op. 43, d. 2242, l. 36.

[298] Tashkent was by no means unique in this regard. In neighboring Kazakhstan, incidences of typhus rose ninefold from 1941 to 1942. Paula Michaels, in her study of public health in Kazakhstan, further attributes the increase in infectious diseases to the medical needs of frontline and wounded soldiers, which put a serious drain on the resources and personnel available for civilian medical services. See Paula A. Michaels, *Curative Powers: Medicine and Empire in Stalin's Central Asia* (Pittsburgh: University of Pittsburgh Press, 2003), 121–22.

[299] RGASPI, f. 17, op. 22, d. 2911, l. 144.

[300] GARF, f. 6822, op. 1, d. 481, l. 30.

[301] N. Ia. Mandel'shtam to B. S. Kuzin, November 8, 1942, in Mandel'shtam, *192 pis'ma*, 687.

[302] Ibid.; Chukovskaia, *Zapiski ob Anne Akhmatovoi*, vol. 2, 23; Ivanova, *Moi sovremenniki*, 145, 148.

[303] Diary of O. A. Boltianskaia, RGALI, f. 2057, op. 2, d. 30, l. 25, entry of March 28, 1943; RGALI, f. 631, op. 15, d. 643, l. 6. According to mortality statistics for the city of Tashkent in 1943, 2,412 people died of various forms of pneumonia, 171 of typhoid fever, 447 of typhus, 726 of dysentery, and 1,699 of tuberculosis. RGAE, f. 1562, op. 20, d. 421, l. 61.

[304] GARF, f. 8114, op. 1, d. 917, l. 34.

[305] Letter to L. Maliugin, February 14, 1942, in Lugovskaia, *Kak znaiu*, 256.

[306] TsGARUz, f. 837, op. 32, d. 3716, l. 67.

[307] GAGT, f. 10, op. 18, d. 376, l. 60.

one Kurdiukova, from Leningrad, both her children.[308] Death was a common occurrence. Valentin Berestov saw an older man die right in front of him: in his diary he recorded that the man "fainted from hunger. . . . He wanted to kiss me. Then he died."[309] Stepanishcheva, reflecting on the camps that used to form by her home near the railway station, recalled that "sometimes, when the camp finally departed, there remained one or two corpses."[310] The general impression is corroborated by municipal statistics. Although mortality rates rose substantially across the country, and especially in urban centers, the rise was particularly dramatic in Tashkent.[311]

• • •

Tashkent was home to tens of thousands of displaced people during the war and ranked among the most significant reception sites for evacuees in the country. It was not for nothing that the poet Iulia Drunina christened the city a "good star." Referring to the "women and children" who flocked to Tashkent during the war, she wrote: "Yes, it really was a good star! And the most generous city on earth."[312] As the many people who were refused entry attests, however, the gates of the city were not open to all. Nor was life in Tashkent easy. Aleksander Wat, reflecting on conditions in the fabled "city of bread," could not but be ironic: "I, too, was in Tashkent: hunger, typhus from hunger."[313] The deprivation and difficulties that characterized daily life in Tashkent were in no small measure a function of the war. Loss of territory and resources coupled with the necessity of shifting economic produc-

---

[308] Lugovskaia later recalled, "I found a wonderful place in this Asiatic cemetery—altogether Russian—spacious and quiet, and a poplar grows at her feet." Letter to L. Maliugin, 1942, in Lugovskaia, *Kak znaiu*, 260. Raisa Yasvoina's brother died of hunger in 1942. Raisa Yasvoina, interview in *Jewish Witness to a European Century*. Russian transcript provided by Centropa.org). Kurdiukova, the wife of a captain who died at the front, lost both children within a few weeks in the winter of 1943–44. TsGARUz, f. 837, op. 32, d. 4145, l. 1.

[309] Berestov, *Izbrannye proizvedeniia*, vol. 2, 221.

[310] Stepanishcheva, "Vot tak i zhizn' proshla," l. 21.

[311] From 1941 to 1942 in the country as a whole, mortality rates rose by 21.7% and by 50% in cities. GARF, f. 9415, op. 3, d. 1406, l. 2. According to Paul Stronski, the death rate in Tashkent in this period rose by 25%. "Forging a Soviet City," 172. Data I have seen suggest that the rise may well have been even higher. Between 1941 and 1942, the number of deaths in the Uzbek capital almost doubled, rising from 15,614 in 1941 to 30,923 in 1942. GARF, f. 9415, op. 3, d. 1406, l. 2. Exactly how dramatic the rise was is difficult to assess given that the population of Tashkent was rising at the same time. As of July 1, 1942, the population of the city was assessed at 700,530 people. RGAE, f. 1562, op. 20, d. 327, l. 101. According to the census of 1939, the prewar population of the city (adjusted to account for an administrative change effected in the borders of the city in the spring of 1941) was 584,955. RGAE, f. 1562, op. 20, d. 244, l. 29. Thus, even taking the rise in population into account, the mortality rates in Tashkent rose by approximately 65% from 1941 to 1942. Although I do not have access to the mortality rates for 1940, one can assume that mortality rates in 1941 were already higher than in 1940.

[312] The poem is quoted in full in Arifov, *Zapiski voennogo kommendanta*, 36.

[313] Wat, *My Century*, 310, my translation.

tion from a civilian to a military footing put a significant strain on the Soviet state and its capacity to provide for the population. At the same time, the war set the limits of the Soviet system into stark relief. Access to scarce state-supplied resources was dependent on status, institutional networks, and connections. Militsa Nechkina later recalled a "conversation between people in the film industry on the train" to Tashkent. "One of them, a prominent cinematographer, almost in tears, said to the other: 'I don't want to be a refugee.' 'You are not a 'refugee,' his friend reassured him. 'You are an honored evacuee' [*pochetnyi evak*]."[314] The friend was quite right. "Honored evacuees" and refugees lived in very different circumstances. That said, not even "honored" evacuees were above the struggle to survive. Ironically, even those who were rescued by the state were sometimes left to languish in the rear. Akhmatova had been flown out of the city of Leningrad, but she nonetheless had to rely on friends to secure access to both shelter and sustenance. As Boris Romanov, likewise flown out of Leningrad, remarked of his evacuation in a letter to a friend: "instead of the salvation of the golden *fond*—illness and poverty."[315] "Illness and poverty" could not but breed frustration with the Soviet state. That said, the country was at war. For the most part, moreover, evacuees regarded the war not simply as "a war," but as "our war."

---

[314] M. V. Nechkina, "V dni voiny," in *V gody voiny: stat'i i ocherki*, ed. Aleksandr Mikhailovich Samsonov (Moscow: Nauka, 1985), 34.

[315] Paneiakh, *Tvorchestvo i sud'ba istorika*, 191.

7

"OUR WAR" IN TASHKENT

Olga Boltianskaia, describing the difficult living conditions in Tashkent in her diary, reflected: "but none of this is as terrible as the fact that thanks to a handful of maniacs the world has been plunged into blood and misery."[1] While the difficulties of daily life weighed heavily on evacuees, they did not lose sight of the larger tragedy of which they were a part. Evacuees were anything but indifferent to the war. Indeed, the war years witnessed a surge in popular patriotism, even among those who had reason to be suspicious of the state. Emblematic in this regard are the comments made to the journalist Hedrick Smith by Ben Levich, a Jewish scientist who had spent the war in evacuation in Kazan. When asked about the "best time of our lives," Levich replied: "the war." Asked to explain, he said, "at that time we all felt closer to our government than at any other time in our lives. It was not their country then, but our country. . . . It was not their war, but our war. It was our country we were defending, our war effort."[2]

Like Levich, many evacuees in Tashkent saw the war as their own. Though far from the field of battle, evacuees lived and breathed the war. Moreover, everyone knew someone on the front lines. As Zinaida Stepanishcheva later wrote of herself and her friend Lusia, also an evacuee: "although our children and our mothers were with us in Tashkent, out of danger, consciousness of the fragility of our husbands' lives, and, consequently, of our own well-being and that of our children, did not leave us for a minute in Tashkent."[3]

[1] Diary of O. A. Boltianskaia, RGALI, f. 2057, op. 2, d. 29, l. 123, entry of November 8, 1941.

[2] The passage is cited in Bernd Bonwetsch, "War as a 'Breathing Space': Soviet Intellectuals and the 'Great Patriotic War,' " in *The People's War: Responses to World War II in the Soviet Union*, ed. Robert W. Thurston and Bernd Bonwetsch (Chicago: University of Illinois Press, 2000), 137.

[3] Z. G. Stepanishcheva, "Vot tak i zhizn' proshla," TsDNA, f. 422, l. 16.

Evacuees perceived the war not only as a tragedy but as an imperative. As Levich remarked, "it was our war effort." Few did not feel some compulsion to participate. In faraway Tashkent, people found their own avenues for contributing to the war. In the process, relations between citizen and state were recalibrated. The war brought some, to borrow Levich's phrase, "closer to the government." It also imbued many Soviet citizens with a stronger sense of community. Smith wrote of his discussions with Soviet citizens in the 1970s that "people often spoke of the war not only as a time of suffering and sacrifice but also a time of belonging and solidarity."[4] It was in this sense, too, that Levich spoke of "our war," casting the struggle as a collective, shared endeavor.

Although the sentiment of solidarity looms large in descriptions of the war, the boundaries of the collective were far from fixed. In Tashkent— where Russians, Ukrainians, and Jews shared the city's streets and stages with the local Uzbek population—the collective was frequently presented in a multinational guise. Tashkent was repeatedly celebrated as an exemplar of the wartime "friendship of peoples." In reality, however, the "our" of "our war" was unstable and ambiguous. It could refer to all Soviet citizens or only to Russians. Its very embrace created boundaries of exclusion. Thus, just as the war forged new feelings of social solidarity, so too did it create new divisions.

ECHOES OF WAR

Tashkent was far from the front lines. In Esther Markish's words, "the rumble of war was scarcely audible in faraway Tashkent."[5] For some evacuees, the city seemed to exist in a time and space that was altogether distinct from the war-ravaged country they had left behind. The most striking sign of their distance from the front lines came at night, in the city lights. Maria Belkina later wrote that "Tashkent during this period lived a spectral life, illuminated at night, not fearful of bright lights (and we had grown unaccustomed to them!). In the evening, on the central streets, there was strolling, the shuffling of feet on asphalt, the babbling of water in the canals, and from some semiprivate restaurants and cafes—music. Small orchestras— violin, cello, piano—and someone, poorly managing with the Russian words, sings."[6] Igor Bakhterev recalled how shocked he and other evacuees were by the "illuminated street lamps and the unblackened windows."[7] Although the most visible, the lights were not the only marker of the gulf that

---

[4] Hedrick Smith, *The Russians* (New York: Ballantine, 1976), 404.

[5] Esther Markish, *The Long Return* (New York: Ballantine, 1978), 126.

[6] Maria Belkina, *Skreshchenie sudeb*, 2d ed. (Moscow: Blagovest Rudomino, 1992), 346.

[7] Igor' Bakhterev, "Tot mesiats v Tashkente," in *Ob Anne Akhmatovoi: stikhi, esse, vospominaniia, pis'ma*, ed. M. M. Kralin (Leningrad: Lenizdat, 1990), 216.

separated Tashkent from the front lines. Kornei Chukovskii was struck by the children who "hurry to school—a sight I did not see in Moscow this year. It seems strange, that in the USSR there are still places where children learn."[8]

These signs of normalcy, however, only thinly masked the ever present war. Even amid the sights and sounds of Central Asia, evacuees could not escape the war. Those who had come to the city as evacuees were often haunted by the war-torn landscapes they had left behind. This was particularly true of children. Lydia Chukovskaia, who interviewed dozens of children in Tashkent for a collection of children's stories about the war, observed that "children who have been evacuated from frontline regions are deeply shaken by what they have endured."[9] As the director of a quarantine center for evacuated children later remarked of those under her care, the "terrible phantoms of fires, murders, and bombardments haunted them for a long time."[10] Random sounds could make evacuee children flinch: a report by a local doctoral candidate in pedagogy noted that the "loud voices of passersby, the siren of a car driving past, the noise of a propeller . . . all awakened troubling memories in the children."[11] In a similar vein, Lydia Chukovskaia later recalled how, on a number of occasions, "I saw teenagers, walking in groups down the street, suddenly dash off in all directions, throwing themselves into the irrigation ditches or lying prostrate on the viscous, clay-like earth, on hearing the approaching roar of an airplane in the distance. The fear of this roar was irresistible, although there never were any enemy planes over Tashkent."[12] Alexander Kovarskii, whose journey into evacuation had exposed him to numerous bombardments, experienced this terror firsthand. He later recalled how for the entire duration of the war and for several years thereafter he had only to hear a motor in the distance to be seized with fear.[13]

Many children were plagued by nightmares. As the doctoral candidate mentioned above reported of the children she encountered, "they slept poorly at night, often crying out in their sleep. . . . They dreamed of bombardments, fires, enemy airplanes."[14] This was certainly true of Faina Barisheva, a young girl from Leningrad who for some time after her arrival in

[8] Kornei Chukovskii, *Dnevnik, 1930–69* (Moscow: Sovremennyi pisatel', 1995), 160, entry of October 24, 1941.

[9] Lidiia Chukovskaia and Lidiia Zhukova, *Slovo predostavliaetsia detiam* (Tashkent: Sovetskii pisatel', 1942), 89.

[10] Quoted in G. Marianovskii, "Tashkentskii vokzal," in *Deti voennoi pory,* ed. E. Maksimova (Moscow, 1984), 31.

[11] The report was on "evacuated children in the children's homes of Tashkent." TsGARUz, f. 94, op. 5, d. 4232, l. 6.

[12] Lidiia Chukovskaia, *Zapiski ob Anne Akhmatovoi,* 5th ed., 2 vols. (Moscow: Soglasie, 1997), vol. 2, 28.

[13] Aleksandr Kovarskii, "Detstvo na ulitse chempiona," *Zhurnal Mishpokha,* no. 14 (2004) (www.mishpoha.org/nomer14/a18.htm).

[14] TsGARUz, f. 94, op. 5, d. 4232, l. 6.

Tashkent was "disturbed by nightmares: she tossed about, screamed, cried for help, and wept." Faina arrived in Tashkent emaciated and sick. Even after she had gained weight and was assured of a continuous supply of good food, she could not leave the dinner table without taking some bit of food that she would subsequently stash under her pillow. When asked about the practice by her new parents, she replied: "And if the fascists come to our house, what will we eat then?"[15] Some children refused to leave their rooms in the children's homes in which they had been placed, afraid of being shot.[16]

While some heard the ringing of bombardments in their dreams, others could think of nothing else. The war preoccupied evacuees, young and old alike.[17] Olga Boltianskaia's diaries tack back and forth between her personal travails (problems with food, her sister-in-law) and developments on the front. An entry in late August began, the "withdrawal from Novgorod and German movement toward Leningrad and Dnepopetrovsk fill my soul with a smarting pain. When will there be a turning point, and will our troops begin to expel them from our land?"[18] Like other evacuees, Boltianskaia made every effort to stay abreast of what was happening on the front lines. As Yuri Tiulin wrote to a friend who was also in evacuation, "like you, we live on news from the front and the singular hope of returning . . . to Petrograd."[19]

The war was a topic of private reflection and public discussion. In their new abodes, among friends and at work, evacuees talked about the war. News from the war, moreover, reverberated through the streets of Tashkent. Igor Bakhterev recalls how for news, many turned to the radio. "The central newspapers took a long time to arrive, the local *Pravda Vostoka* was unsatisfying, and there remained only the radio."[20] Like many others, Bakhterev did not have his own radio but listened to the news at a loudspeaker, in the hall of the Pushkin Hotel. The historian Ekaterina Kusheva likewise recalled, "every morning we gathered at the loudspeaker and listened to the latest news."[21] Nadezhda Mandelstam wrote of herself and Akhmatova in 1943: "we live from one radio announcement to the next. We are at the loudspeakers in the evening, the morning, and the afternoon."[22] The crowds

[15] Enver Arifov, *Zapiski voennogo kommendanta: dokumental'nye ocherki, vospominaniia, povesti* (Moscow: Sovetskii pisatel', 1990), 16.

[16] TsGARUz, f. 94, op. 5, d. 4232, l. 5.

[17] On reactions to the war on the part of the local population, see Paul Stronski, "Forging a Soviet City: Tashkent, 1937–1966" (Ph.D. diss., Stanford University, 2003), 102–6.

[18] Diary of O. A. Boltianskaia, RGALI, f. 2057, op. 2, d. 29, l. 99, entry of August 28, 1941.

[19] Iu. Tiulin to V. A. Znamenskaia, February 10, 1942, RNB, f. 1088, op. 1, d. 154, l. 4.

[20] Bakhterev, "Tot mesiats v Tashkente," 219.

[21] E. N. Kusheva, "Vospominaniia E. N. Kushevoi," *Otechestvennaia istoriia*, no. 4 (1993): 143.

[22] N. Ia. Mandel'shtam to B. S. Kuzin, February 12, 1943, in Nadezhda Mandel'shtam, *192 pis'ma k B. Kuzinu*, ed. N. I. Kraineva and E. A. Perezhogina (St. Petersburg: Inapress, 1999), 699.

that spontaneously formed around the city's loudspeakers were even the subject of one of Vladimir Lugovskoi's wartime poems.[23]

The tenor of news from the front lines had a palpable effect on the city. News of the German capture of Sevastopol in the spring of 1942, for instance, was met by evacuees in Tashkent with deep anxiety. Vsevolod Ivanov wrote in his diary that "the city is in despair over the fall of Sevastopol. . . . Everyone believed that there would be no more retreats."[24] The rapid collapse on the Southern front in 1942 convinced some that Tashkent itself might be subject to attack. According to Ivanov, "everyone is talking about the possibility of flights over Tashkent. An agitator said that 'Tashkent is a frontline city.' In houses you get the sense that those who are accustomed to evacuation are already packing their bags."[25] Ivanov was even told that "they are evacuating factories from Tashkent."[26] More plausible, though no more true, was the belief, allegedly expressed by Kornei Chukovskii, that Tashkent would be cut off from the "center."[27]

Continued defeats and difficult conditions in the rear bred despair and disbelief. As one woman wrote to her husband on the front, invoking the famous first line of Konstantin Simonov's celebrated war poem, "in the newspapers, at the theater, in the cinema, we are told over and over again: 'Wait! Wait for me!' Wait for what? For what? For the end of the war? It's more likely that we'll die before it ends." The unbridled optimism of her husband's letters clearly struck her as naive. Indeed, she went so far as to claim that "I detest the idiotic statements in your letters about the forthcoming victory over Hitler."[28] Another woman in Tashkent was similarly skeptical: "Fedia, you either don't have information about the progress of the war," she wrote, "or you want to lie to us like they lie to us in the rear."[29]

The Soviet victory at Stalingrad marked a turning point in this regard. In the late summer of 1942, Soviet citizens had looked on in horror as the German army laid waste to the city, seizing one district after another and drawing ever closer to the Volga. Soviet forces, however, held on; and in November 1942, the Red Army mounted a successful counteroffensive, encircling the attacking German army. After another two months of fighting, deprived of much-needed supplies and reinforcements, the remains of the embattled German army surrendered. The effect on morale in Tashkent, as in other

[23] The poem, titled "Victory's Salute," was published in *Pravda Vostoka*, November 14, 1943.
[24] Vsevolod Ivanov, *Dnevniki* (Moscow: IMLI RAN, Nasledie, 2001), 103, entry of July 4, 1942.
[25] Ibid., 142, entry of September 25, 1942. As Ivanov's comments intimate, propaganda and agitation about the potential dangers of an air attack on Tashkent became common in 1942. See Stronski, "Forging a Soviet City," 110.
[26] Ivanov, *Dnevniki*, 141, entry of September 24, 1942.
[27] Ibid., 103, entry of July 4, 1942.
[28] GAGT, f. 10, op. 17, d. 55, l. 105.
[29] Ibid., l. 25.

Soviet cities, was dramatic. "Everyone became imbued with a greater certainty of our victory," Valentina Khodasevich recalled.[30] According to Alexander Kovarskii, "people's faces brightened; on the streets one heard laughter more frequently."[31] "The successes of the Red Army cheer everyone up!" Olga Boltianskaia observed in the midst of the German surrender. "Nobody doubts that victory will be ours," she noted a few months later, "but when?"[32]

Evacuees followed the changing fortunes of the war, and every advance of Soviet troops brought them that much closer to home. Stepanishcheva described how her stepfather had a map on which he placed flags indicating the progress of the war.[33] Far from home, such maps adorned the walls of the living quarters of numerous evacuees in Tashkent, including Faina Ranevskaia and Kornei Chukovskii.[34] Documentary newsreels on the war became a venue for those displaced from their homes to gather and recall the places they had left behind. Stepanishcheva described in her memoirs how the documentary film *The Defeat of German Forces Outside Moscow* was shown in Tashkent. "I can't say what kind of film it was—good or bad. We apprehended it not as a film but as a tragic part of our lives. In the hall there were mainly Muscovites and for that reason the film was taken in very emotionally."[35]

News from the front lines was precisely that—emotional. The keen interest with which evacuees followed developments on the front reflected their identification with the war. This was very much "our war." At stake in the conflict were "our land," "our troops," and ultimately "our victory." Not surprisingly, the war elicited a response that was both patriotic and deeply personal. As Olga Boltianskaia put it, "it is terribly difficult for me on account of both the country and myself."[36] This was particularly true for evacuees: the war threatened both their motherland and their home towns. More personally still, it threatened their families.

SEPARATION AND LOSS

Evacuees had escaped the fire of the front lines, but they invariably had husbands, brothers, and fathers, sometimes even sisters and wives, who had stayed behind. As Olga Boltianskaia noted in her first diary entry on arrival

[30] Valentina Khodasevich, *Portrety slovami: ocherki*, 2d ed. (Moscow: Galart, 1995), 323.

[31] Aleksandr Kovarskii, "Detstvo na ulitse chempiona."

[32] Diary of O. A. Boltianskaia, RGALI, f. 2057, op. 2, d. 30, ll. 5, 53, entries of January 20 and June 22, 1943.

[33] Z. G. Stepanishcheva, "Vot tak i zhizn' proshla," l. 28.

[34] See Aleksei Shcheglov, *Faina Ranevskaia: vsia zhizn'* (Moscow: Zakharov, 2001), 85; Chukovskii, *Dnevnik*, 162, entry of April 1, 1942.

[35] Stepanishcheva, "Vot tak i zhizn' proshla," l. 22.

[36] Diary of O. A. Boltianskaia, RGALI, f. 2057, op. 2, d. 29, l. 95, entry of August 15, 1941.

in Central Asia, the "family has fallen to pieces."[37] Couples had been separated, families rent apart. Those who were fortunate enough to be evacuated with their spouses, usually middle-aged or elderly evacuees such as Olga Boltianskaia or Kornei Chukovskii, frequently had children on the front (in Boltianskaia's case one son, in Chukovskii's two). Younger evacuees, who were overwhelmingly female, often remained with their children and even their parents but were almost invariably separated from their husbands.[38] This was the predicament of Maria Belkina, Sophia Abidor, Zinaida Stepanishcheva, and countless others. In his first letter to his wife in Tashkent, Stepanishcheva's husband wrote, "let's hope that our reunion will not be years away."[39] With time, however, such hopes began to fade. As Maria Belkina's husband wrote her in the spring of 1942, "the meeting which we have so dreamed about is still far away. . . . Tashkent is far, over 4,000 kilometers. . . . If you traveled them by foot, you would need 150 days. I would do it, perhaps, if it were possible. But for the time being neither you nor I have the right to hope for a forthcoming meeting."[40] Belkina, who returned from Tashkent earlier than most, would see her husband sooner than he thought. Others, like Stepanishcheva, would wait for years.

Occasionally, those at the front managed to secure sufficient leave to make the journey east. "A big event in our lives," Alexander Kovarskii recalled, "was the arrival of my father in the fall of 1943." He had been wounded and, as a result, had been granted a one-week leave. Kovarskii had been a young child when his father had first left for the army (he had been serving since 1940) and did not recognize the man whom his mother now presented as his father. Kovarskii "knew the father from his mother's stories, but this one, the real one, . . . in one week I could not get used to."[41] (A family picture of husband, wife, and son survives from this time: the portrait was done in a studio in Tashkent; the father is the only person smiling; they are all dressed in what were clearly their best clothes.) Sophia Abidor also received a visit from her husband in Tashkent. As she later recalled, "I was walking with my son, and who was walking toward me but my husband!"[42] Like Kovarskii's father,

---

[37] Ibid.

[38] In some cases, this general pattern was reversed and men were evacuated to the rear without their wives. Many workers, for instance, were evacuated without their families. In other cases, women were mobilized for work in the war effort and were unable to accompany their husbands into evacuation. Boris Romanov, for example, came to Tashkent on his own, because his wife, a doctor, was serving on the front. See V. M. Paneiakh, *Tvorchestvo i sud'ba istorika: Boris Aleksandrovich Romanov* (St. Petersburg: Institut rossiiskoi istorii S.-Peterburgskii filial, Rossiiskaia akademiia nauk, 2000), 190.

[39] Letter to Z. G. Stepanishcheva from her husband, August 1941, TsDNA, f. 422, l. 5.

[40] Quoted in N. A. Gromova, *Vse v chuzhoe gliadiat okno* (Moscow: Sovershenno sekretno, 2002), 145.

[41] Aleksandr Kovarskii, "Detstvo na ulitse chempiona."

[42] Sophia Abidor, interview by Ella Levitskaya, April 2003, in *Jewish Witness to a European Century*. Russian transcript provided by Centropa.org.

Abidor's husband had been wounded and had only thus been granted leave to see his family. Tatiana Okunevskaia's husband was more fortunate: he managed to secure leave without incurring wounds. Okunevskaia later wrote of her husband's arrival in Tashkent that "we both cried," and later, "when we had come to our senses . . . we laughed from happiness."[43]

Although Tashkent was the site of numerous reunions, most evacuees had to rely on the post. The post acquired a special significance during the war. Alexander Kovarskii, whose three uncles and father were all at the front, later recalled "how much joy there was in our room, when the postman delivered postcards or three-cornered letters from them! . . . Small bits of news from the front were read aloud many times; they were wept over with tears of joy. But official notifications also came—of burials. And then behind the tall fences on our street people didn't cry, they sobbed."[44] Kovarskii's own family received their first such notification only months after their arrival in Tashkent. His aunt's husband had been killed near Leningrad. His aunt was pregnant at the time, and for a month after the baby was born, the whole family "cried bitterly." Stepanishcheva's friend Lusia likewise learned of the death of her husband through the post. Stepanishcheva writes: "I was coming home from work, and I saw Lusia and Raisa Andreevna sitting on stools on the terrace and crying. 'What happened?' I asked, fearing to hear the answer. Lusia silently handed me a piece of paper. It was a notification of death for her husband."[45] Such notifications were all too common in Tashkent. As Valentin Berestov later wrote, "in the residence in which I lived with my mother and brother, death could appear with the postman."[46]

Many received no news at all. Berestov and his family "didn't know anything about my father's fate. The last letter we had received from him was in October 1941 after the battle for Kaluga."[47] Similarly, Kornei Chukovskii last heard from his son Boris while still in Moscow, before being evacuated. With every passing day, the hope that he was still alive grew dimmer. He conveyed his concern to his elder son, Nikolai, by telegraph: "We have had no word from Boba for three months."[48] He was more direct with his fellow writer and friend Marshak. Explaining how his personal library had been destroyed (as had his car), he wrote: "it doesn't concern me only because I am sure Boba has died."[49] (In his next letter, penned a few months later, he

[43] Tat'iana Okunevskaia, *Tat'ianin den'* (Moscow: Vagrius, 1998), 106.

[44] Aleksandr Kovarskii, "Detstvo na ulitse chempiona."

[45] Stepanishcheva, "Vot tak i zhizn' proshla," l. 22.

[46] Valentin Berestov, *Izbrannye proizvedeniia*, 2 vols. (Moscow: Izdatel'stvo imeni Sabashnikovykh, 1998), vol. 2, 262.

[47] Ibid.

[48] Telegram of December 7, 1941, in Nikolai Chukovskii, *O tom, shto videl*, ed. E. N. Nikitina (Moscow: Molodaia gvardiia, 2005), 594.

[49] Letter of December 1941, in Kornei Chukovskii, "'Mezhdu nami dolgo byla kakaia-to stena . . .' Pis'ma K. Chukovskogo k S. Marshaku," ed. M. Petrovskii, *Almanakh "Egupets"* 12 (2002): 300.

assumes an altogether different position: "I have a stubborn certainty that my Boba has not died. I have not had any news from him since October 5, but all the same I don't lose hope.")[50] Raisa Yasvoina's father and her uncle were both on the front lines, and not a single letter arrived from either. Although she and her mother must have suspected that they had been killed, it was only when the women returned to Kiev at the end of the war that they could confirm the deaths.[51] Malka Zaltsberg, evacuated from Odessa to Tashkent, retained contact with her husband, who had departed for the front only two days after the German invasion, but their short-lived correspondence came to an end precisely one year later, on June 26, 1942. As an acquaintance later put it, "it was already understood that he did not manage to escape Sevastopol, where he had been stationed with the Primskaia Army, although a weak hope remained until the end of the war and after."[52] Zaltsberg's son, Leonid Averbukh, still has the thirty-four letters (a collection of "postcards, three-cornered letters, and self-made envelopes") that he and his mother received from his father in their year of separation.[53]

People shared their sorrow with family, friends, and even strangers. Stepanishcheva recalls: "once I was standing in line for something. An elderly woman, crying, talked about her grief. Before the war she had a husband, four sons, and a daughter. All six went to the front. Five of them—her husband and her four sons—were killed. She received death notifications for one after the other. And yesterday her daughter was brought to her without either of her legs. Hearing this, the whole line shuddered, and almost every other person could recount a similar story concerning his or her family."[54] This is undoubtedly no exaggeration. By the end of the war, everyone had suffered losses of some kind.

Nor were the losses exclusively on the front lines. Evacuees from Leningrad, of whom there were many in Tashkent, lost countless family members and friends to hunger in the city under siege. Historians estimate that as many as 750,000 civilians died in Leningrad in three years.[55] The Leningrad historian Boris Romanov received news of his losses only shortly after arriving in Tashkent: both his brother and sister perished in the first blockade winter.[56]

[50] Ibid., 301.

[51] Raisa Yasvoina, interview in *Jewish Witness to a European Century* Russian transcript provided by Centropa.org.

[52] Leonid Averbukh, ed., "Moia evreiskaia sem'ia—dinastiia Zal'tsbergov-Averbukhov, 1796–2003," Odesskii evreiskii muzei, 32.

[53] Leonid Averbukh, "Navsegda so mnoi," *Migdal' Times* 58, April/May 2005 (www.migdal.ru/article-times.php?artid=5388).

[54] Z. G. Stepanishcheva, "Vot tak i zhizn' proshla," ll. 28–29.

[55] John Barber, "Introduction: Leningrad's Place in the History of Famine," in *Life and Death in Besieged Leningrad, 1941–44*, ed. John Barber and Andrei Dzeniskevich (New York: Palgrave Macmillan, 2005), 1.

[56] Paneiakh, *Tvorchestvo i sud'ba istorika*, 193.

Anna Akhmatova, who had no family in Leningrad to lose, lost numerous friends.[57] Given the statistics, it could not be otherwise.

Many more evacuees came from subsequently occupied territory, where they had left family and friends behind. Here, losses were particularly significant among the Jewish population. Of the almost three million Soviet Jews who had remained in enemy occupied territory, only a few hundred thousand survived. Although news of their fate was hard to come by, when word did arrive, it was rarely positive. In faraway Uzbekistan, Saul Borovoi knew little about the fate of individual friends in his native Odessa. A journalist who managed to visit the city shortly after its liberation, however, informed Borovoi's brother that "Odessa is a city without Jews."[58] Soldiers and journalists were one source of news; non-Jewish neighbors and friends were another. Deborah Averbukh, many years later, still vividly recalled the day she received a postcard from a former neighbor in Kiev informing her of her parents' murder by the occupying forces.[59]

SERVICE ON THE TASHKENT FRONT

As the war drew to a close, it became common to refer to the "Tashkent front" ironically, as a place where people evaded service on the front lines. Yet few of those who ended up in Tashkent sought to shirk service in the war. Maria Belkina, for instance, protested her evacuation from the outset. In a letter to her husband penned en route to Tashkent, she wrote, "if it weren't for Mitka [her newborn son], I would have left for the front."[60] Her resolve to participate in the war did not diminish in Tashkent, and she embarked on the journey west less than a year after her arrival in evacuation, after her son's first birthday. As she put it many years later, "I had promised myself: as soon as I stop breast-feeding him, I will depart for the front, leaving my son with my parents."[61] Frida Vigdorova, who was in a similar situation, also yearned to be on the front. "In Russia the fate of the country is being decided," she reportedly remarked one afternoon in Tashkent, "and we are sitting here in the muck."[62] Her sense of anguish at being stuck in the rear was clearly expressed in a novel she wrote some twenty years later. In

---

[57] Lidiia Chukovskaia, *Zapiski ob Annoi Akhmatovoi, 1938–1941*, vol. 1, 417, entry of March 24, 1942.

[58] Saul Borovoi, *Vospominaniia* (Moscow: Evreiskii universitet v Moskve, 1993), 285.

[59] Deborah Averbukh, interview by Ella Orlikova, December 2001, in *Jewish Witness to a European Century* (www.centropa.org).

[60] Quoted in Gromova, *Vse v chuzhoe gliadiat okno*, 27.

[61] Belkina did try to enlist in the army but was refused on the grounds of ill health. *Skreshchenie sudeb*, 362–63.

[62] Kena Vidre, "Kakaia ona byla, Frida Vigdorova," *Zvezda*, no. 5 (2000): 112.

the novel, the main character is a woman who, like Vigdorova herself, wanted to go to the front but went to Tashkent instead for the sake of her young daughter Ania. One evening in Tashkent, in her notebook, the woman describes her dilemma: "In Moscow there is a state of emergency, and I am here. Kaluga has fallen to the Germans. My Kaluga. There is fighting around Naro-Fominskaia. And I am here. Doctor Sheveleva put her son in a children's home and went to the front. I look at Ania and I understand: I can't give her to anyone. I might have left her with my mother, but with strangers—I can't. All the same, I need to be there, far from here."[63]

Both Belkina and Vigdorova had chosen evacuation for the sake of their children; they yearned to be at the front, yet there could be no shame in their presence in the rear. Not so for those who did not have parental responsibilities. As one woman evacuated to Siberia wrote to authorities in Moscow: "I am fine here. It is warm, I am well-fed, I can work. But *I do not feel needed here*, and besides that, I cannot shake a *feeling of shame*. After all, I do not have children. Why did I leave Moscow?"[64] An elderly writer in Tashkent made a similar point. In an appeal for permission to return, he noted, "it is difficult to live without work and shameful to die far from the front lines; I can be of use to the motherland."[65] Saul Borovoi, who was deemed eligible for service (just) but chose not to enlist, later recalled, "I was overcome by shame that I was not in the army, that I wasn't doing anything."[66] It is surely indicative that when the writer Kirill Levin, evacuated to Tashkent, decided to write of the war in the capital, his hero was not an evacuee, like the author, but a Muscovite professor "who cannot leave his native city in its moment of danger; he remains there."[67]

For men in particular, the evacuation could be a stigma. Vsevolod Ivanov learned this firsthand. After his departure for Tashkent, he and a group of other writers were evidently "declared deserters" by officials in the Writers' Union.[68] None was made to bear the shame of evacuation more publicly, however, than Vladimir Lugovskoi. Lugovskoi had earned a reputation for himself in the years preceding the war as a poet, a teacher, and a brave man.[69] When the war began, he went to the front, only to return shortly thereafter shaken

[63] Frida Abramovna Vigdorova, *Semeinoe schast'e: povest'* (Moscow: Slovo, 2002), 145.

[64] Emphasis in the original. RGALI, f. 631, op. 15, d. 604, l. 32.

[65] Ibid., d. 597, l. 24.

[66] Borovoi, *Vospominaniia*, 255. On his summons for military service and subsequent release from the obligation to serve as a member of the Academy of Sciences, see ibid., 266–67.

[67] RGALI, f. 631, op. 15, d. 605, l. 8. Levin described the plot for his projected new novel in a letter to authorities in Moscow requesting permission to return to the city. The novel, it seems, was never completed.

[68] Ivanov, *Dnevniki*, 105, entry of July 7, 1942. Among the other writers branded as deserters Ivanov listed Trenev, Fedin, Pasternak, "and others."

[69] See, for example, Konstantin Simonov, "Ego mesto v nashei iunosti," in *Stranitsy vospominaniia o Lugovskom: sbornik*, ed. Elena Leonidovna Bykova (Moscow: Sovetskii pisatel', 1981), 118–23.

and sick. When his family was evacuated in mid-October, there was no question but that he would go with them. His failure to stand up to the challenge of the war was a source of disappointment for many and, for some, derision. Maria Belkina's husband, for example, concluded a letter to his wife with a request to send his best to their mutual friends in Tashkent: "only don't send my greetings to my pseudofriends, runaways like Virta, Lugovskoi, Sobolev. After the war we'll expel them from the Writers' Union."[70] Konstantin Simonov, for whom Lugovskoi was a mentor, was deeply disappointed by his behavior. As he later wrote, "we expected something else of him, expected that he would be one of the strongest and bravest voices of our poetry in that difficult year, expected that of everyone 'Uncle Volodia,' as we called Lugovskoi at the time, would spend the whole war in the army."[71] Lugovskoi was well aware of how others felt about his conduct. He spent the war years, in the words of Olga Grudtsova, his future wife, "burning up with shame."[72]

While Lugovskoi never returned to the field of battle after his initial foray, other evacuated writers did subsequently see service on the front lines. From within the writer's colony in Tashkent, Alexei Tolstoi, Iosif Utkin, Vsevolod Ivanov, and Evgenii Khazin, Nadezhda Mandelstam's brother, all spent time on the front following their respective returns from Central Asia.[73] Back in Moscow, Tolstoi allegedly remarked to a fellow writer, "explaining his arrival," that "I couldn't . . . I found Tashkent distasteful. This evacuation . . it was like you were hiding yourself."[74] Many, however, had little choice but to "hide." The writer Oleg Erberg, while in evacuation in Tashkent, sent numerous appeals to Skosyrev, an official in the Union of Soviet Writers, seeking a posting to the front. His request that Skosyrev "do everything within your power to help me enter the ranks of the active defenders of our motherland" was turned down.[75] "What can I write?" Skosyrev replied. "I can only repeat myself: we cannot summon you, or anyone else, for work in the frontline press. All positions are filled."[76] Skosyrev, moreover, was better positioned than most to understand Erberg's anguish.

---

[70] Quoted in Gromova, *Vse v chuzhoe gliadiat okno*, 31.

[71] Quoted in ibid., 32.

[72] Ol'ga Grudtsova, "Dovol'no, ia bol'she ne igraiu . . . : Povest' o moei zhizni," *Minuvshee*, no. 19 (1996): 75.

[73] On Tolstoi's activities on the front and his wartime writing, see G. P. Trefilovaia, ed., "Iz zapisnykh knizhek A. N. Tolstogo voennykh let," in *A. N. Tolstoi: materialy i issledovaniia*, ed. A. M. Kriukova (Moscow: Nauka, 1985), 417–30. Utkin died in an airplane accident returning from one of his trips to the front in 1944. Vsevolod Ivanov wrote of his trips to the front in his diary. See Ivanov, *Dnevniki*. According to Nadezhda Mandelstam, her brother "wanted to go to the front, actively pursued this goal, and attained it." N. Ia. Mandel'shtam to B. S. Kuzin, August 20, 1944, in Mandel'shtam, *192 pis'ma*, 740.

[74] Thus did Nikolai Nikitin later describe his meeting with Tolstoi in the summer of 1942. Quoted in Viktor Petelin, *Zhizn' Alekseia Tolstogo* (Moscow: Tsentrpoligraph, 2001), 911.

[75] RGALI, f. 631, op. 15, d. 605, l. 221.

[76] Ibid., l. 222.

Having been dispatched to the Uzbek capital on a one-month official trip shortly before the all-out evacuation of Moscow began, Skosyrev had been temporarily stranded there. In one of several letters he dispatched to authorities back in Moscow in the hopes of securing the elusive permit authorizing his return, he set out the position of writers in the Uzbek capital: "In Tashkent at the moment there are as many as a hundred Moscow and Leningrad writers. We are not needed here in these numbers. The Uzbek government doesn't know what to do with us. Neither the journals nor the newspapers here can absorb everything we are writing. And even if they could, I do not want to be out of Moscow. I am a Muscovite, and I have grown accustomed to active work with heavy responsibilities. . . . I need to be there, where I can be of real use to our country." He put it more bluntly in a letter penned a few days later to Fadeev: "I like to work; more than that, I am happy only when I am up to my eyebrows in work. Tashkent with its hundreds of newly arrived Muscovites is hardly an arena of activity. During a war, Soviet writers should not and cannot sit 3,000 kilometers from the front."[77]

Those who, unlike Skosyrev, were forced to "sit 3,000 kilometers from the front" for months and sometimes years tried to make the best of a difficult situation. Many saw their writing as their means of contributing to the war. While in Tashkent, writers worked on a wide range of patriotic publications aimed at supporting the war effort. Alexei Tolstoi, who quickly established his credentials as a patriotic writer while still in Moscow, continued his patriotic output in evacuation. In Tashkent, he completed the first part of his historical play *Ivan the Terrible*, which he later described as "my response to the humiliations to which the Germans were subjecting my homeland. I summoned out of nonexistence into life a great passionate Russian soul—Ivan Groznyi—to fortify my 'outraged conscience.'"[78] Anna Akhmatova composed poems about bravery and victory, which she herself referred to as "patriotic."[79] One such poem, entitled "Courage," was published in *Pravda* on March 8, 1942, and, according to a fellow writer and evacuee, "was very popular in Tashkent."[80] Indeed, the Writers' Union itself commended Akhmatova on the tremendous "resonance" of the poem, and wrote her to request that she send any further poems to the Union for distribution to the country's central presses.[81] That the poem was published at all was due only to the intervention of another evacuee, Frida Vigdorova, who had wanted

[77] Ibid., d. 572, ll. 28, 129.
[78] Quoted in Maureen Perrie, *The Cult of Ivan the Terrible in Stalin's Russia* (New York: Palgrave, 2001), 129. In fact, Tolstoi had been commissioned to write the play before the German invasion.
[79] Chukovskaia, *Zapiski ob Annoi Akhmatovoi*, vol. 1, 381, entry of January 22, 1942.
[80] Svetlana Somova, "'Mne dali imia—Anna': Anna Akhmatova v Tashkente," *Moskva*, no. 3 (1984): 177–93.
[81] RGALI, f. 631, op. 15, d. 758, l. 15.

to serve on the front as a nurse, but did her part in the rear as *Pravda*'s second correspondent in Tashkent.

Academics also contributed to the patriotic output. The historian Militsa Nechkina wrote numerous articles for the popular press to inspire patriotism via stories from Russia's historic past (on the "partisan war in 1812," for instance, or the "eternal traditions of the people's militia").[82] Although the topics were handed down to her from on high, her diaries reveal that she conceived of her war writing as a civic duty. Indeed, she initially had considerable misgivings when she was commissioned to write something on the war of 1812, a topic that in her view could undermine the Soviet war effort. The comparison, she reflected in her diary, was "inadmissible." "It is the second day of the war, and I am going to explain a plan of retreat? I should say—they surrendered Smolensk and that was right? They abandoned Moscow and that was good. 'With the loss of Moscow Russia was not lost'? What, have I lost my mind? . . . I am in doubt—either it is somebody's stupidity or . . . All my civic feelings are against it."[83] One can only surmise that her qualms about the topic lessened after vast tracts of Soviet territory were surrendered.

Many scholars gave talks to workers and to wounded soldiers. Nechkina, for instance, delivered hundreds of lectures while in Tashkent, many of them at hospitals and military academies. Her subjects, invariably patriotic, ranged from the "defeat of Napoleon" to the "failure of schemes for world domination in history."[84] As she later wrote, "lectures, too, wage war."[85] Writers read from their works to provide relief to wounded soldiers. Akhmatova spoke of the opportunity of reciting her poems to such soldiers as a "joy."[86] According to a fellow writer who was present at a number of such visits, Akhmatova's poetry, particularly her love poems, had a profound impact on her audiences: one wounded soldier later referred to her as his "savior."[87] Many evacuees regarded such performances as a form of wartime service. As one writer put it in a letter to the Press Bureau in Moscow:

[82] M. V. Nechkina, "Dnevniki akademika M. V. Nechkinoi," *Voprosy istorii*, no. 7 (2005): 136 n. 9.

[83] Ibid., 122, entry of June 23, 1941.

[84] Nechkina's wartime diary contains a chronicle of her lectures. See ibid., 123–27.

[85] M. V. Nechkina, "V dni voiny," in *V gody voiny: stat'i i ocherki*, ed. Aleksandr Mikhailovich Samsonov (Moscow: Nauka, 1985), 31. This is not to minimize the important role of such lectures in securing the livelihood of those who gave them. Kornei Chukovskii, for instance, complaining in a letter to Marshak that "we are living in poverty," wrote that "I have to earn money the hard way, with lectures and public addresses." Letter of December 1941, in Chukovskii, "Pis'ma K. Chukovskogo k S. Marshaku," 299.

[86] Chukovskaia, *Zapiski ob Annoi Akhmatovoi*, vol. 1, 374, entry of January 11, 1942. According to Chukovskaia, Akhmatova was distressed that she had not been invited to read to wounded soldiers earlier.

[87] Somova, "'Mne dali imia—Anna': Anna Akhmatova v Tashkente."

if I am not on the front lines, I must work in the rear in a frontline manner—
that has been the goal of everything I have done as a writer since my arrival
in Tashkent. It is unlikely that you can experience a feeling of greater satisfaction, pride, and élan than that with which you leave the hospital after
performing among wounded soldiers, commanders, political workers, when
our dear soldiers have enjoyed your poetry and they thank you and ask you
to visit them again and again. . . . Today I did something for victory, you
think.[88]

Even in faraway Tashkent, there were thus many ways of contributing to
the war. While writers toiled away on the "cultural front," evacuated workers did their part on the "labor front." The evacuation of some ninety factories to the region had transformed Tashkent into an important industrial
center where evacuees and locals worked side by side manufacturing aircraft for the army and uniforms for soldiers.[89] Oleg Boldyrev and his father
worked at a factory producing mines, shells, and bombs. Although Oleg was
only eight when he was evacuated to Tashkent with his family, he begged to
be allowed to work, and when he turned ten his father finally relented.[90] The
young Iania Chernina and her mother, who were also evacuees, spent much
of the war at a Tashkent factory producing shells for Soviet katyushas.[91]

The entry of children such as Oleg and Iania into the workforce was emblematic of the total mobilization of Soviet society. On the factory floor,
young and old alike assumed the place of those who had departed for the
front. Their labor enabled the Soviet Union to continue to wage war in the
face of crippling losses and against all odds. The Soviet economy, brought to
the brink of collapse in the first year of the war, survived. Evacuated factories resumed their production in evacuation, albeit with significant delays,
and by the end of 1942, the Soviet Union had outstripped Germany in the
production of aircraft, artillery, and tanks. The increase in output proved
crucial to the outcome of the war. Although it came at the expense of the
civilian economy, Soviet citizens persevered.[92]

People like the Boldyrevs and the Cherninas did their part for the war
effort simply by virtue of their work. Many also contributed to the war effort through voluntary acts: by sewing, collecting, and donating clothing for
soldiers in the army or by giving blood to help the wounded. Iania Chernina

---

[88] B. V. Bobovich, August 31, 1942, RGALI, f. 631, op. 15, d. 758, l. 41.

[89] Stronski, "Forging a Soviet City," 120.

[90] Svetlana Aleksievich, *Poslednie svideteli (sto nedetskikh kolybel'nikh)* (Moscow:
Pal'mira, 2004), 72–73.

[91] Ibid., 134.

[92] On Soviet production and the crucial contribution made by millions of individual Soviet
citizens see Mark Harrison, "The USSR and Total War: Why Didn't the Soviet Economy Collapse in 1942?" in *A World at Total War: Global Conflict and the Politics of Destruction,
1939–1945*, ed. Roger Chickering, Stig Forster, and Bernd Greiner (Cambridge: Cambridge
University Press, 2005), 137–57.

recalled how she was asked to donate something to the defense fund while her mother was at work. "What did we have? We had nothing except a few bonds, which mother had been saving. Everybody was giving something, how could we give nothing?! I donated all the bonds."[93] Stepanishcheva later wrote that she donated blood, in part to earn extra money for her son, but the "main consideration in this decision was, of course, the wish to do something, however small, that would help the front."[94]

Perhaps the most notable of these wartime endeavors were the efforts undertaken on behalf of the war's most vulnerable victims—children. The war in Tashkent saw a massive campaign to aid evacuated children, spearheaded by the Moscow and Leningrad intelligentsia and supported by the republican government and by local elites. This, too, was a way of participating in the war. Kornei Chukovskii, who played an active role in these efforts, wrote about them in a small book he published in 1942 on "children and war." Although, as he explained in a letter to Marshak, some of the material was already outdated, he urged him to "read the chapter on Uzbekistan and children, about how eighty-five thousand evacuated children were given shelter here. In this," he continued, "Soviet civic consciousness has passed one of the most difficult tests."[95]

Leading the way in this campaign was the Commission to Aid Evacuated Children. Although in formal terms the commission was a government body run by republican officials, its "organizer and director," as one official document put it, was Ekaterina Peshkova, the widow of the revered Soviet writer Maksim Gorky and an evacuee.[96] Much of the commission's work, moreover, was carried out by volunteers under the direction of Peshkova. Among her closest aides was her good friend Tamara Ivanova, the wife of the writer Vsevolod Ivanov and another evacuee from Moscow.[97] Tamara Ivanova later recalled that "in Tashkent, in evacuation, Ekaterina Pavlovna [Peshkova] took me under her moral wing."[98] Other notable members included Liudmila Tolstaia and Lydia Chukovskaia, who later recalled how "soon after our arrival in Tashkent, the Ministry of Education engaged me in work of a voluntary nature with the Commission to Aid Evacuated Children. I visited children in children's homes—children from the Ukraine, from Belorussia, Voronezh, Kiev, Kursk, Leningrad—children who had been brought to the deep rear, to Tashkent, from all ends of the country."[99] Chukovskii

[93] Ibid., 135.

[94] Stepanishcheva, "Vot tak i zhizn' proshla," TsDNA, l. 25.

[95] Letter of March 12, 1942, in Chukovskii, "Pis'ma K. Chukovskogo k S. Marshaku," 301. Note that the number cited by Chukovskii was certainly exaggerated.

[96] TsGARUz, f. 94, op. 5, d. 4439, l. 6. On the formal composition of the commission, see ibid., d. 4414, ll. 9–10.

[97] Ibid., d. 4439, l. 6.

[98] Tamara Ivanova, *Moi sovremenniki kakimi ia ikh znala: ocherki* (Moscow: Sovetskii pisatel', 1984), 366.

[99] Chukovskaia, *Zapiski ob Anne Akhmatovoi,* vol. 2, 26.

was also very active in the movement. "Almost every day," he wrote Marshak, "I give lectures, speak at children's homes, and so on. I am a member of the Commission to Aid Evacuated Children—the work has completely engrossed me, as it has Lydia. She works at various children's homes from early in the morning until evening and is writing a book about evacuated children."[100]

The commission's activities were wide-ranging. In addition to the Registration Bureau, the commission established subcommittees responsible for overseeing the republic's children's homes, collecting and distributing clothing, and arranging cultural activities.[101] Members of the commission also sought to raise funds for evacuated children by organizing a series of ticketed events. At one such event held in the summer of 1942, a city park was taken over and transformed into a paid-access market. According to Georgii Efron, who sold tickets at the entrance, the "whole point was that people could purchase various products cheaply. This was supposed to attract many people and thus raise money for children."[102] And raise money it did. Reports on the commission's activities chart a steady inflow of funds, which were then used to subsidize cafeterias and to provide aid to especially needy children.[103]

The visibility of the commission as well as the high profile of the volunteers it attracted to the cause are readily apparent in what was undoubtedly the most famous of its fund-raising events—a concert organized on behalf of evacuated children in 1942, which Esther Markish later described as "a major event in our life in Tashkent."[104] The "pièce de résistance" of the night was Alexei Tolstoi's parody of a contemporary film shoot in which the author and Mikhoels played the role of janitors who were perpetually disrupting the production.[105] "Exactly at the moment when absolute silence was required," Mikhoels's wife subsequently recalled, "they started hammering nails." Then, just when order had been restored, the "reigning silence was

---

[100] Letter of March 12, 1942, in Chukovskii, "Pis'ma K. Chukovskogo k S. Marshaku," 301. Chukovskii took a particularly active role in cultural activities targeting evacuated children. He visited children's homes and served on the committee responsible for organizing cultural events and campaigns. TsGARUz, f. 94, op. 5, d. 4257, ll. 56–57.

[101] TsGARUz, f. 837, op. 32, d. 3691, l. 1.

[102] Georgii Efron, *Dnevniki (1941–1943 gody)*, vol. 2, ed. E. B. Korkina and V. K. Losskaia (Moscow: Vagrius, 2005), 138–39, entry of August 30, 1942.

[103] As of September 1, 1942, the commission had raised 719,000 rubles through voluntary contributions as well as fund-raising events. TsGARUz, f. 837, op. 32, d. 3418, l. 45.

[104] Markish, *The Long Return*, 123.

[105] "Pièce de résistance" is Markish's phrase. Khodasevich described the skit as "very funny," and Svetlana Somova deemed it a "particularly good" performance in a generally "brilliant evening." See Markish, *The Long Return*, 124; Valentina Khodasevich, "Vospominaniia ob A. N. Tolstom," in *Vospominaniia ob A. N. Tolstom*, ed. Z. A. Nikitina and L. I. Tolstaia (Moscow: Sovetskii pisatel', 1973), 254; and Somova, "'Mne dali imia—Anna': Anna Akhmatova v Tashkente."

shattered by wild howls behind the curtains: the janitors were beating up the actor, who was dressed as Hitler."[106] According to Faina Ranevskaia, who played a makeup artist in the skit, each time the actor playing Hitler appeared, "everything began all over again." The director, "almost crying," would plead with the janitors: "Fellows, he's not the real Hitler. He's an actor; he's receiving a salary in our Soviet rubles, he has a ration card for bread and meat!"[107] Meanwhile, between shoots, Ranevskaia would insist on freshening up Tatiana Okunevskaia, who played the heroine in the film. "I would discuss the pressing problems of the day," Ranevskaia recalled, "becoming horrified by the troubles that had fallen to my lot, which in fact were not funny, but presented in a humorous manner they became simpler and lighter, and the audience enjoyed the opportunity to laugh at the things that surrounded them each day, the absurdity of which they no longer noticed."[108]

As Ranevskaia's comments suggest, the concert provided comic relief for an audience that generally had far too few opportunities for laughter. Moreover, for its organizers, the provision of aid to evacuated children forged a sense of community among those who had been displaced by the war. Esther Markish later wrote that, when approached to help out with the organization, "I was only too glad to accept; I'd do anything to brighten up the humdrum existence of the evacuation zone—especially something that would help people who were in a worse situation than we were."[109] Markish recalled a meeting convened to organize a lottery to benefit evacuated children at which "all the ladies from Tashkent's high society were in attendance."[110] The provision of aid to children was not merely, however, a form of sociability. In their activities on behalf of evacuated children, evacuated members of the intelligentsia, many of them women, found an outlet in which they, too, could participate in the war.

Valentin Berestov, a beneficiary of the commission's activities on behalf of children, later wrote: "Ekaterina Pavlovna Peshkova, who founded the commission, revived the prerevolutionary philanthropic tradition. These women, the wives of well-to-do and influential people, were not bureaucrats, although they sat behind office desks in one of the rooms at the Commissariat of Education. They were able, often with the help of their husbands or thanks to their authority, to obtain quite a bit from the bureaucrats for evacuated children, and they themselves retained their independence and a domestic, friendly relationship with the children."[111] Women such as Peshkova and

---

[106] A. Pototskaia-Mikhoels, "O Mikhoelse bogatom i starshem," in *Stat'i, besedy, rechi: Vospominaniia o Mikhoelse*, ed. K. L. Rudnitskii (Moscow: Iskusstvo, 1965), 522.

[107] G. A. Skorokhodov, *Razgovory s Ranevskoi* (Moscow: Olimp', 2002), 266.

[108] Ibid., 267.

[109] Markish, *The Long Return*, 123.

[110] Ibid.

[111] Berestov, *Izbrannye proizvedeniia*, vol. 2, 211–12.

Ivanova did draw, as Berestov rightly pointed out, on a prerevolutionary tradition. Peshkova, in particular, had a long history of philanthropic service. Not only had she provided aid to political prisoners under both the tsarist and the Soviet regimes, but she also had prerevolutionary experience with precisely the type of work she took up in Tashkent: during World War I, Peshkova had chaired the Children's Division of the organization Aid for the Victims of War.[112] At the same time, her activities and those of her colleagues also fit comfortably within a framework of Soviet civic activism organized by the wives of elites for those less fortunate. The *obshchestvennitsa* movement, which originated in the mid-1930s, prompted thousands of wife-activists to descend on canteens and kindergartens in an effort to bring culture and cleanliness to the Soviet working people.[113] The organizers of the Tashkent commission, however, were not the usual contributors to such endeavors—normally the wives of engineers, managers, or Stakhanovites. For a start, they were married to writers, the intellectual elite. Moreover, many of the women on the Commission to Aid Evacuated Children had reason to be suspicious of the state: Chukovskaia's husband had been killed in the terror, and she herself had been subject to police surveillance; Peshkova had long served as an advocate for political prisoners and was only too aware of the broad scope of state-sponsored repression; Esther Markish's brother was in the Gulag. In their wartime activities, however, these women and others found an accommodation with the state.

FREEDOM IN THE WAR: THE INTELLIGENTSIA AND THE STATE

The war brought Soviet citizens closer to the state. Stephen Kotkin has argued that the welfare state of the 1930s constituted a "common ground" between the "dreams of ordinary people" and those of the Soviet state.[114] The war provided another common ground—not of shared dreams, per se, but of shared enemies, shared outrage, and shared hopes. The war itself was shared: it was everyone's war, the state's war, and, in Levich's words, "our war." Propaganda slogans such as "our cause is just—victory will be ours" were echoed in the personal writings of individual Soviet citizens.[115] As Andrei Sakharov later reflected, "I always believed that our country, assisted

---

[112] On Peshkova's activities, see Iaroslav Leont'ev, "Dorogaia Ekaterina Pavlovna," *Russkaia Germaniia*, no. 24 (2005) (www.rg-rb.de/2005/24/mir.shtml).

[113] On the history of the movement, see Mary Buckley, "The Untold Story of Obshchestvennitsa in the 1930s," *Europe-Asia Studies* 48, no. 4 (1996): 569–86; and Rebecca Balmas Neary, "Mothering Socialist Society: The Wife Activists' Movement and the Soviet Culture of Daily Life, 1934–41," *Russian Review* 58, no. 3 (1999): 396–412.

[114] Stephen Kotkin, *Magnetic Mountain: Stalinism as a Civilization* (Berkeley: University of California Press, 1995), 23.

[115] See, for example, S. A. Unkovskaia, "Vospominaniia uchitel'nitsy. Tretaia chast'. Na pensii," RNB, f. 1007, op. 1, d. 8, l. 991.

by our allies, would emerge victorious—there was simply no alternative, and I have no doubt whatsoever that the overwhelming majority of my countrymen felt the same way. The slogan 'Our cause is just' was not simply humbug—no matter who said it."[116]

In many ways, the war served to legitimate Soviet power.[117] One evacuee from Odessa recalled how the war transformed his father's attitudes toward the party. "Later he told me, 'Before the war I in no way espoused communist views, I was a nonparty engineer. But during the war, I understood that the party was the only power capable of organizing resistance to Hitler and achieving victory.'"[118] The war fostered a new sense of identification with Stalin as well. When Stalin delivered a speech in a Moscow Metro station to mark the twenty-fourth anniversary of the October revolution only weeks after the panicky flight from the city, the results were electrifying. Vera Inber, in blockaded Leningrad, wrote of the speech in her diary in almost mystical terms: "Twice the alerts went, and Stalin's speech was immediately relayed again. It came across above the darkness, above the alerts, above the raid. It was stronger than anything. We listened to it, as we stared at the fire, and everything merged for us as one great shining consolation."[119] Georgii Efron, reflecting on the impact of the speech on his way to Tashkent, was convinced that it would "revive Russian patriotism."[120] What was true in November 1941 was doubly so in the following years. Aleksander Wat later observed that "no one in Russia ever had the popularity that Stalin had in that brief period between Stalingrad and the end of the war." Even those who hated Stalin now hailed him as the "savior of Russia!" Members of the Soviet intelligentsia, evacuees with whom Wat spent time during his stay in Alma-Ata, "worshipped Stalin," "everyone did, everyone, no exceptions."[121]

---

[116] Andrei Sakharov, *Memoirs*, trans. Richard Lourie (New York: Knopf, 1990), 40.

[117] On the transformation of the war into a powerful legitimizing myth, see Amir Weiner, *Making Sense of War: The Second World War and the Fate of the Bolshevik Revolution* (Princeton, N.J.: Princeton University Press, 2001), 8; Weiner, "The Making of a Dominant Myth: The Second World War and the Construction of Political Identities within the Soviet Polity," *Russian Review* 55, no. 4 (1996): 638–60.

[118] M. Gauzner, interview by A. Beiderman, M. Gauzner Collection, Odesskii evreiskii muzei.

[119] Vera Inber, *Leningrad Diary*, trans., Serge M. Wolff and Rachel Grieve (London: Hutchinson of London, 1971), 31.

[120] Efron, *Dnevniki*, vol. 2, 97, entry of November 7, 1941.

[121] Aleksander Wat, *My Century: The Odyssey of a Polish Intellectual*, trans. Richard Lourie (New York: New York Review of Books, 2003), 352. In a similar vein, Roy Medvedev, whom John Barber rightly describes as "one of the severest critics of Stalinism," nonetheless acknowledged the leader's importance during the war. He wrote: "Stalin's name became a sort of symbol existing in the popular mentality independently of its actual bearer. During the war years, as the Soviet people were battered by unbelievable miseries, the name of Stalin and faith in him to some degree pulled the Soviet people together, giving them hope of victory." Quoted in John Barber, "The Image of Stalin in Soviet Propaganda and Public Opinion during World War 2," in *World War 2 and the Soviet People*, ed. John Garrard and Carol Garrard (New York: St. Martin's, 1993), 39.

To be sure, the spectacle of panic in the wake of the invasion had bred doubts about Soviet power. It had shaken the faith of some believers and confirmed others in their suspicion of the Soviet state. At the same time, the conviction that the cause was just brought people closer to the state, enabling even those who had suffered at the hands of Soviet power to dedicate themselves to the war effort without hesitation or doubt. Thus did Olga Berggolts turn her back on her years in prison and "plunge" into her work for the war. As she wrote in her diary, "other massive thoughts and feelings possessed my soul."[122] Undoubtedly the most famous expression of this phenomenon is a fictional exchange in the postwar novel *Doctor Zhivago*. In an oft-quoted passage, Boris Pasternak wrote: "And when the war broke out, its real horrors, its real dangers, its menace of real death, were a blessing compared with the inhuman power of the lie, a relief because it broke the spell of the dead letter. It was not only felt by men in your position, in concentration camps, but by everyone without exception, at home and at the front, and they all took a deep breath and flung themselves into the furnace of this deadly, liberating struggle with real joy, with rapture."[123] A similar sentiment was articulated, albeit in less exalted terms, by Saul Borovoi. In his memoirs, he recalled of the beginning of the war that "my first sensation was a kind of internal liberation, satisfaction, that in this war we were on the just side [*na pravoi storone*], an unwavering certainty in our ultimate victory. This sense did not leave me in the difficult days."[124]

The sense of "liberation" experienced by at least some sectors of the Soviet intelligentsia had implications for their creative output. Many artists subsequently reflected that the war enabled them to be more sincere or, in Dmitrii Shostakovich's words, "to express myself."[125] The comments of Shostakovich and others like him prompted one historian to refer to the war as a "breathing space."[126] Such retrospective reflections are necessarily informed by the crackdown on intellectual and cultural life that followed the war. That said, they do reflect something of the wartime spirit, particularly among evacuees. Far from Moscow, evacuees found themselves at least partially released from the institutional and social strictures that governed cultural life. Boris Pasternak expressed this sense well. In a letter to his former wife in Tashkent from Chistopol, he wrote, "We feel freer here than in Moscow, despite the longing [*toska*] for her."[127]

[122] O. F. Berggol'ts, "Iz dnevnikov O. Berggol'ts," *Zvezda*, no. 5 (1990): 180, entry of October 28, 1942.

[123] Boris Pasternak, *Doctor Zhivago*, trans. Max Hayward and Manya Harari (New York: Pantheon, 1997), 507–8.

[124] Borovoi, *Vospominaniia*, 236.

[125] Quoted in Bonwetsch, "War as a 'Breathing Space,'" 146.

[126] Ibid., 137–53.

[127] Letter to E. Pasternak, March 12, 1942, in B. L. Pasternak, E. V. Pasternak, and E. B. Pasternak, *Biografiia v pis'makh* (Moscow: Art-Fleks, 2000), 280.

This is not to say that in Tashkent, or Chistopol, writers were free from intervention in their work. No less a personage than Alexei Tolstoi saw the first installment of his most significant wartime drama, his play about Ivan the Terrible, banned. Although Tolstoi read from the play to critical acclaim for an audience of historians and writers in Tashkent, authorities in Moscow found the play severely lacking. "The play," Party Secretary A. S. Shcherbakov wrote to Stalin, "distorts the historical image of one of the greatest Russian statesmen."[128] Similar charges were made in the press: Tolstoi was accused of depicting Ivan "primarily in the realm of his personal life. The feverish activity of Ivan the Terrible in 'gathering' the Russian lands and establishing a centralized state are not reflected in the play."[129]

The criticism of Tolstoi was simply the most visible indication that the old methods of censorship and public censure were still very much alive. In Tashkent, as elsewhere, it was regular practice for publications to be subject to censorship. Victor Zhirmunskii reported to a colleague in mid-1944 from Tashkent that his latest book, a cowritten piece on the Uzbek epic, "is being industriously read in the 'official channels.'"[130] Moreover, although Akhmatova, for instance, was being published again, only some of her poetry was approved for publication. Just as she was once again granted a public voice for her patriotic output, much of her poetry remained inadmissible, secret, the preserve of small gatherings of fellow writers and close friends. Akhmatova's *Poem without a Hero*, which she had begun in Leningrad but which continued to absorb her in Tashkent, is a case in point. Even though recitations of the poem loom large in memoir accounts of the evacuation in Tashkent, not once was the poem recited on the city's stages. Dmitrii Tolstoi later recalled hearing the poem at his father's house, at a dinner among a group of writers.[131] Valentin Berestov heard it in the more intimate setting of Akhmatova's apartment at 54 Zhukovskaia.[132] Galina Kozlovskaia recalls Akhmatova's reading of the poem at a small gathering she hosted with her husband.[133]

Similarly, Akhmatova restricted her readings from her first and only play to a close circle of friends. The play no longer survives. Akhmatova burned

---

[128] Andrei Artizov and Oleg Naumov, eds., *Vlast' i khudozhestvennaia intelligentsiia: Dokumenty TsK RKP(b)-VKP(b), VChK-OGPU-NKVD, o kul'turnoi politike. 1917–1953 gg.* (Moscow: Mezhdunarodnyi fond Demokratiia, 2002), 478.

[129] M. Khrapchenko, "Sovremennaia sovetskaia dramaturgiia," in *Literatura i iskusstvo*, no. 22, 1942: 3.

[130] Letter of July 1, 1944, in G. F. Blagovoi, ed., "Perepiska V. M. Zhirmunskogo s S. E. Malovym," *Izvestiia RAN. Seriia literatury i iazyka*, no. 2 (2002): 66.

[131] Dmitrii Tolstoi, *Dlia chego vse eto bylo: Vospominaniia* (St. Petersburg: Bibliopolis kompozitor, 1995), 210–11. According to Lydia Chukovskaia's diary, Akhmatova was asked to read the poem when Liudmila Tolstoia invited her to dinner. *Zapiski ob Annoi Akhmatovoi*, vol. 1, 402, entry of February 27, 1942.

[132] Berestov, *Izbrannye proizvedeniia*, vol. 2, 208–9, 214.

[133] Galina Kozlovskaia, "Vstrechi s Akhmatovoi," ed. V. Kiselev, *Arion*, no. 4 (1997) (www.magazines.russ.ru/arion/1997/4/81.html).

it at the end of the decade when she feared a house search following the repeat arrest of her son. The play, according to Nadezdha Mandelstam, was
reminiscent of Kafka, among others. "The theme of the play is the trial before a writers' tribunal of a woman poet who is then sentenced to prison."[134]
Clearly, in Akhmatova's case, the turn to patriotic poetry did not signal a
true reconciliation with the state.

Akhmatova's poetry was only one part of the unofficial literary world of
wartime Tashkent. Also in Tashkent, select writers and others were for the
first time able to read the late Mikhail Bulgakov's *Master and Margarita*,
which his widow, Elena Bulgakova, carefully transcribed while in evacuation. Frida Vigdorova read the book while in Tashkent, as, at least according to one account, did Konstantin Simonov, when he was passing through
the city.[135] Osip Mandelstam's poems were made available to new audiences
as well.[136] The continued existence of an unofficial literary world peopled
by writers whose publications were banned by the Soviet state was one indication that the sense of freedom to which Pasternak and others referred
was nonetheless a relative state. Writers were freer but not free. Suspicion of
the state may have lessened, but it had not disappeared. Many expected,
however, that in the aftermath of the war, the changes would go further.[137]

Lydia Chukovskaia later recalled that the "war was drawing to a close; it
seemed, that in that inconceivable time called 'after the war,' everything
would be new, everything would be different from *before*."[138] Chukovskaia
had fled Leningrad before the war had even begun, in May 1941, in fear of
the NKVD. However, as she subsequently reflected, "neither in Chistopol
nor in Tashkent nor in Moscow did I feel any kind of surveillance." Referring to the "silent war" that had preceded the war with Germany (the war
of the terror), Chukovskaia wrote that "in 1944, it seemed to me that *that*
war had ended."[139]

Chukovskaia's belief in the end of "that war" and the notion of an imminent "rebirth" are reflected in a range of contemporary sources. From
the outset, many believed that the war would change things. Georgii Efron
expressed a common assumption in the fall of 1941, while traveling to
Tashkent: "I am sure that after the war ends things will not resume as they
were before the war, in May 1941—there will be decisive changes."[140]

[134] Nadezhda Mandelstam, *Hope Abandoned*, trans. Max Hayward (New York: Atheneum, 1974), 352–53.

[135] Vidre, "Kakaia ona byla, Frida Vigdorova," 112–13.

[136] Eduard Babaev, *Vospominaniia* (St. Petersburg: Inapress, 2000), 128–29, 132.

[137] Expectations of postwar change, understood in various ways, were widespread among
all sectors of the population. For a general treatment of this topic, see Elena Zubkova, *Russia
after the War: Hopes, Illusions, and Disappointments, 1945–1957*, trans. Hugh Ragsdale
(Armonk, N.Y.: M. E. Sharpe, 1998), 31–39.

[138] Chukovskaia, *Zapiski ob Anne Akhmatovoi*, vol. 2, 32.

[139] Ibid., 33.

[140] Efron, *Dnevniki*, vol. 2, 102, entry of November 8, 1941.

Most, moreover, were quite convinced that these "decisive changes" would be for the better. In evacuation in neighboring Kazakhstan, Academician Vladimir Vernadskii was decidedly optimistic. In February 1942, he wrote in his diary that the "Soviet Union, I have no doubt, will be victorious and will emerge from the ordeal stronger. The union with democratic countries will strengthen our freedom of thought, freedom of religion, freedom of academic inquiry. The police regime is weakened and perhaps will fade into history. After devastation [as a result of the war]—reconstruction."[141] In Tashkent, far from Moscow, such hopes were easily nurtured. Georgii Efron wryly noted in his diary in the late summer of 1942, "many *frondeurs* dream that England and the United States will make our regime more flexible and liberal, that there will be a new NEP, that freedom of speech and of the press will increase, and so on."[142] Alexei Tolstoi may well have been one of the individuals Efron had in mind: the next year, already back in Moscow, Tolstoi was reported to have spoken of the inevitability of a "new NEP," claiming that "without it it will be impossible to rebuild the economy."[143] A further indication of the currency such ideas enjoyed among the writer's colony in Tashkent is the final diary entry made by the young poet Valentin Berestov before leaving for Moscow in the spring of 1944. Berestov, who had studied in Tashkent under Chukovskaia and Mandelstam, expressed what was clearly a fairly common sentiment: "The war will end, but the end will give way to some kind of new beginning. . . . The suffocation of the prewar years has come to an end, has broken up."[144]

The expectations of postwar change underscore the complexities of the wartime reconciliation between select sectors of the intelligentsia and the Soviet state. Theirs was a reconciliation based on a shared enemy and a shared war. Conditioned by the belief that the war would change things, the relationship was not without tension. In some ways, it was a reconciliation with the state not as it was, but as it was sure to become in the aftermath of the war. To be sure, the tension in the relationship between citizen and state was implicit in the very notion of "our war," at least as articulated by Levich. The series of oppositions that structured Levich's comments positioned the Soviet state not as "us" but as "them." "It was not their war," he remarked, referring to the government, "but our war."[145] "Our war," as deployed by

[141] Vladimir Vernadskii, "'Samoe slozhnoe—mozg gosudarstvennogo chekoveka': Iz neopublikovannykh dnevnikov 1942 goda," ed. Inar Mochalov, *Rodina*, no. 12 (2000): 13, entry of February 15, 1942.

[142] Efron, *Dnevniki*, vol. 2, 138, entry of August 29, 1942.

[143] Artizov and Naumov, *Vlast' i khudozhestvennaia intelligentsiia*, 497. Tolstoi's words were reported as part of a report on the mood among intellectuals in Moscow in the summer of 1943.

[144] Berestov, *Izbrannye proizvedeniia*, vol. 2, 256.

[145] Bonwetsch, "War as a 'Breathing Space,'" 137.

Levich, was the "people's war." Who exactly the "people" were, however, was problematic.

THE FRIENDSHIP OF PEOPLES

The pages of *Pravda Vostoka* frequently celebrated the warm welcome extended by Uzbeks to their European brethren. "The Uzbek people has forcefully demonstrated just how strong the friendship of peoples is in our Soviet Socialist State," proclaimed the head of the Tashkent Soviet.[146] Indeed, Tashkent became a symbol of the much acclaimed "friendship of peoples" during the war.[147] Russians, Ukrainians, Jews, Belorussians—all found refuge in the Uzbek capital.[148] In the city's roster of cultural events, moreover, "friendship" with the local Uzbek population was on prominent display. As an Uzbek writer from Tashkent noted at a conference in Moscow, "the war . . . has demonstrated the full force of the friendship of Soviet peoples. This has been demonstrated not only on the front, in battle, and not only on the labor front but also on the creative front."[149] At literary gatherings in Tashkent, Russian poets such as Anna Akhmatova and Vladimir Lugovskoi shared the podium with the Belorussian poet Iakub Kolas and the Uzbek poet Aibek, all "under the banner," as a participant at one such evening put it, "of the friendship of peoples."[150]

A more sustained example of this exchange could be found on the city's stages. Theatergoers in Tashkent were treated to performances of Sholom Aleichem's Yiddish classic *Tevya the Milkman* by Moscow's Jewish State Theater, which, in the spirit of cultural exchange, also staged the revolutionary Uzbek drama *Khamza*. The play was translated from Uzbek into Yiddish by the Jewish writer Der Nister, who was also in evacuation in Tashkent. As the theater director Solomon Mikhoels reported to authorities in

---

[146] GAGT, f. 10, op. 18, d. 31, l. 10.

[147] The term "Friendship of Peoples" became common currency in the mid-1930s. As the historian Terry Martin put it, "by 1938, the Friendship of the Peoples was the officially sanctioned metaphor of an imagined multinational community." Although Russians and Russian culture were privileged in this equation and regarded, in Martin's words, as "the motive force that forged and sustained the friendship," the cultures of the other Soviet peoples were celebrated and even cultivated. *The Affirmative Action Empire: Nations and Nationalism in the Soviet Union* (Ithaca, N.Y.: Cornell University Press, 2001), 432. On the prewar history of the Friendship of Peoples, see ibid., 432–61.

[148] Official statistics on the nationality of evacuees are available only for 1941 and apply to the whole of Uzbekistan rather than the city of Tashkent specifically. According to these statistics, most evacuees in Uzbekistan were Jewish, Russian, or Ukrainian, although there were also small numbers of Belorussians, Poles, evacuees from the Baltics, and Moldavians. RGAE, f. 1562, op. 20, d. 249, ll. 67–68.

[149] RGALI, f. 631, op. 15, d. 638, l. 22.

[150] Aleksandr Deich, *Den' nineishii, den' minuvshii: literaturnye vpechatleniia i vstrechi* (Moscow: Sovetskii pisatel', 1969), 155.

Moscow in 1943, the "theater considered it appropriate to include in its repertoire a play demonstrating the struggle and daily life of the Uzbek people, its heroes, and to thus extract useful lessons about the conditions of life in Soviet Uzbekistan."[151] Although Jewish actors played the parts, the theater invited a number of well-known Uzbek actors to consult on the production, and one of the republic's most famous dancers, People's Artist Mukkaram Turgunbaeva, directed the choreography. The Soviet press trumpeted the production as a "new expression of the close link between the national cultures of the Soviet peoples."[152]

Mikhoels took the process of cultural exchange one step further by agreeing to codirect the Uzbek writer Khamid Almidzhan's play *Mukanna* for the local Khamza theater. According to the report of another Uzbek writer, Mikhoels thereby gave "tremendous help to Uzbek dramatic art. He helped the author in many ways, and the latter was enchanted by all the instructions that Mikhoels gave him."[153] Mikhoels himself, however, clearly felt that the learning process was mutual. In a critique of an English book that presented the encounter of evacuated and Central Asian theatres as "a meeting between East and West," he countered that "this was a meeting of Soviet theatres," rejecting the notion of a colonial relationship. His work on *Mukanna*, he claimed, had convinced him that "the influences were reciprocal."[154]

A similar form of collaboration was on display in Tashkent's universities. According to Khamid Almidzhan, some evacuees had become veritable champions of Uzbek literature. As he reported to central authorities in Moscow, "Zhermunskii is completing a big book about the heroic epic. Zelinskii is working on a history of Uzbekistan. Deich . . . has written a book. They have come to love Uzbek literature and some of them have even learned the Uzbek language during this time. Zhermunskii reads Uzbek literature without a translator."[155] Indeed, the linguist Zhermunskii took advantage of his evacuation to Tashkent to switch his speciality from the dialects of Russia's German colonists (a topic that had already led to his arrest on three occasions and had become particularly sensitive since the onset of the war) to a safer area of study—Turcology. As he wrote in a letter to a fellow linguist,

[151] RGALI, f. 2693, op. 1, d. 194, ll. 8–9. On the structural similarities between Khamza and the theater's more traditional Jewish repertoire, see Jeffrey Veidlinger, *The Moscow State Jewish Theater: Jewish Culture on the Soviet Stage* (Bloomington: Indiana University Press, 2000), 237.

[152] "Uzbekskaia drama v gosete," in *Literatura i iskusstvo*, no. 28 (80), 1943: 3.

[153] RGALI, f. 631, op. 15, d. 638, l. 22.

[154] The book in question was Joseph Macleod, *Actors Cross the Volga: A Study of the 19th Century Russian Theatre and of Soviet Theatres in War* (London: Allen and Unwin, 1946). Mikhoels's comments were made as part of a formal discussion of the book in the theatrical section of the All-Union Society for Cultural Ties Abroad in June 1947. Mikhoels's speech was published in *Stat'i, besedy, rechi: Vospominaniia o Mikhoelse*, 608.

[155] RGALI, f. 631, op. 15, d. 638, l. 8.

Figure 7. Alexei Tolstoi (center) and Alexander Fadeev (second on the left) with Khamid Almidzhan (first on the left) and a number of other Uzbek cultural figures, Moscow, 1943 (courtesy TsGAKFFD RU).

"I am studying the Uzbek language energetically."[156] Ushakov also studied Uzbek, which, as he wrote to a friend, he did with "pleasure." While in Tashkent, he worked on a Russian-Uzbek dictionary.[157] According to Militsa Nechkina, "many began to study the Uzbek language." She herself participated in a circle to learn the language. Nechkina was one of a handful of Russian historians from the Academy of Sciences' Institute of History who collaborated with their new Uzbek colleagues on a collective history of Uzbekistan. As she later recalled, "I wrote a chapter for it on the mass antitsarist movement among Uzbeks at the end of the nineteenth century."[158] Another contributor to the volume, Ekaterina Kusheva, described the book project as an attempt "to repay the hospitality" of their Uzbek hosts.[159]

[156] Blagovoi, "Perepiska V. M. Zhirmunskogo s S. E. Malovym," 62–63.
[157] Letters of December 22, 1941, and February 19, 1942, in O. V. Nikitin, ed., "Poslednie pis'ma D. N. Ushakova G. O. Vinokuru," *Izvestiia RAN. Seriia literatury i iazyka*, no. 1 (2001): 68, 69.
[158] Nechkina, "V dni voiny," 35.
[159] Kusheva, "Vospominaniia E. N. Kushevoi," 143.

By far the most powerful symbol of the much acclaimed Friendship of Peoples, however, was the widely publicized adoption of evacuee children by Uzbek parents.[160] "Here," wrote Kornei Chukovskii, "we find the most touching and poetic form of the indissoluble brotherhood of peoples which is such a solid foundation of our entire Soviet system."[161] Tellingly, such adoptions were the subject of arguably the single most famous Uzbek wartime poem, written by Gafur Guliam and titled "You Are Not an Orphan." In the poem, an adoptive father reassures a young boy who has been separated from his parents: "Are you really an orphan? . . . Relax, my dear [*rodnoi*]!"[162] The poem was translated into Russian by Svetlana Somova, who had been evacuated to Tashkent, and published in *Pravda*. Somova later described the poem's unique reception at a reading she did on the front lines:

> I was reading and felt that there was some sort of special mood in the auditorium. . . . I got to the end, and was surrounded. The commander of the regiment was brought up, a gray-haired major, with tears in his eyes. It turned out that his son had been located thanks to this poem. He had read the following lines in *Pravda*: "If your father is alive, let the shadow of worry not disturb him amid the horror and fire, let him know: his son is with me!" And this man, who had lost his family during the war, wrote a letter—"To Tashkent. To Gafur Guliam," and some days later he received a reply: his son had been found, and was living in a children's home in Tashkent.[163]

According to Guliam, the poem was inspired by the case of the Uzbek blacksmith Shaakhmed Shamakhmudov, who adopted fifteen evacuee children with his wife. The fame of Guliam's verse was such that Shamakhmudov later claimed that his actions had been inspired by the poem. "I was touched by these words," Guliam later commented, "but I had to refute them. It all happened in the reverse order."[164]

Guliam had read about Shamakhmudov and others like him in Tashkent's wartime press. Indeed, the adoptions received widespread publicity,

---

[160] Adoption itself was glorified during the war, in sharp contrast to the immediate postrevolutionary period, when adoption was viewed, in the words of one historian, "as a mask for labor exploitation or as a means to safeguard property." See Laurie Bernstein, "The Evolution of Soviet Adoption Law," *Journal of Family History* 22 (April 1997): 206, 213. In what follows, I use the term adoption to refer to both actual adoptions (*usynovlenie*) and to foster-care arrangements (*patronat*). The terms of care were set out in a directive issued in late November 1941. TsGARUz, f. 837, op. 32, d. 2894, l. 131.

[161] Kornei Chukovskii, *Deti i voina* (Tashkent: Gosudarstvennoe izdatel'stvo UzSSR, 1942), 25.

[162] Gafur Guliam, *Izbrannye proizvedeniia*, vol. 1, ed. A. Akhmedova and R. Farkhadi (Tashkent: Izdatel'stvo literatury i iskusstva imeni Gafura Guliama, 1983), 54.

[163] 163 Somova, "'Mne dali imia—Anna': Anna Akhmatova v Tashkente."

[164] Quoted in A. I. Akbarov, *Gafur Guliam: o zhizni i tvorchestve narodnogo poeta Uzbekistana* (Tashkent: Izdatel'stvo TsK LKSM Uzbekistana "Esh Gvardiia," 1974), 200–201.

Figure 8. The Shamakhmudov Family—Shaakhmed and his wife, Bakhri, pose for a photograph among their adopted evacuee children, Tashkent, 1944 (courtesy TsGAKFFD RU).

and stories about them appeared regularly in the republican press.[165] A newsreel made during the war in Tashkent offers a fairly typical example of the way they were represented. Titled "The Blacksmith Akhmed," the newsreel featured a blacksmith on a collective farm who "gave shelter to and is raising five children of different ages and nationalities who have lost their parents on the front."[166] Lydia Chukovskaia, in her collection of children's stories from the front lines, also emphasized the multinational character of the adoptions. As she wrote in her conclusion, "many Soviet patriots in Uzbekistan took orphaned children into their families. Snub-nosed, blue-eyed children from Riazan, dark-eyed Ukrainians, Jewish children from Bessarabia become full-fledged members of Uzbek families."[167]

Leading the way in the adoptions was the Uzbek political elite. When the writer and wartime correspondent Konstantin Simonov passed through Tashkent in early 1943, he was struck by the genuine pride with which Usman Iusupov, the first secretary of the Uzbek Communist Party, enumerated his republic's contributions to the war effort. If Iusupov was proud of how

[165] See, for example, *Pravda Vostoka*, January 10, 1942, and February 7, 1942.
[166] RGALI, f. 2057, op. 1, d. 375, l. 14.
[167] Chukovskaia and Zhukova, *Slovo predostavliaetsia detiam*, 91.

Figure 9. The Shamakhmudov children having lunch, Tashkent, 1944 (courtesy TsGAKFFD RU).

many evacuated enterprises had found a home in Tashkent, "he spoke with even more inner pride about the adoption of orphans, about how many had been taken in by Uzbek families, even large ones, from children's homes and from receiving and sanitary centers at the train station."[168] In fact, it was none other than Iusupov who initiated one of the first such adoptions. In December 1941, he and his wife took in the four-year-old Leningrad girl Faina Barisheva.[169] Faina's registration card indicates that, until her adoption, she had been living in Tashkent in a children's home.[170] Other notable adoptive parents included the chairman of the Uzbek Council of People's Commisars, his deputy, another party secretary, and the deputy commissar of the NKVD.[171] Such elite adoptions, however, were merely the tip of the

[168] Konstantin Simonov, *Raznye dni voiny. Dnevnik pisatelia, 1942–1945 gody* (Moscow: Grifon M, 2005), 171, 172. Simonov later recalled that the meeting with Iusupov "remains the strongest impression of my days in Tashkent." Ibid., 171.

[169] Arifov, *Zapiski voennogo kommendanta*, 15.

[170] Her registration card can be viewed at http://resources.ushmm.org/uzbekrefugees/getjpg .php/B/13411.jpg.

[171] Arifov, *Zapiski voennogo kommendanta*, 18. A female deputy of Uzbekistan's Supreme Soviet, L. I. Shatokhina, was featured on page 2 of the republican newspaper with a picture of her three-year-old Russian adoptee. *Pravda Vostoka*, January 15, 1942.

iceberg. Many of the most highly publicized cases featured ordinary Uzbek people who had adopted numerous children, such as the blacksmith Shamakhmudov or the "simple" Uzbek woman Bakhrikhon Ashirkhodzhaeva who adopted as many as ten evacuated children.[172] Municipal archives contain ample evidence that people of all backgrounds and social classes participated in the wave of adoptions, albeit not to the same extent. In a fairly typical case, an Uzbek woman, the wife of a lawyer, appealed for permission to adopt an evacuated child, citing her "desire to help our motherland and to demonstrate a Stalinist care for children."[173]

In all, over a thousand evacuee children were adopted in Tashkent alone by a combination of Russian, Tatar, and Uzbek parents.[174] Of the one hundred preschool children who arrived with an Odessa children's home in the fall of 1941, nine had been taken in by local families a few months later.[175] Chukovskaia later recalled that the children who were taken in by local residents "were happier than those who were in the charge of the state."[176] Although information about the fate of such children is incomplete, their conditions were monitored by volunteers associated with the commission. Lectures on themes related to child rearing were prepared for newly adoptive parents in both Russian and Uzbek.[177] More significantly, over the course of 1942, members of the commission made approximately one thousand visits to families to this end.[178] A visit to Bakhrikhon Ashirkhodzhaeva, mentioned above, found that the "apartment is clean . . . , the children are healthy, happy, and the general impression is positive."[179] Of course, not all families took equally good care of their new wards. The Garaschenko family, who had taken in three-year-old Liza Badalbaeva, were brought to court on charges of neglect by the commission, which viewed the family as responsible for the young girl's untimely death. An internal directive dispatched to oblast commissions nonetheless maintained that the "vast majority of children find themselves in wonderful conditions and receive genuine motherly care and comfort . . . in their new families."[180] Chukovskaia, moreover, later recalled of these "new families" that "I saw many good [ones]."[181] Five- or six-year-old Nadia Baranova was clearly among the fortunate. According to a report by one of the commission's voluntary inspectors, her new

172 Arifov, *Zapiski voennogo kommendanta*, 29–33.
173 GAGT, f. 13, op. 3, d. 75, l. 16. For other examples, see ibid., d. 30, 33, 61.
174 As of January 1, 1943, 1,045 children had been taken in by local families. TsGARUz, f. 94, op. 5, d. 4609, l. 16. In 1942 alone, more children were adopted in Tashkent than in the five years preceding the war (1935–1940). See GAGT, f. 13, op. 3, d. 224, l. 30.
175 TsGARUz, f. 94, op. 5, d. 4254, l. 3.
176 Chukovskaia, *Zapiski ob Anne Akhmatovoi*, vol. 2, 27.
177 TsGARUz, f. 94, op. 5, d. 4232, l. 40.
178 Ibid., d. 4609, l. 16.
179 The report is cited in full in Arifov, *Zapiski voennogo kommendanta*, 32.
180 TsGARUz, f. 94, op. 5, d. 4257, l. 53.
181 Chukovskaia, *Zapiski ob Anne Akhmatovoi*, vol. 2, 28.

family "makes a very good impression. The husband and wife both work, and the girl is in day care from the morning until eight in the evening. But they give her a lot of attention. The girl looks good, and is well fed. . . . She has become very attached to her new parents."[182] A similar sense of attachment was felt by Faina Barisheva, the young girl adopted by the party chief Iusupov and his wife. Faina came to see herself as a full-fledged member of the family and remained in Tashkent after the war (her biological parents, it turned out, had both been killed).[183] In a conversation many years later, she was asked: "Many Leningrad children, like you, were saved in those terrible years by Uzbek families. What can you say about this people?" She replied, "It is awkward to talk about oneself. After all, I am an Uzbek."[184] As her case suggests, many children really did find a "native home" in Tashkent.

The warm welcome extended to evacuee children by at least some sectors of the local population makes it clear that the "friendship of peoples" was not strictly confined to cultural venues, academic exchanges, and the pages of the republican press. It was also manifest on an interpersonal level, in relations between evacuees and the Uzbek population. Kornei Chukovskii had nothing but positive things to say about the locals, both in his diary and in his letters to his son. In one of the first such letters posted from Tashkent, he described the Uzbeks as a "wonderful people, considerate and courteous." A couple of months later, he concluded a letter with the note "The Uzbeks are a very good people—I am completely at home among them [*sredi nikh, kak sredi svoikh*]."[185] The mathematician Evgenii Slutskii expressed similar sentiments in a letter to a friend. "I like the local people," he wrote, praising their "orderliness, propriety, and politeness." Slutskii even had plans to study Uzbek, although he feared it would be too difficult.[186] Some evacuees, moreover, made friends among the locals. Militsa Nechkina recalled the "large number of acquaintances and friendships that sprung up between the 'honored evacuees' and the local Uzbek population."[187] Nor were such friendships confined to the cultural elite. The young Alexander Kovarskii found a regular playmate in his Uzbek landlord's son, with whom he roamed the city streets, climbed trees, and engaged in other youthful ventures. As a child, Kovarskii was better able to broach the cultural divide than many of his elders. "I quickly mastered Uzbek," he later recalled, "and I became the link between the old people and the outside world."[188] Not only was he able

[182] GAGT, f. 13, op. 3, d. 75, l. 36.
[183] Arifov, *Zapiski voennogo kommendanta*, 17.
[184] Ibid., 18.
[185] Letters of January 15 and March 9, 1942, in Nikolai Chukovskii, *O tom, shto videl*, 596, 604.
[186] Letter to A. Sofonova, 1942, in A. Sofonova, *Zapiski nezavisimoi: dnevniki, pis'ma, vospominaniia*, ed. Irina Evstaf'eva (Moscow: RA, 2001), 266.
[187] Nechkina, "V dni voiny," 34.
[188] Kovarskii, "Detstvo na ulitse chempiona."

to pick up the language, but he had an easy time finding common ground with Uzbek youth his age. Not all youth, however, crossed the divide quite so easily. Raisa Yasvoina, a young girl at the time, had a number of other Jewish playmates but did not socialize with locals. As she later explained in an interview, "they didn't speak Russian, they spoke in Uzbek."[189]

As Yasvoina's experience suggests, language barriers constituted a real impediment to meaningful social interaction between evacuees and the local Uzbek population. This may account for the striking absence of Uzbeks in the memoirs, diaries, and letters of many evacuees. To some extent, evacuees and locals lived surprisingly separate lives. Saul Borovoi, in neighboring Samarkand, recalled that of all his "Samarkand friends," only one was not an evacuee, and even he had not been born in the region.[190] The lack of interaction is not surprising given the degree to which writers and other cultural elites lived, ate, and worked together in an insular émigré community. Even so, such people still rubbed shoulders with locals on the city's overcrowded trams, winding streets, and busy markets. Moreover, given the acute shortage of housing, many evacuees were quartered with locals, who were forced to "self-condense." Some evacuees later recalled their one-time landlords with fondness. Sophia Abidor, whose family found lodgings in an Uzbek women's house, appears to have had good relations with her landlord, as did the family of Raisa Yasvoina.[191] The Polish refugee Jack Pomerantz likewise had fond memories of the Tajik couple who gave him shelter during his brief sojourn in Tashkent.[192] Another evacuee, born in evacuation in Tashkent, credits her life to her Uzbek landlord: according to her mother, only the care and attention of the Uzbek woman kept her from dying as an infant.[193]

Despite the many instances of friendly relations, however, overcrowding and scarce resources could not but put a strain on relations between locals and the ever-increasing contingent of newcomers. Diaries, letters, and contemporary reports contain ample evidence of tension. Isaak Bakhmatov, who had moved to Tashkent shortly before the war, wrote in late November 1941, that a "slight chill in the attitude of Tashkenters to the arrivees can be observed, as the latter have filled up all the lines, the restaurants and cafes—anywhere one might try to jostle one's way through, all the free space."[194] A "slight chill," however, hardly captured the way some evacuees described

---

[189] Raisa Yasvoina, interview.

[190] Borovoi, *Vospominaniia*, 277.

[191] Sophia Abidor, interview; Raisa Yasvoina, interview.

[192] Jack Pomerantz and Lyric Wallwork Winik, *Run East: Flight from the Holocaust* (Urbana: University of Illinois Press, 1997), 58.

[193] Zinaida Leibovich, interview, in *Jewish Witness to a European Century* (www.centropa .org).

[194] I. M. Bakhmatov to E. M. Bakhmatova, November 21, 1941, TsDNA, f. 45, l. 1. A few days later, he complained that the "writers who have arrived [from Moscow] are depriving me of all my bread (and not me alone)." Letter of November 25, 1941, ibid., l. 6.

their reception. "We evacuees are hated," one woman wrote in a letter to the front.[195] Another woman, describing her desperate situation, wrote: "there are not a few here like myself, and the indifference of the locals is even greater. They regard us as importunate indigents."[196] Often locals resented evacuees. One woman complained to her husband that "meals for children are provided only for evacuees."[197] Another reported that the local military committee had refused her requests for aid. "They say," she wrote, "that I am not an evacuee and I can go without."[198] Saul Borovoi recalled the "local population's insulting attacks on parasitical evacuees. On occasion, 'activists' among the locals demanded that they be given bread first, before the evacuees."[199]

In many ways, the relationship between Uzbeks and newcomers was marked by mutual incomprehension. Sometimes, this took on humorous dimensions. According to Alexander Kovarskii, old Uzbek men used to sit in the shade, sipping hot tea, and look on with amusement as the evacuees from the west "attacked every kiosk with fizzy water and perspired all the more."[200] At other times, it was more ominous, manifesting itself as suspicion. Numerous sources suggest that members of the evacuated intelligentsia feared the Uzbeks. Aleksander Wat recalled that "the Russians, the Jews, the fugitives, the refugees—everyone was expecting a bloodbath."[201] In a similar vein, Georgii Efron recorded in his diary how the intelligentsia "is afraid. . . . In the event of defeat what will happen in Uzbekistan? Everyone says that 'a slaughter will begin.' The Uzbeks will slaughter the Russians and Jews."[202] This rumor, and the fears that fed it, underscores the real limits of the Friendship of Peoples in Tashkent. In its identification of victims, moreover, it points to another dimension of the Friendship of Peoples that was particularly fraught during the war—the status of Jews.

Nowhere were the limits of "our war" more apparent than in the marked hostility toward the Soviet Union's Jewish population. Jews figured prominently among the city's evacuee population. Indeed, in Uzbekistan as a whole, Jews constituted a clear majority among the newcomers—according

---

[195] GAGT, f. 10, op. 17, d. 55, l. 260.

[196] RGALI, f. 962, op. 3, d. 1076, l. 3.

[197] GAGT, f. 10, op. 17, d. 55, l. 31.

[198] Ibid., l. 23.

[199] Borovoi, *Vospominaniia*, 264.

[200] Aleksandr Kovarskii, "Detstvo na ulitse chempiona."

[201] Wat, *My Century*, 336.

[202] Efron, *Dnevniki*, vol. 2, 137, entry of August 29, 1942. Vsevolod Ivanov registered similar fears in his diary. He noted: "Nadezhda Alekseevna does not want to go to Chimgan as she is afraid of the appearance of *basmachi*. The city's police stand on guard without revolvers, they have all been dispatched to the front." *Dnevniki*, 106, entry of July 9, 1942. Evacuees' fears were conditioned by stereotypes about the Uzbek population as well as threats made by Uzbeks themselves. On this, and for other examples of the fear it produced, see Stronski, "Forging a Soviet City," 159–61.

to imperfect statistics from late 1941, they accounted for 63 percent of the total number of evacuees.[203] In addition, the republic received a number of notable Jewish institutions, including the Jewish theaters of Moscow, Kiev, and Odessa. It is perhaps not surprising, then, that Jews occupied an important place in the Friendship of Peoples as it was celebrated in Tashkent. A poem by Gafur Guliam, the same poet whose "You Are Not an Orphan" came to symbolize the Uzbek adoptions, took the lead in this regard. Entitled "I Am a Jew" and written in 1941, the poem was constructed as a challenge to Hitler's racial ideology: the repeated refrain of "I am a Jew" gives way in the end of the poem to "I am a person." As Ilya Ehrenburg put it at a wartime function intended to honor Uzbek literature, "at a time when Hitler had chosen the Jews as a target, there was a poet in the Soviet Union who threw the proud words 'I am a Jew' in the face of the bloody petty tyrant."[204] The poem further praised Jewish participation on the front lines and celebrated the attachment of Jews to their Soviet homeland.

Similar themes were sounded in the theater. At the premiere of the State Jewish Theater's production of *Tevya the Milkman*, the theater was welcomed to Tashkent by an Uzbek actor, who proclaimed that "the grandsons of Tevya the Milkman do not want to be victims any longer. Together with the other peoples of the USSR they are on the field of battle, shattering the darkest and most brutal force—that of Hitlerism."[205] Jewish participation in the war, alongside that of other peoples, was subsequently dramatized by the theater in a production of Peretz Markish's wartime play *An Eye for an Eye*, which dealt with partisan activity in occupied territory. (Notably, however, a short description of the play in *Pravda Vostoka* did not make explicit mention of the Jewish people, noting only that it was dedicated to "the heroic struggle of Soviet partisans.")[206] In an interview about the play published in *Pravda Vostoka*, Mikhoels commented that today Soviet Jews "can pronounce a word which even twenty-five years ago seemed foreign to the Jewish ear. The word is homeland."[207]

Jews received a warmer welcome on the city's stages than on its streets. Tensions between locals and newcomers frequently took on antisemitic overtones. Olga Boltianskaia, shortly after her arrival in Tashkent, was informed by her sister-in-law of the "philistine, Judeo-phobic sentiments in Tashkent."[208] Another evacuee later recalled the locals' "general dislike for the European Jews evacuated to Tashkent from the Ukraine."[209] In some

---

[203] RGAE, f. 1562, op. 20, d. 249, ll. 67–68.

[204] Akbarov, *Gafur Guliam*, 215.

[205] See *Pravda Vostoka*, January 14, 1942.

[206] Ibid., July 19, 1942.

[207] Ibid., May 14, 1942.

[208] Diary of O. A. Boltianskaia, RGALI, f. 2057, op. 2, d. 29, l. 99, entry of August 28, 1941.

[209] A. E. Levitin-Krasnov, *"Ruk tvoikh zhar": 1941–1956* (Tel Aviv: Krug, 1979), 135.

quarters, rumors circulated that the local police, infiltrated by nationalists, "intentionally delayed the prosecution of charges of antisemitism."[210] Leonid Averbukh, who later reflected that he hadn't experienced antisemitism before the war, noted that it was "clearly expressed during the war in Tashkent. It mixed with a hatred of evacuees, who had occupied part of the living space of the native population." Averbukh suffered from the sentiment firsthand: on his way home from school one day, he was attacked by a group of schoolboys who "brutally beat me, their feet against my face" while they assailed him with antisemitic slurs.[211] Mariam Magarik was similarly attacked on the streets of Tashkent by a group of local youth who shouted, as she described it in a poem of 1942, "kill the yid [*zhid*]!"[212] Vladimir Lugovskoi recounted hearing a similar cry.[213] Although antisemitism was clearly present in the city, its pervasiveness should not be overstated. When interviewed many years later, numerous evacuees, including Sophia Abidor and Evgenia Galina, could recall no incidences of antisemitism in Tashkent.[214] Nonetheless, the phenomenon was sufficiently pronounced to receive official notice. In August 1942, the NKVD reported to Beria that the arrival in Uzbekistan "of a significant number of citizens of the USSR of Jewish nationality" had led to problems. According to the report, "anti-Soviet elements, taking advantage of the discontent of some local residents with the compression [*uplotnenie*] of living space, the rise in market prices, and the tendency of some evacuated Jews to set themselves up in the system of trade, supply, and storage organizations, activated counterrevolutionary work directed toward kindling antisemitism. As a result, in Uzbekistan there were three incidents in which Jews were murdered, accompanied by antisemitic cries." In Tashkent, where one of these incidents took place, there were also numerous reported cases of antisemitic remarks and threats. Some focused on the alleged nonparticipation of Jews at the front, and others on the way they had supposedly "squeezed out Uzbeks and Russians" from all the "favorable jobs." Hostility toward Jews was further exacerbated by the housing situation, as one of the examples cited in the NKVD report suggests. According to the NKVD, "the worker Avdeeva announced to a circle of her friends that when

[210] Ivanov, *Dnevniki*, 118, entry of July 24, 1942. This rumor was passed on to Vsevolod Ivanov by the Jewish poet M. Golodnyi.

[211] Leonid Averbukh, interview by Nicole Tolkachova, 2003, in *Jewish Witness to a European Century,* cassette 1, side B. Russian transcript provided by Centropa.org.

[212] Mariam Isaakovna Magarik, "Mnogie veterany pishut nam pis'ma . . . stikhi," *Vestnik KEROOR "Da"*, no. 5 (www.corbina.net/~synrus/da5.html).

[213] Lugovskoi's account is reported by Georgii Efron, who noted in his diary with some skepticism that Lugovskoi boasted of beating up the individual in question. See Efron, *Dnevniki*, vol. 2, 136, entry of August 29, 1942. Other examples of antisemitism in Tashkent can be found in Stronski, "Forging a Soviet City," 161–62.

[214] Sophia Abidor, interview; Evgenia Galina, interview by Ella Levitskaya, April 2003, in *Jewish Witness to a European Century* (www.centropa.org). A similar testimony was given by Rakhil Givand-Tikhaya in her interview by Vladimir Zeidenberg, in *ibid.*

Hitler comes, she would exterminate all the Jews who had been quartered in her apartment."[215]

Although Tashkent was perhaps particularly ripe with tension of this sort, it was in no sense unique. A Jewish evacuee in the capital of neighboring Kazakhstan protested to authorities in Moscow: "there is such hatred here of evacuees, especially of Jews, that it is simply horrible and the local authorities do nothing. Evacuees are not given work, especially if they notice their nationality."[216] In Frunze, the capital of the adjoining republic of Kyrgyzstan, party authorities reported numerous antisemitic incidents and rumors.[217] According to a writer evacuated to the city, demobilized soldiers "openly say that Jews have refused to participate in the war and that they sit in the rear in warm places. . . . I was a witness to how Jews were thrown out of lines; even women were beaten up by legless cripples."[218]

The role of demobilized soldiers, and the nature of their comments, underscore the way in which the war and the evacuation gave shape to a new form of popular antisemitism. The novelty and pervasiveness of such attitudes is readily apparent in the observations of Vladimir Petrov, who found himself in Alma-Ata at the height of the evacuation. Having spent the previous six years in the Gulag, Petrov noted one change in particular after his release: antisemitism, a "phenomenon wholly strange to me." "Where I had happened to be before the war," he wrote, "there was almost none of it." Petrov was nothing short of "astonished" when he witnessed a group of Moscow students rudely throw a Jewish man out of a restaurant to claim his table for themselves, referring to the bewildered man as a parasite, and suggesting both that Jews were evading army service and that they had stolen money during the Moscow panic and were living in the rear "like kings."[219] Petrov's impressionistic account is corroborated by a report sent to Vyshinskii at the Central Procuracy Office in Moscow. The report noted a steep rise in antisemitic activity in Kazakhstan. Whereas twenty people had been charged with antisemitic actions in the first half of 1942 in the entire republic, just over double that were charged on the same counts in the month of

---

[215] G. B. Kostyrchenko, ed., *Gosudarstvennyi antisemitizm v SSSR: ot nachala do kul'minatsii, 1938–1953* (Moscow: Mezhdunarodnyi fond Demokratiia; Materik, 2005), 33. Others blamed Jews for the war. Thus was the wife of the Yiddish poet Peretz Markish reportedly denied food in the countryside surrounding Tashkent. According to Vsevolod Ivanov, the "peasants said to her, 'We won't sell to Jews, we have the war thanks to you.'" *Dnevniki*, 105–6, entry of July 7, 1942.

[216] A. Ia. Livshin and I. B. Orlov, eds., *Sovetskaia povsednevnost' i massovoe soznanie, 1939–1945* (Moscow: Rosspen, 2003), 409.

[217] See Zeev Levin, ed., "Antisemitism and the Jewish Refugees in Soviet Kirgizia, 1942," *Jews in Russian and Eastern Europe* 50, no. 1 (2003): 196–98.

[218] RGASPI, f. 17, op. 125, d. 190, l. 16.

[219] Vladimir Petrov, *My Retreat from Russia* (New Haven: Yale University Press, 1950), 41–42.

August in Alma-Ata and Semipalatinsk oblasts alone.[220] Nor were such incidents confined to Central Asia. In Siberia, in Sverdlovsk oblast, there was even a pogrom, in which the aggressors launched their attack with cries "here's your second front—kill the yids!"[221]

Expressions of antisemitism, manifest across the country, underscore just how precarious the Friendship of Peoples really was. As the incident related by Petrov suggests, ethnic harmony was threatened both by conflicts between locals and newcomers and by strains within the evacuee community itself. In some sense, however, at least for Jews, the most disturbing threat to the Friendship of Peoples came not from the unruly streets of Tashkent or Alma-Ata but from the very pinnacle of power in Moscow. Vsevolod Ivanov first got wind of a change in central policy while in Tashkent—a fellow writer, Gusev, returned to report the "Slavicization" of the board of a literary journal.[222] Frida Vigdorova was likewise informed of the new policy in evacuation in Tashkent, allegedly by Chukovskaia, on the latter's return from a trip to Moscow. As recounted by another evacuee, who accompanied Vigdorova on the visit, Chukovskaia reported: "'They say that there is beginning to be state antisemitism: they just fired the head of TASS—a Jew.' This was probably the spring of 1943. We didn't believe it."[223]

Even for those directly affected, the emergence of state antisemitism was difficult to fathom. The Jewish actress Faina Ranevskaia, also in evacuation in Tashkent, was one of the early victims of the Kremlin's new policy. Though the director Sergei Eisenstein, in evacuation in Alma-Ata, had chosen her for a new part for his latest film, *Ivan the Terrible*, he was unable to secure authorization for her to play the role. Cast by Eisenstein in the role of Princess Evfrosinia Staritskaia, Bolshakov, the head of the Committee for Cinematography in the USSR, deemed Ranevskaia unsuitable for the role as her "semitic traits are very pronounced, especially on the big screen."[224] Eisenstein protested, to no avail. Ranevskaia herself remained unaware of the reasons behind her dismissal, for a long time blaming Eisenstein himself.[225]

One of the few Tashkenters to observe the workings of the new policy firsthand was the film director Mikhail Romm. In a letter to Stalin penned in early 1943 about the difficult conditions facing Soviet cinematography, Romm concluded with "one question about which I can turn to none except you." Referring to the recent replacement of numerous figures in the film

[220] Kostyrchenko, *Gosudarstvennyi antisemitizm v SSSR*, 34.

[221] GARF, f. 5446, op. 81a, d. 361, l. 182. Saul Borovoi, evacuated initially to the Krasnodar region in southern Russia, later recalled that a "hostile attitude to the Jews, who constituted a notable proportion of evacuees, became more and more apparent." *Vospominaniia*, 254.

[222] Ivanov, *Dnevniki*, 136, entry of September 17, 1942.

[223] Kena Vidre, "Kakaia ona byla, Frida Vigdorova," 112.

[224] Kostyrchenko, *Gosudarstvennyi antisemitizm v SSSR*, 30.

[225] Shcheglov, *Faina Ranevskaia*, 98.

industry, he noted that "all those fired turned out to be Jews, while those who replaced them were non-Jews." This, he continued, had led some to speak of "anti-Jewish tendencies within the Cinematography Committee." He himself had not been unaffected: "in the past few months I have frequently had occasion to recall my Jewish roots, although until now, in twenty-five years of Soviet power, I never thought of this, for I was born in Irkutsk, I grew up in Moscow, I speak only Russian, and I have always felt myself to be a Russian, full-fledged [*polnotsennyi*] Soviet person."[226]

In his "recollection" of his Jewish identity, Romm was not an isolated case. Indeed, his words to Stalin closely echo the words of Ilya Ehrenburg, pronounced shortly after the German invasion. "I grew up," Ehrenburg said, "in a Russian city. My native language is Russian. I am a Russian writer. Now, like all Russians, I am defending my homeland. But the Nazis have reminded me of something else: my mother's name was Hannah. I am a Jew."[227] Whereas Ehrenburg was "reminded" of his Jewish identity by the Nazis, Romm's recollections of his "Jewish roots" were thrust on him by the Soviet state.[228] The place of Jews within the Soviet polity was changing. It is not that Romm and others like him had not been previously identified as Jews, both by the state and by themselves. Indeed, Romm had been registered as a Jew on his arrival in Tashkent: the line beside "place of birth" is empty on his registration card, but the line beside nationality is not.[229] Wartime registration cards, moreover, were based on information in prewar passports. Since the introduction of the passport system in the early 1930s, all Soviet citizens of Jewish origin who chose to identify themselves as such (and many did) carried passports that clearly labeled them as Jews.[230] While in Tashkent, however, the brief notation "Jew" (abbreviated in Russian to *Evr*) had become weightier. For Romm and others, it was increasingly difficult to be both a Jew and a "full-fledged Soviet person." One is reminded of Gafur Guliam's poem, in which the repeated refrain of "I am a Jew" gives way in the final verses to "I am a person." The poem had been written and published to

[226] Artizov and Naumov, *Vlast' i khudozhestvennaia intelligentsiia*, 484. See also Mikhail Romm, *Kak v kino: ustnye rasskazy*, ed. Ia. I. Groisman (Nizhnii Novgorod: Dekom, 2003), 120–25.

[227] Quoted in Yuri Slezkine, *The Jewish Century* (Princeton, N.J.: Princeton University Press, 2004), 288.

[228] Elena Bonner later described a similar transformation in her sense of identity during the war in response to the surge in popular antisemitism. Reflecting on the war, she wrote: "I survived it and became Jewish . . . in the outburst of military antisemitism . . . with the crude officers' anecdotes and stories that the Jews were conducting the war in Tashkent." Quoted in Marius Broekmeyer, *Stalin, the Russians, and Their War, 1941–1945*, trans. Rosalind Buck (Madison: University of Wisconsin Press, 2004), 142.

[229] A copy of his registration card can be seen at http://resources.ushmm.org/uzbekrefugees/getjpg.php/R/6697.jpg.

[230] On the tendency of Soviet citizens of Jewish origin to self-identify as Jews, see Slezkine, *Jewish Century*, 285.

much acclaim in 1941. It is hard to imagine it would have met a similarly positive reception only a year or two later.

At the same time as Jews were being excluded from the family of Soviet peoples, the relationship among the various peoples was being recalibrated. As the war progressed, Russia was increasingly championed as the "leading" nation of the country, the "first among equals," and the Russian prerevolutionary past was accordingly rehabilitated.[231] The critical reception accorded the collective history of Uzbekistan, written as a joint venture between evacuated historians and their local Uzbek colleagues, is telling in this regard. The book, particularly the chapters by Nechkina, glorified the indigenous anti-tsarist movements of the late nineteenth and early twentieth centuries. Nechkina wrote of the "heroic struggle of the people of Uzbekistan" against the "national-colonial oppression" meted out from Moscow.[232] When it was written, in 1942, it seemed a perfect exemplar of the Friendship of Peoples. The parameters of the Friendship of Peoples, however, soon changed. In 1943, a collective history of Kazakhstan, edited by one of Nechkina's colleagues in evacuation in Alma-Ata and stressing the progressive role of anti-tsarist movements in the region, became the object of a sustained controversy. Initially nominated for a Stalin Prize, it was subsequently subjected to sharp criticism for its failure "to demonstrate the 'leading role of the Russian people in the formation and development of a multinational state in Russia.' "[233] For Nechkina, one of the editor's closest allies, the writing was on the wall. Although the history of Uzbekistan, published in 1947, never attained the same notoriety, it, too, was criticized for its failure to highlight the positive role played by Russians in bringing enlightenment and development to the region.[234] In the pantheon of wartime heroes, there was evidently little place for local resisters of Russian power. Rather, even in Tashkent, pride of place belonged to the Russian tsar Ivan the Terrible, a man who was credited with expanding that power. He was the subject of Alexei Tolstoi's play; a poem by Vladimir Lugovskoi, commissioned by Sergei Eisenstein as a script for his film; a historical seminar; and a handful of

---

[231] To be sure, the privileging of Russia and Russian culture predated the war and was implied by the Friendship of Peoples. However, the shift to a Russian nationalist line became decidedly more pronounced in the latter half of the war. See David Brandenberger, *National Bolshevism: Stalinist Mass Culture and the Formation of Modern Russian National Identity, 1931–1956* (Cambridge, Mass.: Harvard University Press, 2002), 130–31.

[232] S. V. Bakhrushin, ed., *Istoriia narodov Uzbekistana*, vol. 2 (Tashkent: Izdatel'stvo AN UzSSR, 1947), 357, 370.

[233] Reginald E. Zelnik, *Perils of Pankratova: Some Stories from the Annals of Soviet Historiography* (Seattle: Herbert J. Ellison Center for Russian, East European, and Central Asian Studies, University of Washington, 2005), 38–39, 45. See also Brandenberger, *National Bolshevism*, 123–32.

[234] See Lowell Tillett, *The Great Friendship: Soviet Historians on the Non-Russian Nationalities* (Chapel Hill: University of North Carolina Press, 1969), 157.

significant historical studies.[235] It is indicative of the renewed emphasis on Russia's heroic past that Nechkina, who had been sharply critical of attempts to glorify Ivan in the past, now praised the efforts of her colleagues.[236]

• • •

On arrival in Tashkent, the dramatist Aleksander Deich had been greeted by Khamid Almidzhan, the head of the Uzbek Union of Writers. "I hope that you will not regard Tashkent as a room to wait out the end of the war," he had said, "but that it will be a native home for you, which you will remember for the rest of your life."[237] Some evacuees did regard the cities and towns that had given them refuge in precisely this light. Boris Pasternak, in a letter to his son in Tashkent penned shortly after his own return to Moscow, reflected that neither his dacha nor his apartment in Moscow "seem like home to me." Rather, it was Chistopol, the "terrible hole which frightened everyone," that possessed that quality for him. "I am sure that Tashkent will possess the same qualities for you," he wrote. "In the future, you will probably be grateful to it."[238] "At the time I could not understand my father's words about our future gratitude to Tashkent," Evgenii Pasternak recalled many years later. "I thought that Tashkent could not possibly evoke any tender thoughts in either me or my mother, I couldn't wait to get to Moscow."[239] Although numerous writers and other well-placed figures expressed gratitude for the hospitality of their Uzbek hosts, which Kornei Chukovskii described in his diary as "inexhaustible," few, even among these groups, regarded Tashkent as a "native home."[240] Only Akhmatova embraced Tashkent as her own: "Who dares to tell me, that here / I am in a foreign land?"[241] In a statement that was probably typical of many evacuees, Tatiana Lugovskaia wrote, "it is better to live in the cold but in your homeland [*na rodine*]."[242] Lydia Chukovskaia agreed. She recalled that although Akhmatova came to love Tashkent, she never could. "It is easy to die in a foreign land . . . ," she

[235] The most notable historical works, both published by evacuees in Tashkent, were R. Iu. Vipper's *Ivan Groznyi* and S. V. Bakhrushin's book of the same name. On representations of Ivan the Terrible in Tashkent, see Perrie, *Cult of Ivan the Terrible*, 92–99, 129–36.

[236] See Perrie, *Cult of Ivan the Terrible*, 19, and Nechkina's review of Vipper's book on Ivan IV in *Pravda Vostoka*, January 16, 1942.

[237] Deich, *Den' nineishii*, 155.

[238] Letter to E. B. Pasternak, December 12, 1942, in Boris Pasternak and Evgenii Pasternak, *Sushchestvovania tkan' skvoznaia: Boris Pasternak perepiska s Evgeniei Pasternak, dopolnennaia pis'mami k E. B. Pasternaku i ego vospominaniiami* (Moscow: Novoe literaturnoe obozrenie, 1998), 454.

[239] Ibid., 458.

[240] Chukovskii, *Dnevnik*, 160, entry of October 30, 1941. Militsa Nechkina later wrote, "Tashkent welcomed us with great hospitality, as its own." "V dni voiny," 34.

[241] Quoted in Babaev, *Vospominaniia*, 9.

[242] Letter to L. Maliugin, 1942, in Tat'iana Lugovskaia, *Kak znaiu, kak pomniu, kak umeiu. Vospominaniia, pis'ma, dnevniki* (Moscow: Agraf, 2001), 260.

began a poem in early 1942, "only one should not live in a foreign land, not for nothing is it foreign."[243] As these comments suggest, for most evacuees Tashkent remained inescapably alien. Although the city's inhabitants contributed to "our war," Uzbekistan was not "our land." The motherland was not here, in Central Asia, but there, in the war-torn landscape to the west.

Evacuees pined for the places they had left behind. Stepanishcheva described how at work, when there was a free moment, she and her colleagues used to "recall our prewar Moscow. Everything in that life of ours seemed wonderful and attractive. We forgot the communal apartments, the lines, the ration system, the persistent shortage of goods, the arrests of our relatives and acquaintances—we remembered only the good."[244] A similar nostalgia for places left behind permeates the correspondence of evacuees. Tatiana Lugovskaia wrote to a friend, "I remember snow as if it were a pastry, and the Moscow air raids and everything else I remember as some kind of very rich event in my life."[245] In Tashkent, as elsewhere, evacuees yearned to return to their homes. In Nadezhda Mandelstam's words, "everyone dreams of Moscow."[246] The return, however, was in many ways as complicated as the search for refuge. Moreover, only with their return could evacuees assess the true significance of their "Central Asian evaco-interlude,"[247] as one writer aptly termed it, and the extent to which the "old life" really was a thing of the past.

---

[243] "Na chuzhoi zemle umeret' legko . . . Tol'ko zhit' nelz'ia na chuzhoi zemle. Nedarom ona chuzhaia." Lidiia Chukovskaia, *Po etu storonu smerti: iz dnevnika 1936–1976* (Paris: YMCA Press, 1978), 28 January, 1942.

[244] Stepanishcheva, "Vot tak i zhizn' proshla," l. 25.

[245] Letter to L. Maliugin, February 14, 1942, in Lugovskaia, *Kak znaiu,* 256.

[246] N. Ia. Mandel'shtam to B. S. Kuzin, September 19, 1942, in Mandel'shtam, *192 pis'ma,* 684.

[247] "Iz dnevnikov A. M. Faiko," ed. N. G. Koroleva, in Tsentral'nyi gosudarstvennyi arkhiv literatury i iskusstva SSSR, *Vstrechi s proshlym,* vol. 5 (Moscow: Sovetskaia Rossiia, 1984), 304, entry of November 23, 1943.

8

THE RETURN

"Everyone is leaving Tashkent, one after another," Nadezhda Mandel-stam observed in the fall of 1943.[1] The city was indeed, in Tatiana Lugov-skaia's words, "emptying out,"[2] so much so that Anna Akhmatova reported in a letter of late September that "everyone has left Tashkent."[3] The "evaco-interlude" was drawing to a close. By the fall of 1943, the fortunes of war had shifted. The Red Army had halted its long retreat and was now on the offensive. Tashkent, like other Soviet cities, was abuzz with news of liberation. Evacuees began to pack their bags.

The reevacuation began as a trickle in 1942 but accelerated dramatically in 1943 and especially 1944, as increasingly large swathes of territory were returned to Soviet rule. Statistics on departures from Tashkent roughly mirror developments on the front, albeit with a significant delay: they record successive waves of people departing first for Moscow (especially in 1943 and 1944), then for Kharkov, followed by Kiev, then Leningrad, and finally Odessa.[4] The seemingly inexorable flow of people, however, should not obscure the obstacles encountered by those seeking to return. Although evacuation had always been envisioned as a temporary measure, the process of return was anything but automatic. Much like the evacuation itself, the state conceived of the reevacuation as a form of managed migration. The continued strain and shortages of war as well as authorities' long-standing

---

[1] N. Ia. Mandel'shtam to B. S. Kuzin, August 29, 1943, in Nadezhda Mandel'shtam, *192 pis'ma k B. Kuzinu*, ed. N. I. Kraineva and E. A. Perezhogina (St. Petersburg: Inapress, 1999), 715.

[2] Letter to L. Maliugin, 1943, in Tat'iana Lugovskaia, *Kak znaiu, kak pomniu, kak umeiu. Vospominaniia, pis'ma, dnevniki* (Moscow: Agraf, 2001), 276.

[3] A. A. Akhmatova to I. N. Tomashevskaia, September 27, 1943; Z. B. Tomashevskaia, "Ia—kak peterburgskaia tumba."

[4] RGAE, f. 1562, op. 20, d. 461, ll. 85–86; d. 549, ll. 29–30; d. 551, ll. 1–2.

suspicion of unorganized migration made them anxious to control the flow of people. Evacuees accordingly had to go to considerable lengths to acquire permission to return. Thus did evacuation draw ever closer to exile.

The journey home bore little resemblance to the journey into evacuation. In the aftermath of the invasion, evacuees had set out for destinations unknown, with little idea of what awaited them. Now they returned to places they had lived in for years, places that had occupied their dreams, their waking hours. Yet the return was replete with uncertainties of its own. Evacuees returned to a land that had been transformed by the war. The succession of invasion, occupation, and liberation had left no place untouched. It was not just the physical landscape that had changed. Soviet society had also changed, as had the social order. While evacuees found themselves as reliant as ever on networks and connections, they now had to confront the fact that they were returning not simply as writers or workers but as evacuees, as people who had spent the war in the rear, far from the front lines. All too often, evacuation became a source of stigma. For the Soviet Union's many Jewish evacuees, the return was particularly fraught. Not only did they return to a land "without Jews," but they returned, whether they liked it or not, as Jews. By the end of the war, this identity was anything but neutral. For all evacuees, the return was a complicated affair, and the legacy of evacuation long-lasting.

THE REGULATION OF RETURN

Although not all hastened to make the journey home, many were eager to depart. "I cannot remain in Tashkent any longer," Evgenia Pasternak wrote to her former husband.[5] Some were driven from Tashkent by the living conditions, which were, as one woman put it in a petition to depart, "truly difficult."[6] Others sought respite from the climate. The "climate here is dangerous for me and I need to leave," one Odessite wrote in an appeal to return.[7] Olga Boltianskaia was so affected by the Tashkent climate that her doctor advised her to leave the city as soon as possible, to escape the "heat and the stuffiness."[8] Many had simply grown weary of life in a faraway and foreign city. "I have had it up to here with Asia," proclaimed the writer Paustovskii, in evacuation in neighboring Kazakhstan, in a letter to Fadeev, head of the Union of Soviet Writers. "Remaining here is not only

---

[5] Letter of July 1, 1943, in Boris Pasternak and Evgenii Pasternak, *Sushchestvovania tkan' skvoznaia: Boris Pasternak perepiska s Evgeniei Pasternak, dopolnennaia pis'mami k E. B. Pasternaku i ego vospominaniiami* (Moscow: Novoe literaturnoe obozrenie, 1998), 464.

[6] RGALI, f. 631, op. 15, d. 649, l. 67.

[7] GAOO, f. P17, op. 4, d. 20, l. 62.

[8] Diary of O. A. Boltianskaia, RGALI, f. 2057, op. 2, d. 30, l. 44, entry of May 24, 1943.

pointless . . . but is becoming a form of self-destruction. Outside Russia, I can no longer live nor work."[9]

More significant than the frustration with life in evacuation was the fervent desire to return home. As one Odessite in Tashkent put it in a letter seeking help in the process of return: "I want to be in Odessa, Odessa, Odessa!"[10] Indeed, evacuees yearned for the places they had left behind. "I am dying to be back in Moscow," Tatiana Lugovskaia wrote in a letter to a friend.[11] Similarly, Kochetkov "pine[d] for Moscow in such a frenzied manner that it seems I simply won't survive, unless I return to my homeland this spring."[12] Nor were such sentiments confined to writers. A worker from Moscow's Stalin automobile factory, evacuated to Ulianovsk, later recalled the "craving" to return to Moscow that prevailed among the factory's workers. Although acutely aware of the difficult living conditions in Moscow, "they were drawn there, . . . back to Moscow. . . . These attitudes were called, at the time, 'suitcase moods' [chemodannoe nastroenie]."[13]

In Tashkent, as elsewhere, the first to undertake the journey home were residents of Moscow, which had narrowly escaped occupation. Vsevolod Ivanov noted in his diary in early September 1942, that "everyone is preparing to leave for Moscow."[14] Although many prepared, only a select and privileged few initially departed. Ivanov himself left in late October, Kornei Chukovskii in January. Nadezhda Mandelstam aptly described the situation in a letter that fall: "whoever can—or rather, whoever has received a summons—returns."[15]

As Mandelstam's comment suggests, the "reevacuation," like the evacuation itself, was regulated by state authorities. Wartime restrictions on freedom of movement, which made train travel dependent on the permission of the police, remained in effect until the summer of 1946.[16] Permits for train travel, in turn, were frequently contingent on the presentation of a summons issued by authorities in the intended destination. Return thus depended on the authorization of various agencies, including municipal or regional soviets as well as the local police. Valentin Berestov, in his memoirs,

[9] N. I. Dikushina, ed., *Aleksandr Fadeev: pis'ma i dokumenty iz fondov Rossiiskogo gosudarstvennogo arkhiva literatury i iskusstv* (Moscow: Izdatel'stvo Literaturnogo instituta im. A. M. Gor'kogo, 2001), 237.

[10] I. T. Liandres to A. V. Nedvedskii, June 18, 1944, "Komplekt pis'ma odessitov A. V. Nedvedskomu s pros'boi pomoshch' vernutsia v Odessu prednaznachennyi N. A. Litovchenko," Odesskii evreiskii muzei.

[11] Letter to L. Maliugin, July 22, 1942, in Lugovskaia, *Kak znaiu*, 262.

[12] RGALI, f. 631, op. 15, d. 650, l. 3.

[13] TsAGM, f. 415, op. 16, d. 293, ll. 80–81.

[14] Vsevolod Ivanov, *Dnevniki* (Moscow: IMLI RAN, Nasledie, 2001), 130, entry of September 5, 1942.

[15] N. Ia. Mandel'shtam to B. S. Kuzin, September 19, 1942, in Mandel'shtam, *192 pis'ma*, 684.

[16] M. N. Potemkina, *Evakuatsiia v gody Velikoi Otechestvennoi voiny na Ural: liudi i sud'bi* (Magnitogorsk: Magnitogorskii gosudarstvennyi universitet, 2002), 182–83.

lists the range of documents required for the journey west. He recalls how his mother permitted him to leave Tashkent before the rest of the family as he "would soon be sixteen, the end of my freedom of movement—passport, summons, permit, registration. . . . A Muscovite, an employee [who worked with Berestov's mother], agreed to enter me in her permit as her son."[17]

Thus began, for many evacuees, yet another bureaucratic odyssey, this time in search of the paperwork that would secure the passage home.[18] Like the evacuation itself, the return required the mobilization of institutional, patronage, and personal networks, a task made more difficult by distance. Consider the case of Olga Boltianskaia, who had been evacuated to Tashkent in organized fashion as the wife of a film director. The first attempt to secure her return to Moscow was spearheaded by her son, who had been demobilized due to an injury and was conveniently located in Moscow, where he could appeal directly to officials on the Cinematography Committee.[19] Her husband later initiated a more sustained attempt following his own summons back to the capital to continue his work. Shortly after his return, he wrote to an official on the committee, who then forwarded the request to another official, but it took sheer coincidence (running into a third official at the right moment) for him to have his wife and younger son inserted on the lists of those slated to return.[20]

Boltianskaia's case exemplifies the crucial role played by institutional networks as well as the sustained efforts that were required of evacuees. These efforts are readily apparent in the voluminous archives of the Writers' Union, whose officials were inundated with requests for return. "I once again beg you, Peter Georgievich [Skosyrev]," one such letter began, "to do everything possible so that my family and I can return to Moscow. . . . I know I have already plagued you with my letters and telegrams."[21] The writer Pavel German was not far off the mark when he wrote Skosyrev, in an appeal of his own, that "I can well imagine the flood of letters and telegrams with requests for summons that you receive from every corner of the country."[22]

---

[17] Valentin Berestov, *Izbrannye proizvedeniia*, 2 vols. (Moscow: Izdatel'stvo imeni Sabashnikovykh, 1998), vol. 2, 248.

[18] To be sure, some evacuees returned as part of an organized mass reevacuation to a specific region, and thus faced few of the bureaucratic obstacles encountered by others. Such mass reevacuations, however, were authorized only for specific regions and accounted for only a small percentage of the returning population. In 1944, for example, only 12% of those who returned from evacuation in the Russian Republic were reevacuated in organized fashion on the orders of the government. The vast majority of reevacuees (1,699,200 of a total of 1,928,600) were either reevacuated by a ministry, department, or organization or returned in "unorganized" fashion. GARF, f. A-327, op. 2, d. 710, ll. 38–39.

[19] Diary of O. A. Boltianskaia, RGALI, f. 2057, op. 2, d. 30, l. 45, entry of May 24, 1943.

[20] Much to everyone's dismay, however, their housekeeper, whom Boltianskii presented as his "foster daughter," was not included in the list on the grounds that she was over sixteen and thus could not be considered a dependent. Ibid., ll. 85, 87, entries of August 1 and 23, 1943.

[21] RGALI, f. 631, op. 15, d. 642, l. 85.

[22] Ibid., d. 759, l. 75.

Although the letters varied in their details, each one was designed to justify a summons, not simply to request one. "Life here has become unbearable in all respects," one evacuated writer in Tashkent wrote. She recognized that life in Moscow would not be easy, but "all the difficulties . . . will be excused by the fact that I am home."[23] Supplicants cited moral hardship as well as material difficulties in their appeals. "If my spiritual condition does not improve, I fear that it may end badly," Berestinskii warned in the conclusion to the letter cited above. "This is not empty chatter."[24] In a similar vein, Kochetkov informed Skosyrev, "it seems that I simply won't survive, unless I return to my homeland this spring." Insisting that "I will be more useful in Moscow now than here," Kochetkov sought to persuade Skosyrev, "my dear friend," that he could act on this request "with a clean conscience. All the more so, since my family is portable: there is just my wife."[25] Kochetkov was one of numerous evacuees to couch his request in the register of service to the country. Skosyrev had used the same language himself in the first winter of the war when he, too, had found himself stranded in Tashkent.[26] In a similar spirit, some sought to justify their requests with reference to ostensibly pressing projects that could be completed only in Moscow. The writer Kirill Levin appealed to Skosyrev for an urgent summons to Moscow to complete a story about General Brusilov, for which he needed access to materials located in the capital: "The thought that this important and much needed work . . . will not be realized is unbearable to me." (In a separate letter to another official written less than two months earlier, he described another current project, this one a novel set in wartime Moscow, that likewise necessitated his immediate return.)[27]

Writers were privileged by their proximity to power. Successful supplicants were included on lists submitted to the highest authorities in the land. Fadeev appealed to Molotov himself for authorization for the return of Vladimir Lugovskoi and his extended family (including their housekeeper who was presented as his sister).[28] Molotov was likewise called on to approve the reevacuation of a list of evacuated writers and their families submitted by Skosyrev in June 1943, a list that included Kochetkov as well as Faiko and numerous others.[29]

The cultural and intellectual elite, however, were by no means the only ones to benefit from institutional connections. Factories and other institutions routinely requested summons from city authorities on behalf of their former workers and employees. Berta Pashkova, for instance, was issued a summons to return from Tashkent to Odessa on the basis of an appeal by

[23] Ibid., d. 605, l. 150.
[24] Ibid., d. 642, l. 86.
[25] Ibid., d. 644, l. 3.
[26] Ibid., d. 572, l. 28.
[27] Ibid., d. 605, ll. 7, 8.
[28] Ibid., d. 650, l. 16.
[29] Ibid., d. 649, ll. 43, 45.

the administration of the municipal sewer system, which had employed her before the war as an accountant. In a similar vein, Rosa Livshits was summoned from Tashkent back to Odessa to resume her post as director of a home for invalids, which she had held for several years before the war. Both of these women would be needed to help establish the postwar order. So too, evidently, would the tailor Khaim Rakhgendler, who was summoned from Tashkent back to Odessa to work in a special clothing workshop serving the local party and Soviet elite.[30]

Others were reevacuated with the organizations that employed them in evacuation. Zinaida Stepanishcheva, who had been evacuated in individual fashion, accepted a low-paying job in Tashkent in an evacuated institute with the sole aim of facilitating her return home. Although her new salary was less than the one she had received at the veterinary institute in which she had already found work, the new job was with an institute from Moscow. As one of her future colleagues pointed out to her, "organizations will return to Moscow first, and individuals only later. As a member of the institute you will return with us. But alone, how will you get out of here?" Stepanishcheva's gamble paid off. When the institute was summoned back to Moscow, she was included on the list of those slated to return.[31]

Those who were "alone" were compelled to navigate more circuitous channels. Georgii Efron, the adolescent son of the deceased poet Marina Tsvetaeva, appealed to the wife of Alexei Tolstoi with a letter intended, in his words, to "spur her to action that will aid my reevacuation."[32] The letter evidently had the desired effect: the Tolstois appealed on Efron's behalf to Skosyrev, who agreed to include Efron on the next list of writers slated to return.[33] An evacuee from Odessa who lacked any direct institutional connections of his own appealed to two friends, both editors of a journal in Odessa, in a bid to secure his return. Although he had not been previously employed by the journal, he wrote that "your summons is the only way for me to get out of here." "I know it is not easy, but you can do it if you want to, and, in the name of our friendship, you must do it! . . . I beg you to do what I ask of you. In any case, I won't give you a minute's peace . . . until I receive a summons from you."[34]

---

[30] GAOO, f. R1234, op. 7, d. 289, l. 104; d. 290, l. 81; d. 289, l. 231.

[31] Z. G. Stepanishcheva, "Vot tak i zhizn' proshla," ll. 21, 36.

[32] Quoted in N. A. Gromova, *Vse v chuzhoe gliadiat okno* (Moscow: Sovershenno sekretno, 2002), 261.

[33] Georgii Efron, *Dnevniki (1941–1943 gody)*, vol. 2, ed. E. B. Korkina and V. K. Losskaia (Moscow: Vagrius, 2005), 201, 223, 266–67, entries of March 25, April 29, and May 14, 1943. However, even with the permit, Efron was not able to leave Tashkent for another two to three months as he was unable to procure a train ticket. As he put it in his diary, "I can't get a ticket on my own (the 'normal' way—going and buying a ticket—is out of the question, for there are thousands of people and fights there, I don't have any kind of *blat*, and I am not in a position to pay an 'agent' 1,000 rubles)." Ibid., 285, entry of July 5, 1943.

[34] I. T. Liandres to A. V. Nedvedksii, June 18, 1944, "Komplekt pis'ma odessitov A. V. Nedvedkomu s pros'boi pomoshch' vernutsia v Odessu," Odesskii evreiskii muzei.

As these examples suggest, personal networks could be as important as institutional ones. Evgenia Pasternak is a case in point. Her appeal to the Union of Soviet Artists, of which she was a member, was unsuccessful, whereupon she asked her former husband, a writer, for help. Unsure which organization would actually issue the summons (the Moscow Division of the Union of Soviet Artists, the Organizational Committee of the Union of Artists, or the Committee of the Arts), she nonetheless insisted, "your intervention and request would have some effect, knowing how much you are respected and liked in our milieu." Failing that, she suggested that he might simply go through the Union of Soviet Writers, for "all the [writers'] families have already left for Moscow, and not only the wives and children but in general all the relations and relatives, house-keepers, cousins, . . . and so on."[35]

Family members played a particularly prominent role in the process. Consider the case of the Eliutins, friends living with Stepanishcheva in Tashkent. "A permit for Raisa Andreevna was acquired by her son, efforts on behalf of an aunt were made by the aunt's husband, but Liusia was a widow; there was no one to make efforts on her behalf and she had no permit."[36] Among the many female evacuees in Tashkent, those who could turned to husbands, sons, and brothers at the front for help in securing the summons required to return. Thus an appeal for the return of Odessite Rosalia Glushkin, in evacuation in Tashkent with her three young children, was submitted by her husband, an officer in the army.[37] In many cases, the men who sought to secure summons for their wives had been wounded in the war. Appeals on behalf of Rosa Mirlik, Zinaida Levina, and Bella Khamut, all of whom were in Tashkent with their children, came from invalids, whose petitions underscored their new state of dependence on their families: as Bella Khamut's husband put it, "I cannot be alone."[38] The state of dependence was clearly mutual. Without their husbands' intervention, these women would be stranded in Central Asia. While Levina, for instance, had worked before the war, her position as an accountant in the Odessa hotel trust did not, presumably, put her high on the list of those slated to return. Levina's husband put it plainly in his appeal: "she cannot leave due to the absence of a summons."[39] Those whose husbands had died in the war had a particularly difficult time. Stepanishcheva's friend Lusia had no one to petition on her behalf and did not receive a summons. Liubov Radulianskaia, who lost her husband and her father at the front, would have been in a similar position had it not been for

[35] Letter to B. L. Pasternak, July 1, 1943, in Pasternak and Pasternak, *Sushchestvovania tkan' skvoznaia*, 464.
[36] Z. G. Stepanishcheva, "Vot tak i zhizn' proshla," l. 37.
[37] GAOO, f. R1234, op. 7, d. 289, l. 270.
[38] Ibid., l. 182; d. 290, l. 429; d. 289, l. 240.
[39] Ibid., d. 290, l. 429.

the intervention of her brother, who survived the war as a military tailor and submitted a petition on her behalf.[40]

The general pattern whereby women depended on men to secure their return reflected the gender dynamics of the war and the evacuation: the vast majority of adults in evacuation were women, and the majority of those in a position to petition on behalf of family members were men. There were, however, numerous exceptions, spawned both by the extraordinary death toll among men and the increasingly important role played by women in the war effort and the tasks of reconstruction. By the end of the war, women accounted for over half of the national workforce.[41] Moreover, there were a substantial number of women serving on the front lines who could count on the military to support their appeals.[42] One such woman, in a petition requesting the return of her family from Tashkent, noted, "I am the only able-bodied member of the family remaining." Her father had died in evacuation only days before the end of the war, her mother was sick and no longer able to work, her sixteen-year-old sister was still too young, and her slightly older brother was blind and thus also unable to work. Her only able-bodied brother had died on the front. The commander of her division, who wrote supporting her appeal, noted that the entire family now depended on her.[43]

By the end of the war, many women were in the same predicament. Dora Dvoretskaia, who had spent the war in evacuation in Uzbekistan, was one of them. Her parents were both sick and her husband had died from wounds inflicted at the front in 1942. An electrical engineer, she had returned to her native Odessa in early 1945, leaving her elderly parents and young child in Samarkand. As she later explained, they "did not have warm clothing, and I didn't know what the state of our apartment was, so I had to leave them in Samarkand." Now, she appealed for permission for their return as her dependents.[44] Rosa Livshits, who had been summoned from Tashkent to Odessa to resume her work as director of a home for invalids, made a similar appeal. Although Livshits had brought her six-year-old granddaughter with

[40] Ibid., d. 289, l. 74.

[41] In 1945, 56% of people employed in the Soviet economy were women, as opposed to the prewar figure of 39%. Although the overall workforce shrank in this period, the absolute number of women rose by almost three million. See Sheila Fitzpatrick, "War and Society in Soviet Context: Soviet Labor before, during, and after World War II," *International Labor and Working-Class History* 35 (1989): 42.

[42] Current estimates put the number of women who served in the Red Army at around eight hundred thousand. See John Erickson, "Soviet Women at War," in *World War 2 and the Soviet People*, ed. John Garrard, Carol Garrard, and Stephen White (New York: St. Martin's, 1993), 50. On the participation of women in the army, see also Suzanne Conze and Beate Fieseler, "Soviet Women as Comrades-in-Arms," in *The People's War: Responses to World War II in the Soviet Union*, ed. Robert W. Thurston and Bernd Bonwetsch (Urbana: University of Illinois Press, 2000), 211–34.

[43] GAOO, f. R1234, op. 7, d. 290, ll. 398, 396.

[44] Ibid., l. 48.

her to Odessa, she had left her daughter Sonia, the girl's mother, and her son, an invalid, in Tashkent. Her appeal on her children's behalf, which was supported by the oblast administrators in charge of the home in which she worked, was the best chance Sonia and her brother had: Sonia's husband had been killed in the war, and Rosa's other son, their brother, had died of his wounds the previous summer.[45]

In addition to institutional and personal connections, the success of the appeals made by evacuees or on their behalf depended on the timing of their requests and the places they sought to return to. Moscow, though never occupied, was subject to restrictions from the outset. As early as September 1941, any return to the city required the explicit authorization of municipal authorities.[46] In January 1942, access to the city was further restricted by a decree that forbade organizations from reevacuating their employees without the permission of both the city soviet and the Moscow party organization.[47] Even in 1944, when the State Defense Committee established a three-month window to review requests for reevacuation to the capital, those who lacked living space were refused entrance and a full 20 percent of requests were turned down.[48] Access to the Ukrainian capital of Kiev, though not nearly as restrictive, was nonetheless limited to those with a "transfer, agreement, or invitation to work here by an institution, organization, or enterprise." Those "arriving in the city in an unorganized manner" were, at least in theory, denied entrance.[49] Return to Leningrad, once the blockade was lifted, was particularly tightly controlled. As late as the spring of 1945, the government stipulated that only children evacuated with children's organizations would be automatically permitted to return, and that all others had to receive special authorization.[50] It was only in September and October of that year, months after the war had already ended, that a more general reevacuation to Leningrad was initiated.[51] As in the case of Moscow, authorization to return required proof of living space. Similar conditions were imposed, in somewhat weaker form, in Odessa, Kiev, and Kharkov.[52]

---

[45] Ibid., ll. 81–83.

[46] GARF, f. 259, op. 40, d. 3035, ll. 77–78.

[47] The decree is reprinted in K. I. Bukov, M. M. Gorinov, and A. N. Ponomarev, eds., *Moskva voennaia, 1941–1945. Memuary i arkhivnye dokumenty* (Moscow: Mosgorarkhiv, 1995), 381.

[48] GARF, f. 5446, op. 46, d. 2244, l. 27. According to the passport division, 9,447 reevacuees were refused registration in Moscow. GARF, f. 9415, op. 3, d. 1412, l. 15.

[49] Martin J. Blackwell, "Regime City of the First Category: The Experience of the Return of Soviet Power to Kyiv, Ukraine, 1943–1946" (Ph.D. diss., Indiana University, 2005), 67.

[50] TsGASPb, f. 7384, op. 17, d. 1514, l. 46.

[51] GARF, f. A-327, op. 2, d. 720, l. 5.

[52] In Kiev, the requirement was imposed only in 1946. Blackwell, "Regime City of the First Category," 141. In Odessa, such measures appear to have been in effect somewhat earlier, in that people who lacked living space were often denied registration. As one Odessite explained in an attempt to secure the return of his family in the summer of 1946, he had been demobilized in December 1945, but "given that my apartment was destroyed and I did not have living

Restrictions were much less firm in a host of regions recently liberated from the enemy. Much to the chagrin of central authorities in Moscow, regional officials made little effort to control the flood of people. As one report by authorities in the Russian Republic put it, the "oblast executive committees of liberated regions have allowed the mass return of evacuees to their previous places of residence." The result was a "disruption of the normal functioning of railway stations" and the "threat of outbreaks of epidemics."[53] In an attempt to impose a semblance of order on the process, the Russian republican government passed a resolution in the spring of 1944 prohibiting authorities in liberated regions from undertaking any large scale reevacuation "without the special authorization of the government." It further demanded that liberated regions come up with "reevacuation plans," to be submitted for approval.[54] Although government decrees subsequently authorized the return of evacuees to a range of different regions, most appeared after the war had already ended and did not include all regions.[55] Moreover, in mid-November 1944, the State Defense Committee called an all-out halt to reevacuations for the duration of the winter.[56] In accordance with this decree, return to many places was temporarily forbidden. In Odessa, the city soviet had standard forms drawn up which informed their recipients that "your request for permission to return to Odessa cannot at present be fulfilled due to circumstances beyond our control." As municipal authorities informed one individual requesting permission to return to his native city, "in accordance with a government decision . . . , entry into Odessa, without specific permission, is temporarily forbidden until April 1, 1945." Insisting on the "necessity" of maintaining the ban, the letter further invoked the "difficult conditions associated with the beginning of winter and the tense situation in the city in terms of supplying the population with fuel, housing, bread, light and water."[57]

As the letter from authorities in Odessa makes clear, the reevacuation put a strain on newly liberated areas. With limited housing stock and a severe shortage of supplies, these regions were hardly in a position to receive a steady stream of new inhabitants. The mass return of evacuees threatened cities and their residents with shortages of food and other goods and with a range of infectious diseases. At the same time, the task of rebuilding necessitated a return of select sectors of the workforce.[58] Population levels in

---

space, I was not able to secure a summons for my family." GAOO, f. R1234, op. 7, d. 363, l. 222. It was common in appealing for permission to return to include proof of living space. See, for example, GAOO, f. R1234, op. 7, d. 194.

[53] GARF, f. A-327, op. 2, d. 377, l. 31.

[54] Ibid., l. 29.

[55] See Potemkina, *Evakuatsiia v gody Velikoi Otechestvennoi voiny na Ural*, 181–82.

[56] GARF, f. A-327, op. 2, d. 710, l. 39.

[57] GAOO, f. R1234, op. 7, d. 290, ll. 449, 104.

[58] For a discussion of the difficulties these conflicting goals could engender, see Blackwell, "Regime City of the First Category," chaps. 1 and 2.

formerly occupied territory had dropped dramatically, and many evacuees specialized in fields that would be required for rebuilding. People such as the engineer Dora Dvoretskaia were thus summoned to their native city despite the dire conditions.[59]

The imperative to rebuild, however, could cut both ways. Whereas the demands of reconstruction necessitated the return of some, the need to keep the economy running mitigated against the return of others, such as workers employed in evacuated factories. In a bid to maintain production and to avoid the inevitable economic disruption that would follow the transfer of a factory or a large portion of its workforce, a substantial number of factories were kept in evacuation. General reevacuation plans explicitly targeted people "not working in industrial enterprises."[60] Unauthorized departures, moreover, carried substantial risk. Stricter labor laws introduced in 1940 and tightened during the war made departure from work a criminal offense.[61] The central newspaper of Uzbekistan, *Pravda Vostoka*, contained cautionary tales of what might happen should one attempt an unauthorized return. In early January 1942, the paper contained an article about three men who had been evacuated with their factory, which was engaged in the production of defense-related materials. The paper reported that "on December 27, 1941, the men willfully abandoned their place of work and went to Moscow." According to the article, only one week later they were arrested and sentenced to eight years in prison.[62] Such draconian measures remained in effect well into the postwar period.[63]

As a result, many workers had to remain indefinitely "in evacuation." In one city after another, evacuated workers voiced their frustration. "This whole time, three and a half years, we lived and continue to live like soldiers at war, that is, we have nothing except a suitcase and a knapsack," complained a group of workers from Kharkov at a factory in Sverdlovsk.[64] Although the life of a soldier was acceptable in a country at war, it was no longer so once the war had ended. For evacuated workers, many of whom conceived of their wartime work as a fulfillment of military duty, return seemed like a just reward for their sacrifices and service rendered. "Evacuees in Siberia worked for four years in difficult conditions for the front," an evacuated worker in Omsk exclaimed. "The war is over; when will the factory be reevacuated?"[65] A collective letter to the Supreme Soviet from evacuated workers in Ordzhonikidze expressed a similar sentiment: "When the military situation demanded sacrifices and deprivation of us, when, to save the motherland, we

[59] GAOO, f. R1234, op. 7, d. 290, l. 48.
[60] GARF, f. A-327, op. 2, d. 720, l. 9.
[61] Fitzpatrick, "War and Society in Soviet Context," 41, 44.
[62] *Pravda Vostoka*, January 9, 1942.
[63] Fitzpatrick, "War and Society in Soviet Context," 46.
[64] GARF, f. 7253, op. 65, d. 579, l. 65.
[65] RGASPI, f. 17, op. 88, d. 649, l. 232.

had to leave our elders, our wives, and our young children to the mercy of fate—we did this." Now, however, they wanted, and expected, to go home. As a group of miners from the Donbass put it, "we worked selflessly during the war. Now the war has ended; let us return to our children."[66]

For those denied permission to return, evacuation became a form of exile. "The war has ended; why do they want to forcefully keep us in Siberia?" a factory worker in Omsk asked.[67] Workers expected an end to their wartime sacrifices and were frustrated by authorities' refusal to permit them to return home. State policy, however, though clearly disappointing, was hardly surprising. The insistence on keeping workers in place was consistent both with immediate prewar policies and with developments during the war. It grew out of a system in which individuals were regarded as state resources and the state managed migration. It further reflected the stratification of Soviet society, which the collective sacrifice of the war years had done little to diminish.

In one respect, however, the reevacuation constituted a significant departure from prewar practices—in the treatment of the Soviet Union's Jewish population. The fate of Isaak Notkin, an evacuee in Tashkent and a member of Kiev's Industrial Institute, is emblematic of the new state of affairs. In a letter to Mikhoels, head of the Jewish Anti-Fascist Committee, Notkin described a strange succession of events:

> Finally that wonderful time arrived. Hopes were turning into reality. . . . Kiev was liberated. Lists were composed of workers of the Kiev Industrial Institute who were to be reevacuated to Kiev, and I, of course, was included on the lists. There was not a doubt among a single comrade or colleague regarding me. You can well imagine my disbelief and horror when it turned out that on the list of the institute's teachers who were to be reevacuated to Kiev my name was nowhere to be found.[68]

In the conclusion to his letter he asked: "Why don't I have the right to return to the place where I studied, worked, lived, was happy and suffered? How am I different from others who are analogous to me in formal terms and are no better than me when it comes to work?"[69] The answer to this question, though difficult to countenance, was clear. Notkin was Jewish.

Although Notkin did not explicitly identify his nationality as the source of his problems, others did. According to another member of the same institute, who also wrote Mikhoels, sixteen people had been left off the lists, "the overwhelming majority" of them Jews. "Although it seems absolutely unimaginable that there could be an antisemite active somewhere in our country,"

[66] GARF, f. 7253, op. 65, d. 579, l. 66.
[67] RGASPI, f. 17, op. 88, d. 649, l. 232.
[68] GARF, f. 8114, op. 1, d. 917, l. 34.
[69] Ibid., l. 35.

Notkin's colleague wrote, he could not explain what had happened except as a "manifestation of antisemitism."[70]

This was one of countless appeals dispatched to Members of the Jewish Anti-Fascist Committee about one and the same phenomenon—the refusal to permit Jews to return to their hometowns in previously occupied territory. In response, the committee wrote to Molotov: "Jewish workers who were temporarily evacuated by Soviet authorities to the remote rear are encountering obstacles in returning to their former places of residence. Even though the evacuees include skilled workers who could be of great benefit in the reconstruction of the devastated cities and villages, they are not being permitted to return."[71] Anecdotal evidence confirms the committee's arguments. Boris Rubenchik later recounted how his parents wanted to return to their native Odessa at the end of the war, but his father, an academic, was "explicitly not invited to return to Odessa University" (the same thing happened to a good friend of theirs) even though both were members of the Ukrainian Academy of Sciences.[72]

In a similar vein, the Jewish historian Saul Borovoi, who spent much of the war in the Uzbek city of Samarkand, later recalled how the directors of Odessa University, where he worked before the war, contacted some of his colleagues to make arrangements for their reevacuation. Having heard nothing himself, he contacted the director and received a "very evasive reply." In his memoirs, he recalls how "strange, at first glance seemingly implausible rumors began to circulate." The rumors held that Jews who had not obtained the status of full professor would not be permitted to return to Odessa and would instead be "turned over to the ministry to be appointed to jobs at its discretion." "The rumor," according to Borovoi, "was confirmed." He further recounts that on the journey back, at a station outside Odessa, "an older woman [baba], seeing me on the platform of the train, triumphantly cried: 'Where are you going? In Odessa there are no residence permits for Jews.'"[73]

The difficulties Borovoi and others encountered notwithstanding, the woman's claim was clearly exaggerated. Jews did receive permits to return to the city, and in large numbers. Among the countless Jews who were summoned back to their native Odessa from Tashkent were Berta Pashkova, Rosa Livshitz, and Khaim Rakhgendler. Despite persistent rumors regarding a directive stipulating the institution of quotas for Jews, no such document has ever been uncovered in former Soviet archives.[74] Nonetheless, there

[70] Ibid., d. 908, l. 15.

[71] Quoted in Mordechai Altshuler, ed. and trans., "Antisemitism in Ukraine toward the End of the Second World War," *Jews in Eastern Europe*, no. 3 (1993): 43.

[72] Boris Rubenchik, *Mesta i glavy zhizni tseloi* (St. Petersburg: Aleteiia, 2004), 45.

[73] Saul Borovoi, *Vospominaniia* (Moscow: Evreiskii universitet v Moskve, 1993), 284–85.

[74] Mordechai Altshuler has argued that "there is some evidence" that Ukrainian authorities "tried to limit, to the extent possible, the number of permits granted to Jews" to return to

were clearly substantial restrictions. Available evidence suggests that the at-tempt to restrict Jewish resettlement was directed at one sector of the Jewish population in particular, the cultural and intellectual elite. Those affected were employed in the cultural sphere, broadly defined: in institutes and acad-emies, in museums, and on theater boards. They were victims of the new policy that had already become apparent in Tashkent in 1942 and 1943, the same policy that had prevented Faina Ranevskaia from securing a role in Sergei Eisenstein's *Ivan the Terrible* and had prompted Mikhail Romm to write Stalin in distress over the removal of Jews from responsible positions in the film world. Whereas Jewish intellectuals and cultural figures often had difficulty securing permission to return, Jewish accountants, tailors, and engineers came back to their native cities in large numbers. Such "ordi-nary" Jews did face obstacles, but their difficulties were those common to all Soviet citizens. They were the difficulties born of wartime conditions and of a system in which residence rights were jealously guarded by the state.

THE ALTERNATIVES: "SPONTANEOUS REEVACUATION" AND PERMANENT EVACUATION

Those denied authorization to return—whether writers, workers, or Jews— had several choices. Among the Jewish members of Kiev's Industrial Insti-tute, some went to Moscow, others to Leningrad, and some remained in Tashkent. A fourth group returned to Kiev on their own, presumably secur-ing the passage home through connections, bribery, or simple evasion.[75] A friend in the military smuggled Maria Belkina back into Moscow, trans-porting her in his airplane and subsequently hiding her in the back of his car as his "personal goods."[76] Stepanishcheva's friend Liusia bribed one of the train's conductors to notify her of verifications, at which point "she hid under the bottom seat and was barricaded in with bundles and suitcases." The final leg of the journey Liusia made first by suburban train and then, once she reached the outskirts of Moscow, by foot. "Of course, it was a very risky journey," Stepanishcheva commented, "I probably would not have done it, but at that time many traveled in this way."[77] Among the many who returned without the required papers were factory workers who fled their

---

liberated districts. "Antisemitism in Ukraine," 42. As Gennadii Kostyrchenko concludes, how-ever, the absence of a written order does not preclude the transmission of oral instructions to the same effect. *Tainaia politika Stalina: Vlast' i antisemitizm* (Moscow: Mezhdunarodnye ot-nosheniia, 2001), 249.

[75] A hairstylist and her family reportedly paid 10,000 rubles to return to Kiev. Blackwell, "Regime City of the First Category," 63.

[76] Maria Belkina, *Skreshchenie sudeb*, 2d ed. (Moscow: Blagovest Rudomino, 1992), 362–63.

[77] Stepanishcheva, "Vot tak i zhizn' proshla," TsDNA, f. 422, l. 37.

factories rather than remain indefinitely in evacuation. At one factory in Omsk, workers estimated that as many as eight hundred people had left. Flight, however, was not an option for all. As one group of workers complained: "we, of course, have to stay here, because if you want to flee, you need money, and we don't have any."[78]

As these examples suggest, official regulations complicated but by no means forestalled the process of "spontaneous reevacuation," as the phenomenon was quickly christened.[79] Authorities complained about the "suitcase mood" of evacuees and their "willful departure from places of resettlement," but were frequently unable to control the flow of people.[80] Even where regulations were strictest, "spontaneous reevacuation" took on substantial proportions. "There are masses of people returning from evacuation," one Muscovite noted in her diary in early February 1942. "The *propiska* is difficult, but that doesn't stop anyone."[81] In the words of a report issued by passport authorities in Moscow two years later, a "large number of citizens have been brought to Moscow by enterprises or have willfully returned without permits and are currently living without registration."[82]

Although the need for a *propiska* certainly did not stop everyone, it did stop some. Nadezhda Mandelstam, for example, rejected a potential opportunity to return to Moscow with Akhmatova on the grounds that she would most certainly be denied registration.[83] Registration both conferred legal status and entitled residents to rations, which remained a crucial avenue of food distribution. Thus one young woman who returned to Moscow alone and without permission found herself starving in Moscow.[84] Data on departures from Tashkent sketch a telling story of the degree to which state controls inhibited many Muscovites from returning to their homes. Writers' impressions notwithstanding, most Muscovites remained in Tashkent until 1944, and some remained well into 1945 and even 1946.[85]

---

[78] RGASPI, f. 17, op. 117, d. 530, ll. 56, 54.

[79] GARF, f. A-327, op. 2, d. 68, l. 13.

[80] Ibid., d. 366, l. 52; d. 68, l. 11.

[81] N. M. Ponikarova, "Moskva, ispytanie voiny (leto 1941—vesna 1942)," *Moskovskii zhurnal*, no. 5 (1999): 29.

[82] GARF, f. 9415, op. 3, d. 1412, l. 14. In Kiev, the vast majority of returning evacuees had not received permission to return. After their arrival, however, many were successfully registered by the local police, even though they lacked the required documentation. Blackwell, "Regime City of the First Category," 138–39. Martin Blackwell has suggested that city authorities were willing to tolerate high levels of "unorganized" reevacuation in anticipation of future labor needs. Ibid., 154.

[83] N. Ia. Mandel'shtam to B. S. Kuzin, December 26, 1943, in Mandel'shtam, *192 pis'ma*, 722.

[84] GARF, f. 5446, op. 70, d. 10, l. 42.

[85] Although almost nine thousand Muscovites returned home in 1943, the number was even greater the next year, when over twelve thousand returned to their homes. Thereafter, the number of returning evacuees steadily declined from almost four thousand in 1945 to just over

Official regulations were not the only thing holding people back. Many were worried about what awaited them should they return. As Lydia Chukovskaia put it in a conversation with a number of other writers in 1942, "at present Moscow equals Tashkent's difficult daily life+ice+bombs."[86] Despite difficult conditions in evacuation, evacuees had worked hard to create a life for themselves in their new locales. In rural areas in particular, people had planted gardens and did not want to depart before harvesting the fruits of their labor.[87] Many, moreover, now had local jobs. Nadezhda Mandelstam, who as late as February 1944 described herself as "possessed by one idea—Moscow," wrote to a friend the following month: "I decided to remain in Tashkent, even though they are evidently sending me a permit for Moscow soon. But I think I'll let well enough alone. Here I have a place to live and a good job. . . . All this leads me to what is at first glance a very strange decision—I am turning down the possibility of returning home."[88] For many, a place to live was a deciding factor. In Gorky oblast, resettlement authorities reported in late 1945, "there are cases in which people refuse to return, as they have homes here, property, and in their hometowns there is nothing but ashes."[89] Similar considerations made Deborah Averbukh reluctant to return to Kiev. Her prewar home had been destroyed, and, as she later commented, "I didn't want to study there, in the ruins." Only the encouragement of her colleagues led her to reconsider her decision.[90]

The combination of official restrictions and individual reluctance significantly extended the evacuation. Two months after the war had ended, as many as 1.5 million evacuees remained in the Russian Republic alone. Although the numbers subsequently dwindled, there were still half a million evacuees in the republic by the end of 1946.[91] Thereafter, the numbers are deceptive. By the end of 1947, entire categories of evacuees had simply been "taken off the books," most prominently those compelled to remain with their factories as well as residents of Moscow and Leningrad who could not obtain living space in their native cities.[92] Henceforth, these people would no longer be considered evacuees. Subsequent counts of the evacuated population

---

fifteen hundred in 1946. RGAE, f. 1562, op. 20, d. 461, ll. 85–86; d. 549, ll. 29–30; d. 551, ll. 1–2.

[86] Lidiia Chukovskaia, *Zapiski ob Annoi Akhmatovoi, 1938–1941*, 5th ed., 2 vols. (Moscow: Soglasie, 1997), vol. 1, 385, entry of January 25, 1942.

[87] RGASPI, f. 17, op. 126, d. 9, l. 58.

[88] N. Ia. Mandel'shtam to B. S. Kuzin, February 19, 1944, and March 6, 1944, in Mandel'shtam, *192 pis'ma*, 726, 727.

[89] GARF, f. A-327, op. 2, d. 428, l. 95.

[90] Deborah Averbukh, interview by Ella Orlikova, December 2001, in *Jewish Witness to a European Century* (www.centropa.org).

[91] GARF, f. A-327, op. 2, d. 724, l. 2; d. 748, l. 2.

[92] See, for example, ibid., d. 738, l. 18. According to M. N. Potemkina, the number of those taken off the books was over two hundred thousand. *Evakuatsiia v gody Velikoi Otechestvennoi voiny na Ural*, 205.

shrank accordingly. A tally conducted in the middle of 1948 included only those who had opted to remain permanently in evacuation. The official count was twenty thousand, although in reality it was certainly higher.[93] Although comparable data for the Republic of Uzbekistan or the city of Tashkent are not available, we know that a significant number of people chose to remain. Mandelstam stayed in Tashkent for several years after the war. Many others remained until the end of their days, or until another wave of emigration brought them to Canada, Israel, the United States, or one of the other post-Soviet successor states. Most evacuees, however, departed.

THE JOURNEY HOME

The journey home was for many less arduous than the journey into evacuation. Zinaida Stepanishcheva later wrote: "we did not travel to Moscow in the same way as we had traveled to Tashkent. The train was a passenger train; we had a sleeper car. But they evidently had not managed to disinfect the car; lice crawled all over the walls."[94] Predictably, those who traveled in "organized" fashion traveled in greater comfort than those who set out on their own. Saul Borovoi recalled that the journey to Odessa from Samarkand, via Tashkent, lasted two months. Despite the length of the journey, he noted that the "echelon consisted of passenger cars, and we did not experience the difficulties that fell to the lot of those who attempted to get home on their own."[95] Olga Boltianskaia was optimistic as she set out on the journey from Tashkent to Moscow: "we will travel well; our traveling companions are cinematographers, cultured people, and I hope it will be clean and calm."[96] The Writers' Union did its utmost to facilitate the process of writers' reevacuation. Skosyrev asked Abdurakhmanov in late March 1943, to help with the reevacuation of writers. "I am sure that you will find a way to ease their journey to Moscow, not least in terms of supplies."[97] The Writers' Union provided Akhmatova with a car, and she and several other writers, including Vsevolod Ivanov, returned to Moscow by plane.[98]

Descriptions of the journey home almost invariably center on the change in landscape. Elena Bulgakova, in a letter to Lugovskoi, still in Tashkent, described her "unusual agitation" and "happiness" on the train as the bare

[93] GARF, f. A-327, op. 2, d. 748, l. 6. As indicated above, some of those who had chosen to remain had already been removed from the count of evacuees in 1947. See ibid., d. 738, l. 32, as well as Potemkina, *Evakuatsiia v gody Velikoi Otechestvennoi voiny na Ural*, 205. Moreover, this tally did not include those who still sought to return.

[94] Stepanishcheva, "Vot tak i zhizn' proshla," l. 37.

[95] Borovoi, *Vospominaniia*, 286.

[96] Diary of O. A. Boltianskaia, RGALI, f. 2057, op. 2, d. 30, l. 90, entry of September 10, 1943.

[97] RGALI, f. 631, op. 15, d. 650, l. 42.

[98] Eduard Babaev, *Vospominaniia* (St. Petersburg: Inapress, 2000), 15.

steppe of Kazakhstan gave way to a green landscape covered in bushes, trees, and forests.[99] Kornei Chukovskii traveled home in winter but was no less moved: "We are rejoicing in the birch trees, pine trees, snow, and ice," he wrote his daughter Lydia.[100] In a similar vein, Mariam Magarik, in a poetic rendition of her journey from Tashkent to Moscow written shortly after her return, rejoiced when her train passed Chkalov—the "end of Asia!"— and celebrated her first sighting of "Russia's sweet soil."[101]

The return was in many ways a journey back to the familiar, especially for Muscovites, who returned to a city that had been spared many of the ravages of war. Vsevolod Ivanov recorded his first impressions of Moscow on the Metro back from the airport. "My first sensation in the Metro car was happiness. Why? Because it was clean? Yes, perhaps: the residents here are cleaner, more discreet. But there's another thing—there are no Uzbeks, and everywhere you hear the Russian language. I harbor no grudge against the Uzbeks, to the contrary—I like them, but all the same, Moscow is Moscow!"[102]

Even in Moscow, however, the homecoming was often incomplete. Vsevolod Ivanov spent his first several months back in Moscow in a hotel, as his former home, in the writers' building on Lavrushinskii Lane, was intact but uninhabitable. Vladimir Lugovskoi's apartment, according to Elena Bulgakova, who returned to Moscow several months before Lugovskoi, was in terrible condition. "The wife of one Kornev, a writer, with her two three-year-old boys, lives there now. . . . The dirt is unimaginable." Neither the water nor the sewage were in working order, and many of the window panes were gone.[103] Boris Pasternak returned from Chistopol to find his apartment occupied by antiaircraft gunners.[104]

As these examples attest, not all those who returned to their native cities could go home. Across the country, in towns large and small, evacuees found their former homes destroyed, uninhabitable, or occupied by other residents. For some, return thus marked the onset of a new period of homelessness. As Deborah Averbukh later recalled, "I had no place to stay. Our house was destroyed." Averbukh's home in Kiev was one of many local residences—25 percent of the prewar total—that did not survive the war.[105] The rates for

[99] Quoted in Gromova, *Vse v chuzhoe gliadiat okno*, 240.
[100] Letter of January 31, 1943, in Kornei Chukovskii and Lidiia Chukovskaia, *Perepiska: 1912–1969*, ed. E. Ts. Chukovskaia and Zh. O. Khavkina (Moscow: Novoe literaturnoe obozrenie, 2004), 320.
[101] Mariam Isaakovna Magarik, "Mnogie veterany pishut nam pis'ma . . . stikhi," *Vestnik KEROOR "Da"*, no. 5 (www.corbina.net/~synrus/da5.html).
[102] Ivanov, *Dnevniki*, 176, entry of October 26, 1942.
[103] Quoted in Gromova, *Vse v chuzhoe gliadiat okno*, 249.
[104] Pasternak, letter of November 5, 1943, in *The Correspondence of Boris Pasternak and Olga Freidenberg*, ed. Elliott Mossman, trans. Margaret Wettlin (New York: Harcourt Brace Jovanovich, 1982), 228.
[105] Deborah Averbukh, interview. On the destruction of Kiev's housing see Blackwell, "Regime City of the First Category," 235.

other cities in formerly occupied territory were even higher. In Odessa, local authorities estimated that the city lost one-third of its housing during the war.[106] The housing crisis was particularly acute in the Belorussian cities of Minsk, Vitebsk, Gomel, and Mogilev, where authorities estimated that only 23 percent of the housing stock remained intact.[107]

Residents could not always go back even to intact housing. As one state prosecution official from the Dnepropetrovsk region wrote of returning evacuees: "Their living space has been occupied, in part on the orders of the housing division, after the liberation of the city, and in part during the occupation."[108] In some cases, squatters had moved in. Kharkov had suffered such great dislocation that, according to the oblast prosecutor, not a single person lived in the apartment where he or she had resided before the war.[109] In these circumstances, it was inevitable that many evacuees would return to find their living quarters already inhabited.

THE ADJUDICATION OF HOUSING CLAIMS

Although returnees could reclaim their apartments, they seldom succeeded without a battle. Boris Romanov, who returned to Leningrad to find his living quarters occupied, found himself embroiled in an "apartment war" that lasted a year and a half.[110] In 1945, such "apartment wars" accounted for almost half of the complaints regarding housing submitted to the Supreme Soviet.[111] The struggle to reclaim occupied housing was often the final step in bringing the "evaco-interlude" firmly to a close. For many, this was also the first step in the transition to life after the war. As such, it functioned as an important marker of people's place in the postwar order. For evacuees, this place was far from certain. Not only were their legal rights poorly defined, but they were also at a distinct disadvantage in the newly emerging hierarchy of entitlement.

In legal terms, although the vast majority of evacuees did not actually own their prewar apartments, they did have rights as tenants.[112] To be sure,

---

[106] GAOO, f. R1234, op. 7, d. 288, l. 45.

[107] RGASPI, f. 17, op. 88, d. 718, l. 20. For a discussion of the longevity of the postwar housing crisis, see Elena Zubkova, *Russia after the War: Hopes, Illusions, and Disappointments, 1945–1957*, trans. Hugh Ragsdale (Armonk, N.Y.: M. E. Sharpe, 1998), 102–3.

[108] GARF, f. 8131, op. 21, d. 21, l. 10.

[109] Ibid., d. 23, l. 154.

[110] Quoted in V. M. Paneiakh, *Tvorchestvo i sud'ba istorika: Boris Aleksandrovich Romanov* (St. Petersburg: Institut rossiiskoi istorii S.-Peterburgskii filial, Rossiiskaia akademiia nauk, 2000), 206.

[111] The precise figure was 45.2%. Also note that the number of housing-related complaints had reportedly doubled in 1945. GARF, f. 7253, op. 65, d. 579, ll. 127, 129.

[112] Although there was private ownership of housing, most urban housing was owned by city soviets and by a host of other organizations including enterprises, trade unions, and minis-

according to a law from 1937, an absence of over six months from one's apartment could result in a loss of occupancy rights, as could failure to pay rent for three months. That law, however, operated in ordinary times, and officials in the prosecutor's office recognized the problems inherent in applying these regulations during times of war. Central archives contain dozens of letters from state prosecutors and judicial officials in recently liberated territories asking how and whether to apply the existing legislation.[113] "When should the six-month period begin," one prosecution official queried, "from the day of evacuation or from the day the place was liberated from the Germans? How should we respond if the people in question have not paid their rent? Can we apply section 30 of the law of October 17, 1937?" In a clear indication that the official himself had his doubts about the applicability of these laws to the current situation, he concluded with one final question: "Is there no plan to issue a new law in relation to the housing rights of evacuees?"[114]

To the presumed dismay of prosecution and judicial officials, whose repeated queries testify to their continued struggles to make sense of the complex situation (which had raised, in the words of the chairman of an oblast court, "extraordinary difficulties"), no such law was ever issued.[115] Moreover, those who failed to pay their rent were routinely deprived of the rights to their apartment, in accordance with the 1937 legislation. The writer Alexander Kochetkov was one of those affected. Although Fadeev pleaded that Kochetkov's "extraordinarily difficult living conditions [in Tashkent] impeded him from paying for his room," such special circumstances, which were in fact quite common, were rarely taken into account.[116]

Even so, the housing rights of evacuees were at times defended and upheld. When the Council of People's Commissars drafted a proposal stipulating that those returning to Leningrad would be accorded housing from the general stock (rather than provided with their previous living space), prosecution officials objected: "One cannot agree with this proposal. It cannot be considered right that tenants who were evacuated from Leningrad and who in good conscience fulfilled all their responsibilities should be deprived of their right to their living space."[117]An only slightly less extreme measure

----

tries. In Odessa, for example, 87.6% of the prewar housing stock was in the public sector. Of that, local soviets owned the vast majority, 94.7%. GAOO, f. R1234, op. 7, d. 288, l. 45. On the various forms of housing tenure and their evolution, see Gregory D. Andrusz, *Housing and Urban Development in the USSR* (London: Macmillan in association with the Centre for Russian and East European Studies, University of Birmingham, 1984), 29–110.

[113] See, for example, GARF, f. 8131, op. 21, d. 21, ll. 10, 92.

[114] Ibid., op. 19, d. 59, l. 11.

[115] Ibid., op. 21, d. 21, l. 104.

[116] RGALI, f. 631, op. 15, d. 650, l. 102. There is no record of the success of Fadeev's appeal, but his petition on behalf of another evacuated writer in a similar situation was refused. Ibid., d. 649, l. 60.

[117] Ibid., l. 77.

proposed by the State Defense Committee with respect to Moscow met with a no less categorical response. The draft resolution proposed that evacuees who had failed to return to Moscow by January 1, 1944, should lose their claim to their prewar housing. Once again, prosecution officials responded, "one cannot agree with this proposal," arguing: "we cannot permit a situation in which tenants who left Moscow as part of the evacuation, and who have fulfilled all their obligations . . . , can be deprived of their rights to their living space only because they were unable, for one reason or another, to return to their place of permanent residence in Moscow by January 1, 1944." Clearly, in the minds of central prosecution officials, the involuntary nature of evacuees' departure, coupled with the unspoken difficulties attendant on return, mitigated against the application of the six-month rule. If any doubts remained, however, the prosecution official added one final, and in his view decisive, argument: "If one takes into consideration the fact that this proposal mostly affects the families of those serving in the army (judicial practice has shown that the principal group of people who have not yet returned to Moscow from evacuation are the families of service people), then it becomes clear that this point of the draft cannot be accepted."[118]

As these proposals makes clear, evacuees' rights to their former apartments were precarious. Proposals similar to those put forward in Moscow and Leningrad were advanced in a host of formerly occupied cities as well. In Odessa, authorities proposed an expiration date on tenants' rights, and in Voronezh, local authorities, "on their own initiative," simply abolished all rights to previously occupied living space.[119] Although such proposals appear to have foundered in each case on the objections of the state prosecution (in Voronezh the city soviet's decision was not approved by legal organs), they underscore the feeble foundations on which such rights rested. In addition, they point to a tendency toward geographical differentiation, which the war had done little to diminish. Universal laws, applicable to the entire space of the Soviet Union, were mediated by a series of individual resolutions applicable to specific cities, thereby establishing spatially differentiated rights for reevacuees.

Frontline service led to further differentiation in reevacuees' rights. In the exchange over housing rights in Moscow, the prosecutor ultimately chose to defend the rights of returnees not as "evacuees" but as the "families of service people." The choice of words was not accidental. In the wartime and postwar order, the rights of service people and their families emerged as a powerful category of entitlement. A government resolution issued on Au-

---

[118] Ibid., l. 36.
[119] See, respectively, GAOO, f. P9, op. 3a, d. 123, l. 81; and GARF, f. 8131, op. 21, d. 21, l. 92.

gust 5, 1941, guaranteed to those serving in the Red Army and their families the right to return to their former living space.[120] For this group, and this group alone, moreover, the requirement to pay the rent, a key part of the 1937 legislation, was waived.

The government did not, however, recognize all wartime service as equal. Workers shipped to factories in Siberia and the Urals might feel that they, too, had made sacrifices for the war, but they were effectively excluded from the postwar hierarchy of entitlement. In February 1942, a government resolution deprived workers and employees evacuated with factories and enterprises of their right to their former housing.[121] The resolution struck workers as manifestly unfair. As one worker put it in a letter excerpted by the censors: "The workers have given all their strength to defeat the enemy, and they want to return home, to their own people, their own homes. And now it turns out we have been deceived. They've shipped us out of Leningrad, and they want to leave us in Siberia. In this case we workers should say that our government has betrayed us and our work."[122] Similar sentiments were expressed by workers from Moscow.[123] Even some officials doubted its correctness. In Kalinin, for example, the head of the people's court wrote in 1944 to the prosecutor's office in Moscow that the rejection of workers' claims to their former housing was, in his opinion, "essentially incorrect," as no other housing for these people existed.[124] His query, however, received a definitive answer: evacuated workers had "lost their right to the living space they occupied before the evacuation."[125] Only if, before the war, the worker happened to have lived with someone currently serving in the army would he or she have a chance of reclaiming the apartment—or so one Moscow prosecutor interpreted the law.[126]

Wartime behavior emerged as a basis for exclusion in a more punitive sense as well—those who had voluntarily departed with the Germans and now sought the return of their former living space, for example, were explicitly deprived of their rights.[127] Moreover, people who had occupied the apartments of evacuees on "their own initiative" (*samovol'no*), either with

[120] GARF, f. 5446, op. 1, d. 195, ll. 88–89.
[121] The resolution, entitled "on Freeing Up the Living Space of Local Soviets and Enterprises Previously Occupied by Workers and Employees Evacuated to the East," was reprinted in *Pravda*, February 17, 1942.
[122] RGASPI, f. 17, op. 117, d. 530, ll. 56–57. Quoted in Zubkova, *Russia after the War*, 37.
[123] See RGASPI, f. 17, op. 88, d. 137, ll. 70–71.
[124] GARF, f. 8131, op. 21, d. 21, l. 50.
[125] Ibid., l. 51.
[126] Ibid., op. 19, d. 59, l. 46.
[127] See, for example, the unequivocal instructions to this effect issued by the central state prosecution office to prosecution officials in Dnepropetrovsk oblast. GARF, f. 8131, op. 21, d. 21, l. 11.

the sanction of the occupying powers or with no sanction at all, were subject to administrative eviction and not entitled to the protections afforded by a legal process.[128]

The war thus created new categories of entitlement and exclusion, but behavior during the war did not entirely determine the new postwar hierarchies.[129] Prewar elites saw their privileges ensconced and strengthened in legislation that secured their return to their previous apartments. The cultural and scientific elite enjoyed such privileges, as did the party and state apparatus. It comes as little surprise that Boris Pasternak and Vladimir Lugovskoi both ultimately succeeded in reclaiming their prewar apartments. In some cases, the state both guaranteed elites the return of their prewar housing and assured them of living space, from which they could not be evicted, even if their own housing had been destroyed (a right it did not extend, at least in theory, to the families of service people). Party authorities in Odessa, for example, appealed to state prosecution officials to exempt certain categories of citizens from expulsions, namely the "Soviet and party *aktiv*, war invalids, and scholars, who returned to Odessa in conjunction with a decree of the Central Committee or oblast authorities. In practice, this is what happens: some comrades arrive, receive living space, and then a family that used to live in the apartment returns from evacuation, and the comrades are resettled in another apartment, and another family returns. Again resettlement—where should we resettle the comrades next?"[130]

Of course, the hierarchy of entitlement established by central and regional directives did not seamlessly translate into a corresponding hierarchy on the ground. The gulf between theory and practice was in part a product of bureaucratic corruption and bribery, of which there is ample evidence in the archives.[131] It was also a product, however, of competing conceptions of entitlement. Correspondence among prosecutors, the dictates of local officials, and the petitions of individuals all suggest that the claims of the families of servicemen enjoyed widespread support. Appeals for the return of housing rarely failed to mention service on the front lines. In the consider-

[128] See, for example, GARF, f. 8131, op. 19, d. 59, l. 26. Similar procedures were applied in Moscow. See ibid., op. 21, d. 21, l. 3.

[129] On the war's partial erasure of previous stigmas, see Amir Weiner, *Making Sense of War: The Second World War and the Fate of the Bolshevik Revolution* (Princeton, N.J.: Princeton University Press, 2001).

[130] GAOO, f. P9, op. 3a, d. 123, l. 81. In Odessa, elites were further exempt from the postwar reduction in the amount of living space to which each individual was entitled. The measure applied to "academics, scholars, cultural figures, leading engineering and technical workers, directors of enterprises and organizations and other workers who are entitled to supplementary living space." GAOO, f. R6105, op. 1, d. 3, l. 8.

[131] In Odessa, for instance, eighteen members of the city housing bureau were arrested in the fall of 1945 on charges of corruption. The individuals in question had allegedly accepted bribes, in the words of an NKVD report on the topic, in return for the "illegal signing of orders for the occupation of living space and the illegal settlement of apartments." GAOO, f. P9, op. 3a, d. 123, l. 77.

ation of municipal government and even prosecution officials, moreover, service appears to have constituted a much stronger ground for the reclamation of living space than evacuation. It was typical, for instance, that when the rights of a returning evacuee came into conflict with the desires of local industry, the prosecutors upheld the rights of the former not because the living space was rightfully his but because of his connection to the army. "Citizen Reznikov," the prosecutor claimed in one such case, "is the father of a *frontovik* and in conjunction with the Sovnarkom decision of August 5, 1941, he has an indisputable right to his former living space, regardless of whether or not he has documents permitting him to enter Odessa."[132]

More striking still, the rights of service people's families were widely considered to trump the rights of other groups. Military families did have special rights, as laid out in the August 1941 resolution. The resolution, however, entitled the families of service people to the return of their own living space. It did not entitle them to the prewar living space of others. Not, at least, in theory. In practice, evacuees often had their rights to regain their former living space abrogated in favor of the rights of the families of servicemen. Consider the following case: one reevacuee who returned to Odessa attempted to evict a resident who had settled in her apartment "willfully." Although the courts upheld the eviction order, the resident who had occupied the apartment was permitted to retain it "as she is also the family of a serviceman."[133] Another woman returning from evacuation and seeking to reclaim her former living space sought to strengthen her case by pointing out that her husband was at the front. It turned out, however, that they had divorced shortly before the war. Did the divorce thus deprive her of the right to her apartment? The military official writing on behalf of those about to be evicted certainly thought so.[134] Although the archives contain no trace of how the conflict was resolved, it would not be surprising if the petitioner's claim was denied. The correspondence of regional judicial officials suggests that, in practice, the families of service people were often endowed with rights for which there was in fact no legal foundation. The chairman of the Kursk oblast court, for instance, was convinced that the law prevented evacuees from reclaiming their former housing if the families of service people had occupied it with official sanction. Although the deputy prosecutor of the Soviet Union informed the chairman in no uncertain terms that he had misinterpreted the existing legislation and risked violating the "legal interests" of evacuees, such assumptions appear to have been widespread.[135]

In practice, then, it would seem that officials on the ground substantially extended the rights of military families, encroaching on the less well-defined

[132] GAOO, f. P17, op. 4, d. 140, l. 47.
[133] GAOO, f. P9, op. 3, d. 400, l. 52.
[134] GAOO, f. P22, op. 9, d. 310, l. 418.
[135] GARF, f. 8131, op. 21, d. 21, ll. 104, 106.

but nonetheless recognized rights of others. This does not mean that all families of service people succeeded in reclaiming their former apartments.[136] The housing crisis was extreme, the operation of the housing and judicial organs slow. Even an invalid, whose rights to housing were in theory well protected, found himself compelled to live on a balcony for four months in Odessa.[137] As party officials themselves acknowledged in a meeting of the city's party bureau, there were serious "deficiencies" in the way local authorities were handling the housing problem, as a result of which even "war invalids, the families of service people, and party, Soviet, and economic workers who have come from the east lose a tremendous amount of time searching for an apartment and receive apartments only after lengthy appeals and pressure on the part of leading party and Soviet authorities."[138] There does, however, seem to have been a consensus among officials (and certain sectors of the population as well) that the sacrifices of those who served at the front had conferred on them and their families an entitlement not enjoyed by other groups.

At a distinct disadvantage in the emerging hierarchy of entitlement were Jews. As in the reevacuation more generally, Jews seeking to reclaim housing in the previously occupied territories faced particular difficulties. Saul Borovoi later recalled how in 1944 his old neighbor in Odessa "wrote that our furniture had been preserved and that she was waiting for us. Later, evidently having better understood the situation, she realized that she had rushed the invitation, and she did everything not to let us back into our old apartment." Borovoi was unable to reclaim either his old apartment or the majority of his belongings. His neighbor, who had occupied the apartment, "kept part of my books, my stamp collection, and many domestic objects for herself."[139] Leonid Averbukh and his mother encountered similar difficulties on their return to Odessa, where they found their prewar apartment occupied by an antisemitic district party official. Only by threatening the official with legal action were they able to reclaim a couple of rooms in the apartment. As Averbukh later observed, "we were the family of a serviceman

[136] Mark Edele concludes: "while as a rule the eviction process worked to the advantage of veterans, there were cases when they had to fight for years for their housing. Such cases occurred if the apartment or room which the veteran had inhabited before the war was occupied either by an individual with competing legal rights, with superior connections, or by an institution which could claim to be more important than an individual veteran." "A 'Generation of Victors?' Soviet Second World War Veterans from Demobilization to Organization, 1941–1956" (Ph.D. diss., University of Chicago, 2004), 216.

[137] GAOO, f. P17, op. 4, d. 140, l. 5.

[138] RGASPI, f. 17, op. 44, d. 1784, l. 167. A similar point was made in a report on complaints submitted to the Supreme Soviet in 1945. Noting that the supplicants included "service people and their families returning from evacuation, invalids of the patriotic war, and more recently demobilized service people," the report blamed the situation on the "fact that local organs of power fulfill the resolution of the government on this question in an insufficiently energetic manner." GARF, f. 7253, op. 65, d. 579, l. 129.

[139] Borovoi, *Vospominaniia*, 285, 288.

who had died at the front, so the law was on our side."[140] The difficulties encountered by Borovoi and Averbukh were in many ways typical. In the spring of 1944, the chairman and executive secretary of the Jewish Anti-Fascist Committee wrote to Molotov asserting that Jews "are encountering obstacles in their reevacuation to their native areas." The letter went on: "even those few who manage, through various ways, to get to their native towns where their grandfathers and great-grandfathers had lived find that their homes have been occupied since the German occupation. Thus those returning are left without a roof over their heads."[141] The committee representatives clearly believed that Jews were encountering exceptional obstacles in their efforts to reclaim their housing.

Letters sent to the committee seem to corroborate their suspicion. Across the formerly occupied territories, there were reports of Jews being barred from reclaiming their prior abodes. The predicament that one Jewish Odessite described in a letter to Ilya Ehrenburg was in many ways typical: "I was in evacuation for three years, I returned to my native city recently. The things and furniture in my apartment had been stolen; my apartment was occupied. I have two sons who are officers defending the motherland, and for seven days I had to sleep in the front entrance before a neighbor felt sorry for me and let me into his apartment. The bureaucrats in the housing division have still not given me an order for an apartment."[142]

Even the intervention of the bureaucrats from the housing division did not always resolve the situation. Consider the case of a Jew from Kiev who had returned from evacuation to find his apartment occupied. As he put it in his own letter to Ehrenburg, "despite a whole slew of resolutions from the procuracy office of the Kaganovich district of Kiev and resolutions of the soviet of the same district about freeing up a room for my family, the room has still not been vacated." According to the letter writer, the individual who had occupied the room, and who happened to live on the floor below in the same building, "acts from the outside [*deistvuet so storony*], imperceptibly, and all the decisions concerning the vacation of the room for my family come to nothing." As a result, the letter writer's wife and children were living in Moscow without housing; and his sister-in-law, who had gone ahead to Kiev, was living in the communal kitchen of their former apartment.[143]

Whereas the difficulties encountered by Jews are incontrovertible, the sources of their problems are more difficult to identify. Were the "bureaucrats

---

[140] Leonid Averbukh, interview by Nicole Tolkachova, in *Jewish Witness to a European Century*, cassette 3, side A. Russian transcript provided by Centropa.org.

[141] Shimon Redlich, *War, Holocaust, and Stalinism: A Documented Study of the Jewish Anti-Fascist Committee in the USSR* (Amsterdam: Harwood Academic Publishers, 1995), 243.

[142] Mordechai Altshuler, Yitzhak Arad, and Shmuel Krakowski, eds., *Sovetskie evrei pishut Il'e Erenburgu, 1943–1966* (Jerusalem: Prisma-Press, 1993), 148.

[143] Ibid., 149–50.

in the housing division" simply slow, perhaps corrupt, or was this a case of antisemitism? How should we explain the large number of Jews who had difficulties reclaiming their apartments? In part, the prominence of Jews among supplicants seeking to reclaim former housing reflects their over-representation among the returning population as a whole. Jews had consti-tuted a full quarter of the evacuee population, and accordingly constituted a substantial proportion of the reevacuees.[144] It was also, however, a prod-uct of antisemitism.

Antisemitism had risen substantially over the course of the war. Fueled by the widespread perception that Jews had fled the front lines, it was further inflamed by the "apartment wars" that followed the reevacuation. Housing was at once both a site and an important source of popular antisemitism. One Soviet Jew directly attributed the "unfriendly" reception accorded to reevacu-ated Jews to the fact that "disputes arise over the return of apartments and demands for the return of plundered property when it is found."[145] Another Soviet Jew, a resident of Odessa, went so far as to claim that the antisemitism in his native city "doesn't particularly worry me, as I qualify it exclusively as a phenomenon of love for Jewish property, and, insofar as it is in practice al-ready stolen, there is reason to believe that the lovers of such property will soon understand that there is no basis for the manifestation of hateful feelings toward the Jewish nation."[146] "Love for Jewish property" was undoubtedly important, but it was hardly an "exclusive" source of hostility toward Jews.

Signals from above also stimulated antisemitism. Although central authori-ties do not seem to have elaborated a systematic policy of exclusion, central policies do, in part, account for the obstacles encountered by Jews. The period of reevacuation corresponded with a series of initiatives divesting Jews of their responsibilities in the arts, in academia, and in party and government organi-zations. Given these policies, it is hardly surprising that there were rumors in Odessa that Jews would not be permitted to return to the city. State-sponsored discrimination, in other words, fed and reinforced the notion that the postwar polity would not include Jews. The rumors both confirmed the local popula-tion's conviction that Jews had no right to reclaim their housing and embold-ened efforts to assure that Jews could not reclaim it should they try.

EVACUATION'S AFTERMATH

Eventually, most of those who returned, Jews and non-Jews alike, did find accommodation of one sort or another. Saul Borovoi obtained a place to

---

[144] According to data compiled by Soviet authorities as of December 12, 1941, 26.94% of evacuees were listed as Jews. RGAE, f. 1562, op. 20, d. 249, ll. 67–68.

[145] Redlich, *War, Holocaust and Stalinism*, 226.

[146] Altshuler, Arad, and Krakowski, *Sovetskie evrei pishut Il'e Erenburgu*, 140.

live (albeit a room in a communal apartment) by virtue of his status as an academician.[147] Others received housing from municipal authorities or from their workplace. In the meantime, some, like Rakhil Givand-Tikhaya, were given shelter by neighbors.[148] Others, like Vsevolod Ivanov, were put up in hotels. Still others slept in the unoccupied corners of communal apartments, in kitchens, and even on balconies.[149]

Zinaida Stepanishcheva was one of the few to find her prewar residence intact. She describes returning to Moscow and entering her family's home, a room in a communal apartment: "everything was neatly arranged, clean, and cozy. On the table there was a letter and some sausage—a present from my husband. We felt that we had come home."[150] As the letter on the table suggests, however, not even Stepanishcheva's return home was complete. Her return signaled only a partial reconstitution of the family hearth, for Stepanishcheva's husband had left Moscow only the day before. The family would not be reunited for another year and a half.

For those who were fortunate and whose family members had survived the war, such delays were not uncommon. Even once the war had ended, many men continued to serve in the army. Although demobilizations began in June 1945, mass demobilization did not end until February 1948.[151] The search for family members lost "in evacuation," moreover, continued well into the postwar era. As late as the spring of 1949, a woman from Odessa wrote to the Resettlement Bureau asking for help locating her missing son, who had been evacuated from Odessa with his school in 1941.[152] Similar letters were dispatched on behalf of Fedor Kulchanovskii, who had been evacuated from the Ukraine as a four-year-old in 1941 and had been missing ever since. Fedor was living safely in Tashkent, as the adopted son of the blacksmith Shaakhmed Shamakhmudov, but requests by his family about his whereabouts yielded nothing: Fedor had been entered in the official ledgers as Fedor Kulchakovskii, not Fedor Kulchanovskii. Only in the 1980s, when an enterprising journalist put the pieces of the puzzle together, was Fedor reunited with his grandmother. One hundred years old at the time of their reunion, the woman had reportedly refused to die before locating her long-deceased daughter's missing child.[153] Anna Matsueva was equally determined to find her missing daughter. In desperation, Matsueva had given

[147] Borovoi, *Vospominaniia*, 289.

[148] Rakhil Givand-Tikhaya, interview.

[149] Elena Zubkova claims that many years after the war ended, there were still people living in dugouts, ruins, and "other places unfit for human habitation." *Russia after the War*, 102–3.

[150] Stepanishcheva, "Vot tak i zhizn' proshla," l. 39.

[151] Edele, "A 'Generation of Victors?'" 63–66.

[152] GARF, f. A-327, op. 2, d. 763, l. 106.

[153] See Diana Ledi, Blog, April 13, 2008 (http://diana-ledi.livejournal.com/129407.html); Anatolii Zolozov, "Ukraintsy Iuldash Shamakhmudov, Khudaiberdy Gadoev i drugie," *Zerkalo nedeli* 51 (December 30—January 5, 2001, www.zn.ua/3000/3150/29924).

her eldest daughter into the care of another woman on the streets of Tashkent. The woman subsequently left the city, leaving neither a name nor a forwarding address. Matsueva searched for her daughter for years after the war, but only after her death, in 2000, did her younger daughter finally locate her missing sister.[154]

Even those reunited with their families sometimes faced difficulties readjusting. Anna Akhmatova's relationship with the man she planned to marry, whom she referred to in Tashkent as her husband, ended on the railway station platform in Leningrad. He had gone mad. Both Maria Belkina and Tatiana Lugovskaia ended up separating from their husbands. "As [Belkina] said, people had grown unaccustomed to one another and were very tired. She even wanted to write a novel about how husbands and wives who remained alive after the war had to grow accustomed to each other all over again."[155]

· · ·

Slowly, evacuees got settled and prepared for life "after the war." Lydia Chukovskaia later described this period: "The war was ending; it seemed that in that inconceivable period referred to as 'after the war,' everything would be new, would be different from *before*."[156] Many shared such expectations, which had been nurtured in evacuation, only to be disappointed. The return and the close of the war signaled the end neither of the labor camp system nor the system of censorship and political control. Some of those who returned from evacuation, such as Akhmatova, would soon find themselves the targets of renewed repression. As noncombatants, moreover, evacuees were often marginalized. Those returning from Central Asia or Siberia received no hero's welcome. On his return to Leningrad, Nikolai Punin noted: "between those who remained and those who returned you hear the following conversations: 'So, you sat it out in the rear?' They respond: 'And you were waiting for the Germans?' "[157] As this exchange suggests, evacuees were sometimes stigmatized for having spent the war in the rear. One Leningrader who had remained in the city later described the resentment of evacuees. "There were cases," he recalled, "in which individual workers treated those who arrived in a hostile fashion, called them deserters, accused them of saving their skins in the rear while those who remained at the factory had lived through tremendous difficulties. It had to be explained. After all, these peo-

[154] Einara Tomm, "Sestry," *Desnitsa*, December 18, 2002, no. 51 (194) (www.province.ru/publishing/index-izdanie.html).

[155] Gromova, *Vse v chuzhoe gliadiat okno*, 277.

[156] Lidiia Chukovskaia, *Zapiski ob Anne Akhmatovoi*, vol. 2, 32.

[157] N. Punin, *Mir svetel liuboviu: dnevniki, pis'ma*, ed. L. A. Zykov (Moscow: Artist. Rezhisser. Teatr, 2000), 385, entry of July 24, 1944.

ple had not been at a resort; they, too, had had a tough time."[158] In some cases, evacuees found themselves pushed out of jobs they had held before the war. Amir Weiner has shown how in the party apparatus of the Vynnitsa region evacuees were deemed "unsuitable for the tasks of the postwar era" and marginalized.[159]

The stigma attached to evacuation was nowhere more marked and as enduring as in the emergence and flowering of a new wartime myth—that of the "Tashkent front," where Jews were widely said to have "fought" the war. The essentials of the myth are contained in the comments made by a war veteran to a Jew on a city bus in 1948: "all you Jews are cunning and didn't fight in the war, you were all sitting in Tashkent while we fought."[160] The association of Jews and Tashkent was forged as early as 1942. Shortly after his return to Moscow in the fall of that year, Vsevolod Ivanov recorded in his diary how a fellow writer, Korneichuk, refusing a request to write an article about antisemitism, blamed the Jews themselves for the phenomenon: "Why did they carry off their bureaucratic paunches to Tashkent, leaving Hitler the artisans in Vynnitsa, Zhitomir, Berdichev?"[161] Although the notion of the "Tashkent front" seems to have originated on the Soviet home front, it also circulated in occupied territory. In the final months of the German occupation, Nazi propaganda often advanced claims that the Jews were not fighting or were fighting on a "third front" in Tashkent.[162]

The alleged nonparticipation of Jews, symbolized by their supposed flight to the rear, became a staple of postwar humor. In the words of a demobilized Jewish soldier, a resident of Kiev, "'Tashkent' itself became an anti-Soviet word and in part a hooligan one. In coming across a Jew (a participant in the war with medals and other awards), an antisemite would mock him with a question such as, 'Where did you buy that award, in Tashkent?' or, if he was a war invalid, 'So you fell under a tram in Tashkent, eh?'"[163] Jokes circulated that the "Jews have taken the cities of Alma-Ata and Tashkent by storm" and the "Jews took Tashkent without a fight."[164] The "Tashkent front"

[158] Quoted in Potemkina, *Evakuatsiia v gody Velikoi Otechestvennoi voiny na Ural*, 195.

[159] Weiner, *Making Sense of War*, 61. Weiner notes that resentment of evacuees corresponded with, and was reinforced by, resentment of Russians: the latter were over-represented among evacuees, whereas most Ukrainians had seen service on the front lines. Ibid., 59.

[160] Altshuler, Arad, and Krakowski, *Sovetskie evrei pishut Il'e Erenburgu*, 293. Further evidence of the prevalence of the notion of the "Tashkent front" can be found in Weiner, *Making Sense of War*, 115.

[161] Ivanov, *Dnevniki*, 201, entry of November 20, 1942.

[162] Il'ia Al'tman, *Zhertvy nenavisti: anatomiia kholokosta* (Moscow: Sovershenno sekretno, 2002), 47.

[163] Quoted in Blackwell, "Regime City of the First Category," 371. Blackwell cites another example in which a Jewish officer was labeled a "Tashkent partisan" by two Red Army soldiers. Ibid., 364.

[164] The first joke was reported to Ilya Erenburg in 1947 by a Soviet Jew evacuated to Alma-Ata. Altshuler, Arad, and Krakowski, *Sovetskie evrei pishut Il'e Erenburgu*, 276. For the

thus became a byword for Jewish cowardice and nonparticipation in the war, underscoring the centrality of the wartime experience and the experience of evacuation in giving shape to postwar antisemitism in the Soviet Union.

The myth further underscores the ambiguous status of the evacuation more generally in the wartime and postwar Soviet Union. A passage in an article in a postwar Ukrainian newspaper highlights the connection. The Ukrainian author writes of Kiev after the liberation: "It was already clear, to a certain extent, who fought at the front and who in Fergana and Tashkent, who returned as rebuilders and restorers and who to trade in beer and soft drinks and win back apartments." The article cast aspersions not only on Jews (whom the author did not need to mention by name, so closely was Tashkent associated with them) but on the evacuation as a whole. Some readers responded to it in precisely these terms in a series of letters to *Pravda*. One letter, which criticized the author for "stamp[ing] shame on Soviet cities," concluded with a question: "Cannot a reevacuated person, demanding his apartment back, also be a rebuilder and be useful to the country?" Another respondent, who pointed to the lack of honors awarded to evacuees, asked: "has not the time come in the pages of your newspaper or in other places to put forth the question about changing relations toward the reevacuated?"[165]

In their angry responses, the authors of these letters attempted to inscribe the evacuation into a respectable wartime history, to claim a place for evacuees among the victors and heroes of the war. Theirs, however, was an uphill battle. Although the evacuation was alternately heralded in official publications as an example of the state's efficiency or benevolence, it continued to be denigrated on the streets. For evacuees, moreover, it often became a mark of shame. Vladimir Lugovskoi considered remaining in Tashkent, so great was his shame and his anxiety about his reception back in Moscow.[166] Such sentiments were more common among men of fighting age but were not confined to them. Tatiana Lozinskaia wrote to a fellow Leningrader soon after her return to the city that those who had lived through the blockade had a "stern and severe expression in their eyes. And I always feel somewhat ashamed in front of them."[167] The trials and tribulations of evacuation fit uneasily into the official rubrics established to organize the wartime experience in the postwar Soviet Union. Mariam Magarik wrote a series of poems in Tashkent about life in evacuation. Many years later, she sent them

---

second, which a Jewish survivor of the Odessa ghetto recalls hearing after his return to the city, see Leonid Moiseiovich Dusman, *Pomni! Ne povtori!* (Odessa: Druk, 2001), 63.

[165] Quoted in Blackwell, "Regime City of the First Category," 370–73.

[166] Gromova, *Vse v chuzhoe gliadiat okno*, 245. In his memoirs, Saul Borovoi recalls his feelings of shame that he was not in the army. *Vospominaniia*, 255, 270.

[167] T. B. Lozinskaia to N. P. Antsiferov, 24 September, 1944, OR RNB, f. 27, op. 1, d. 280, l. 29.

to a Jewish publication in Moscow, explaining that she had written many poems about various subjects: "Some—the patriotic ones—were published. But these, the evacuation ones, I showed no one, fearing condemnation for daring to write about something personal while the entire country was fighting and toiling."[168]

[168] Mariam Isaakovna Magarik, "Mnogie veterany pishut nam pis'ma . . . stikhi."

CONCLUSION

The Memory and Meaning of Evacuation

Several years ago, the distinguished Russian filmmaker Samarii Zelikin set about making a documentary on the evacuation. To his surprise and that of his coproducer, there were, as yet, no films on the topic, "however strange it may seem."[1] Despite a long-standing cult of the war in the Soviet Union and its successor states, only a handful of books had examined the evacuation. Compared with the thousands of works published on the war, the evacuation has been singularly neglected. As an article about Zelikin's film put it, "over the course of the almost sixty years since Victory Day, the words 'battle,' 'partisan,' and 'occupation' were heard much more frequently in all possible contexts than the word 'evacuation.'"[2] Although a documentary film made for television and produced by one of the country's distinguished documentary filmmakers might seem to mark a new stage in the public memory of evacuation, the film was in some sense the exception that proved the rule: only one television station expressed interest in the film, and although it was shown in the midst of the Victory Day holidays, interested viewers were required to stay up late into the night, leading one reviewer to compare "the fate of *Evacuation*" to "the fate of evacuees."[3] In the words of another reviewer, the film "was shown in the middle of the night, where all sorts of truths (especially bitter, difficult ones) have been relegated."[4]

---

[1] Aleksei Dykhovichnyi, "Nashe kino. Film ob evakuatsii," interview with Samarii Zelikin and Grigorii Libergal on *Spravochnoe biuro*, Radio Ekho Moskvy, December 28, 2004 (www.echo.msk.ru/programs/buro/33731).

[2] Ekaterina Barabash, "Poezd idet na vostok. 'Otkrytaia Rossiia' zapuskaet dokumental'nyi proekt 'Evakuatsiia.'" *Nezavisimaia gazeta*, December 10, 2004 (http://dlib.eastview.com/sources/article.jsp?id=7147657).

[3] Iurii Bogomolov, "Voina voinoiu o voine," *Rossiiskaia gazeta*, May 10, 2006 (www.rg.ru/2006/05/10/a108539.html).

[4] Irina Petrovskaia, "Novye pesni o glavnom," *Izvestiia*, 12 May 2006.

And yet, as Zelikin remarked, for the millions of people who lived through it, the "evacuation is one of the strongest impressions of that time."[5] The filmmaker himself was evacuated as a young boy. He recalls how he and his mother were almost left behind in Kharkov; the journey into evacuation; the birth of his sister en route; the anxiety on arrival. The evacuation was the "most vivid" memory of his childhood.[6] The same could be said for many of the one hundred people he interviewed for the film. When he himself was interviewed on the radio, moreover, the station was inundated with calls. Listeners were eager to share their own experiences as children in evacuation and to recount the stories of their parents and grandparents.[7]

The centrality of evacuation in individual and family memory stands in sharp contrast to its long-standing position on the margins of the public memory of the war. The dominant myth of the war, propagated in the post-war era to legitimize the Soviet state, had little place for the evacuation. The evacuation served as a powerful reminder of all that went wrong in the Soviet-German war—the desperate days of 1941 and the panic that seized party members, government officials, soldiers, and ordinary Soviet citizens. Tales of evacuation threatened to undermine the state's carefully constructed history of the war as a vindication of the communist party and the Soviet system. When Alexander Fadeev, head of the Union of Soviet Writers, por-trayed the evacuation of the southeastern Ukrainian town of Krasnodon as a disorderly, spontaneous affair in his Stalin-Prize-winning novel *Young Guard*, he ran afoul of the censors. In his revised edition, the panic and disorder were replaced by the organized, deliberate actions of the party and the populace. For authorities in the postwar years, tales of evacuation could be troubling.

The volatility of memories of evacuation is underscored by an exchange about Zelikin's film in the pages of the daily *Moskovskie novosti*. In 2004, the newspaper published an interview with Zelikin in which he spoke at length about the hardships of evacuation but also presented it, following a number of historians, as the "most significant, most large-scale operation that the So-viet Union undertook during the Great Patriotic War."[8] A couple of months after the article appeared, the newspaper received and published a response. The author began by stating that the "theme of evacuation is eternally painful for me." His mother, he writes, had requested permission to evacuate but had been denied. Instead of saving the civilian population, Soviet authorities had saved themselves. Some of the town's Jews who survived had written a letter at the time. "It ends," he writes, "with the words: 'The Bolshevik bosses are to blame.'"[9]

---

[5] Dykhovichnyi, "Nashe kino. Film ob evakuatsii."

[6] Iurii Arpishkin, "Pro beglikh," *Moskovskie novosti*, December 17, 2004 (http://dlib .eastview.com/sources/article.jsp?id=7173533).

[7] Dykhovichnyi, "Nashe kino. Film ob evakuatsii."

[8] Arpishkin, "Pro beglikh"; Barabash, "Poezd idet na vostok."

[9] Boris Dekhtiar, "Obratnaia sviaz'. Pomniu pro vragov," *Moskovskie novosti*, Feburary 4, 2005.

This was neither the first nor the last time that the evacuation was invoked to indict the Soviet state. In the immediate postwar years, Victor Kravchenko, a defector from the Soviet Union, included the evacuation in his long list of Soviet crimes. His account of the evacuation is a piercing indictment of the regime—both for its criminal oversight in failing to evacuate the population from countless cities across the front lines and for the "new Soviet system of class privilege" that "made itself manifest in the crudest way" in the course of the operation.[10] Although Kravchenko's was a lone voice in the Soviet era, key elements of his critique have been reprised in post-Soviet Russia. They have surfaced with particular force in discussions of the evacuation of Leningrad, where the failure to secure the evacuation of the population led to tremendous loss of life. In the words of one of the city's prominent journalists, the "truth [regarding the evacuation] was hidden by all means possible because it would very quickly become an indictment not only of particular leaders but of the entire communist regime."[11]

A similar volatility is evident in the memory of life in evacuation. This was the one aspect of evacuation that did occupy a place in public memory, particularly in the regions that received evacuees. In Uzbekistan, the adoption of orphaned children by the local population was a mainstay in the memory of the war. The extraordinary adoption of fifteen evacuated children by the blacksmith Shamakhmudov and his wife, which inspired Gafur Guliam's poem *You Are Not an Orphan*, was made the subject of an award-winning film of the same name in the early 1960s and of a novel several years later.[12] In the early 1980s, a monument was even created to commemorate the blacksmith and his family. Erected in a prominent position in front of the Palace of the Friendship of Peoples in Tashkent, it featured the blacksmith and his wife, surrounded by a dozen of their children, welcoming yet another orphaned child into their embrace. The monument was featured in guidebooks as one of the city's prime attractions, a site of pride for Uzbeks and a defining tribute to the Uzbek contribution to the war.

Today, the myth of the Friendship of Peoples is fraying. In the spring of 2008, the statue of the blacksmith and his adoptive family was removed on orders from on high. The Palace of the Friendship of Peoples is being replaced by a Palace of Independence.[13] Many of the descendants of those who once sought refuge in the city or moved there as migrants have left, concerned about their status in an independent Uzbek state.[14] But it is not only the

[10] Victor Kravchenko, *I Chose Freedom: The Personal and Political Life of a Soviet Official* (Garden City, N.Y.: Garden City Publishing, 1947), 365.

[11] Sergei Achil'diev, "Genotsid. Obrechennyi gorod," *Rossiia* 3 (27 January 2005).

[12] The story of the novel is modeled on the Shamakhmudov family: Rakhmat Faizi, *Ego velichestvo chelovek*, trans. G. Markov and O. Markovaia (Moscow: Izvestiia, 1976).

[13] Aleksei Volosevich, "Uzbekistan: v tsentre Tashkenta snesen samyi izvestnyi pamiatnik druzhbe narodov," April 12, 2008 (www.ferghana.ru/article.php?id=5665).

[14] See Hilary Pilkington, *Migration, Displacement, and Identity in Post-Soviet Russia* (London: Routledge, 1998), 128.

situation in Uzbekistan that has changed. In Russia itself, people remember their reception in evacuation in very different ways.

Discussions of Zelikin's film again offer a case in point. Zelikin observed of his interviewees that when asked to speak about "relations between evacuees and locals," "almost nobody speaks about hostility." "There was a surprising unity," Zelikin commented. "Perhaps it stemmed from faith in victory. Perhaps from the common enemy." The film was dedicated to the woman who gave his own family shelter in Siberia. Although they had their fights, Zelikin would always remember the hot water she prepared on the night of their arrival for his newborn baby sister.[15] He struck a similar note in another interview:

> Imagine Muscovites, Leningraders, or Odessites who find themselves in a district town in Uzbekistan. They find themselves in a milieu that is completely foreign, with different customs and ideas about how people should conduct themselves in the course of daily life. An interpenetration of culture took place. . . . Inevitably there were conflicts, but people got on and helped one another. And this experience of coexistence is still relevant, and perhaps even more relevant today than it was sixty years ago.[16]

In discussions of the film, Zelikin did not deny the tension between evacuees and locals but chose to stress the mutual aid and sense of solidarity. Not so the films' reviewers. One noted television critic put it bluntly: "The myth about the extraordinary friendship of all Soviet people in the desperate years of the war fades under the weight of the mournful testimony of eyewitnesses of the events: evacuees, whom locals were compelled to take in, were the object of open hostility, and even hatred."[17]

Whether recalled with nostalgia or bitterness, for those who lived through it the evacuation was an experience not to be forgotten. In historical scholarship and fiction it is common to focus on the "frontline experience" as a defining moment in the lives of an entire generation. For the many people who did not serve on the front, however, the evacuation rather than the front defined their wartime experience. As Iania Chernina later remarked, "Tashkent is my war."[18] Evacuation constituted a journey into the unknown, from which few returned unchanged. Samarii Zelikin observed, "in the moment when we crossed the threshold of our home and set out for the train station, my world was completely transformed."[19] As he put it on another occasion, "my generation was in many ways formed by the evacuation."[20]

[15] Dykhovichnyi, "Nashe kino. Film ob evakuatsii."
[16] Arpishkin, "Pro beglikh."
[17] Petrovskaia, "Novye pesni o glavnom."
[18] Svetlana Aleksievich, *Poslednie svideteli (sto nedetskikh kolybel'nikh)* (Moscow: Pal'mira, 2004), 132.
[19] Arpishkin, "Pro beglikh."
[20] Barabash, "Poezd idet na vostok."

As the examples above make clear, memories of the evacuation construct different versions of the Soviet past. The evacuation is alternately presented as a formidable Soviet accomplishment and as a moment of breakdown and betrayal. It is remembered as a rescue operation and a source of suffering, a period of solidarity and one of isolation and ethnic tension. In reality, it was all these things. The evacuation was a humanitarian initiative, but it was crucially mediated by existing social and spatial hierarchies that shaped whose lives the state sought to protect. As a rescue operation, it was restricted by the ideological imperative to remain steadfast in the face of the enemy. There is a certain irony, moreover, in the fact that many were saved by evacuation only to be left to languish in the rear. The evacuation similarly saved countless Jews from almost certain death, at the same time as it sparked a new wave of popular antisemitism that fed into, and was nurtured by, the selective antisemitism of the Soviet state. Although the war shook many peoples' faith in the Soviet system, perhaps at no time was identification with the Soviet state and Stalin greater. Although the evacuation was not forced, it did have a coercive dimension. It was carried out, moreover, within the confines of a regulatory system that threatened to transform evacuation into exile. The story of the evacuation demonstrates the Soviet state's success in mobilizing both resources and popular support at the same time as it underscores the state's fragility and limitations.

Index

Page numbers with an *f* indicate figures